Research Series on the Chinese Dream and China's Development Path

Drawing on a large body of empirical studies done over the last two decades, this Series provides its readers with in-depth analyses of the past and present and forecasts for the future course of China's development. It contains the latest research results made by members of the Chinese Academy of Social Sciences. This series is an invaluable companion to every researcher who is trying to gain a deeper understanding of the development model, path and experience unique to China. Thanks to the adoption of Socialism with Chinese characteristics, and the implementation of comprehensive reform and opening-up, China has made tremendous achievements in areas such as political reform, economic development, and social construction, and is making great strides towards the realization of the Chinese dream of national rejuvenation. In addition to presenting a detailed account of many of these achievements, the authors also discuss what lessons other countries can learn from China's experience.

He Tian · Yanbin Lv · Xiaomei Wang
Editors

Report on the Rule of Law Index in China 2

Springer

Editors
He Tian
Institute of Law
Chinese Academy of Social Sciences
Beijing, China

Yanbin Lv
Institute of Law
Chinese Academy of Social Sciences
Beijing, China

Xiaomei Wang
Institute of Law
Chinese Academy of Social Sciences
Beijing, China

Translated by
Xiaoqing Bi
Beijing, China

Published with financial support of the Innovation Program of the Chinese Academy of Social Sciences.

ISSN 2363-6866 ISSN 2363-6874 (electronic)
Research Series on the Chinese Dream and China's Development Path
ISBN 978-981-19-9596-5 ISBN 978-981-19-9597-2 (eBook)
https://doi.org/10.1007/978-981-19-9597-2

Jointly published with Social Sciences Academic Press
The print edition is not for sale in China (Mainland). Customers from China (Mainland) please order the print book from: Social Sciences Academic Press.

This Springer imprint is published by the registered company Springer Nature Singapore Pte Ltd.
The registered company address is: 152 Beach Road, #21-01/04 Gateway East, Singapore 189721, Singapore

Series Preface

Since China's reform and opening began in 1978, the country has come a long way on the path of Socialism with Chinese characteristics, under the leadership of the Communist Party of China. Over 30 years of reform, efforts and sustained spectacular economic growth have turned China into the world's second largest economy, and wrought many profound changes in the Chinese society. These historically significant developments have been garnering increasing attention from scholars, governments, and the general public alike around the world since the 1990s, when the newest wave of China studies began to gather steam. Some of the hottest topics have included the so-called "China miracle", "Chinese phenomenon", "Chinese experience", "Chinese path", and the "Chinese model". Homegrown researchers have soon followed suit. Already hugely productive, this vibrant field is putting out a large number of books each year, with Social Sciences Academic Press alone having published hundreds of titles on a wide range of subjects.

Because most of these books have been written and published in Chinese, however, readership has been limited outside China—even among many who study China—for whom English is still the lingua franca. This language barrier has been an impediment to efforts by academia, business communities, and policy-makers in other countries to form a thorough understanding of contemporary China, of what is distinct about China's past and present may mean not only for her future but also for the future of the world. The need to remove such an impediment is both real and urgent, and the *Research Series on the Chinese Dream and China's Development Path* is my answer to the call.

This series features some of the most notable achievements from the last 20 years by scholars in China in a variety of research topics related to reform and opening. They include both theoretical explorations and empirical studies, and cover economy, society, politics, law, culture, and ecology, the six areas in which reform and opening policies have had the deepest impact and farthest-reaching consequences for the country. Authors for the series have also tried to articulate their visions of the "Chinese Dream" and how the country can realize it in these fields and beyond.

All of the editors and authors for the *Research Series on the Chinese Dream and China's Development Path* are both longtime students of reform and opening and recognized authorities in their respective academic fields. Their credentials and expertise lend credibility to these books, each of which having been subject to a rigorous peer review process for inclusion in the series. As part of the Reform and Development Program under the State Administration of Press, Publication, Radio, Film, and Television of the People's Republic of China, the series is published by Springer, a Germany-based academic publisher of international repute, and distributed overseas. I am confident that it will help fill a lacuna in studies of China in the era of reform and opening.

Shouguang Xie

Contents

Chapter 1
Rule of Law in China: Situation in 2018 and Prospect for 2019

Innovation Project Team on the Rule of Law Index

Abstract In 2018, which was the 40th anniversary of reform and opening up, as well as the first year since the 19th National Congress of the Communist Party of China, China further improved the leadership system of ruling the country by law, comprehensively advanced the construction of the rule of law in the fields of legislation, law-based government, judicial reform, criminal law, civil, commercial and economic laws, and social law, made great strides forward and achieved remarkable results in ruling the country by law in an all-round way. In 2019, China still needs to make efforts to break through institutional bottlenecks, further improve supporting measures, boost economic construction, and bring grassroots social governance under the rule of law.

Keywords Ruling the country by law in an all-round way · Law-based government · Reform of the judicial system · Social rule of law

In 2018, China ushered in the 40th anniversary of reform and opening up. Over the past four decades, China has always adhered to the principles of emancipation of the mind, seeking truth from facts, advancing with the times, and being pragmatic, steadfastly upheld the guiding ideology of Marxism and the basic principles of scientific socialism, and made remarkable advancements in economic development. At the same time, it has vigorously constructed the rule of law, comprehensively

---

Leaders of the Project Team: Tian He, director of Center for Studies of National Rule of Rule Index, Chinese Academy of Social Sciences (CASS) and a research fellow at the CASS Institute of Law; Lv Yanbin, a research fellow and head of the Department of Survey and Studies of National Situation of Rule of Law, CASS Institute of Law. Members of the Project Team: Ma Ke, Wang Xiaomei, Wang Yiming, Deng Li, Lu Chao, Ren Lei, Liu Xiaomei, Liu Hongyan, Liu Yanpeng, Qi Jianjian, Li Xia, Zhang Peng, Zhang Zhongli, Lin Xiaoxiao, Yue Xiaohua, Hu Changming, Zhong Wei, Yao Jia, Li Yanjie, Xu Hui, Huang Fang, Huang Zhongshun, Dou Haiyang. Authors of this report: Wang Yiming, an assistant research fellow, CASS Institute of Law, Tian He, and Lv Yanbin.

Innovation Project Team on the Rule of Law Index (✉)
Institute of Law, Chinese Academy of Social Sciences, Beijing, China
e-mail: 13263169197@163.com

H. Tian et al. (eds.), *Report on the Rule of Law Index in China 2*,
Research Series on the Chinese Dream and China's Development Path,
https://doi.org/10.1007/978-981-19-9597-2_1

advanced law-based governance, gradually perfected the legal system of socialism with Chinese characteristics, provided more powerful institutional and legal guarantee for the system whereby the people become masters of the country, and comprehensively developed the human rights undertaking. The year 2018 was the first year since the 19th National Congress of the Communist Party of China as well as a crucial year in the all-round implementation of the general goal of comprehensively advancing the rule of law, building a socialist system of rule of law with Chinese characteristics, and constructing a socialist state under the rule of law. The Central Committee on Comprehensively Governing the State by Law was established, and its first meeting was held. This was an important institutional arrangement made by China to improve the system of and working mechanism for the Party's leadership over the law-based governance of China, promote the institutionalization and legalization of the Party's leadership, and strengthen the Party's leadership in the whole process and all aspects of the law-based governance, so as to provide long-term and stable legal guarantee for building a moderately prosperous society in all aspects, comprehensively deepening the reform, and strengthening Party's self-governance. It can be said that, in 2018, China made great strides and achieved remarkable results in all aspects of law-based governance.

1.1 Legislative Work

2018 was a busy year for China's legislation. In order to implement the task of comprehensively advancing law-based governance, the legislature made outstanding progress in improving the Constitution and its implementation mechanism, deepening the reform, perfecting the economic regulation mechanism, and strengthening the ecological and environmental protection.

1.1.1 Improving the Constitution and Its Implementation Mechanism

In 2018, the 13th National People's Congress (NPC) deliberated on and adopted at its first session the Amendments to the Constitution, which establish the guiding position of the Scientific Outlook on the Development and the Xi Jinping Thought on Socialism with Chinese Characteristics for a New Era in the country's political and social life, improved the measures for ruling the country by law and implementing the Constitution, enriched the contents relating to adherence to and strengthening the CPC's overall leadership, revised the terms of office for the state president and added provisions on the National Supervisory Commission. Modifications were made to the Decision of the NPC Standing Committee (NPCSC) on Implementing the Constitutional Oath-Taking System, so as to demonstrate the authority of the Constitution, encourage and educate state personnel to be loyal to and abide by the Constitution, and strengthen the implementation of the Constitution. In accordance with the relevant provisions of the Constitution, the 13th NPC decided at its first session to establish the Constitution and Law Committee of the NPC, which shall, on the basis of continuing to carry out the unified deliberation of draft laws and other work, assume the additional duties such as promoting the implementation of the Constitution, interpreting the Constitution, promoting the examination of the compliance with the Constitution, strengthening constitutional supervision and cooperating with other organs in the publicity of the Constitution.

1.1.2 Legislation on Deepening the Reform

In 2018, the legislation on the setup of government institutions and allocation of their functions was further improved. The deliberation on and adoption of the Supervision Law marked the initial completion of the reform of the national supervision system. The amended Criminal Procedure Law improves the linking mechanism between criminal procedure and supervision, and provides for the procedures for transferring a case by supervisory authorities for prosecution, thereby ensuring the smooth reform of the national supervision system.

To ensure the smooth and orderly adjustment of the responsibilities and work of administrative organs in the process of institutional reform, the NPCSC adopted the Decision on the Adjustment of the Responsibilities of Administrative Organs as Prescribed by Law in the Institutional Reform of the State Council, which clarifies the responsibilities and roles of relevant organs during and after the institutional reform. To meet the needs of institutional reform, the NPCSC has adopted a series of decisions on the amendment of laws, including the Decision to Amend Six Laws Including the Frontier Health and Quarantine Law (and the Law on Import and Export Commodity Inspection, the National Defense Education Law, the Mental Health Law, the Counterterrorism Law, and the National Intelligence Law), the Decision on the Exercise of the Marine Right Safeguarding and Law Enforcement Functions and Powers by the China Coast Guard, and the Decision to Amend Fifteen Laws Including the Law on the Protection of Wild Animals (and the Metrology Law, the Law on the Prevention and Control of Atmospheric Pollution, the Law on the Protection of Disabled Persons, the Law on the Protection of Rights and Interests of Women, the Advertising Law, the Law on Energy Conservation, the Law on Desert Prevention and Transformation, the Law on Promotion of Agricultural Mechanization, the Law on Agricultural Product Quality Safety, the Circular Economy Promotion Law, the Tourism Law, the Law on Environmental Protection Tax, the Law on Public Libraries, and the Law on Vessel Tonnage Tax). The State Council passed the Decisions on Adjustment of the Responsibilities of Administrative Organs in the Institutional Reform and adopted the Decision on Issues concerning the Adjustment of Functions of Administrative Organs Prescribed by Administrative Regulations as Involved in the Institutional Reform of the State Council, which further clarifies issues relating to the adjustment of the responsibilities of the administrative organs. Moreover, in line with the institutional reform, the State Council also promulgated a decision to amend 10 administrative regulations.

To meet the need to further promote the reform of the classification of civil servants, the legislature revised the Civil Servant Law. The revised law confirms and consolidates the reform of the parallel system of posts and ranks of civil servants, the talent selection and appointment system, and the classified administration and recruitment of civil servants, thereby providing a legal guarantee for the construction of a high-quality professional team of civil servants.

With respect to judicial reform, the Law on People's Assessors further improves the people's assessor system; the revised Organic Law of People's Courts and Organic Law of People's Procuratorates provide legal bases for the reform of the quota systems of judges and procurators; the Decision of the NPCSC on the Establishment of the Shanghai Financial Court provides for the jurisdiction and the appointment and removal of personnel of the Shanghai Financial Court; and in December 2018, the Standing Committee of the 13th NPC deliberated at its seventh meeting the draft of revised Law on Judges and the draft of revised Law on Public Procurators.

1.1.3 Legislation on Enhancing Economic Regulation

In the process of formulating the E-Commerce Law, the legislature had adhered to the principles of promoting development, being problem-oriented, and attaching equal importance to both standardization and guarantee. The law was enacted to promote the healthy and sustainable development of e-commerce, solve prominent problems in the development of e-commerce, standardize the operational behavior of the entities of e-commerce, and strengthen the protection of the lawful rights and interests of e-commerce consumers.

To unify the adjudicative standards for intellectual property cases, further strengthen the judicial protection of intellectual property, optimize the legal environment for scientific and technological innovation, and speed up the implementation of the innovation-driven development strategy, the Standing Committee of the 13th NPC adopted at its sixth meeting the Decision on Several Issues concerning Judicial Procedures for Patent and Other Intellectual Property Cases. The State Council promulgated the revised Regulations on Patent Agency, which focus on improving the quality of patent agencies, lowering the entry threshold for the patent agency industry, cracking down on "unlicensed agents", and advocating for the provision of patent agency assistance services.

Efforts had been made to further revise and improve the tax law. The revised Individual Income Tax Law integrates four kinds of labor incomes, including wages and salaries, labor remuneration, author remuneration, and royalties, into a comprehensive tax. The Vehicle Purchase Tax Law and the Law on Farmland Occupation Tax were adopted, which, in accordance with the idea of the parallel tax system, keep the current tax system framework and the level of the tax burden unchanged, adjusted only several taxes, upgrading the legislation on these two kinds of tax from "interim regulations" to law.

1.1.4 Legislation on Strengthening Ecological and Environmental Protection

The Standing Committee of the 13th NPC adopted at its fourth meeting the Resolution on Comprehensively Tightening Ecological and Environmental Protection and Lawfully Promoting Triumph in the Uphill Battle for Prevention and Control of Pollution, which requires people's congresses at all levels and their standing committees to use the law as a weapon to control and treat pollution and protect the ecology and environment by relying on the rule of law.

The Soil Pollution Prevention and Control Law, adopted in 2018, specifies the principles to be adhered to in the prevention and control of soil pollution, including giving priority to prevention and protection, adopting classified management, controlling risks, implementing the pollution accountability system, and encouraging public participation. In accordance with the Decision of the State Council to Amend and Repeal Certain Administrative Regulations adopted on March 19, 2018, a series of administrative regulations in the field of ecology and environment, including Regulations on the Administration of River Courses, Regulations on the Administration of the Prevention and Control of Damages to the Marine Environment Caused by Pollution Derived from Coastal Engineering Construction Projects, Regulations on the Administration of Reservoir Dam Safety, Regulations on Urban Water Supply, Regulations on the Implementation of the Forest Law, Regulations on the Biosafety Management of Pathogenic Microorganism Laboratories, Regulations on the Administration of the Import and Export of Endangered Animals and Plants, Regulations on the Administration of the Prevention and Control of Damages to the Marine Environment Caused by Pollution Derived from Marine Engineering Construction Projects, Regulations on the Prevention and Control of Vessel-Source Pollution of the Marine Environment, and Regulations on the Administration of Ozone Depleting Substances, were revised, thereby strengthening the protection and clarifying the responsibility of relevant parties.

1.1.5 Legislation on Carrying Forward the Spirit of Patriotism

To strengthen the protection of heroes and martyrs, uphold and carry forward their spirit and the spirit of patriotism, foster and practice the core values of socialism, and unleash the strong spiritual power to realize the Chinese Dream of the great rejuvenation of the Chinese nation, the Law on the Protection of Heroes and Martyrs adopted by the NPCSC clearly stipulates that the state protects, honors, and commemorates heroes and martyrs, strengthens the publicity and education on the deeds and spirit of heroes and martyrs, and upholds the dignity and lawful rights and interests of heroes and martyrs.

1.2 Law-Based Government

In 2018, China steadily promoted the construction of a law-based government, advanced the comprehensive reform of the Party and state institutions in an orderly manner, further standardized administrative legislation, achieved new progress in the reforms of "simplification of administrative procedures, decentralization of powers, combination of decentralization with appropriate control, and optimization of services", continuously strengthened the standardization of administrative law enforcement, consistently explored and pushed forward the reform of the administrative reconsideration system, and made significant breakthroughs in the reform of the administrative litigation system.

1.2.1 Implementing the Institutional Reform to Adapt to the Development of the New Era

All the previous reforms of the Party and state institutions since 1982 had been aimed at adapting to and promoting the reform of the economic system and social management system, especially focusing on such basic government functions as economic adjustment, market regulation, social management, public service, and ecological and environmental protection.

In 2018, to further adapt to the needs of reform and optimize the operation of power, China launched a new round of reform of the Party and state institutions. The Decision on Deepening the Institutional Reform of the Party and State and the Plan for Deepening the Institutional Reform of the Party and State were adopted at the Third Plenary Session of the 13th CPC Central Committee, and the State Council Institutional Reform Proposal was deliberated on and adopted at the First Session of the 13th NPC, thereby opening the prelude to the deepening of the reform of government institutions in the new era. This round of reform embodies elasticity in strength, systematization in scope, pertinence in emphasis, wholeness in thinking, specialization in organization integration, integrity in function allocation, hierarchy in reform measures, internationality in content, progressivity in implementation, and synergy and legality in safeguard measures. As such, it can be regarded as the most farsighted and courageous one of all the institutional reforms in the past 40 years since the beginning of the reform and opening-up.

Statutory authority is the basic concept of the modern rule of law. The Decision of the CPC Central Committee on Deepening the Institutional Reform of the Party and State clearly points out that, where the implementation of the institutional reform proposal requires the enactment or amendment of any laws or regulations, relevant proceedings shall be initiated in a timely manner; the functions of the Party and state institutions shall be improved, the responsibilities shall be performed and the institutions and staffing shall be managed efficiently in accordance with law, so as to ensure that the reform is carried out on the track of rule of law. To this end, the Decision of NPCSC on Issues concerning Adjustments to Functions of Administrative Organs Prescribed by Laws as Involved in the Institutional Reform of the State Council, and the Decision of the State Council on Issues concerning the Adjustment of Functions of Administrative Organs Prescribed by Administrative Regulations as Involved in the Institutional Reform of the State Council have clarified at different levels issues concerning the adjustment of the functions and responsibilities of administrative organs prescribed by administrative regulations as involved in institutional reform of the State Council.

In accordance with the unified arrangement made by CPC Central Committee, the institutional reform of the central and state organs had been implemented by the end of 2018. The reform plans for provincial-level Party and government institutions had been submitted to the CPC Central Committee for approval at the end of September 2018, and the institutional adjustment was basically completed by the end of 2018. The reform of Party and government institutions below the provincial level have been carried out under the unified leadership of the provincial Party committees and reported to the Central Party Committee for the record before the end of 2018. All tasks of the reform of local Party and government institutions would be basically completed by the end of March 2019.

1.2.2 Strengthening Administrative Legislation by Focusing on Standardization and Supervision

Administrative legislation is an important part of the legislative system in China. The recordation and review of administrative regulations, local regulations and judicial interpretations is an important power entrusted to the NPCSC by the Constitution and laws as well as an important work carried out by the NPCSC in performing its constitutional supervision duties, ensuring the implementation of the Constitution and laws, and upholding the unity of the national legal system. In December 2017, the Standing Committee of the 12th NPC heard at its 31st meeting the first report by the Legislative Affairs Commission of the NPCSC on its work of recordation and review of administrative regulations since the 12th NPC in 2017. This was not only an important measure for implementing the requirements of strengthening the implementation and supervision over the implementation of the Constitution, promoting the constitutional review, and upholding the authority of the Constitution put forward in the report to the 19th National Congress of the CPC but also a historic breakthrough in the system of recordation and review of normative documents.

To further standardize and institutionalize the work of recordation and review of normative documents, the NPCSC is currently studying and drafting the provisions on the normative document recordation and review work, which will clarify the definition of normative documents, the scope of recordation by people's congresses, the retrospective effect of normative documents after being revoked or corrected, etc. They will play an important role in promoting the normative document recordation and review work carried out by people's congresses at all levels.

In view of the practice of arbitrary issuance of documents and issuance of "weird" documents by some local government departments in recent years, the General Office of the State Council issued the Notice on Strengthening the Development and Supervisory Administration of Administrative Regulatory Documents, which contains comprehensive and systematic provisions on the concept, formulation procedures and the supervision and management of administrative normative documents, thereby bringing the formulation, issuance, and management of administrative normative documents onto the track of the rule of law. Moreover, the General Office of the State Council issued the Guiding Opinions on Comprehensively Implementing the Legality Review Mechanism for Administrative Regulatory Documents to further clarify the legality review mechanism for administrative normative documents.

1.2.3 Relying on Judicial Interpretation to Improve the Administrative Litigation System

Administrative litigation is the wind vane of law-based government practices, and the operation of administrative litigation directly reflects the prospects of administration by law in China. More than three years after the implementation of the new Administrative Litigation Law, many institutional designs in the new Law are still at the initial stage of practice. For this reason, the administrative litigation system in 2018 had yielded prominent improvements in the field of judicial interpretation.

The Interpretation of the Supreme People's Court on the Application of the Administrative Litigation Law further clarifies the scope of accepting cases in administrative litigation, refines the qualifications of the plaintiff and the defendant as subjects of litigation, enhances the operability of the summary procedure and the mediation system, and improves the applicability and operability of the law. The judicial interpretation also contains special and detailed rules on such systems as the appearance of the persons in charge of administrative agencies in court to respond to a lawsuit, the organ of reconsideration serving as the joint defendant, and incidental review of normative documents. The introduction of this judicial interpretation will greatly stimulate the vitality of China's administrative litigation system, and better guide the institutional adjustment and practical operation of administrative litigation.

Moreover, the Supreme People's Court and the Supreme People's Procuratorate jointly issued the Interpretations of Several Issues Concerning the Application of Law in Procuratorial Public Interest Litigation Cases, which explain in detail the types of application, threshold elements, evidentiary materials, judgment types, and other issues relating to public interest administrative litigation cases. As a result, it is expected that the overly general standards on the public interest litigation system in Article 25 Paragraph 4 of the Administrative Litigation Law will be gradually unified in the judicial practices of various regions, thereby changing the situation of lack of uniformity in the judicial application of the administrative public interest litigation system in different regions.

1.2.4 Deepening the Reforms of "Simplification of Administrative Procedures, Decentralization of Powers, Combination of Decentralization with Appropriate Control, and Optimization of Services" and Transforming Government Functions

The reforms of "simplification of administrative procedures, decentralization of powers, combination of decentralization with appropriate control, and optimization of services", which are designed to promote the deep transformation of government functions and enable the market to play a decisive role in resource allocation, is a self-revolution carried out by the government to reshape its relationship with the market, as well as a key step towards achieving economic stability in recent years.

In accordance with the general arrangement made by the State Council for accountability inspection in 2018 and based on the comprehensive self-examination carried out by all government departments in all regions, the State Council conducted on-the-spot inspections on the implementation of major decisions and arrangements made by CPC Central Committee and the State Council in all regions. One of the important aspects of the inspection is to examine the implementation of the reforms of "simplification of administrative procedures, decentralization of powers, combination of decentralization with appropriate control, and optimization of services", focusing on simplifying administration and decentralizing powers, improving interim and *ex-post* regulation, optimizing government services, and reducing taxes and fees. The inspection team also conducted a comprehensive survey of important indicators of the business environment. The results of the inspection show that, while streamlining administration and delegating powers, local governments had innovated ways to strengthen interim and *ex-post* regulation, and improved the efficiency of regulation. However, in some regions, there were still problems of "delegating powers only on papers or in name, but not in practice or reality"; some adopted policies had not been implemented in a timely manner; the supervision over some approval processes was still inadequate; the "information islands" needed to be effectively linked, and the working style of some local government departments needed to be improved.

In order to deepen the reforms of "simplification of administrative procedures, decentralization of powers, combination of decentralization with appropriate control, and optimization of services", the Coordinating Group of the State Council for Advancing the Transformation of Government Functions was renamed the Coordination Group for Advancing the Transformation of Government Functions and the Reforms of "Simplification of Administrative Procedures, Decentralization of Powers, Combination of Decentralization with Appropriate Control, and Optimization of Services". On the basis of deepening the reforms of "simplification of administrative procedures, decentralization of powers, combination of decentralization with appropriate control, and optimization of services" in all regions and departments, the Coordination Group, as a deliberation and coordination agency of the State Council, carries out researches on major policies and measures in important fields and key links of the reforms, identifies major issues to be submitted to the executive meeting of the State Council for deliberation, coordinates the solution of key and difficult problems, guides and urges all regions and departments to implement reform measures, so as to stimulate the market vitality, and give full play to social creativity.

1.2.5 Implementing the "Three Systems" to Standardize Administrative Law Enforcement

Focusing on transparent, standard, and law-based law enforcement, the State Council launched the pilot projects on the system of publication of administrative law enforcement actions, the system of whole-process recording of law enforcement actions, and the system of legal review of major law enforcement decisions in 2017. The pilot work on these three systems has achieved remarkable results on the basis of summing up experiences. It has laid a sound foundation for building a law-based government and is of great significance for the government to perform its duties according to the law, standardize administrative law enforcement behavior, restrict its own power, and minimize the abuse of power.

As an important measure for implementing the spirit of the 19th National Congress of the CPC and accelerating the construction of a law-based government, the three systems were fully implemented in the administrative law enforcement agencies at all levels in 2018. The valuable experiences from the pilot work on these three systems have been integrated into the daily law enforcement activities of all law enforcement agencies throughout the country.

By combining administrative law enforcement and precision popularization of law, China has innovated the ways of enforcing and popularizing the law. The Work Guidance on Precision Popularization of Law in the Process of Administrative Law Enforcement, issued by the Judicial Bureau of Shanghai Municipality, provides that, in case of refusal to cooperate with enforcement and other situations, administrative law enforcement agencies (personnel) may interview the legal representatives or main leaders of the administrative counterparts by appointment or visit without an appointment. An interview can be made under the following circumstances: two or more violations of the same legal provisions in the same year; refusal to cooperate with administrative law enforcement; bad attitude in accepting administrative penalties; and other prominent problems. In an interview, the popularization of and education on law will be focused on the identification of facts, admission of evidence, application of law, social harm, etc. involved in the illegal act, so as to encourage the administrative counterpart to choose solutions or rectification measures that are in line with relevant legal provisions. The main methods of precision popularization of law in the process of administrative law enforcement include active notification, answering of questions, explanation of law, persuasion, and administrative interview.

1.3 Reforming the Judicial System

The reform of the judicial system is a key link in the continuous development and improvement of the socialist judicial system with Chinese characteristics, an important guarantee for continuously standardizing the operation of judicial power, strengthening the capacity building of judicial organs, and upholding judicial justice and enhancing judicial credibility, as well as an important aspect of comprehensive law-based state governance. Since the 19th National Congress of the CPC, the CPC Central Committee has put forward a series of new tasks in promoting the reform of the judicial system, and drawn up the general blueprint and implementation plans for the reform of the judicial system in the new era. In 2018, China further implemented the new tasks set by the CPC Central Committee for the reform of the judicial system and made remarkable progress in various aspects of the reform.

1.3.1 Implementing the Overall Arrangement for the Reform of the Judicial System

The Decision of the CPC Central Committee on Deepening the Reform of the Party and State Institutions and the Plan for Deepening the Reform of the Party and State Institutions, adopted at the Third Plenary Session of the 19th CPC Central Committee in February 2018, clearly stipulated the institutional reforms of the CPC Central Commission for Political and Legislative Affairs, the Supreme People's Procuratorate and the Ministry of Justice, thereby providing organizational guarantee for the reform of the judicial system in the new era. On August 24th, the Central Committee on Comprehensively Governing the State by Law held its first meeting to reaffirm the deepening of the reform of the judicial system, thoroughly study the comprehensive reform supporting the judicial accountability system, and speed up the construction of a new judicial power operation mechanism with consistency between powers and responsibilities.

At the Central Political and Legal Work Conference held on January 22, 2018, it was proposed that the reform of the judicial system should be deepened in a comprehensive way in four aspects: advancing the construction of the judicial responsibility system and accelerating the building of a new mechanism for the operation of judicial power with consistency between powers and responsibilities; deepening the reform of the litigation system and realizing the unity of fairness and efficiency at a higher level; deepening the reform of public security and judicial administration systems, and building the capacity for maintaining security and stability and serving economic and social development; and further promoting strict, standardized, fair and civilized law enforcement, and striving to create a fair, transparent and predictable legal environment.

At the beginning of 2018, the National Court Work Conference, the National Conference of the Presidents of People's Procuratorates and the National Conference of the Directors of Public Security Departments were held and the Ministry of Justice officially issued the Opinions on Accelerating the Reform of Judicial Administration, which make arrangements for the top-level design and for judicial reform in various judicial organs in the new era.

1.3.2 Coordinating with the Reform of the National Supervision System

In accordance with the requirements of the Third Plenary Session of the 19th CPC Central Committee on the establishment of the National Supervision Commission, the functions, institutions, as well as 44,151 procurators of the anti-corruption, anti-malfeasance and crime prevention departments of four levels of procuratorates in China had all been transferred on time at the beginning of March 2018.[1] The adoption of the Supervision Law and the revision of the Criminal Procedure Law provide a clear legal basis for the reform of the supervision system.

1.3.3 Continuing to Deepen the Reform of the Judicial Responsibility System

The reform of judicial responsibility system is the key to the reform of the judicial system. In 2018, the Organic Law of People's Courts and the Organic Law of People's Procuratorates were revised, and the reform of the personnel quota system of judges and prosecutors was confirmed at the legal level, providing a solid institutional guarantee for deepening the reform of judicial responsibility system.

---

[1] See the Work Report of the Supreme People's Procuratorate Submitted to the First Session of the Thirteenth National People's Congress on March 9, 2018, at http://www.sppgovcn/spp/gzbg/201803/t20180325_372171.shtml, last visited January 24, 2019.

In June 2018, the Supreme People's Court issued the Opinions on the Coordinated Operation of Case Docketing, Trial, and Enforcement by People's Courts, which made arrangements for further clarifying the division of responsibilities and coordination of work within people's courts and promoting the smooth linkage between and efficient operation of case docketing, trial and enforcement of judgments. In order to ensure the effectiveness of the reform of the judicial responsibility system, the Supreme People's Court has especially issued the Implementation Opinions on the Judicial Accountability System and the Guiding Opinions on Improving the Working Mechanism for Presiding Judges' Meetings of People's Courts (For Trial Implementation).

1.3.4 Strengthening the Personnel, Financial and Material Guarantees for the Administration of Justice

Personnel, finance and material are the foundation of the healthy operation of justice. In 2018, China strengthened the personnel, finance and material guarantees for the administration of justice by setting up specialized adjudication organs, reforming internal institutions and unifying professional qualification examinations.

The establishment of special judicial organs or departments is also an important part of judicial reform. In 2018, the Supreme People's Court set up an international commercial court, led the establishment of an international commercial expert committee, supported the settlement of international commercial disputes in the Belt and Road Initiative through mediation and arbitration, and promoted the establishment of a diversified dispute resolution mechanism that effectively links litigation with mediation and arbitration. In accordance with the plan adopted by the Central Committee for Comprehensively Deepening Reform, Shanghai Financial Court, Beijing Internet Court and Guangzhou Internet Court were established one after another.

The Supreme People's Procuratorate has also reshaped its internal institutions in accordance with the principles of meeting the needs of the people, highlighting professional orientation, integrating arrest and prosecution, and adhering to unity and standardization. To promote the handling of public interest litigation cases by people's procuratorates, the Central Committee for Comprehensively Deepening Reform adopted at its third meeting the Plan for Establishing the Public Interest Litigation Procuratorate Office of the Supreme People's Procuratorate, stressing that the establishment of the Public Interest Litigation Procuratorate Office of the Supreme People's Procuratorate should be guided by the principles of strengthening legal supervision, improving case handling effect and promoting professional construction, so as to build a public interest litigation procuratorial organ with scientific configuration and efficient operation, and provide organizational guarantee for the better performance of procuratorial public interest litigation duties.

In 2018, China started the first national unified legal professional qualification examination. The personnel serving as legal arbitrators for the first time, and civil servants of administrative authorities engaging in the review of decisions of administrative penalty, administrative reconsideration, administrative ruling and legal consulting must pass the examination and obtain a legal professional qualification, so as to embody the quasi-judicial nature of the above professions and the protection of the rights of citizens and legal persons.

1.3.5 Standardizing the Operation of Judicial Power

Developing judicial openness in both depth and width. In April 2018, the Supreme People's Court issued the Provisions on the Disclosure of Trial Process Information on the Internet by People's Courts, which clearly require that the information about the process of trial of criminal, civil, administrative, and state compensation cases by people's courts should be disclosed to the parties and their legal representatives, agent *ad litem*, and defenders participating in the litigation on the Internet, thereby providing clear norms and guidance for effectively improving the transparency of the trial process. Starting from September 1, 2018, the courts of 31 provinces, autonomous regions, municipalities directly under the Central Government, and Xinjiang Production and Construction Corps all began to disclose the information about the process of examination and approval of newly received cases to the parties and their agents through a unified platform, thus effectively improving the transparency of the case trial process and greatly enhancing judicial credibility. The Opinions on Further Deepening Judicial Openness issued by the Supreme People's Court, based on various previous documents on judicial openness, make new arrangements for deepening judicial openness by further deepening the content and scope, perfecting and standardizing the procedures, strengthening the construction and management of platform carriers, and strengthening organizational guarantee.

Reforming and improving the system of people's assessors. The newly adopted Law on People's Assessors provides for the selection of people's assessors, the distinction between the trial of facts and the trial of law, the scope of participation in a trial, the mechanism for withdrawal and punishment, and the guarantee for the performance of duties, and once again makes it clear that people's assessors have the same rights as judges. The Notice of the Supreme People's Court on Implementing in a Deep-going Way the Law on People's Assessors makes arrangements for people's assessors to participate in trial activities and for their training, management, and guarantee. In addition, the Ministry of Justice, the Supreme People's Court, and the Ministry of Public Security jointly issued the Measures for the Selection and Appointment of People's Assessors, which focus on building a team of high-quality people's assessors with broad representation and solid mass base, optimizing the conditions of selection, refining the selection procedures and enhancing the operability of the selection work.

Strengthening procuratorial supervision. In 2018, the procuratorial supervision by procuratorial organs over adjudicative committees and judges was significantly strengthened. Firstly, strengthening the supervision over adjudicative committees. Since the Procurator-General of the Supreme People's Procuratorate and the Deputy Procurator-General in charge of civil and administrative procuratorial work became non-voting members of the Adjudicative Committee of the Supreme People's Court, the presidents and vice presidents of procuratorates at all levels had participated in the discussions of 385 civil cases by the adjudicative committees of people's courts at their corresponding levels in 2018. Secondly, strengthening the supervision over civil litigation. In 2018, people's procuratorates at various levels made procuratorial proposals on such situations of violations of law as obviously exceeding the standard, passive enforcement, selective enforcement, and unlawful disposal of property subject to enforcement, and arranged for special campaigns to supervise the enforcement in civil non-litigation cases, focusing on supervising over violations of law in the enforcement of legal documents in such cases, and promoting the standardization of arbitration and notarization. Thirdly, strengthening the supervision over criminal proceedings. In 2018, procuratorial organs throughout the country strengthened the supervision over criminal proceedings mainly in the aspects of the production of evidence by the public prosecution, legitimate rights and interests of detainees, compulsory medical treatment, and criminal petition. Fourthly, improving procuratorial public interest litigation. The Interpretation of the Supreme People's Court and the Supreme People's Procuratorate on Several Issues concerning the Application of Law in Cases of Procuratorial Public Interest Litigation clarifies that procuratorial organs act as "public interest litigation prosecutors" in initiating public interest litigation, refines the acceptance procedures of procuratorial public interest litigation cases, and implements the registration system. In 2018, the number of procuratorial public interest litigation cases increased drastically. From January to November, procuratorial organs across the country filed 89,523 cases of public interest litigation, made 78,448 procuratorial recommendations and announcements, and filed 2,560 lawsuits, thereby playing an increasingly important role in protecting national interests and public interests.

1.3.6 Fully Protecting the People's Litigation Rights

1.3.6.1 Guaranteeing and Standardizing Lawyers' Participation in Court Trial Activities and Their Litigation Rights

In April 2018, the Supreme People's Court and the Ministry of Justice issued the Notice on Lawfully Protecting Lawyers' Rights in Proceedings and Regulating Lawyers' Participation in the Trial Activities, which focuses on the protection of lawyers' rights and the code of conduct for lawyers at the trial stage, enables lawyers to have more rules to go by when participating in trial activities, and emphasizes that people's courts at all levels and their staff should respect and protect lawyers' litigation rights.

1.3.6.2 Cracking Down on False Litigation and Abuse of Litigation Rights

In September 2018, the Supreme People's Court and the Supreme People's Procuratorate promulgated the Interpretation on Several Issues concerning the Application of Law in the Handling of Criminal Cases regarding False Litigation, with a view to severely cracking down on six typical false litigation behaviors, such as fabricating civil legal relations and fabricating civil disputes by means of forging evidence and false statements.

1.3.6.3 Promoting the Construction of a Diversified Dispute Resolution Mechanism

In order to cope with the frequent occurrence of social contradictions and disputes in the period of rapid social development, people's courts at all levels have taken diversified dispute resolution mechanisms as an important supplement to adjudication.

At the conference commemorating the 55th anniversary of Comrade Mao Zedong's instructions to study and popularize the "Fengqiao Experience" and the 15th anniversary of Party General Secretary Xi Jinping's instructions to adhere to and develop the "Fengqiao Experience", the head of the CPC Central Commission for Political and Legislative Affairs pointed out that judicial workers should adhere to and develop the "Fengqiao Experience" in the new era, accelerate the modernization of grassroots social governance, strive to build a higher-level of Safe China, and constantly enhance the people's sense of gain, happiness and security.

In February 2018, the People's Courts Mediation Platform, developed and constructed by the Supreme People's Court, was put into trial operation in courts throughout the country. Parties to disputes can apply for mediation on the platform, and courts can push similar cases to the parties, and guide them to choose mediation methods for resolving their disputes.

In April 2018, the Commission for Political and Legal Affairs of the CPC Central Committee, the Supreme People's Court, the Ministry of Justice, the Ministry of Civil Affairs, and the Ministry of Human Resources and Social Security jointly promulgated the Opinions on Strengthening the Building of the People's Mediator Team, which provide for the qualifications of mediators of people's mediation commissions at the township (sub-district) level.

The Opinions on Launching a Pilot Program on Diversified Resolution of Disputes Involving Overseas Chinese in Certain Regions, the Opinions on Comprehensively

Advancing the Establishment of Diversified Mechanism for the Resolution of Securities and Futures Disputes, and the Notice on Determining the First Group of International Commercial Arbitration and Mediation Institutions Included in the "One-Stop" Diversified Mechanisms for Resolving International Commercial Disputes, issued by the Supreme People's Court in conjunction with relevant departments, have further clarified the mechanisms for the diversified resolution of disputes in related fields.

1.3.7 Making Every Effort to "Basically Overcome Difficulties in Enforcement"

2018 was the decisive year for "basically overcoming difficulties in enforcement". Since 2016, China has launched a campaign to "win a decisive victory in overcoming difficulties in enforcement" in courts throughout the country, intensified enforcement, and made full use of information technology to overcome the systematic and institutional obstacles that impede the enforcement of court judgments. In order to supplement the rules on enforcement, the Supreme People's Court issued 12 judicial interpretations or normative documents of the nature of judicial interpretation that especially adjust enforcement procedures, including Provisions on Several Issues concerning Enforcement Compromise, Provisions on Several Issues concerning Guarantee for Enforcement and Provisions on Several Issues concerning the Determination of the Reference Prices for Disposition of Property by People's Courts. To strengthen the long-term mechanism for basically overcoming enforcement difficulties, the Standing Committee of the 13th National People's Congress included the Civil Enforcement Law in the second-class projects of its legislative plan. At the 6th meeting of the Standing Committee of the 13th National People's Congress held on October 24, 2018, the Supreme People's Court delivered the Report on the Work of People's Courts in Overcoming "Enforcement Difficulties", which gave a comprehensive report to the NPCSC on the origin and task objectives of the work of "basically overcoming the enforcement difficulties", the progress and achievements made in the work, and the problems and difficulties currently existing in the work.

In 2018, the National Development and Reform Commission, the Supreme People's Court, and the former Ministry of Land and Resources issued the Notice of Imposing Punitive Measures on Dishonest Judgment Debtors to Restrict Their Real Estate Transactions to jointly take disciplinary measures for restricting real estate transactions by dishonest judgment debtors; and relevant government departments and 12 Internet financial companies jointly established a disciplinary mechanism for punishing dishonest judgment debtors; and in September 2018, the General Office of the National Development and Reform Commission, the General Office of the Supreme People's Court, the Comprehensive Department of the Civil Aviation Administration of China, and the General Office of China Railway Corporation jointly issued the Notice on the Implementation of Relevant Work on Appropriately

Restricting Particular Seriously Dishonest Persons from Travelling by Train and Civil Aircraft within a Certain Period, which stipulated the collection, enforcement and removal of information on the list of dishonest persons.

1.3.8 Accelerating the Construction of Smart Justice

Following the issuance of the Opinions on Accelerating the Construction of Smart Courts in 2017, the Supreme People's Court continued to promote the construction of smart courts in 2018. On the basis of summarizing local experiences, the Notice on Further Accelerating the Synchronous Generation and Deep Application of Electronic Files with Cases includes the Technical Requirements for Synchronous Generation and Deep Application of Electronic Files with Cases, which provide guidance from the perspective of construction and application as well as the Management Requirements for Synchronous Generation and Deep Application of Electronic Files with Cases, which standardize the work from the perspective of organization and implementation. It also summarizes the local practical experience of centralized and decentralized generation modes of electronic files, which can be used for reference by courts throughout the country in adopting working modes suitable for themselves and their jurisdictions as soon as possible.

The Supreme People's Procuratorate issued the Opinions on Deepening the Construction of Intelligent Procuratorial Work (2020–2025), which specify the plans for the development of intelligent procuratorial work during the period between 2020 and 2025. The National Action Guide for the Intelligent Procuratorial Work of Procuratorial Organs (2018–2020) provides a road map for comprehensively building an intelligent procuratorial ecology in the new era before the end of 2020.

In 2018, the Ministry of Justice had also studied and arranged for network security and informatization work, such as "digital rule of law and intelligent justice", requiring relevant organs to take integration as the theme, integrate resources to the maximum extent, optimize resource allocation through the application of information technology, and innovate government service and legal service modes, so that the people can have more sense of gain, happiness and security by benefiting from achievements in the development of scientific and technological information technology.

1.4 Criminal Law

Improving the criminal law system means, on the one hand, upholding public interests and protecting the legitimate rights and interests of the public and victims of crime by cracking down on illegal and criminal acts, and, on the other hand, protecting the legitimate rights and interests of criminal suspects and defendants by standardizing the exercise of criminal judicial power. In 2018, the development of criminal justice showed an obvious trend towards institutionalization, with constant improvement of the top-level design. China implemented the Party's policies by amending the Criminal Procedure Law, summed up the judicial experience of leniency for pleading guilty and accepting punishment, and incorporated it into law; strengthened international pursuit of fugitives and recovery of stolen assets, and promoted the institutionalization of anti-corruption through the system of trial in absentia stipulated in the Law on International Criminal Judicial Assistance and the Amendment to the Criminal Procedure Law; promoted judicial democracy by perfecting the criminal jury system; responded to economic and social demands by strengthening the criminal judicial protection of private entrepreneurs and their property rights; stabilized social order by launching a new round of special campaign against organized criminal gangs; implemented the trial-centered reform of the litigation system by promoting the pilot reform of full coverage of criminal defense; and strengthened procuratorial supervision and safeguarded the legitimate rights and interests of the parties by improving the open examination of criminal petitions.

1.4.1 Revising and Improving the Criminal Procedure System

The Criminal Procedure Law involves the protection, restriction or deprivation of personal rights, property rights and litigation rights in the process of exercising the power of criminal punishment by the state. The Third Amendment to the Criminal Procedure Law, adopted at the Sixth Meeting of the Standing Committee of the 13th National People's Congress aims to link the Criminal Procedure Law with the Constitution and ensure the smooth progress of the reform of the national supervision system. To this end, it adjusts investigative powers of people's procuratorates, transfers the power to investigate duty crimes to the National Supervision Commission, while preserving the power of people's procuratorates to carry out investigations on their own initiatives cases of false imprisonment, extortion of a confession by torture, or illegal search or any other crime that infringes upon a citizen's rights or undermines the fair administration of justice committed by judicial personnel by taking advantage of their functions and powers; improves the linkage between supervision cases and criminal proceedings, including the linkages between supervisory investigation and examination and prosecution, and between custody and compulsory measures, and preserves the power of procuratorates to return a case back to a public security organ for supplementary investigation and the power to carry out supplementary investigation on their own; and revises the definition of investigation and the provisions on lawyers' meeting with criminal suspects, surveillance in designated residence and technical investigation measures during the investigation of the crime of bribery. In order to enrich the means and strengthen the work of anti-corruption and international pursuit of fugitives and recovery of stolen assets, the law establishes the system of criminal trial in absentia. In addition, it also establishes the principle of leniency for pleading guilty and accepting punishment, and added corresponding new provisions on summary adjudication procedures, and duty lawyers.

1.4.2 Carrying Out Special Campaigns Against Organized Criminal Gangs

In 2018, a nationwide special campaign against organized criminal gangs had been carried out, combining the crackdown on crimes committed by organized criminal gangs and the fight against corruption and "swatting flies" at the grassroots level. It involved a wide range and a large number of crimes, focusing on key areas, key industries and key fields, severely punishing the organizers, ringleaders, and backbone members of organized criminal gangs of underworld nature and their "protective umbrellas" in accordance with law, and investigating and handling major cases involving organized crimes, especially those about which the people had expressed strong concerns.

Arrangements for the special campaign against organized crimes have been made in the Notice on Launching the Special Campaign against Organized Crimes issued by the CPC Central Committee and the State Council and the Work Plan for the Supervision over the National Special Campaign against Organized Crimes issued by the General Office of the CPC Central Committee and the General Office of the State Council. The Guiding Opinions on Certain Issues Concerning the Handling of Criminal Cases Involving Organizations of a Gangland Nature and Gang-like Groups, jointly issued by the Supreme People's Court, the Supreme People's Procuratorate, the Ministry of Public Security, and the Ministry of Justice, made arrangements for public security, procuratorial, adjudicative and judicial administrative organs to give full play to their functions, cooperate closely with each other to form a synergy, and strengthen the construction of a long-term mechanism for the prevention and punishment of organized crimes.

1.4.3 Strengthening International Criminal Judicial Assistance

To implement the spirit of the 19th CPC National Congress, advance the rule of law in an all-round way, promote national legislation against corruption and the work of international pursuit of fugitives and recovery of stolen assets, the Standing Committee of the 13th National People's Congress passed at its sixth meeting the Law on International Criminal Judicial Assistance, which strengthens international cooperation and eliminates the institutional obstacles between China and foreign countries in combating transnational crimes, provides the domestic legal basis for China to fulfill its obligations under international conventions such as the United Nations Convention against Corruption, the United Nations Convention against Transnational Organized Crime and relevant bilateral treaties, and enhances the awareness and ability of Chinese judicial organs to actively carry out treaty-based international cooperation.

1.4.4 *Protecting the Legitimate Rights and Interests of Entrepreneurs in Accordance with Law*

Entrepreneurs are the core force in social and economic development. In 2018, judicial organs strengthened criminal judicial protection for entrepreneurs and their property rights. In accordance with the Opinions on Creating a Healthy Growth Environment for Entrepreneurs, Promoting Excellent Entrepreneurship, and Giving Full Play to Entrepreneurs' Role issued by the CPC Central Committee and the State Council, the Supreme People's Court issued the Notice on Giving Full Play to the Judicial Function to Create a Good Legal Environment for Entrepreneurs' Innovation and Entrepreneurship, and the Ministry of Justice issued the Opinions on Giving Full Play to the Role of Judicial Functions to Create a Good Legal Environment for the Development of Private Enterprises, so as provide a solid legal guarantee and create a good legal environment for the development of private enterprises. The Supreme People's Court published 13 typical cases in which the people's courts gave full play to their judicial functions to protect property rights and entrepreneurs' legitimate rights and interests, demonstrating the determination and strength of the people's courts to strengthen the protection of property rights and entrepreneurs' legitimate rights and interests in accordance with law.

1.4.5 *Promoting the Full Coverage of Lawyers' Defense*

The pilot work on the full coverage of lawyers' defense in criminal cases is an important measure for promoting the trial-centered reform of the criminal procedure system and the legal protection of human rights, which is of great significance to the development of the rule of criminal law. In 2018, the pilot work was carried out in various provinces in the country. In May 2018, the Government of Guangdong Province started to implement the system of full coverage of lawyers' defense in criminal cases in an all-round way, and the Guangdong High People's Court and the Guangdong Provincial Department of Justice jointly formulated the Implementation Measures for the System of Full Coverage of Lawyers' Defense in Criminal Cases (for Trial Implementation), making Guangdong the only province in China to achieve full coverage of lawyers' defense in criminal cases in courts at all three levels in the province.

1.4.6 *Strengthening Procuratorial Supervision and Trial Supervision*

With respect to strengthening procuratorial supervision and trial supervision, the Third Circuit Court of the Supreme People's Court announced that it would further promote the criminal petition and retrial work in the circuit area, raise the awareness of the harmfulness of misjudged cases by clarifying and refining criminal law rules and criminal policies, and focusing on overcoming difficulties in retrial and problems with case filing standards, so as to effectively correct unjust and wrong cases. In May 2018, the Criminal Petition Department of the Supreme People's Procuratorate issued the Notice on Deepening the Special Supervision Activities of Public Examination of Criminal Petitions, requiring the criminal petition departments of procuratorates at all levels to continuously increase the public examination of criminal petition cases, further expand the scope of the activities, and simplify operational procedures.

1.4.7 *Safeguarding the Legitimate Rights and Interests of Detainees*

With respect to safeguarding the legitimate rights and interests of detainees, the Supreme People's Procuratorate issued the Notice on Launching Special Activities of Supervising the Protection of the Legitimate Rights and Interests of Detainees by Procuratorial Organs Throughout the Country, requiring that the legitimate rights and interests of detainees be strictly protected by supervising prisons, detention centers and other executive organs to carry out the execution of penalties and criminal coercive measures in accordance with the law and in a standardized manner.

1.4.8 *Advancing the Work of State Compensation and Judicial Assistance*

In 2018, judicial organs at all levels had worked together to advance the work of state compensation and judicial assistance. In recent years, the criminal compensation standards for infringement upon personal freedom announced by the Supreme People's Procuratorate and the Supreme People's Court have been increasing year after year, which reflects the importance they attached to the rectification and remedy of miscarriages of justice. In May 2018, the Criminal Petition Department of the Supreme People's Procuratorate and the Supreme People's Court both issued notices demanding the criminal petition departments of procuratorial organs at all levels and the people's courts at all levels to implement the new daily compensation standard of RMB 284.74 yuan when handling cases of state compensation for infringing upon personal freedom, an increase of RMB 25.85 yuan over the previous year. In November 2018, the Supreme People's Court issued 10 typical cases of state compensation and judicial assistance to provide guidance to courts in the whole country on the uniform application of laws and protection of the legitimate rights and interests of the parties when handling cases of state compensation and judicial assistance.

1.5 Civil, Commercial and Economic Law

In 2018, China continued to strengthen the legislation in key fields of civil, commercial and economic law, ensure the implementation of reform achievements, and strive to create a good business environment.

1.5.1 Responding to Major Theoretical Issues and Judicial Practical Needs Through Legislative and Judicial Work

In the construction of civil rule of law in 2018, China mainly focused on the solution of urgent problems in the compilation of the Civil Code and in the civil judicial practice.

With respect to civil legislation, the Legislative Affairs Commission of NPCSC, on the basis of separate civil laws such as the Property Law, the Guarantee Law, the Contract Law, the Tort Liability Law, the Marriage Law and the Inheritance Law and related judicial interpretations, compiled the drafts of various books of the Civil Code, namely the "consultation drafts" prepared by the Civil Law Office of the Commission on October 31, 2017 and March 15, 2018. The drafts included 6 books, namely the books on "property rights", "contracts", "personality rights", "marriage and family", "inheritance" and "tort liability", with a total of 1034 articles. They were submitted by the Chairmen's Meeting of NPCSC to the Fifth Meeting of the Standing Committee of the 13th National People's Congress for deliberation on August 27, 2018, and have now entered the stage of solicitation of public opinions.

With respect to judicial interpretation, because the General Principles of the Civil Law and the General Provisions of the Civil Law are inconsistent with each other in the provisions on extinctive prescription, and in order to correctly apply the provisions in the General Provisions of the Civil Law and protect the legitimate rights and interests of the parties, the Supreme People's Court issued the Interpretation on Several Issues concerning the Application of the Extinctive Prescription Rules in the General Provisions of the Civil Law, which effectively solved the legal application problems caused by the parallel application of the old and new laws.

In order to correctly handle cases involving marital debt disputes and equally protect the legitimate rights and interests of all parties, the Supreme People's Court adopted the Interpretation on Issues concerning the Application of Law in the Trial of Cases Involving Marital Debt Disputes, which defines the concept of marital debt, makes "the joint signatures of husband and wife" the core standard for the identification of marital debts, and clarifies such issues as the identification of the needs of everyday family life, the distribution of the burden of proof, and the relationship with a third party. The Supreme People's Court also issued the Notice on Properly Handling Private Lending Cases according to Law, with a view to giving full play to the evaluation, education and guidance functions of civil and commercial trials, properly handling private lending disputes, and preventing and eliminating various risks.

1.5.2 Strengthening Securities Supervision and Alleviating the Legislative Delay

Since the current round of revision of the Securities Law started in 2013, the revised law has always been in a state of being ready to come out. During this period, A-shares fluctuated abnormally, and it became necessary to be prudent in implementing many new systems. In 2018, the revision of the Securities Law was still listed as "an item prepared for deliberation", and its adoption was once again delayed. Normative documents always play an important role in China's securities legal norms. In 2018, China Securities Regulatory Commission issued dozens of normative documents on the offering of securities, listed companies, information disclosure and market transactions, which have played an important role in "governing" the market. They include Rules of China Securities Regulatory Commission on Administrative Penalty Hearings, Interim Measures for the Supervision and Administration of Regional Equity Markets, Decision of China Securities Regulatory Commission to Amend Seven Sets of Rules Including the Measures for the Administration of Securities Registration and Clearing, Decision to Amend the Provisions of the China Securities Regulatory Commission on the Procedures for the Implementation of Administrative Licensing, Measures for the Supervision over and Administration of Integrity in the Securities and Futures Markets, Decision to Amend the Measures for the Administration of the Initial Public Offerings and Listing of Stocks, Decision to Amend the Measures for the Administration of the Initial Public Offerings and Listing of Stocks on ChiNext, Decision to Amend the Measures for the Administration of the Offering and Underwriting of Securities, Decision on Amending the Measures of China Securities Regulatory Commission for the Issuance Examination Committee, Measures for the Administration of Stock Exchanges, Measures for the Administration of the Margin Trading and Short Selling Business of Securities Companies, Measures for the Compliance Management of Securities Companies and Securities Investment Fund Management Companies, Measures for the Administration of Foreign-Funded Securities Companies, Measures for the Supervision and Administration of Money Market Funds, and Measures for the Administration of Risk-Based Regulatory Indicators of Futures Companies. Meanwhile, in April 2018, the People's Bank of China, China Banking and Insurance Regulatory Commission, China Securities Regulatory Commission, and the State Administration of Foreign Exchange jointly issued Guiding Opinions on Regulating the Asset Management Business of Financial Institutions, which are of positive significance to the development of large asset management.

Securities regulatory authorities continued to strictly examine the issuance of IPOs. By mid-October 2018, the pass rate of A-share IPOs was 60.14%, which was significantly lower than that in 2016 and 2017. Protecting small and medium investors is an important task of market supervision. At the beginning of 2018, Shenzhen Stock Exchange and Shanghai Stock Exchange made specific explanations on the application of the rules on the implementation of Several Provisions on the Reduction of Shares Held in a Listed Company by the Shareholders, Directors, Supervisors, and Senior Executives of Listed Companies, adopted in 2017.

With respect to the delisting system, ST Gene, ST Kunji, ST Alkene Carbon, Zhonghong Shares, and ST Changsheng were delisted and entered the delisting consolidation period for trading. On November 16, 2018, Shenzhen Stock Exchange issued the Implementation Measures of the Shenzhen Stock Exchange for Compulsory Delisting of Listed Companies Due to Major Violations of Law. The legalization and normalization of delisting have become another important system regulating the securities market in China.

1.5.3 Improving Commercial Legislation and Building a Commercial Environment that Meets the Needs of the Times

China's economy has entered a new stage of transition from high-speed growth to high-quality development. In this new era, in order to cross the threshold of this development stage and promote high-quality economic development, it is necessary to continuously enhance China's economic innovation and competitiveness, consolidate the foundation of the real economy, implement the innovation-driven development strategy, and deepen the reform. Commercial law is the main carrier of the rules of the market economy. Adapting to the theme of the times and the changes in the economic environment is an integral part of the development and perfection of commercial law. Looking back at the development of commercial law in 2018, rule of law events in response to the advent of the new era had occurred in many fields.

With the approval of the CPC Central Committee and the State Council, the National Development and Reform Commission and the Ministry of Commerce issued the Negative List of Market Access (2018 Edition), which indicates that China has fully implemented the negative list system of market access, and all kinds of market players can equally enter into the industries, fields and businesses outside the negative list in accordance with law. It is also an important measure for opening up to the outside world.

Business environment is a productive force, and the rule of law is the best business environment. A law-based, internationalized and facilitating business environment is the inherent requirement for achieving high-quality development and modernizing the capacity for and system of state governance. Since the beginning of 2018, local governments at all levels have continued to promote the reform of "simplification of administrative procedures, decentralization of powers, combination of decentralization with appropriate control, and optimization of services". Some local governments have achieved positive results and accumulated useful experiences in facilitating the start-up and operation of enterprises, innovating supervision concepts and methods, and providing quality public services; the State Council summed up and promoted advanced experiences in a timely manner, requiring all local governments to be problem-oriented and demand-oriented, take the advanced as benchmarks, carry out exploration and innovation, and continuously optimize the business environment; and relevant ministries and commissions under the State Council promoted business environment evaluation, strived to build a business environment evaluation system with Chinese characteristics, and to provide goal guidance for building a world-class business environment highland. The State Council issued the Plan for Further Deepening the Reform and Opening-up of China (Guangdong), (Tianjin) and (Fujian) Pilot Free Trade Zones, which sums up the innovative experiences of the three pilot free trade zones, points out the direction for their future high-quality development, and provides safeguards for the further development of free trade zones. In July 2018, the National Development and Reform Commission and the Ministry of Commerce jointly issued the Special Administrative Measures (Negative List) for the Access by Foreign Investment in Pilot Free Trade Zones (2018 Version), which cancel or relax restrictions on the access by foreign investment in more plot fields, thereby further expanding the scope of opening-up. In addition, the State Council also issued the Work Plan for Optimizing Port Business Environment to Enhance Cross-border Trade Facilitation.

Asset management service plays a positive role in meeting the wealth management needs of residents, enhancing the profitability of financial institutions, optimizing the social financing structure, and supporting the real economy. In recent years, China's financial institutions and some non-financial institutions have been very active in the asset management business. However, due to the inconsistent regulatory rules and standards, there have been such phenomena as multi-layer nesting of products and rigid redemption, which have interfered with macro-control to a certain extent and increased the cross-industry and cross-market transmission of risks. The Guiding Opinions on Regulating the Asset Management Business of Financial Institutions, jointly issued by the People's Bank of China, the Insurance Regulatory Commission of the Bank of China, China Securities Regulatory Commission and the State Administration of Foreign Exchange, embody the idea of implementing functional supervision under guidance of the principle of "attaching more importance to substance than form", aiming directly to eliminating arbitrage space caused by standard differences under the separate supervision system.

In order to improve the financial trial system and create a good financial legal environment, the Central Government decided to set up the Shanghai Financial Court, which has the jurisdiction over first-instance financial, civil and commercial cases involving such matters as securities, futures trading, trust, insurance, bills, letters of credit and other types of cases that should be accepted by an intermediate people's court in Shanghai Municipality. The establishment of Shanghai Financial Court was another reform measure aimed at trial specialization after the specialization of the trial of environmental resource cases. It will focus on the tasks of financial work, service the real economy, prevent and control financial risks, deepen financial reform, improve the quality, efficiency and judicial credibility of financial trials, enhance China's discourse power in the making of international financial transaction rules, and improve the financial judicial system with Chinese characteristics.

1.5.4 Making More Progress in Judicial and Administrative Law Enforcement Work in the Field of Intellectual Property

To implement the national intellectual property strategy in a deep-going way and build itself into an intellectual property power, China had made progress in the revision of the Trademark Law, the Patent Law and the Copyright Law in 2018. However, due to the fierce gaming between stakeholders and theoretical controversies over related issues, the legislative process in this field had been slow.

A positive reform trend had been shown in the system of judicial protection of intellectual property. The Opinions on Strengthening Reform and Innovation in the Field of Intellectual Property Adjudication, issued by the General Office of the CPC Central Committee and the General Office of the State Council, have become the first landmark programmatic document specifically on intellectual property adjudication, establishing the guiding ideology, basic principles, reform objectives and key measures for the intellectual property adjudication of people's courts in the new era. The Plan of the Supreme People's Court for Initiation of Judicial Interpretations in 2019 included two intellectual property judicial interpretations that were to be completed before the end of 2018, namely, Interpretation on Several Issues concerning the Trial of Administrative Cases Involving Patent Granting and Confirmation and the Interpretation of the Supreme People's Court on Several Issues Concerning the Application of Laws in Handling Cases of Pre-litigation Act Preservation in Intellectual Property Disputes.

The new round of institutional reform integrates the responsibilities of the National Intellectual Property Administration, the trademark management responsibilities of the State Administration for Industry and Commerce, and the geographical indication management responsibilities of the General Administration of Quality Supervision, Inspection and Quarantine, and re-establishes the National Intellectual Property Administration under the State Administration of Market Regulation, so as to solve the problems of separate management and repetitive law enforcement in the field of trademarks and patents, and improve the intellectual property management system. The examination and registration of intellectual property had been carried out closely around the theme of the reform of "simplification of administrative procedures, decentralization of powers, combination of decentralization with appropriate control, and optimization of services".

In the process of intellectual property administrative law enforcement, investigating and handling cases of infringement upon intellectual properties and counterfeiting cases by administrative organs to make up for the lack of judicial protection of intellectual property has become a prominent feature of intellectual property law enforcement in China at the current stage.

1.5.5 Amending the Individual Income Tax Law to Further Optimize the National Taxation Structure

In 2018, the Individual Income Tax Law was amended with a view to optimizing the tax rate structure, improving pre-tax deduction, standardizing and strengthening the tax base, and strengthening tax supervision. The amended Individual Income Tax Law embodies the following changes: improving the provisions on taxpayers (establishes the determination standard of 183 days for resident individuals and non-resident individuals); making a general provision on business income, rather than subdividing the relevant subjects; modifying some tax rates and optimizing and adjusting the tax rate structure, including the application of 3–45% differential progressive tax rates for comprehensive income, 5–35% excess progressive tax rates for business income, and 20% tax rate for interest, dividends, bonus income, property lease income, property transfer income and accidental income; raising the basic expense to be deducted from the amount of comprehensive income, setting up special additional deductibles, including newly-added income from remuneration for labor services and income from author's remuneration and royalties, with the amount of taxable income calculated by reducing 20% expenses from the income; adding expenses for supporting elderly parents as special additional deductions, with the specific scope, standards and implementation steps of the new special additional deductibles determined by the State Council and reported to the NPCSC for the record; adding new provisions against tax evasion; adding new provisions on tax declaration; adding corresponding information disclosure procedures, etc. In December 2018, the State Council issued the Regulations on the Implementation of the Individual Income Tax Law and the Interim Measures for Additional Special Deductions for Individual Income Tax, and the State Taxation Administration issued the Administrative Measures for the Filing of Individual Income Tax Withholding Returns (for Trial Implementation). Generally speaking, this tax reform involved such matters as taxpayers, tax items, tax rates and procedures, fully reflecting the level of social and economic development and the regulatory role of taxation.

1.6 Social Law

As an important branch law in China's socialist system of law, social law takes the protection and realization of citizens' social rights as its own responsibility at the micro level, and concerns the people's livelihood and well-being at the macro level. It is also an important aspect of enabling the people to share the fruits of reform and opening up. In 2018, China continued to improve its legal system and strengthen law enforcement and judicial protection in the fields of labor and employment, social security and protection of vulnerable groups.

1.6.1 Improving Labor, Employment and Social Security Systems

Employment is the greatest livelihood. On December 5, 2018, the Ministry of Human Resources and Social Security, the National Development and Reform Commission, and the Ministry of Finance jointly issued the Guiding Opinions on Advancing Comprehensive Public Employment Services, which stipulate that China will adhere to the employment priority strategy and active employment policy, provide all-round public employment services, achieve full coverage of urban and rural permanent residents by public employment services, ensure that all kinds of employers equally enjoy public employment services, improve the whole-process employment services for workers, strengthen the whole-process recruitment and employment guidance for employers and the whole-process entrepreneurship services, and implement the whole-process employment assistance and lifelong vocational skills training.

Old-age insurance is a major livelihood issue of great concern to the people. On March 26, 2018, the Ministry of Human Resources and Social Security and the Ministry of Finance jointly issued the Guiding Opinions on Establishing the Mechanism for the Determination of Basic Old-age Insurance Benefits and Regular Adjustment of Basic Pensions for Urban and Rural Residents, which focus on solving the problems of low level of old-age insurance for urban and rural residents, the imperfect mechanism for the determination and normal adjustment of the benefits of the insurance, and the weak incentive and restraint mechanism for payment. The Notice on Raising the Minimum Standard of Basic Pension for Urban and Rural Residents in 2018, issued by the Ministry of Human Resources and Social Security and the Ministry of Finance, initiated the work of uniformly raising the basic pension for urban and rural residents in 2018, marking the start of the operation of the normal adjustment mechanism for basic pension for urban and rural residents.

1.6.2 Strengthening Social Assistance and Guaranteeing the Right to Subsistence and the Right to Development

Social assistance, as an important part of the social security system, plays a very important role in adjusting the allocation of resources, realizing social equity, and maintaining social stability. In 2018, China continued to strengthen its social assistance system.

The Notice of the General Office of the Ministry of Civil Affairs on Piloting Comprehensive Reform of Social Assistance aims at improving the social assistance system, strengthening the overall planning of social assistance resources, optimizing the social assistance process, building social assistance capacity, and innovating the supervision and inspection mechanism for social assistance.

The Implementation Opinions on Effectively Carrying out Social Assistance Work of Subsistence Guarantee in the Three-year Decisive Battle against Poverty, jointly issued by the Ministry of Civil Affairs, the Ministry of Finance and the Poverty Alleviation Office of the State Council, require governments at various levels to adhere to the basic strategy of precision poverty alleviation and the principle of expanding the coverage of social assistance to all those in need, providing subsistence allowances, making overall plans, establishing linkages, and providing correct guidance, optimize policy supply, improve guarantee measures for poverty alleviation such as rural subsistence allowances, assistance and support for people in extreme poverty, and temporary assistance, give full play to the role of social assistance in winning the fight against poverty, and ensure the basic livelihood of the poor people who have completely or partially lost their ability to work and cannot rely on industrial employment to help them get rid of poverty. In October 2018, the Ministry of Civil Affairs, the National Development and Reform Commission and the Office of the Leading Group for Poverty Alleviation and Development of the State Council jointly issued the Action Plan for the Construction and Renovation of Support Service Facilities (Nursing Homes) for Poor People in Deep Poverty Areas to accelerate the construction and transformation of support service facilities for destitute people in deep poverty areas, enhance the capacity for centralized support service for destitute people, and give full play to the role of social assistance in poverty alleviation.

With respect to temporary assistance, the Opinions of the Ministry of Civil Affairs and the Ministry of Finance on Further Strengthening and Improving Temporary Assistance were promulgated to solve such problems as lack of timeliness in assistance, low level of assistance, insufficient system efficiency, and inadequate guarantee of work.

In order to improve the protection of disabled children, the Opinions of the State Council on Establishing a Rehabilitation Assistance System for Disabled Children clearly stipulate the objects, standards and procedures of rehabilitation assistance for disabled children.

1.6.3 Bringing Medical and Health Industry Management Under the Rule of Law

The medical and health industry concerns people's lives and health, and its regulation relies on the gradual improvement of the relevant institutions. In 2018, the (Draft) Vaccine Administration Law, which was the first Chinese legislation on vaccine administration, was submitted to the Seventh Meeting of the Standing Committee of the 13th National People's Congress for deliberation. The draft law adheres to the strategic and public welfare nature of vaccines, highlights the special requirements for vaccine administration, and clearly stipulates that the state implements a stricter access system for vaccine production enterprises than for general pharmaceutical production enterprises and constructs the strictest supervision system covering the whole process and life cycle of vaccines, thereby increasing the cost of offenders for violation of law and implementing the system of responsibility of market players. At the same time, the draft law stipulates that the state formulates the development plan and industrial policy of the vaccine industry, encourages the scale and intensified vaccine production, and continuously improves the technology and quality of vaccine production.

The Guiding Opinions of the General Office of the State Council on Reforming and Perfecting the Comprehensive Supervision System of Medical and Health Industry provide that, in the reform of the comprehensive supervision system of medical and health industry, China should adhere to the principles of government dominance, comprehensive coordination, law-based regulation, localized whole-industry administration, social co-governance, openness and fairness, reform and innovation, and improvement of efficiency, etc., thereby clarifying the subjects and responsibilities of regulation and strengthening the whole-process regulation mechanism.

The Opinions of the General Office of the State Council on Promoting the Development of Internet plus Medical and Health Services provide that China will improve the Internet plus medical and health service system and its supporting system, and strengthen the regulation and security guarantee of the industry.

1.6.4 Deepening the Refined Development of the Rule of Law in the Field of Charity

In order to specify detailed measures for implementing the Charity Law and further promote the rule of law in the field of charity, the Central Government and various departments under it continued to actively issue normative documents on promoting the development of the charity industry in 2018.

Firstly, both the government and charitable organizations have rules to follow in information disclosure. At the beginning of 2018, the General Office of the State Council issued the Opinions on Promoting the Disclosure of Government Information in the Field of Social Welfare Undertakings, which incorporate social public services and welfare undertakings of high concern to the public and strong public welfare nature into the scope of key disclosure, and put forward specific requirements for government information disclosure in the fields of poverty alleviation, social assistance and social welfare, education, basic medical and health service, environmental protection, disaster relief and accident rescue, and public culture and sports; and the Ministry of Civil Affairs issued the Measures for Information Disclosure of Charitable Organizations in August 2018, which contain detailed provisions on the subjects, content, ways and requirements of information disclosure of charitable organizations, highlight the disclosure of information about property activities and public fundraising of charitable organizations, and form a synergy with the relevant systems provided for in the Charity Law and Administrative Measures for Public Fundraising by Charitable Organizations in protecting the legitimate rights and interests of donors, volunteers and beneficiaries and safeguarding the public's right to know.

Secondly, the construction of a charity credit system has been put on the agenda. At the beginning of 2018, the Ministry of Civil Affairs issued the Measures for the Administration of Credit Information of Social Organizations to strengthen the administration of credit information of social organizations by drawing on the practice of administration of enterprise credit information in the reform of the commercial registration system; and forty departments and units, including the National Development and Reform Commission, the People's Bank of China and the Ministry of Civil Affairs, jointly signed the Memorandum of Cooperation in Implementing Joint Incentives for Trustworthiness and Joint Disciplinary Actions against Dishonesty of Relevant Subjects in the Field of Charitable Donations, which establishes a credit information sharing mechanism in the field of charitable donations, and clarifies incentive objects, incentive measures, disciplinary objects and disciplinary measures, with a view to enhancing charity credibility, creating a good charity environment, and promoting the construction of a national social credit system. Finally, promoting the development of "Internet plus" in the field of public interest and charity. In September 2018, the Ministry of Civil Affairs issued the Action Plan for Internet Plus Social Organizations (Social Work and Volunteer Service) (2018–2020) to deal with the existing problems in the fields of social organization, social work and volunteer service, such as weak foundation of informatization, limited scope of information disclosure and insufficient Internet service.

In the drafting of the Charity Law, the legislature attached great importance to the design of the chapter on legal liability. In the implementation stage, attention should be paid to the application and the impact of this law in the concrete litigation practice. Although there are only no more than 20 judgment documents related to Charity Law on China Judgments Online, these judicial documents can nevertheless show the ecology of public interest and charity in China to a certain extent. For example, cases of charitable donation contracts resulting from the ownership and use of surplus donations have become a social hot spot and news focus and are of representative significance for understanding, interpreting, and applying Article 57 (the principle of similar purposes) of the Charity Law. Generally speaking, the substitution effect of the charity legal system in China's judicial proceedings is not significant but far-reaching, just like the influence and significance of the charity industry in the whole social life.

1.6.5 Making Unprecedented Legislative, Judicial, and Law Enforcement Efforts in the Field of Ecology

Great achievements had been made by China in environmental legislation in 2018. Firstly, the concept of ecological civilization construction was incorporated into the Constitution, and all aspects of the work of ecological civilization construction are guaranteed by the Constitution. In this constitutional amendment, "implementing the new development concept", "ecological civilization" and "beauty" were written into the preamble of the Constitution, showing that the Party and the state attach great importance to ecological and environmental issues. This not only is of great significance to China's ecological civilization construction but also provides a constitutional guarantee for meeting people's needs for a better ecology and environment, and a new impetus for improving the legal system of ecology and environment.

Secondly, taking the legislative work plan as the carrier to promote the formulation and revision of laws and administrative regulations related to the construction of the ecological civilization. The ecological legislative activities of the NPCSC entered an active period in 2018. The Law on Prevention and Control of Water Pollution, revised in 2017, came into force on January 1, 2018, and the Law on Prevention and Control of Soil Pollution has already been adopted by the NPCSC and will come into force on January 1, 2019. At the Sixth Meeting of the Standing Committee of the 13th National People's Congress, 15 laws, including the Wildlife Protection Law, were revised to support the implementation of the institutional reform of the State Council in 2018, and timely rationalize and clarify the responsibilities of relevant administrative supervision departments involved in the laws.

Finally, environmental law enforcement is becoming increasingly rule-based and standardized. The new round of institutional reform has had a great impact on environmental law enforcement agencies. The Plan for Deepening the Reform of Party and State Institutions clearly integrates the responsibilities of the Ministry of Environmental Protection with those of the other six departments, and the newly formed Ministry of Ecology and Environment uniformly exercises various functions of pollution emission regulation and ecological protection administrative law enforcement. This was another major institutional reform since the State Environmental Protection Administration was upgraded to become the Ministry of Environmental Protection in July 2008. The Central Ecological Environmental Protection Supervision Office and other departments have been set up under the Ministry of Ecology and Environment to form a normalization system for the supervision of ecological and environmental protection. The Ministry of Ecology and Environment issued the Guiding Opinions on Further Deepening the Reform of "Simplification of Administrative Procedures, Decentralization of Powers, Combination of Decentralization with Appropriate Control, and Optimization of Services" in the Field of Ecology and Environment to Promote High-quality Economic Development, which highlight further decentralization and strengthen environmental supervision and law enforcement. In 2018, China promulgated a series of ministerial rules on environmental law enforcement, including Measures for Soil Environmental Management of

Industrial and Mining Lands (for Trial Implementation), Measures for Public Participation in Environmental Impact Assessment, Measures for Environmental Radiation Monitoring and Information Disclosure of Associated Radioactive Mine Development and Utilization Enterprises (for Trial Implementation), and Measures for the Administration of Pollutant Discharge Licensing (for Trial Implementation), revised the Classified Administration Catalogue of Environmental Impact Assessments for Construction Projects, and abolished the Measures for the Inspection of the Collection of Pollutant Discharge Fees and other relevant rules and normative documents on the collection of pollutant discharge fees. The standardization of law enforcement has been strengthened through the promulgation of the Guiding Opinions of the Ministry of Ecology and Environment and the National Development and Reform Commission on Issues Concerning the Determination of the "Total Investment" of Construction Projects during Eco-Environmental Law Enforcement (for Trial Implementation), Notice of the Ministry of Ecology and Environment on Issuing the Sample of a Pollutant Discharge Permit Commitment Letter, the Application Form for a Pollutant Discharge Permit, the Format of a Pollutant Discharge Permit and other relevant documents. In addition, the release of special programs such as the Three-Year Action Plan for Keeping Our Skies Blue, the Aquatic Biodiversity Protection Plan for Key River Basins, and the Action Plan for Fighting Pollution in Agriculture and Rural Areas have further promoted administrative law enforcement in key areas.

To thoroughly implement the Central Government's major plan for "taking tough steps to forestall and defuse major risks, carry out targeted poverty alleviation, and prevent and control pollution", the Supreme People's Procuratorate issued the Opinions on Giving Full Play to Procuratorial Functions to Provide Judicial Guarantee for Winning the "Three Critical Battles" (No. 8 [2018] of the Supreme People's Procuratorate) and the Notice on Giving Full Play to Procuratorial Functions to Help Fight the Tough Battle of Pollution Prevention and Control.

1.6.6 Strengthening the Institution-Building and the Practice of Public Interest Litigation

In 2018, China made major progress in the promotion of the public interest litigation system and its practice. The CPC Central Committee, the State Council, the NPCSC, the Supreme People's Court, the Supreme People's Procuratorate, the Ministry of Natural Resources, the Ministry of Ecology and Environment, the Ministry of Civil Affairs and the Ministry of Justice all promoted the public interest litigation through the issuance of normative documents.

The Opinions of the CPC Central Committee and the State Council on Comprehensively Strengthening Ecological and Environmental Protection and Resolutely Fighting the Uphill Battle for the Prevention and Control of Pollution, the Resolution of NPCSC on Comprehensively Tightening Ecological and Environmental Protection and Lawfully Promoting Triumph in the Uphill Battle for Prevention and

Control of Pollution, Article 25 of the Law on the Protection of Heroes and Martyrs, and Article 97 of the Law on the Prevention and Control of Soil Pollution have established the institutional foundation for the multi-field public interest litigation system, and Article 16 of the Law on People's Assessors clearly stipulates that where a people's court tries a first-instance case of public interest litigation, people's assessors and judges shall form a seven-member collegial panel for the trial of the case. The Supreme People's Court and the Supreme People's Procuratorate promulgated 13 normative documents concerning the public interest litigation system, and 9 of the departmental normative documents and departmental working documents issued by relevant ministries and commissions of the State Council in 2018 involve the public interest litigation system.

1.7 Prospect for the Development of the Rule of Law in China in 2019

1.7.1 Comprehensively Promote Law-Based Governance and Safeguarding the Deepening of Reform and Opening-Up

Since the Third Plenary Session of the Eleventh CPC Central Committee, China has gone through a 40-year arduous journey of reform and opening-up from exploration to comprehensive advancement and to comprehensive deepening. As Confucius said, "One should no longer suffer from perplexities at the age of 40". The exploration in past 40 years has finally enabled China to see clearly the future direction of this development path.

At the beginning of reform and opening-up, faced with the complex social environment and the inertia of existing institutional mechanisms, China mainly relied on the introduction of supporting policies for the implementation and promotion of the reform and opening-up; since the basic strategy of governing the country by law was formally put forward at the 15th National Congress of the CPC in 1997, the rule of law has taken over the "baton" and become the backbone and the biggest social consensus in promoting and guaranteeing the reform and opening-up. The rule of law is the concentrated embodiment of the modernization of the state governance system and capacity. The new measures for the deepening of the reform that have been adopted one after another and the "the Belt and Road Initiative" have raised new demands and posed new challenges for the development of the rule of law.

At its 18th National Congress, the CPC put forward the goal of "deepening reform and opening up in an all-round way" and the task of "advancing the rule of law in an all-round way", which have developed synchronously and echoed each other, leading to brilliant achievements.

At its 19th National Congress, the CPC pointed out that advancing law-based governance in all fields is a profound revolution in state governance. China must promote the rule of law and strive to ensure scientific lawmaking, strict law enforcement, impartial administration of justice, and the observance of law by everyone. In the future construction of the rule of law, China will continue to focus on these aspects of the work, so as to guarantee the comprehensive deepening of reform and opening up. To this end, it must further integrate the leading institutions of the rule of law at the local level, strengthen organization and leadership, and establish a scientific and effective evaluation mechanism for the implementation of the rule of law.

1.7.2 Breaking Through the Bottlenecks of the Existing System and Ensuring that Reform and Development Are Based on Law

With the continuous deepening of the reform and the acceleration of the pace of development, many legal systems that were "ready to come out" but had not been able to come out for a long time should also move with the times to keep up with the pace of the reform and development.

For example, the compilation of the Civil Code, which is currently being steadily advanced, is the top priority of China in improving its civil legal system. Formulating a scientific and advanced civil code with Chinese characteristics that conforms to the national conditions of China at the primary stage of socialism on the basis of various separate civil laws is an important step and the inevitable direction of development towards the construction of law-based governance. Before the compilation of the Civil Code is completed, China should carry out an effective review of the application of civil legal norms and further promote the case guidance system. This not only is conducive to the concrete application of abstract legal provisions but also can make up for the defects in legislation and the delay in the adoption of legal rules in light of practical needs. In the field of securities regulation, although the abnormal fluctuation of A-shares led to the consensus that the revision of the Securities Law should be prudent, the long delay in the revision of the Securities Law will result in more difficult problems, and the market will also face more uncertain risks.

For another example, against the background of the institutional reform aimed at incorporating government legislative affairs departments into judicial administrative departments, the questions of how to further promote the reform of the administrative reconsideration system and how to connect the administrative reconsideration system and administrative litigation system are worthy of study and attention; and the Plan for the Reform of Administrative Reconsideration System (Exposure Draft) has been formulated, but the amendment of the Administrative Reconsideration Law has not yet been put on the agenda.

For another example, clarifying the relationship and connection between public interest litigation and private interest litigation should be the key task in the construction of the public interest litigation system. Administrative public interest litigation needs to be further integrated and embedded into the traditional litigation framework. More detailed procedural design still needs to be made in order to deal with the differences between the administrative public interest litigation mode and traditional subjective litigation mode in such concrete matters as plaintiff qualification, trial procedure, evidence rules, and judgment types, so as to avoid the conflict of application of rules under the two litigation modes.

1.7.3 Exploring and Improving Relevant Supporting Systems to Ensure the Smooth Implementation of the Institutional Reform

The institutional reform of the central Party and state organs had been completed by the end of 2018, and all local institutional reform tasks will be basically completed by the end of March 2019. The smooth implementation of the institutional reform plan is precisely the starting point of the gradual adaptive change of corresponding supporting systems. With the operation of the reformed institutions, the old institutions will inevitably become "outdated". If they are not adjusted in time, this disharmony will become increasingly prominent, and even affect the effect of institutional reform. For example, in the field of administrative law, which has a great impact on society, institutional reform has resulted in some new problems relating to the legality review of administrative normative documents, law enforcement competence, administrative reconsideration, and the implementation of the administrative litigation system, which urgently need to be adjusted and clarified by legislation.

1.7.4 Improving Supporting Measures and Comprehensively Summing up the Experience of Judicial Reform

The judicial reform with the reform of the judicial responsibility system as the core is now advancing in all directions and has become the key to standardizing judicial behavior, upholding judicial justice, and enhancing judicial credibility. The supporting measures still need to be further improved in the future. In the reform of the judicial responsibility system, the guarantee of the handling of cases by quota-based judges and procurators, the improvement of their case-handling quality, the implementation of provisions on their benefits, and the guarantee of their personal safety, the selection of judges' assistants, the smoothness of the channels of their promotion, and the guarantee of auxiliary personnel still need to be tracked and paid attention to. Enforcement is a crucial link in judicial organs' numerous tasks that affects the realization of the rights and interests of the winning party and the authority of judicial organs. The Supreme People's Court plans to basically overcome the enforcement difficulties in two to three years, and has achieved remarkable results in building a big pattern of implementation linkage, improving the capacity for "identification of persons and property inquiry" and for the realization of property, and standardizing enforcement behavior. In the future, it is still necessary to further strengthen and improve enforcement legislation, reinforce the linkage mechanism of the whole society, and focus on building a long-term enforcement mechanism.

1.7.5 Creating a Law-Based Business Environment to Promote Economic Construction and Opening-Up

Further optimizing the business environment has been the focus of China's economic construction in recent years. As early as in 2017, Party General Secretary Xi Jinping emphasized the need to create a stable, fair, transparent and predictable business environment. In 2018, it was proposed at the Central Economic Work Conference that China should promote stable economic growth in a coordinated way, advance reform, make structural adjustments, improve living standards, guard against risks, ensure stability, see that the economy operates within an appropriate range, and devote more efforts to ensure stability in employment, financial operations, foreign trade, foreign investment, domestic investment, and expectations, bolster market confidence, and enhance the people's senses of satisfaction, happiness and security. All these require the optimization of the business environment, which is closely related to the construction of the rule of law in the final analysis.

Firstly, China should further standardize administrative power in accordance with law, deepen the reforms of "simplification of administrative procedures, decentralization of powers, combination of decentralization with appropriate control, and optimization of services", and safeguard economic and social development.

In 2019, governments at various levels should speed up the implementation of the Notice on Focusing on Enterprises' Concerns and Further Promoting Implementation of Business Environment Optimization Policies issued by the General Office of the State Council in 2018, create a market environment of fair competition, promote foreign investment, facilitate trade, improve the quality and efficiency of administrative approval services, reduce the production and operation costs of enterprises, protect property rights and strengthen regulation. The core of this document is still the proper meaning of the reforms of "simplification of administrative procedures, decentralization of powers, combination of decentralization with appropriate control, and optimization of services". Therefore, the reform measures aimed at optimizing the business environment are bound to include more legal actions in 2019.

Secondly, China should give a positive legal response to the new economy and new business forms. With the continuous emergence of new business forms and models, the concept of government regulation has been constantly updated. In the Government Work Report of 2017, the State Council pointed out that "the regulatory rules for emerging industries should be formulated based on the principles of encouraging innovation, inclusiveness and prudence". On September 20, 2018, the

CPC Central Committee and the State Council issued Several Opinions on Improving and Promoting the Consumption System and Mechanism to Further Stimulate the Consumption Potentiality of Residents, which mentioned "inclusive and prudent" regulation three times. In the future, active and prudent supervision strategies should be adopted for the new economy and new business forms to promote their rule-based healthy development.

Thirdly, the prevention of financial risks should be the focus of the improvement of the legal business environment. Financial legislation should be foresighted and time-sensitive, so as to adapt to the rapidly changing development trend of the financial industry in the Internet era, while the improvement of the business environment is inevitably based on the standardized and healthy development of the financial industry. In the construction of financial rule of law, China must solve the existing problems and introduce forward-looking measures in a timely manner to deal with possible risks in the future.

Finally, China should emphasize the importance of intellectual property protection in safeguarding the business environment. The revision of major laws in the field of intellectual property, such as the Copyright Law, the Patent Law and the Trademark Law, will continue. As the revision of these laws involves more or less the functional adjustment and institutional reform of relevant competent government departments, it will probably not progress very smoothly. In addition, the government should impose heavier penalties on those who infringe upon intellectual property. In the process of business activities and brand building, enterprises need the market to provide a fair and just environment and protect their intangible assets of brands from being eroded as a result of infringements upon intellectual property rights. China should completely change the situation in which it is difficult for enterprises to uphold their rights in intellectual property cases. In the punishment of infringers, importance should be attached not only to the amounts of fines but, more importantly, also to weakening the capacity for infringement and preventing those who seriously and repeatedly infringe upon intellectual properties from participating in market operations. The intellectual property courts in Beijing, Shanghai and Guangzhou will continue to make useful attempts to solve the problems of prolonged litigation, difficulty in adducing evidence, and low compensation in the trial of intellectual property cases. The judgments of major intellectual property cases should guide social and economic development. The dividends released by the reform of the intellectual property administration system will also accelerate the brand building and innovation-driven development strategy.

1.7.6 Preventing and Controlling Social Risks and Solving the Dilemma of Grassroots Social Governance

In 2018, there were occasional mass incidents in some places, which indicated that there were flaws in the introduction and implementation of local government policies, and the ability to deal with mass incidents still needed to be improved. In recent years, the difficulties and dilemmas encountered by Party committees and governments at all levels in social governance show that the traditional means and models of social governance have been unable to meet the new requirements of the Party and the state for social governance, and some deep-seated institutional contradictions in the performance of government duties need to be solved urgently.

Many incidents endangering public safety in 2018 should be paid great attention to. Namely, in the transitional period when social contradictions are concentrated and prominent, social risk management and control are facing a severe test, and there is an urgent need for a legal response.

The report to the 19th National Congress of the CPC proposes to establish a social governance model based on collaboration, participation, and common interests, step up institution building in social governance and improve the law-based social governance model under which Party committees exercise leadership, the government assumes responsibility, non-governmental actors provide assistance, and the public gets involved, strengthen public participation and rule of law in social governance, and make such governance smarter and more specialized. This shows that the rule of law plays a crucial role in promoting the formation of a new pattern of social governance. In the future construction of social rule of law, China should focus on improving the state governance capacity, proceed from standardizing government decision-making, preventing and controlling decision-making risks, dealing with emergencies, and repairing social relations and other subtleties, establish a scientific social risk evaluation mechanism, and improve the social risk perception, prevention and control system, so as to raise the level of modernization of state governance system and capacity in an all-round way.

Chapter 2
Report on the Indices of Government Transparency in China (2017)—From the Perspective of Information Disclosure on Government Websites

Innovation Project Team on the Rule of Law Index

Abstract In 2017, The Center for Studies of National Rule of Rule Index, Chinese Academy of Social Sciences (CASS) and the Innovation Project Team on the Rule of Law Index, Institute of Law, CASS conducted an assessment of the open government work of 54 departments of the State Council, 31 provincial-level governments, 49 governments of larger cities and 100 county-level governments, focusing on such aspects of the work as decision-making, administrative services, implementation and results, disclosure of information in key fields, policy interpretation and response to public concerns, and information disclosure upon application. This report analyzes the progress made and problems faced by various assessment targets in the open government work, and puts forward corresponding countermeasures and suggestions.

Keywords Open government work · Government transparency · Rule of law index · Government website

In 2017, the Center for Studies of National Rule of Rule Index, Chinese Academy of Social Sciences (CASS) (hereinafter referred to as the "Project Team") continued to investigate and assess the open government work at all levels. This report summarizes and analyzes the results of the investigation and assessment.

Leaders of the Project Team: Tian He, director of Center for Studies of National Rule of Rule Index, Chinese Academy of Social Sciences (CASS) and a research fellow at the CASS Institute of Law; and Lv Yanbin, a research fellow and head of the Department of Survey and Studies of National Situation of Rule of Law, CASS Institute of Law. Members of the Project Team: Wang Xiaomei, Wang Yiming, Li Yanjie, Hu Changming, Xu Bin, Liu Yanpeng, Ma Xiaoling, Wang Shushan, Wang Xiaoli, Wang Zhan, Wang Xin, Mao Yuxiang, Feng Tianyang, Zhu Ying, Ren Yuxi, Xiang Lin, Yan Wenguang, Ruan Yuqing, Yang Deshi, Wu Hongqiang, Zhang Runze, Chen Kexin, Jin Junzhou, Zhou Tianqi, Jing Han, Hou Bingjie, Xu Kaiwen, Qin Yijian, Gao Yunhao, Huang Enhao, Ge Yantong. Main authors of the report: Lv Yanbin.

Innovation Project Team on the Rule of Law Index (✉)
Institute of Law, Chinese Academy of Social Sciences, Beijing, China
e-mail: 13263169197@163.com

H. Tian et al. (eds.), *Report on the Rule of Law Index in China 2*,
Research Series on the Chinese Dream and China's Development Path,
https://doi.org/10.1007/978-981-19-9597-2_2

2.1 Targets, Indices and Methods of Assessment

The assessment targets in 2017 included 54 departments of the State Council, 31 provincial-level governments, 49 governments of larger cities and 100 county-level governments. The 100 county-level governments covered by this assessment were the pilot district and county governments selected in the Notice of the General Office of the State Council on Issuing the Plan for Conducting the Pilot Program of Standardizing and Regularizing Grassroots Open Government Work.

The indices of assessment in 2017 were set by the Project Team in accordance with the Regulations on the Disclosure of Government Information, the Notice of the General Office of the CPC Central Committee and the General Office of the State Council on Issuing the Opinions on Comprehensively Advancing Open Government Work, the Detailed Rules of the General Office of the State Council for the Implementation of the Opinions on Comprehensively Promoting Open Government Work, and the Key Tasks of Open Government Work in 2017 issued by the General Office of the State Council. The grade I indices used for the assessment of open government work of departments of the State Council and local governments at all levels include openness of decision-making, the openness of administrative service, the openness of implementation and results, information disclosure in key fields, policy interpretation and response to public concerns, and disclosure upon application (see Tables 2.1, 2.2, 2.3 and 2.4).

The index of openness of decision-making mainly examined the pre-disclosure of major decisions by various departments of the State Council and governments at all levels, as well as the openness of the results of handling suggestions and

Table 2.1 Government transparency index system (for departments of the State Council)

Grade I indices	Grade II indices
Openness of decision-making (20%)	Pre-disclosure of major decisions (60%)
	Openness of the results of handling of suggestions and proposals (40%)
Openness of administrative service (25%)	Disclosure of government service information (40%)
	Disclosure of "double random" inspection information (30%)
	Disclosure of administrative penalty information (30%)
Openness of implementation and results (10%)	Annual report on the construction of a law-based government (100%)
Information disclosure in key fields (25%)	Disclosure of normative documents (50%)
	Openness of financial budget and final accounts (50%)
Policy interpretation and response to public concerns (20%)	Policy interpretation (70%)
	Response to public concerns (30%)

Table 2.2 Government transparency index system (for provincial-level governments)

Grade I indices	Grade II indices
Openness of decision-making (20%)	Pre-disclosure of major decisions (60%)
	Openness of the results of handling of suggestions and proposals (40%)
Openness of administrative service (25%)	Openness of power list (10%)
	Disclosure of government service information (35%)
	Disclosure of "double random" inspection information (25%)
	Disclosure of administrative penalty information (30%)
Openness of implementation and results (15%)	Disclosure of audit results (30%)
	Annual report on the construction of a law-based government (30%)
	Government work report (40%)
Information disclosure in key fields (20%)	Disclosure of normative documents (40%)
	Openness of financial budget and final accounts (35%)
	Ranking of urban water environment quality (25%)
Policy interpretation	Policy interpretation (70%)
	Response to public concerns (30%)

proposals by various departments of the State Council and provincial-level governments. The index of openness of administrative service mainly examined the disclosure of government service information, "double random" inspection information and administrative penalty information by departments of the State Council and governments at all levels with corresponding functions and powers, as well as the disclosure of power lists by governments at all levels. The index of disclosure of implementation and results mainly examined the disclosure of audit results and government work reports by governments at all levels, the disclosure of annual reports on the construction of a law-based government by departments of the State Council and governments at all levels, and the disclosure of annual reports on government information disclosure by governments of larger cities and county-level governments. The index of information disclosure in key fields mainly examined the disclosure of normative documents and financial budgets and final accounts by departments of the State Council and governments at all levels. The Project Team also carried out spot inspections on the disclosure of urban water environment quality rankings by provincial-level governments, disclosure of centralized drinking water source quality monitoring information and shantytown renovation information by governments of larger cities, and the disclosure of education information by county-level governments. The Index of policy interpretation and response to public concerns included

Table 2.3 Government transparency index system (for governments of larger cities)

Grade I indices	Grade II indices
Openness of decision-making (15%)	Pre-disclosure major decisions (100%)
Openness of administrative service (25%)	Disclosure of power lists (10%)
	Disclosure of government service information (35%)
	Disclosure of "double random" inspection information (25%)
	Disclosure of administrative penalty information (30%)
Openness of implementation and results (20%)	Disclosure of audit results (30%)
	Annual report on the construction of a law-based government (30%)
	Government work report (30%)
	Annual report on government information disclosure (10%)
Information disclosure in key fields (25%)	Disclosure of normative documents (25%)
	Disclosure of financial budget and final accounts (20%)
	Disclosure of monitoring information about the quality of centralized drinking water sources (30%)
	Disclosure of information about shantytown renovation (25%)
Policy interpretation and response to public concerns (15%)	Policy interpretation (70%)
	Respond to concerns (30%)

two grade II indices: policy interpretation and response to public concerns. The index of information disclosure upon application only assessed the smoothness of channels of application by letter and the standardization of reply of 100 county-level governments.

The Project Team analyzed the situation of implementation of the disclosure requirements by various assessment targets by observing the relevant information disclosed on their web portals and the websites of their relevant departments. Beginning on September 27, 2017, it sent applications for the disclosure of government information by registered letter to 100 county-level governments. The content of the application was the following: "Have you provided public cultural service to migrant workers in your administrative area and their wives and children who were left behind in rural areas during the period from January 1, 2016 to now? If yes, please disclose information about the general situation of the completion of this public cultural service." The time period for assessment for different assessment targets varied, but the deadline was generally set as November 10, 2017.

Table 2.4 Index system of government transparency index (for county-level governments)

Grade I indices	Grade II indices
Openness of decision-making (10%)	Pre-disclosure major decision-making (100%)
Openness of administrative service (25%)	Disclosure of power lists (10%)
	Disclosure of government service information (35%)
	Disclosure of "double random" inspection information (25%)
	Disclosure of administrative penalty information (30%)
Openness of implementation and results (20%)	Disclosure of audit results (30%)
	Annual report on the construction of a law-based government (30%)
	Government work report (30%)
	Annual report on government information disclosure (10%)
Information disclosure in key fields (20%)	Disclosure of normative documents (30%)
	Disclosure of financial budget and final accounts (30%)
	Information disclosure in the field of education (40%)
Policy interpretation and response to public concerns (15%)	Policy interpretation (70%)
	Response to public concerns (30%)
Disclosure upon application (10%)	Smoothness of channels (40%)
	Standardized responses (60%)

2.2 General Situation of Assessment Results

In 2017, the departments of the State Council with the highest scores in the assessment included the Ministry of Industry and Information Technology, the General Administration of Quality Supervision, Inspection and Quarantine, the Ministry of Commerce, the Ministry of Transport, the Ministry of Environmental Protection, the Ministry of Land and Resources, the Ministry of Finance, the Ministry of Culture, the Ministry of Education, the General Administration of Customs and the State Forestry Administration (see Table 2.5 for the assessment results). The provincial-level governments with the highest scores in the assessment included the governments of Guizhou Province, Sichuan Province, Beijing Municipality, Yunnan Province, Guangdong Province, Henan Province, Anhui Province, Shandong Province, Shanghai Municipality and Hubei Province (see Table 2.6 for the assessment results). The governments of larger cities with the highest scores in the assessment included: those of Hefei, Suzhou, Guangzhou, Chengdu, Zhengzhou, Ningbo, Yinchuan, Qingdao, Zibo and Shenzhen (see Table 2.7 for the assessment results). And the county-level governments with the highest scores in the assessment included those of Putuo District of Shanghai Municipality, Ningguo City of Anhui Province, Jiangbei District of Ningbo City of Zhejiang Province, Xicheng District of Beijing Municipality, Hongkou District of Shanghai Municipality, Pudong New Area of Shanghai Municipality, Luyang District of Hefei City of Anhui Province, Huizhou District of Huangshan City of Anhui Province, Lingbi County of Anhui Province and Rugao City of Jiangsu Province (see Table 2.8 for assessment results).

2.3 Bright Spots Found in the Assessment

In 2017, which was the second year of comprehensive and deep promotion of the open government work, the State Council issued a series of documents on promoting the open government work, including the Opinions of the General Office of the CPC Central Committee and the General Office of the State Council on Comprehensively Promoting the Open Government Work, sending an increasingly clear message that governments and their departments at all levels should promote in an all-round way the whole-process openness of decision-making, implementation, administration, service and results, give play to the three-in-one and complementary role of information release, policy interpretation and response to public concerns, and expand public participation in an all-round way to enable the public to fully and deeply participate in all aspects of state governance. The assessment shows that China had achieved remarkable results in the open government work in the whole country in 2017.

2.3.1 Prominent Results Had Been Achieved by Governments at Various Levels and Their Departments in Guiding the Open Government Work in Their Respective Fields and Regions

The open government work needs corresponding operational rules and standards, and the open government work of governments at all levels cannot be carried out without guidance from higher-level governments. The assessment shows that over the years, various local departments had defined the standards on the open government work in their respective regions by issuing relevant documents and unifying the open platform, standardized the construction of the platform of openness, and raised the level of openness in their respective fields and regions.

In the field of environmental protection, the Ministry of Environmental Protection issued the Notice on Issuing the Government Information Disclosure Guide for Environmental Impact Assessment of Construction Projects (for Trial Implementation) (No. 103 [2013], General office of the Ministry of Environmental Protection),

Table 2.5 Results of assessment of indices of government transparency of departments of the State Council

Ranking	Departments of the State Council (20%)	Openness of decision-making	Openness of administrative service (25%)	Openness of implementation and results (10%)	Information disclosure in key fields (25%)	Policy interpretation and response to public concerns (20%)	Total score (out of 100)
1	Ministry of Industry and Information Technology	51.50	96.00	0.00	75.00	93.33	71.72
2	General Administration of Quality Supervision, Inspection and Quarantine	59.50	90.70	100.00	75.00	33.33	69.99
3	Ministry of Commerce	57.50	79.40	70.00	50.00	93.33	69.52
4	Ministry of Transport	73.00	68.20	0.00	73.57	96.67	69.38
5	Ministry of Environmental Protection	51.50	66.20	50.00	75.00	86.67	67.93
6	Ministry of Land and Resources	53.50	80.90	0.00	87.50	73.33	67.47
7	Ministry of Finance	64.00	82.60	0.00	75.00	73.33	66.87
8	Ministry of Culture	38.00	48.20	0.00	100.00	93.33	63.32
9	Ministry of Education	44.00	62.50	0.00	75.00	96.67	62.51

(continued)

Table 2.5 (continued)

Ranking	Departments of the State Council (20%)	Openness of decision-making	Openness of administrative service (25%)	Openness of implementation and results (10%)	Information disclosure in key fields (25%)	Policy interpretation and response to public concerns (20%)	Total score (out of 100)
10	General Administration of Customs	44.00	78.29	0.00	73.57	78.33	62.43
	State Forestry Administration	32.00	56.23	0.00	98.57	86.67	62.43
12	Ministry of Civil Affairs	44.00	94.86	0.00	50.00	83.33	61.68
13	Ministry of Human Resources and Social Security	38.00	53.71	50.00	75.00	83.33	61.45
14	National Bureau of Statistics	65.50	54.29	0.00	75.00	80.00	61.42
15	State Administration of Work Safety	43.00	62.50	0.00	75.00	90.00	60.98
16	China Food and Drug Administration	56.00	49.40	50.00	72.14	71.67	60.92
17	Ministry of Agriculture	51.50	53.50	0.00	75.00	90.00	60.43
18	Ministry of Science and Technology	64.00	36.80	0.00	73.57	100.00	60.39
19	State Oceanic Administration	56.00	42.80	50.00	75.00	73.33	60.32

(continued)

Table 2.5 (continued)

Ranking	Departments of the State Council (20%)	Openness of decision-making	Openness of administrative service (25%)	Openness of implementation and results (10%)	Information disclosure in key fields (25%)	Policy interpretation and response to public concerns (20%)	Total score (out of 100)
20	State Administration for Industry and Commerce	51.50	51.50	0.00	75.00	83.33	58.59
21	National Development and Reform Commission	71.00	67.40	0.00	50.00	75.00	58.55
22	State Administration of Cultural Heritage	51.50	28.00	0.00	100.00	80.00	58.30
23	Civil Aviation Administration of China	19.50	40.00	0.00	100.00	96.67	58.23
24	China Banking Regulatory Commission	38.00	66.80	0.00	75.00	71.67	57.38
25	State Intellectual Property Office	38.00	54.20	70.00	50.00	83.33	57.32
26	National Tourism Administration	32.00	28.00	0.00	100.00	93.33	57.07
27	State Railway Administration	38.00	36.80	0.00	100.00	75.00	56.80
28	China Meteorological Administration	46.00	54.29	0.00	75.00	73.33	56.19

(continued)

Table 2.5 (continued)

Ranking	Departments of the State Council (20%)	Openness of decision-making	Openness of administrative service (25%)	Openness of implementation and results (10%)	Information disclosure in key fields (25%)	Policy interpretation and response to public concerns (20%)	Total score (out of 100)
29	National Public Complaints and Proposals Administration	4.00	82.00	0.00	72.14	73.33	54.00
30	Ministry of Water Resources	44.00	54.80	0.00	50.00	90.00	53.00
31	China Securities Regulatory Commission	24.00	83.60	0.00	50.00	73.33	52.87
32	National Energy Administration	56.00	42.90	50.00	50.00	65.00	52.43
33	Ministry of Public Security	32.00	72.70	0.00	50.00	76.67	52.41
34	National Audit Office	32.00	36.00	100.00	50.00	71.67	52.23
35	General Administration of Sports	23.50	52.57	0.00	75.00	73.33	51.26
36	State Post Bureau	38.00	51.80	0.00	50.00	90.00	51.05
37	Ministry of Housing and Urban–Rural Development	23.50	77.60	0.00	50.00	71.67	50.93

(continued)

Table 2.5 (continued)

Ranking	Departments of the State Council (20%)	Openness of decision-making	Openness of administrative service (25%)	Openness of implementation and results (10%)	Information disclosure in key fields (25%)	Policy interpretation and response to public concerns (20%)	Total score (out of 100)
38	State Administration of Press, Publication, Radio, Film and Television	46.00	50.10	0.00	50.00	73.33	48.89
39	State Tobacco Monopoly Administration	40.00	52.10	0.00	50.00	76.67	48.86
40	State Taxation Administration	10.00	18.40	70.00	73.57	78.33	47.66
41	People's Bank of China	10.00	76.50	0.00	50.00	65.00	46.63
42	Ministry of Foreign Affairs	45.50	74.17	0.00	73.57	0.00	46.03
43	State Administration of Foreign Exchange	4.00	34.80	0.00	75.00	83.33	44.92
44	State Administration of Religious Affairs	4.00	45.60	0.00	100.00	36.67	44.53
45	State Bureau of Surveying, Mapping and Geo-Information	10.00	52.10	0.00	50.00	80.00	43.53
46	State Grain Administration	6.00	26.00	0.00	75.00	80.00	42.45

(continued)

Table 2.5 (continued)

Ranking	Departments of the State Council (20%)	Openness of decision-making	Openness of administrative service (25%)	Openness of implementation and results (10%)	Information disclosure in key fields (25%)	Policy interpretation and response to public concerns (20%)	Total score (out of 100)
47	China Insurance Regulatory Commission	23.50	54.80	0.00	50.00	50.00	40.90
48	National Health and Family Planning Commission	10.00	18.20	80.00	50.00	60.00	39.05
49	National Administration of Traditional Chinese Medicine	17.50	36.57	0.00	50.00	68.33	38.81
50	Ministry of Justice	0.00	67.00	0.00	50.00	43.33	37.92
51	China Earthquake Administration	0.00	26.60	0.00	50.00	93.33	37.82
52	State-owned Assets Supervision and Administration Commission of the State Council	4.00	0.00	70.00	50.00	83.33	36.97
53	National Ethnic Affairs Commission	0.00	0.00	0.00	100.00	58.33	36.67
54	State Administration of Foreign Experts	0.00	7.60	0.00	50.00	36.67	21.73

Table 2.6 Results of assessment of indices of transparency of provincial-level governments

Ranking	Provincial-level governments	Openness of decision-making (15%)	Openness of administrative service (25%)	Openness of implementation and results (10%)	Information disclosure in key fields (25%)	Policy interpretation and response to public concerns (20%)	Total score (out of 100)
1	Guizhou Province	70.00	68.45	64.00	86.67	96.67	77.38
2	Sichuan Province	69.50	68.35	100.00	57.17	96.67	76.75
3	Beijing Municipality	44.50	73.50	76.00	92.22	96.67	76.45
4	Yunnan Province	44.00	80.95	94.00	67.42	96.67	75.95
5	Guangdong Province	63.50	78.20	86.80	46.08	96.67	73.82
6	Henan Province	51.50	79.20	50.00	75.17	96.67	71.97
7	Anhui Province	51.00	61.13	65.00	85.17	93.33	70.93
8	Shandong Province	19.50	94.30	85.00	59.33	93.33	70.76
9	Shanghai Municipality	38.50	73.40	79.60	59.33	96.67	69.19
10	Hubei Province	20.50	69.23	85.00	76.33	96.67	68.76
11	Fujian Province	30.00	56.20	100.00	66.33	96.67	67.65
12	Tianjin Municipality	50.00	62.63	66.40	65.89	90.00	66.79
13	Hunan Province	38.00	70.95	85.00	47.08	90.00	65.50
14	Heilongjiang Province	28.50	63.00	85.00	68.83	86.67	65.30
15	Jiangsu Province	41.50	82.63	94.60	22.75	86.67	65.03

(continued)

Table 2.6 (continued)

Ranking	Provincial-level governments	Openness of decision-making (15%)	Openness of administrative service (25%)	Openness of implementation and results (10%)	Information disclosure in key fields (25%)	Policy interpretation and response to public concerns (20%)	Total score (out of 100)
16	Guangxi Zhuang Autonomous Region	38.00	66.48	94.00	25.58	93.33	62.10
17	Shaanxi Province	6.00	65.23	85.00	61.17	96.67	61.82
18	Henan Province	21.00	71.20	68.00	46.00	96.67	60.73
19	Gansu Province	10.00	49.78	70.00	82.17	96.67	60.71
20	Zhejiang Province	20.50	48.90	79.60	65.83	93.33	60.10
21	Chongqing Municipality	12.00	66.05	44.00	81.33	90.00	59.78
22	Ningxia Hui Autonomous Region	6.00	57.43	74.60	73.33	90.00	59.41
23	Shanxi Province	24.00	76.18	52.40	51.25	86.67	59.29
24	Hebei Province	34.50	44.30	94.60	54.83	80.00	59.13
25	Jiangxi Province	6.00	49.25	88.00	61.83	86.67	56.41
26	Inner Mongolia Autonomous Region	25.50	54.33	58.60	57.50	86.67	56.30
27	Liaoning Province	26.00	46.45	73.60	41.50	78.33	51.82
28	Qinghai Province	14.50	54.80	82.60	39.17	73.33	51.49
29	Jilin Province	19.50	55.38	50.00	1.75	93.33	44.26

(continued)

Table 2.6 (continued)

Ranking	Provincial-level governments	Openness of decision-making (15%)	Openness of administrative service (25%)	Openness of implementation and results (10%)	Information disclosure in key fields (25%)	Policy interpretation and response to public concerns (20%)	Total score (out of 100)
30	Xinjiang Uygur Autonomous Region	4.00	44.18	52.00	31.00	83.33	42.51
30	Tibet Autonomous Region	10.00	45.00	55.00	41.50	35.00	36.80

Table 2.7 Results of assessment of transparency of governments of larger cities

Ranking	Larger cities	Openness of decision-making (15%)	Openness of administrative service (25%)	Openness of implementation and results (20%)	Information disclosure in key fields (25%)	Policy interpretation and response to public concerns (15%)	Total score (out of 100)
1	Hefei	42.50	69.53	97.85	97.92	100.00	82.81
2	Suzhou	54.50	82.55	82.29	89.58	96.67	82.17
3	Guangzhou	92.50	66.55	87.47	74.92	100.00	81.74
4	Chengdu	47.50	76.43	91.51	78.68	100.00	79.20
5	Zhengzhou	42.50	88.95	67.54	87.01	96.67	78.37
6	Mingbo	75.00	61.25	76.51	89.10	93.33	78.14
7	Yinchuan	72.50	84.58	68.00	74.92	90.00	77.85
8	Qingdao	32.50	88.70	74.68	84.58	96.67	77.63
9	Zibo	44.50	87.20	72.07	79.33	90.00	76.22
10	Shenzhen	82.00	60.90	91.71	60.39	96.67	75.46
11	Shengyang	47.50	75.45	85.81	76.92	86.67	75.38
12	Fujian	47.50	90.65	62.59	71.17	100.00	75.10
13	Xiamen	67.50	68.00	86.88	67.10	90.00	74.78
14	Shantou	47.50	74.48	82.07	64.10	93.33	72.18
15	Guiyang	37.50	89.90	57.28	69.10	100.00	71.83
16	Changsha	20.00	69.18	90.63	77.35	93.33	71.76
17	Fushun	32.50	91.68	53.72	78.68	90.00	71.71
18	Xi'an	32.50	88.95	62.76	62.33	100.00	70.25
19	Nanjing	32.50	65.18	72.40	78.68	93.33	69.32

(continued)

Table 2.7 (continued)

Ranking	Larger cities	Openness of decision-making (15%)	Openness of administrative service (25%)	Openness of implementation and results (20%)	Information disclosure in key fields (25%)	Policy interpretation and response to public concerns (15%)	Total score (out of 100)
20	Handan	44.50	78.23	64.77	61.10	93.33	68.46
21	Wuhan	52.50	74.00	80.34	50.00	90.00	68.44
22	Dalian	0.00	78.58	85.24	72.43	90.00	68.30
23	Harbin	32.50	67.30	84.20	62.00	90.00	67.54
24	Hangzhou	42.50	63.00	75.46	67.35	86.67	67.05
25	Benxi	32.50	75.43	89.72	46.25	90.00	66.74
26	Xuzhou	57.50	77.05	61.48	55.76	83.33	66.62
27	Haikou	32.50	88.25	83.87	44.58	76.67	66.36
28	Jinan	42.50	74.30	77.17	51.33	86.67	66.22
29	Nanchang	32.50	81.45	60.01	63.33	83.33	65.57
30	Zhuhai	40.00	72.35	76.29	49.10	86.67	64.62
31	Jilin	32.50	59.95	64.00	75.00	86.67	64.41
32	Wuxi	47.50	66.95	62.31	53.10	96.67	64.10
33	Lanzhou	32.50	70.20	61.00	61.25	93.33	63.94
34	Nanning	32.50	72.90	65.03	55.42	90.00	63.46
35	Taiyuan	32.50	63.23	67.79	64.10	86.67	63.26
36	Huainan	42.50	48.80	67.21	72.67	80.00	62.18
37	Tangshan	32.50	79.88	66.22	48.92	73.33	61.32
38	Qiqihar	32.50	87.73	36.91	59.10	80.00	60.96

(continued)

Table 2.7 (continued)

Ranking	Larger cities	Openness of decision-making (15%)	Openness of administrative service (25%)	Openness of implementation and results (20%)	Information disclosure in key fields (25%)	Policy interpretation and response to public concerns (15%)	Total score (out of 100)
39	Luoyang	32.50	72.50	87.61	55.76	36.67	59.96
40	Anshan	20.00	77.73	53.35	42.68	90.00	57.27
41	Kunming	32.50	72.73	47.14	67.43	43.33	55.84
42	Hohhot	42.50	57.28	6.33	79.92	86.67	54.94
43	Changchun	42.50	67.35	37.17	43.67	86.67	54.56
44	Xining	32.50	70.38	68.04	55.67	18.33	52.74
45	Baotou	0.00	62.83	36.50	68.92	73.33	51.24
46	Urumqi	0.00	54.85	21.48	77.77	86.67	50.45
47	Datong	10.00	86.03	21.96	43.00	76.67	49.65
48	Shijiazhuang	0.00	59.85	33.51	28.25	80.00	40.73
49	Lhasa	0.00	59.50	19.56	22.58	40.00	30.43

Table 2.8 Results of assessment of indices of transparency of county-level governments

Ranking	Provinces	County-level governments	Openness of decision-making (10%)	Openness of administrative service (25%)	Openness of implementation and its results (20%)	Information disclosure in key fields (20%)	Policy interpretation and response to public concerns (15%)	Information disclosure upon application (10%)	Total score (out of 100)
1	Shanghai Municipality	Putuo District	80.00	70.38	100.00	61.14	100.00	100.00	82.82
2	Anhui Province	Ningguo City	32.50	72.90	55.77	74.71	100.00	100.00	72.57
3	Zhejiang Province	Jiangbei District of Ningbo City	50.00	86.55	54.17	58.14	71.67	100.00	69.85
4	Beijing Municipality	Xicheng District	32.50	65.88	62.01	62.36	100.00	100.00	69.59
5	Shanghai Municipality	Hongkou District	57.50	55.60	63.51	63.14	90.00	100.00	68.48
6	Shanghai Municipality	Pudong New District	32.50	69.50	92.47	66.14	36.67	100.00	67.85
7	Anhui Province	Luyang District of Hefei City	47.50	70.40	67.11	72.00	61.67	80.00	67.42
8	Anhui Province	Huizhou District of Huangshan City	62.50	53.93	49.61	75.36	83.33	100.00	67.23
9	Anhui Province	Lingbi County of Suzhou City	62.50	54.95	86.41	29.50	93.33	100.00	67.17

(continued)

Table 2.8 (continued)

Ranking	Provinces	County-level governments	Openness of decision-making (10%)	Openness of administrative service (25%)	Openness of implementation and its results (20%)	Information disclosure in key fields (20%)	Policy interpretation and response to public concerns (15%)	Information disclosure upon application (10%)	Total score (out of 100)
10	Jiangsu Province	Rugao City	32.50	82.75	57.76	42.14	83.33	100.00	66.42
11	Beijing Municipality	Dongcheng District	32.50	62.55	74.41	45.50	96.67	90.00	66.37
12	Jiangsu Province	Jianye District of Nanjing City	20.00	70.63	81.61	66.00	33.33	100.00	64.18
13	Anhui Province	Dingyuan County of Chuzhou City	62.50	41.85	50.11	72.07	86.67	100.00	64.15
14	Anhui Province	Jinzhai County of Liu'an City	72.50	64.28	81.85	37.50	75.00	40.00	62.44
15	Jiangsu Province	Shuyang County of Suqian City	0.00	70.90	74.11	33.50	75.00	100.00	60.50
16	Beijing Municipality	Haidian District	10.00	63.08	71.47	54.00	96.67	40.00	60.36
17	Zhejiang Province	Yihu City	0.00	57.90	89.34	54.50	58.33	70.00	58.99
18	Guangdong Province	Luohu District of Shenzhen City	47.50	51.40	81.28	43.50	48.33	90.00	58.81

(continued)

Table 2.8 (continued)

Ranking	Provinces	County-level governments	Openness of decision-making (10%)	Openness of administrative service (25%)	Openness of implementation and its results (20%)	Information disclosure in key fields (20%)	Policy interpretation and response to public concerns (15%)	Information disclosure upon application (10%)	Total score (out of 100)
19	Zhejiang Province	Jiangshan City	32.50	58.25	60.51	60.50	65.00	70.00	58.76
20	Zhejiang Province	Jiashan County of Jiaxing City	32.50	57.45	59.84	40.14	61.67	100.00	56.86
21	Beijing Municipality	Changping District	62.50	38.53	37.68	50.00	81.67	100.00	55.67
22	Guangdong Province	Gaoyao District of Zhaoqing City	32.50	49.90	69.10	58.00	33.33	90.00	55.14
23	Beijing Municipality	Chaoyang District	32.50	52.45	22.80	62.00	78.33	100.00	55.07
24	Anhui Province	Yi'an District of Tongling City	62.50	50.33	36.40	43.36	86.67	70.00	54.78
25	Zhejiang Province	Ouhai District of Wenzhou City	0.00	57.73	53.37	50.36	61.67	100.00	54.43
26	Shanghai Municipality	Xuhui District	32.50	44.65	41.19	50.14	96.67	70.00	54.18
27	Anhui Province	Mengcheng County of Bozhou City	10.00	48.20	38.08	60.00	75.00	100.00	53.92

(continued)

Table 2.8 (continued)

Ranking	Provinces	County-level governments	Openness of decision-making (10%)	Openness of administrative service (25%)	Openness of implementation and its results (20%)	Information disclosure in key fields (20%)	Policy interpretation and response to public concerns (15%)	Information disclosure upon application (10%)	Total score (out of 100)
28	Ningxia Hui Autonomous Region	Helan County of Yinchuan City	32.50	38.53	61.40	47.50	61.67	100.00	53.91
29	Shanghai Municipality	Jinshan District	40.00	52.08	34.00	67.14	40.00	100.00	53.25
30	Ningxia Hui Autonomous Region	Pingluo County of Shizuishan City	0.00	51.78	86.17	31.36	58.33	80.00	53.20
31	Ningxia Hui Autonomous Region	Qingtongxia City	7.50	69.03	52.44	13.50	76.67	100.00	52.69
32	Henan Province	Ruzhou City	20.00	61.63	48.24	33.50	58.33	100.00	52.50
33	Guangdong Province	Pingyuan County of Meizhou City	10.00	48.45	68.53	45.50	36.67	100.00	51.42
34	Guangdong Province	Chancheng District of Foshan City	84.50	38.83	44.76	43.50	36.67	100.00	51.31
35	Henan Province	Changyuan County	32.50	76.58	38.37	27.50	36.67	100.00	51.07

(continued)

Table 2.8 (continued)

Ranking	Provinces	County-level governments	Openness of decision-making (10%)	Openness of administrative service (25%)	Openness of implementation and its results (20%)	Information disclosure in key fields (20%)	Policy interpretation and response to public concerns (15%)	Information disclosure upon application (10%)	Total score (out of 100)
36	Hunan Province	Wuling District of Changde City	10.00	45.23	70.00	45.36	36.67	100.00	50.88
37	Guangdong Province	Boluo County of Huizhou City	32.50	41.15	48.76	39.14	61.67	100.00	50.37
38	Zhejiang Province	Linhai City of Taizhou City	0.00	72.20	50.17	37.14	33.33	90.00	49.51
39	Guangdong Province	Xinxing County of Yunfu City	20.00	36.90	62.37	46.50	61.67	70.00	49.25
40	Yunnan Province	Tengchong City of Baoshan City	22.50	50.95	59.60	25.50	47.50	100.00	49.13
41	Henan Province	Jiyuan City	10.00	68.88	48.29	41.50	58.33	40.00	48.93
42	Hunan Province	Zixing City	27.50	36.35	53.10	54.00	36.67	100.00	48.76
43	Guizhou Province	Bozhou District of Zunyi City	0.00	46.93	38.41	67.50	36.67	100.00	48.41

(continued)

Table 2.8 (continued)

Ranking	Provinces	County-level governments	Openness of decision-making (10%)	Openness of administrative service (25%)	Openness of implementation and its results (20%)	Information disclosure in key fields (20%)	Policy interpretation and response to public concerns (15%)	Information disclosure upon application (10%)	Total score (out of 100)
44	Sichuan Province	Xinjin County of Chengdu City	20.00	51.53	50.15	35.50	61.67	70.00	48.26
45	Jiangsu Province	Tianning District of Changzhou City	0.00	45.45	34.12	26.50	93.33	100.00	47.49
46	Zhejiang Province	Gongshu District of Hangzhou City	32.50	63.50	35.96	32.14	36.67	90.00	47.25
47	Shaanxi Province	Weiyang District of Xi'an City	25.00	47.08	21.88	39.50	90.00	70.00	47.04
48	Hunan Province	Liuyang City	10.00	31.85	62.04	58.00	65.00	40.00	46.72
49	Guizhou Province	Liuzhi Special Zone of Liupanshui City	60.00	57.25	38.68	43.50	36.67	40.00	46.25
50	Sichuan Province	Yanting County of Mianyang City	32.50	36.80	74.05	44.14	36.67	40.00	45.59

(continued)

Table 2.8 (continued)

Ranking	Provinces	County-level governments	Openness of decision-making (10%)	Openness of administrative service (25%)	Openness of implementation and its results (20%)	Information disclosure in key fields (20%)	Policy interpretation and response to public concerns (15%)	Information disclosure upon application (10%)	Total score (out of 100)
51	Jiangsu Province	Suzhou Industrial Park	10.00	49.58	27.33	27.50	80.00	90.00	45.36
52	Guizhou Province	Xingyi City of Qianxinan Buyi and Miao Autonomous Prefecture	20.00	56.25	23.53	38.14	43.33	100.00	44.90
53	Heilongjiang Province	Longsha District of Qiqihar City	0.00	57.30	38.87	40.00	30.00	100.00	44.60
54	Guizhou Province	Zhenfeng County of Qianxinan Buyi and Miao Autonomous Prefecture	20.00	45.75	38.07	46.36	68.33	40.00	44.57
55	Shaanxi Province	Jingbian County of Yulin City	32.50	29.03	56.71	40.14	36.67	90.00	44.38
56	Jiangsu Province	Binhu District of Wuxi City	20.00	54.43	38.21	37.50	30.00	90.00	44.25

(continued)

Table 2.8 (continued)

Ranking	Provinces	County-level governments	Openness of decision-making (10%)	Openness of administrative service (25%)	Openness of implementation and its results (20%)	Information disclosure in key fields (20%)	Policy interpretation and response to public concerns (15%)	Information disclosure upon application (10%)	Total score (out of 100)
57	Heilongjiang Province	Dulbert Mongolian Autonomous County of Daqing City	0.00	54.43	30.67	39.36	46.67	90.00	43.61
58	Yunnan Province	Kaiyuan City of Honghe Hani and Yi Autonomous Prefecture	0.00	48.95	39.20	17.00	61.67	100.00	42.73
59	Guizhou Province	Nanming District of Guiyang City	0.00	25.30	7.68	62.50	81.67	100.00	42.61
60	Yunnan Province	Chuxiong City of Weichu City	32.50	49.45	38.34	28.50	30.00	90.00	42.48
61	Inner Mongolia Autonomous Region	Xincheng District of Hohhot City	0.00	53.50	38.53	58.14	36.67	40.00	42.21
62	Inner Mongolia Autonomous Region	Baotou Rare Earth High-tech Zone	0.00	49.50	19.86	56.50	68.33	40.00	41.90

(continued)

Table 2.8 (continued)

Ranking	Provinces	County-level governments	Openness of decision-making (10%)	Openness of administrative service (25%)	Openness of implementation and its results (20%)	Information disclosure in key fields (20%)	Policy interpretation and response to public concerns (15%)	Information disclosure upon application (10%)	Total score (out of 100)
63	Inner Mongolia Autonomous Region	Ulanhot City of Xing'an League	0.00	56.95	37.16	50.00	36.67	40.00	41.17
64	Yunnan Province	Maitreya City of Honghe Hani and Yi Autonomous Prefecture	0.00	29.38	36.96	45.50	61.67	80.00	41.09
65	Guizhou Province	Fenggang County of Zunyi City	20.00	38.53	38.68	38.07	33.33	90.00	40.98
66	Guangdong Province	Haizhu District of Guangzhou City	44.50	37.30	55.67	36.50	3.33	80.00	40.71
67	Sichuan Province	Wanyuan City of Dazhou City	52.50	42.63	22.07	22.50	43.33	90.00	40.32
68	Yunnan Province	Yaoan of County of Chuxiong Yi Autonomous Prefecture	0.00	52.90	50.53	6.50	36.67	100.00	40.13

(continued)

Table 2.8 (continued)

Ranking	Provinces	County-level governments	Openness of decision-making (10%)	Openness of administrative service (25%)	Openness of implementation and its results (20%)	Information disclosure in key fields (20%)	Policy interpretation and response to public concerns (15%)	Information disclosure upon application (10%)	Total score (out of 100)
69	Henan Province	Shangjie District of Zhengzhou City	0.00	34.75	60.33	34.14	51.67	40.00	39.33
70	Heilongjiang Province	Dongning City of Mudanjiang City	0.00	61.85	37.77	21.50	20.00	90.00	39.32
71	Henan Province	Tangyin County of Anyang City	0.00	41.18	38.34	9.50	61.67	100.00	39.11
72	Jiangsu Province	Xinyi City	10.00	51.78	24.51	27.50	36.67	90.00	38.84
73	Hunan Province	Zhuzhou County of Zhuzhou City	0.00	29.60	45.09	40.14	33.33	90.00	38.45
74	Heilongjiang Province	Tangyuan County of Jiamusi City	0.00	26.75	53.53	36.14	65.00	40.00	38.37
75	Sichuan Province	Shifang City	0.00	48.80	30.00	35.50	18.33	100.00	38.05

(continued)

Table 2.8 (continued)

Ranking	Provinces	County-level governments	Openness of decision-making (10%)	Openness of administrative service (25%)	Openness of implementation and its results (20%)	Information disclosure in key fields (20%)	Policy interpretation and response to public concerns (15%)	Information disclosure upon application (10%)	Total score (out of 100)
76	Yunnan Province	Suijiang County of Zhaotong City	0.00	37.20	49.59	25.50	64.17	40.00	37.94
77	Sichuan Province	West District of Panzhihua City	0.00	52.50	68.25	9.50	33.33	40.00	37.68
78	Shaanxi Province	Huazhou District of Weinan City	10.00	28.50	22.44	41.00	51.67	90.00	37.56
79	Hunan Province	Pingjiang County of Yueyang City	0.00	37.80	20.04	46.36	33.33	90.00	36.73
80	Shaanxi Province	Bin County of Xianyang City	0.00	42.68	22.80	11.50	51.67	100.00	35.28
81	Hunan Province	Lanshan County of Yongzhou City	10.00	29.18	15.67	46.14	36.67	90.00	35.16
82	Heilongjiang Province	Daoli District of Harbin City	0.00	35.63	30.00	53.50	33.33	40.00	34.61
83	Inner Mongolia Autonomous Region	Keshiketeng Banner of Chifeng City	7.50	26.93	68.37	3.50	30.00	80.00	34.36

(continued)

Table 2.8 (continued)

Ranking	Provinces	County-level governments	Openness of decision-making (10%)	Openness of administrative service (25%)	Openness of implementation and its results (20%)	Information disclosure in key fields (20%)	Policy interpretation and response to public concerns (15%)	Information disclosure upon application (10%)	Total score (out of 100)
84	Sichuan Province	Xichang City of Liangshan Yi Autonomous Prefecture	0.00	25.48	53.94	38.14	36.67	40.00	34.29
85	Shaanxi Province	Ziyang County of Ankang City	32.50	23.65	38.53	12.50	30.00	100.00	33.87
86	Sichuan Province	Hejiang County of Luzhou City	17.50	41.20	21.88	15.50	33.33	90.00	33.53
87	Heilongjiang Province	Mishan City	0.00	36.20	37.28	29.50	6.67	90.00	32.41
88	Henan Province	Huangchuan County of Xinyang City	20.00	17.88	21.28	28.14	36.67	100.00	31.85
89	Ningxia Hui Autonomous Region	Haiyuan County of Zhongwei City	0.00	34.03	23.17	18.50	30.00	100.00	31.34
90	Shaanxi Province	Ansai District of Yan'an City	32.50	56.68	8.53	14.14	30.00	40.00	30.45
91	Inner Mongolia Autonomous Region	Haibowan District of Wuhai City	0.00	48.85	30.00	17.50	30.00	40.00	30.21

(continued)

Table 2.8 (continued)

Ranking	Provinces	County-level governments	Openness of decision-making (10%)	Openness of administrative service (25%)	Openness of implementation and its results (20%)	Information disclosure in key fields (20%)	Policy interpretation and response to public concerns (15%)	Information disclosure upon application (10%)	Total score (out of 100)
92	Heilongjiang Province	Zhaodong City of Suihua City	7.50	31.65	52.51	23.50	15.00	40.00	30.11
93	Hunan Province	Hengyang County of Hengyang City	20.00	29.20	7.38	23.00	30.00	100.00	29.88
94	Henan Province	Xiangfu District of Kaifeng City	0.00	27.63	22.54	1.50	58.33	90.00	29.46
95	Sichuan Province	Qingchuan County of Guangyuan City	7.50	23.43	7.81	19.50	46.67	100.00	29.07
96	Inner Mongolia Autonomous Region	Xianghuang Banner of Xilin Gol League	0.00	31.93	38.01	20.50	30.00	40.00	28.18
97	Inner Mongolia Autonomous Region	Kailu County of Tongliao City	0.00	50.43	6.12	17.50	36.67	40.00	26.83
98	Shaanxi Province	Qishan County of Baoji City	0.00	16.08	22.00	11.50	36.67	100.00	26.22
99	Ningxia Hui Autonomous Region	Pengyang County of Guyuan City	0.00	57.08	10.00	1.50	33.33	40.00	25.57

(continued)

Table 2.8 (continued)

Ranking	Provinces	County-level governments	Openness of decision-making (10%)	Openness of administrative service (25%)	Openness of implementation and its results (20%)	Information disclosure in key fields (20%)	Policy interpretation and response to public concerns (15%)	Information disclosure upon application (10%)	Total score (out of 100)
100	Henan Province	Luolong District of Luoyang City	7.50	11.00	20.88	39.50	36.67	40.00	25.08

which contains clear provisions on the disclosure of information about the examination and approval of environmental impact assessment documents, environmental protection acceptance check of construction projects and examination and approval of qualification for environmental impact assessment of construction projects, especially the content elements of the above matters. The assessment shows that all 31 provincial-level governments disclosed the results of administrative approval in the field of environmental protection.

In the field of food and drug safety, China Food and Drug Administration successively issued the Measures for the Administration of the Routine Supervision and Inspection of the Food Production and Operation, Measures for the Administration of Food Safety Spot Inspections, Opinions on Effectively Carrying out the Work of Food Safety Spot Inspection and Information Release, Notice on Issuing the Regulations on the Administration of Spot Inspection for Drug Quality Supervision, and Regulations on the Administration of Spot Inspection for Drug Quality Supervision, which contain clear provisions on the content, time and method of disclosure of information about spot inspection for food and drug supervision. The assessment shows that the China Food and Drug Administration, 31 food and drug administrative departments of provincial-level governments, 47 food and drug administrative departments of governments of larger cities, and 59 food and drug administrative departments of county-level governments disclosed the results of random spot inspections they had made in 2017. The disclosure rate was high.

In the field of affordable housing projects, the Ministry of Housing and Urban–Rural Development successively issued the Notice on Disclosing Information about Urban Affordable Housing Projects, the Notice on Effectively Carrying out the Work of Disclosing Housing Security Information in 2012, and the Notice on Effectively Carrying out the Work of Government-subsidized Housing Projects in Urban Areas in 2013, which contain detailed provisions on the subjects, the content elements and the time of information disclosure. This assessment shows that 22 governments of larger cities published their land-use plans for shantytown renovation in 2017, 35 governments of larger cities published on their web portals or websites of their housing and construction departments their annual construction plans for shantytown renovation in 2017, and 34 governments of larger cities disclosed on their web portals or the websites of their housing and construction departments information about the progress of shantytown renovation projects in 2017, accounting for 44.90%, 71.43% and 69.39%, respectively, of the totals, which indicated a relatively high level of information disclosure in this field.

With respect to the construction of a government service platform, some provincial-level governments, such as those of Guizhou Province, Hunan Province and Guangdong Province, had built a unified government service platform in the whole province, which discloses in a concentrated manner the government service information provided by provincial, municipal, county and township governments, and unifies the content elements and arrangement methods of the government service guide, thereby making it convenient for both the management by the government and the use by the public and enterprises.

2.3.2 *The Quality of Pre-disclosure of Major Decisions Had Been Improved Significantly*

Pre-disclosure of major decision-making matters involving the vital interests of the masses and high social concern, and extensive solicitation of opinions and suggestions from the public are conducive to enhancing the scientific, democratic and credible natures of decision-making and reducing obstacles to the implementation of decisions on the one hand, and to expanding public participation and forming a positive relationship between the government and the people on the other hand. Therefore, the Opinions on Promoting the Open Government Work in an All-round Way require governments at all levels to implement the system of pre-disclosure of major decisions, important reform programs, major policy measures and key engineering projects that involve the vital interests of the masses and need to be widely known by the public, with the exception of those that should be kept confidential according to law. Drafts of decisions and their basis should be announced to the public before decision-making, and public opinions should be widely solicited through hearing, investigation and research, consultation and media communication, and the information about the collection and adoption of public opinions should be announced in an appropriate way. In 2017, remarkable progress was made in the pre-disclosure of major decisions by governments at various levels and departments under them.

Firstly, clarifying the scope of major decision-making matters by making a catalog list. Although the relevant documents issued by the General Office of the State Council require the advancement of pre-disclosure of major decisions, the scope of major decision-making matters is only generally expressed as "important reform programs, major policy measures, and key projects that involve the vital interests of the masses and need to be widely known by the public", providing little guidance to government departments at various levels in concrete operations. For this reason, some local governments adopted the innovative method of drawing up and publishing the catalog of major decision-making matters at the beginning of the year that contains detailed information about the major decision-making matters, undertaking departments, decision-making times, and forms of public participation. The assessment shows that 6 governments of larger cities and 2 county-level governments, namely those of Guangzhou, Handan, Suzhou, Wuhan, Shenzhen, Zibo, Haizhu District of Guangzhou City and Chancheng District of Foshan City in Guangdong Province, published on their websites the catalogs of major decision-making matters in 2017. The Government of Guangzhou City published the Catalog of Major Administrative Decision-making Matters and Hearing Matters of Guangzhou Municipal People's Government in 2017 in the column of "Regulations and Official Documents—Documents of General Office of Municipal Government" on its portal website.

Secondly, actively giving feedback on the opinions collected in the pre-disclosure of major decisions. At the stage of pre-disclosure of major decisions, it is necessary not only to solicit opinions and suggestions from the public but also to give feedback on the collected opinions, explaining the overall situation of public opinion solicitation, the adoption and the reasons for non-adoption of the collected opinions, so as to show respect for the public and meet the requirement of positive interaction between the government and the people. The assessment shows that one department of the State Council, 4 provincial-level governments, 6 governments of larger cities, and 10 county-level governments disclosed on their web portals or the websites of their legislative affairs departments complete feedback information, including the overall situation of solicitation of public opinions, the adoption and the reasons for non-adoption of collected opinions. For example, the Government of Sichuan Province published the feedback information about the solicitation of public opinions under the "Feedback on the Results of Public Opinion Solicitation" column on its portal website, and give a text explanation of the contents in this column; the Government of Putuo District of Shanghai Municipality published tables of feedbacks on solicitation of opinions, which contained detailed information about the source of opinions, the content of feedback, whether each piece of collected opinion had been adopted or not, and the reasons for the adoption or non-adoption of each piece of opinion.

2.3.3 The Disclosure of the Results of Administrative Approval Was Refined to Facilitate Public Access

The common practice of disclosing the results of administrative approval is to set up "double publication" columns on the government portal website, disclose the results in a concentrated manner and classify them according to government departments, or disclose them on the enterprise credit information website. The assessment shows that some assessment targets refined the classification of administrative approval items according to their type, time and applicant. For example, under the "Production Safety License Disclosure" column on its web portal, the Work Safety Administrative Department of Chengdu City in Sichuan Province divided the results of administrative approval into the following 13 categories: licenses for trading in hazardous chemicals; licenses for the production of hazardous chemicals; licenses for the safe use of hazardous chemicals; licenses for trading in (wholesaling of) fireworks and firecrackers; work safety licenses for non-coal mining enterprises; licenses for construction projects involving hazardous chemicals; licenses for occupational health projects under construction projects; review of hidden danger rectification plans; licenses for the examination of the design of safety projects under non-coal mining construction projects; licenses for the examination of design of safety facilities for metal smelting construction projects; certifications of record for the business operation of Category II non-pharmaceutical precursor chemicals; certifications of record for the production of Category II non-pharmaceutical precursor chemicals; and certifications of record for the production of Category III non-pharmaceutical precursor chemicals. Further classification of information was made under each of the 13 categories. For another example, the Government of Guizhou Province has made a detailed classification of the results of administrative approval disclosed on its web portal. At its online service hall, advanced searches on these results can be made by departments handling the application, the time period of application, the applicant, and other keywords. And on the website of the National Development and Reform Commission, the results of administrative approval can be searched by the time of completion of the handling of the application, and the type of the subject matter, so that the results of administrative approval could be conveniently found, analyzed and utilized.

2.3.4 *The Degree of Information Disclosure in Some Administrative Law Enforcement Fields Was Relatively High*

Implementing the administrative law enforcement publication system is an important measure for standardizing the market law enforcement order, an important path to building a transparent and credible government, and an effective means to streamline administration, delegate more powers, improve regulation, and effectively transform government functions. The assessment shows that the degrees of disclosure of lists of administrative penalty items, the results of administrative penalty in some areas, and the results of random spot inspection were relatively high.

Firstly, the assessment targets had generally published the list of administrative penalties. The assessment shows that 31 provincial-level governments (or 100% of the total), 48 governments of larger cities (or 97.96% of the total) and 100 county-level governments (or 100% of the total) published the list of administrative penalties imposed by various departments under them.

Secondly, the situation of disclosure of the results of administrative penalties in the field of environment protection and food and drug safety was also satisfactory. In the field of environmental protection, the environmental protection departments of 41 governments of larger cities (or 83.67% of the total) published the administrative penalties they had imposed in 2017. In the field of food and drug safety, the food and drug administrative departments of 42 governments of larger cities (or 87.76% of the total) and 74 county-level governments (or 74% of the total) published the administrative penalties they had imposed in 2017.

Thirdly, the situation of disclosure of the results of random spot inspection in the field of environment protection and food and drug safety was also satisfactory. The assessment shows that most of the assessment targets disclosed the results of random spot inspections in the field of food and drug supervision in 2017. China Food and Drug Administration, 31 food and drug supervision departments of provincial-level governments, 47 food and drug supervision departments of governments of larger cities, and 59 food and drug supervision departments of county-level governments disclosed the results of random spot inspections they had made in 2017.

2.3.5 *The Disclosure of Information About Implementation and Its Results in Some Fields Was Relatively Standardized*

Truthfully and accurately disclosing the implementation of the government's major decision-making arrangements is conducive to strengthening public supervision over policy implementation, increasing government transparency, enhancing government credibility, and building a law-based and responsible government. The assessment shows that the disclosure of information about implementation and its results by governments at all levels and their departments was satisfactory.

Firstly, the assessment shows that some assessment targets periodically published their work summaries and work arrangements, showing a strong coherence in their work. With respect to work arrangement, 18 provincial-level governments, 27 governments of larger cities, and 35 county-level governments disclosed information about the breakdown and division of government tasks in 2017 and clarified the work items and responsible departments, which was conducive to the smooth carrying out of the work. For example, the governments of Tianjin Municipality, Fushun City, Tianning District of Changzhou City in Jiangsu Province, etc., published their work task decomposition tables in 2017 with clear contents.

With respect to work summaries, two provincial-level governments, seven governments of larger cities and 14 county-level governments disclosed by stages the information about the implementation of their work plans in 2017 on their web portals. Moreover, some assessment targets, such as the governments of Zhuzhou County of Zhuzhou City in Hunan Province and Huizhou District of Huangshan City in Anhui Province, disclosed on a monthly basis the information about the implementation of their work plans in the current month and the work plan for the next month, thereby not only embodying the coherence of government work but also enabling the public to know the progress of relevant work in time and strengthening their supervision over government work.

Secondly, the annual reports on the construction of a law-based government were relatively standardized and focused in content. Most of the reports were able to cover all aspects of the construction of a law-based government in accordance with the requirements of the Plan for Building Rule of Law Government (2015–2020), giving a detailed description of the situation of the construction of a law-based government with respect to the performance of government functions, improvement of relevant systems and institutions and decision-making quality, law enforcement, supervision, conflict resolution, and the improvement of the quality personnel and making specific explanations on related issues in light of local practice. Many administrative organs also stressed the work arrangements with respect to key fields (such as the report of the Government of Zhuhai City in Guangdong Province), leadership responsibility (such as the report of the Government of Tangshan City in Hebei Province), and safeguarding measures (such as the report of the Government of Jinan City in Shandong Province), thus making the contents of the reports more comprehensive. Many departments of the State Council had, in light of the nature and characteristics of their respective work, made practical attempts at innovating the construction of a law-based government. For example, the Ministry of Transportation stressed in its report the efforts it had made in speeding up the legislation on transportation and the construction of a comprehensive system of administrative regulations in the field of transport, and the report of the Ministry of Environmental Protection especially mentioned the key points of its work of strengthening environmental governance and ecological protection through the construction of the rule of law.

2.3.6 *The Information Disclosure in Some Key Fields Was Satisfactory*

Firstly, the disclosure of information about the budget and final accounts by various departments of the State Council was standardized. The assessment shows that 53 departments of the State Council published their budget statements in 2017 and related tables and their final account statements in 2016 and related tables. The budget statements of all departments of the State Council contained such information as to their duties and functions, institutional setup, the increase or reduction of budget and expenditure, the allocation of operational expenditure, and government procurement. The expenditure statements of the general public budget were detailed down to functionally classified item-level subjects, and the basic expenditure statements of the general public budget were also detailed down to the sub-item-level of specific economic categories. This shows that, on the one hand, all departments attached great importance to the disclosure of their budget and final accounts and, on the other hand, the Ministry of Finance had carried out effective work and achieved remarkable results in guiding various departments of the State Council in the disclosure of budget and final accounts.

Secondly, the disclosure of information about the quality of the centralized source of drinking water was satisfactory. The assessment shows that 41 governments of larger cities disclose information about the quality of water sources on a monthly basis; 42 governments of larger cities disclosed the monitoring information about the quality of water from water supply plants, and 42 governments of larger cities disclosed the monitoring information about the quality of water from the faucets of users. Moreover, some assessment targets disclosed information about the quality of the centralized source of drinking water at frequencies higher than that required by law. Compared with 2016, some assessment targets made remarkable progress in the disclosure of information about the quality of the centralized source of drinking water in 2017. For example, Urumqi Water Affairs Bureau and Qiqihar Housing and Urban–Rural Development Bureau did not disclose the information about the quality of water from the water supply plants in 2016, but disclosed the information as required in 2017.

2.3.7 *The Situation of Policy Interpretation and Response to Public Concerns Was Generally Satisfactory*

Timely issuance of policy interpretations by administrative organs on government websites is an important measure for reducing resistance to the implementation of policies, increasing government credibility and social cohesion, stabilizing market expectation and safeguarding the right of to know, the right of participation, and the right of supervision of the public. The assessment shows that the overall situation of policy interpretation by administrative organs was satisfactory, and the quality of construction of the website interactive platform was relatively high.

Firstly, interpreting policies by principal persons-in-charge of the adopting organs authoritative. Publicizing and interpreting policies by principal persons-in-charge of the adopting organs by attending press conferences and accepting interviews is one of the most credible interpretation methods conducive to publicizing government policies and measures. The assessment shows that 47 departments of the State Council, 30 provincial-level governments, 45 governments of larger cities and 18 county-level governments published on their portal websites the information about the interpretation of policies by principal persons-in-charge of the adopting organs.

Secondly, adopting innovative and highly readable forms of policy interpretation. Using such popular and easy-to-understand methods as charts, illustration, audio, and video to explain policies is conducive to the understanding of policies by the public and enhances the affinity and acceptability of policies. The assessment shows that most departments of the State Council were able to interpret policies in an innovative way and use concise and lively illustrations to demonstrate the main ideas of the policies, rather than mechanically copying the texts of policy documents, on their websites. For example, the illustrated interpretation of the Interim Measures for the Management of Leading Personnel of Primary and Secondary Schools on the website of the Ministry of Education used clear structure and texts to demonstrate in a concise and easily understandable way various conditions and requirements provided for in the Interim Measures.

Thirdly, making preliminary efforts to run policy interpretation throughout the whole process of the making, promulgation, and implementation of policies. Moving the link of policy interpretation to the stage of solicitation of public opinions on draft policy decisions is conducive to improving the pertinence of public participation, the quality and effect of decision-making openness, as well as the effect of policy interpretation in later stages. The assessment shows that 10 departments of the State Council, 3 provincial-level governments, 3 governments of larger cities, and 5 county-level governments published the interpretations or explanations of draft decisions. Some assessment targets, such as the Government of Putuo District of Shanghai Municipality, published the explanations of decisions in synchronization with draft decisions in the column of the solicitation of public opinions or in a separate column, while some others, such as the Government of Zhuhai City in Guangdong Province and the Government of Jinshan District of Shanghai Municipality, attached the explanations of decisions to the draft decisions as downloadable files. Strengthening the explanation of policy implementation is conducive to improving the acceptability and communication effect of government work. The assessment shows that some assessment targets, such as the governments of Fujian Province, Zhejiang Province and Shenzhen City in Guangdong Province, published the interpretation information of audit reports on their websites. Take Zhejiang Province as an example. The website of the Provincial Audit Bureau gave detailed explanations, in the form of Q&A, of the characteristics of audit work reports, the general situation of financial revenue and expenditure, the follow-up auditing of the implementation of major policy measures, the concrete situation of auditing in the field of the people's livelihood, and clues of major violations of laws and regulations identified in the audit, thereby increasing the affinity of auditing reports with the public. Some assessment targets, such as the Government of Shandong Province, interpreted the contents of the government work report and explained the main bright spots in the implementation of government work.

Fourthly setting up interactive platforms under government websites to respond to public opinions and proposals. In addition to responding to major public opinion issues, setting up an interactive platform between the government and the people on government portal websites to respond to public personal concerns is also an important way to enhance the credibility of the government and build a positive relationship between the government and the people. The assessment shows that 51 departments of the State Council, 30 provincial-level governments, 48 governments of larger cities and 97 county-level government portals had set up online interactive platforms, such as leaders' mailboxes, message boards and online consultation; 41 departments of the State Council, 30 provincial-level governments, 49 governments of larger cities and 95 county-level governments published feedback information about the solicitation of public opinions.

2.4 Problems Identified in the Assessment

Despite the above-mentioned achievements in 2017, some common problems remained to be solved in the open government work.

2.4.1 The Standards for Open Government Work in Some Areas Needed to Be Clarified

Firstly, the scope of major decision-making matters was not clearly defined. The Opinions on Comprehensively Advancing the Open Government Work issued by the General Office of the CPC Central Committee and the General Office of the State Council, and the Detailed Rules for Implementing the Opinions on Comprehensively Promoting Open Government and the Key Tasks of Open Government Work in 2016 issued by the General Office of the State Council all demanded the pre-disclosure of major decisions. With respect to the scope of major decision-making items, however, they only contain a very general expression of "major reform plans, policy measures and construction projects involving the vital interests of the masses, and therefore need to be widely known by the public". As a result, lower-level governments and the departments under them were at a loss as to what to do, some even used this provision to shirk their responsibilities.

Secondly, the methods of disclosing the results of random spot inspection and the investigation and handling of the problems found in the inspection were not clear. Although the Notice of the General Office of the State Council on Rolling Out the Random Inspection Regulating the Interim and Post-Event Supervision clearly requires the relevant government organs to strengthen the application of the results of spot inspections, publish the results of spot inspections and the investigation and handling of the problems found in the inspection, and accept the supervision by the public over this work, and these requirements were written into the Key Tasks of Open Government Work in 2016 and the Key Tasks of Open Government Work in 2017 by the General Office of the State Council, spot inspection was only a method of administrative regulation or examination, and there was no clear requirement that the results of spot inspections must be distinguished from other types of inspection or clearly labeled. Moreover, the investigation and handling of the problems discovered in spot inspections may take many forms, such as the circulation of notice and imposition of penalties. However, the information about the circulation of notice and imposition of penalties alone does not tell us which of them are the measures taken as a result of spot inspections. Moreover, although there is a linkage between the results of spot inspections and the results of investigation and punishment, there was no clear requirement that these two kinds of results should be published in conjunction with each other.

2.4.2 Pre-disclosure of Decisions Needed to Be Strengthened Urgently

Firstly, most major decisions had not been made public in advance. The Opinions of the General Office of the CPC Central Committee and the General Office of the State Council on Promoting the Open government work in an All-round Way clearly require that major decisions should be actively pre-disclosed and public participation should be expanded. For decision-making matters with high social concern, except for those that should be kept confidential according to law, relevant information should be disclosed to the public before decision-making, and timely feedback should be given on the adoption of opinions. However, the assessment shows that 29 departments under the State Council, 13 provincial-level governments, 8 governments of larger cities, and 56 county-level governments did not disclose the information about the solicitation of opinions on drafts of major decisions in 2017 on their own web portals or the websites their legislative affairs departments; 52 departments of the State Council, 24 provincial-level governments, 36 governments of larger cities and 87 county-level governments did not disclose the feedback on the opinions collected on major decision drafts in 2017 on their own portal websites or the websites of their legislative affairs offices.

Secondly, feedbacks on solicited opinions on major draft decisions were not detailed enough and too perfunctory in content. The assessment shows that two provincial-level governments, seven governments of larger cities and two county-level governments disclosed only the information about the overall situation of solicitation of opinions, but not the information about the adoption of solicited opinions. Among them, one provincial government and four governments of larger cities only disclosed the number of opinions collected, but did not explain the main points of the solicited opinions. One department of the State Council, one provincial government and one county-level government only disclosed the overall situation of solicited opinions and their adoption, but did not explain the reasons for the non-adoption of solicited opinions, thus reducing the persuasiveness and credibility of decision-making.

2.4.3 The Disclosure of Government Service Information Was Not Detailed Enough and Needed to Be Improved

Firstly, the content of the guides to government service matters was not comprehensive. The Guiding Opinions on Accelerating the Work of "Internet Plus Government Affairs Service" stipulate that governments at various levels should standardize and improve their service guides, which should contain such information as bases and conditions of handling of applications, application materials, procedures, and time limits, charging standards and points for attention. However, the assessment shows that the guides to government services provided by some assessment targets did not include such core elements as the bases and conditions of handling of applications, application materials, procedures and time limits, and charging rates. The government service guides published by 22 departments of the State Council, 18 provincial-level governments, 21 governments of larger cities, and 63 county-level governments failed to include all the above-mentioned elements. For example, China Securities Regulatory Commission directly copied the relevant provisions of laws and administrative regulations on the conditions for the application of some of its government services; and on the website of the Government of Huizhou District of Huangshan City in Anhui Province, the time limit for the application for government services was given as "application handling time: Monday to Friday".

Secondly, the content of the guide to government service matters was not clear. Guides to government services should give clear and unequivocal instructions to citizens and enterprises on how to use government services. The assessment shows that the guides to government services of some assessment targets contained vague expressions regarding the basis and conditions for handling applications, application materials, locations, and charging rates of government services that could easily cause confusion among citizens and enterprises. The assessment shows that the information about the bases of the handling of applications for government services given by 40 departments of the State Council, 14 provincial-level governments, 30 governments of larger cities, and 70 county-level governments included only the titles of laws or administrative regulations and the article numbers, or only the titles of laws or administrative regulations, without the concrete content of the relevant provisions; the information about conditions for application for government services given by 35 departments of the State Council, 12 provincial-level governments, 24 governments of larger cities and 67 county-level governments contained such vague expressions as "others" and "etc."; the information about the application materials for government services given by 37 departments of the State Council, 8 provincial-level governments, 11 governments of larger cities and 38 county-level governments also contained such vague expressions as "others" and "etc."; and the service guides published by 10 departments of the State Council, 9 provincial-level governments, 18 governments of larger cities and 36 county-level governments failed to give clear information about the locations of handling of some government affairs.

Thirdly, the content of the guide to government service matters was inaccurate. The contents of the Guide to Administrative Services should be accurate so as not to mislead the masses. However, guides to government services were disclosed at multiple platforms, such as the online service column of government web portals, the online government service center, and the websites of various government departments. This could easily result in the inconsistency of the guides to the same government service disclosed on different platforms. The assessment shows that one provincial-level government, 2 governments of larger cities, and 32 county-level governments had disclosed inconsistent guides to the same government service at different platforms, including inconsistency in the title and article numbers of laws and regulations on which the government service was based, the application materials, the time limit of handling the applications, and service recipients. The guides to government services published by some assessment targets at different platforms, although consistent in content, were different in the level of elaboration: some were very details while others were very brief.

2.4.4 *The Disclosure of Administrative Law Enforcement Information Still Needed to Be Improved*

Firstly, the level of disclosure of information about "double random" inspection was low. The Notice of the General Office of the State Council on Rolling Out the Random Inspection Regulating the Interim and Post-Event Supervision requires governments at various levels to make and publish lists of items of random inspections, strengthen the utilization of the results of random inspections, and disclose to the public the results of random inspections and the investigation and handling of the problems found in the inspections. However, the assessment shows that 20 departments of the State Council did not disclose the list of random spot inspections they had carried out, and 20 provincial-level governments, 24 governments of larger cities, and 79 county-level governments did not disclose on their web portals the list of random spot inspections carried out by various government departments at their corresponding level. Among them, some governments disclosed on their web portals only the lists of items of random inspection by some of the departments under them. Moreover, the level of disclosure of results of random inspections by departments of the State Council was low. 37 departments of the State Council did not disclose on their websites the results of random inspections they had carried out in 2017.

The level of disclosure of the results of random inspections in the field of production safety was not high either. The production safety departments under 28 provincial-level governments, 38 governments of larger cities, and 87 county-level governments did not disclose the results of the random inspections they had carried out in 2017.

Secondly, the level of disclosure of administrative penalty results was still not satisfactory. Disclosure of the results of administrative penalties is a kind of supervision over the exercise of the power of administrative penalties by administrative organs and gives full play to the role of government information in regulating and servicing market subjects. However, the assessment shows that 34 departments of the State Council did not disclose the results of administrative penalties they imposed in 2017. Of course, we cannot rule out the possibility that some departments had not made any administrative penalty decisions in 2017; 16 provincial-level quality supervision departments, 16 provincial-level industrial and commercial administrative departments, 19 provincial-level intellectual property administrative departments, 63 county-level urban management comprehensive administrative law enforcement departments, and 71 county-level production safety supervision departments did not disclose the results of administrative penalties they had imposed in 2017. These assessment results also show that the degree of disclosure of administrative penalties varied from department to department.

2.4.5 The Disclosure of Information About the Results of Some Government Operations Was Still Not Satisfactory

Firstly, the disclosure of audit results was not satisfactory. The Key Tasks of Open Government Work in 2016, Key Tasks of Open Government Work in 2017, and Opinions on Strengthening Audit Work issued by the General Office of the State Council all require governments at all levels to deepen the disclosure of audit results, effectively monitor the implementation of major policies and measures adopted by the CPC Central Committee and the State Council, and especially intensify the efforts in disclosing typical examples of problems and their rectifications, so as to promote the implementation of policies. However, the assessment shows that the audit departments of 6 provincial-level governments, 25 governments of larger cities, and 83 county-level governments did not disclose their budget implementation audit reports in 2016; and the audit departments of 11 provincial-level governments, 30 governments of larger cities and 79 county-level governments did not disclose separate special audit reports. Among them, some described the special audit results in the budget implementation audit reports at their corresponding levels, but did not disclose separate special audit reports.

Secondly, the level of disclosure of annual reports on the construction of a law-based government was not high. According to the Implementation Outline for Building a Law-based Government (2015–2020), governments at or above the county level and departments under them should report their work on the construction of a law-based government in the previous year to the relevant units in the first quarter of each year and such reports should be disclosed to the public through newspapers, periodicals, and government websites. However, the assessment shows that 42 departments of the State Council, 7 provincial-level governments, 14 governments of larger cities, and 66 county-level governments did not publish their annual reports on the construction of a law-based government in 2016 on their own web portals or the websites of their legislative affairs offices.

Thirdly, there were defects in the contents of some government work reports, which affected the credibility of the government. A government work report should include two parts: the summarization of the work in the current year and the arrangement for the work for the next year. As an important embodiment of the construction of a responsible government, governments at various levels should make commitments on the tasks to be accomplished in the next year and give information about the fulfillment of the commitments they have made in the previous year in their annual government work reports. However, the assessment shows that some assessment targets gave no information about the fulfillment of some of the commitments they had made in the annual work reports of the previous year. For example, the annual work report of the Government of Shanxi Province in 2016 failed to give full information about the work of actively and steadily advancing the new-type urbanization. The annual work reports of some assessment targets even contained no summarization of the work in the current year or report on the fulfillment of the work arrangements for the previous year. For example, the work report of the Government of Chaoyang District of Beijing Municipality in 2016 only contained a review of its work in the past four or five years, without a summarization of the concrete work it carried out in 2015. The same problem existed in the 2016 government work report of Tengchong City of Baoshan City in Yunnan Province.

2.4.6 There Were Still Shortboards in Information Disclosure in Key Fields

Firstly, the situation of disclosure of information about the review, recordation, and validity indication of normative documents was not satisfactory. Normative documents, also called "red-heading documents", refer to the documents adopted by administrative organs that can be applied repeatedly and affect the rights and interests of an unspecific majority of people. This year's assessment covered only the disclosure of normative documents with legal effect below that of administrative rules. Normative documents are the basis of the activities of administrative organs as well as of the general public and are thus closely related to the vital interest of the general public. Therefore, the information about their formulation, issuance, recordation, review, and abolition must be disclosed to the public. The Opinions of the State Council on Strengthening the Building of a Law-based Government (No. 33 [2010] of the State Council) clearly require governments at various levels and the relevant government departments to strengthen the informatization, periodically disclose catalogs of administrative rules and other normative documents they have reviewed through recordation, strengthen the review of administrative regulations, rules, and normative documents, establish a regular review system for administrative rules and normative documents, carry out a review of administrative rules every 5 years and normative documents every 2 years, disclose to the public the results of the reviews, and explore the establishment of the validity period system of normative documents. The Key Tasks of Open Government Work in 2017, issued by the General Office of the State Council, also required the timely disclosure of information about the abolition and invalidation of policy documents and the indication of the validity of the original documents published on government websites. However, the assessment shows that 14 provincial-level governments, 40 governments of larger cities, and 92 county-level governments did not disclose the information about the recordation and examination of normative documents in 2017 on their own portals or the websites of their legislative affairs office. 25 departments of the State Council, 15 provincial-level governments, 22 governments of larger cities, and 61 county-level governments did not disclose the results of the reviews of normative documents in recent three years on their own portals or the website of their legislative affairs offices. 41 departments of the State Council, 15 provincial-level governments, 33 governments of larger cities, and 77 county-level governments did not set a validity column in the normative document column or catalog on their portal website or the websites of their legislative affairs offices, or indicate the validity on the front pages of specific normative documents, or specify the validity period at the end of the documents.

Secondly, the disclosure of budget and final accounts of some local governments was not standardized. The Notice of the Ministry of Finance on Issuing the Operating Procedures for the Disclosure of Local Budgets and Final Accounts provides for the most basic requirements for the government budget and final account sheets that should be disclosed by governments at various levels. However, the assessment shows that one provincial-level government and 6 county-level governments disclosed only the budget and final accounts of various departments under them, but not their own budget and final accounts, on their web portals or the websites of their financial departments. With respect to the disclosure of budget statements, 19 provincial-level governments, 25 governments of larger cities, and 72 county-level governments failed to disclose all six budget statements (the income statement of the general public budget; the expenditure statement of the general public budget; the expenditure statement at the same level of the general public budget; the basic expenditure statement at the same level of the general public budget; the tax refund and transfer payment statement of the general public budget; and the statement of the quota and balance of the general debts of the government). Among them, seven provincial-level governments, four governments of larger cities, and 17 county-level governments did not disclose any government budget statement for 2017.

Thirdly, the degree of disclosure of information in the field of compulsory education was still relatively low. In the Key Tasks of Open Government Work in 2017, the General Office of the State Council required governments at various levels to advance the work of openness of the compulsory education enrollment policy, and governments at the county level to disclose information about the conditions of schools and the scope, conditions and results of enrollment of schools of compulsory education. However, the assessment shows that 49 county-level governments did not disclose the enrollment scopes of primary schools in their own administrative areas, and 57 county-level governments did not disclose the enrollment scopes of middle schools in their own administrative areas. Among them, although the Government of Dongcheng District of Beijing Municipality had established a compulsory education enrollment work system, the information in this system was not open to the public. Although we cannot rule out the possibility that the government published the results of the division of districts of compulsory education by posting the notices in such places as physical bulletin boards, billboards, school gates, etc., these methods could no longer satisfy people's need to have access to information at any time and any place in an information age. Therefore, governments should further improve their method of disclosure and get as much information online as they can. With respect to admission conditions, 44 county-level governments did not disclose information about the primary and secondary school admission requirements for ordinary children and 37 county-level governments did not disclose information about the primary and secondary school admission requirements for children of migrant workers. With respect to school information, 34 county-level governments did disclose such information. With respect to the results of school enrollment, only 4 county-level governments disclosed the results of compulsory education enrollment in 2017.

2.4.7 *The Issuance of Policy Interpretations Still Needed to Be Improved*

The Key Tasks of Open Government Work in 2017, issued by the General Office of the State Council, provided that governments at various levels and departments under them must, in accordance with the principle of "whoever drafts a policy shall be responsible for its interpretation", realize the synchronized organization, synchronized examination and approval, and synchronized release of policy documents and plans and materials for their interpretation. The Detailed Rules for Implementing the Opinions on Comprehensively Promoting Open Government Work, issued by the General Office of the State Council, provide that, when a government document is issued, the related interpretation materials and documents should be issued in synchronization with the document on the government website or other media. The synchronized issuance of policy documents with policy interpretation can enhance the timeliness of policy interpretation, and the relevance reading of policy interpretations and policy documents can greatly facilitate the access to and the understanding of policy documents by the public. However, the assessment shows that 29 departments of the State Council, 29 provincial-level governments, 18 governments of larger cities, and 23 county-level governments released policy interpretation information more than three days after their release of policy documents on their web portals. Some assessment targets, such as the governments of Zhejiang Province, Luohu District of Shenzhen City in Guangdong Province, and Jiangbei District of Ningbo City in Zhejiang Province, even released policy documents several days after the release of the interpretations of the policies. The websites of 32 departments of the State Council, 11 provincial-level governments, 30 governments of larger cities, and 37 county-level governments did not provide linkage to corresponding policy documents under items of policy interpretations. On some of these websites, only policy interpretations, but no corresponding policy documents could be found.

2.4.8 *There Were Still Legal Risks in the Disclosure of Government Information upon Application*

Disclosure of government information upon application is an important aspect of the system of government information disclosure. The assessment shows that some assessment targets did not give replies to applications for the disclosure of government information within the prescribed time period or gave non-standard replies to applications. Firstly, some assessment targets were still unable to give timely replies to applications: 29 county-level governments did not give replies to applications within the legally prescribed time period. Secondly, the replies were not given in the standardized form. The written replies given by 18 county-level governments did not have an official seal affixed on them or clearly indicate the replying organs. Among them, most grassroots governments replied to the applications using personal emails, rather than official office emails, and some of these personal emails used inappropriate nicknames as their addresses, which affected the standardization of government information disclosure. Statistics show that only the county or district governments in Shanghai and Beijing used emails with the domain name ".gov" in replaying applications for the disclosure of government information. Thirdly, the content of replies was not standardized. When giving the applicants unfavorable replies, administrative organs should cite legal basis, explain the reasons for the decision, and indicate channels of remedy. However, the assessment shows that, among the 16 county-level governments that had given unfavorable replies to the applications, two did not cite the legal basis for their decisions, nine did not explain the reasons for their decisions, and ten did not indicate the channels of remedy. Among them, the replies given by two county-level governments did not contain any information about the legal basis, the reasons for the non-disclosure, or channels of remedy. For example, the reply given by the Government of Xuhui District of Shanghai Municipality only contained the following simple statement: "Your letter has been received. After review, we decide that the content of the letter is of the nature of consultation." Fourthly, the replies were not discrete. For example, the reply given by the Government of Xinjin County in Sichuan Province to the application by the Project Team contained a draft normative document that was labeled "not to be disclosed".

2.4.9 The Construction of an Open Platform for the Openness of Government Affairs Needed to Be Strengthened

Government web portals are the primary platforms of openness of government affairs and the quality of their construction directly affects the quality of the openness of government affairs. However, the assessment shows that the setup of columns on the websites of some governments or the departments under them was still not standardized. Some had established multiple platforms with no linkage between them.

Firstly, there was a lack of standardization in the setup of the columns on government web portals. Governments should set up special columns for different kinds of information on their portal website, and disclose relevant information in a centralized and classified way, so as to facilitate the management of government information by administrative organs and the access to such information by the public. However, the assessment shows that the setup of columns by many assessment targets on their web portals was not elaborate enough. Both the Key Tasks of Open Government Work in 2017, issued by the General Office of the State Council, and the Notice of the Ministry of Finance on Issuing the Operating Procedures for the Disclosure of Local Budgets and Final Accounts clearly require that, beginning from 2017, local financial departments at various levels should set up a uniform platform (or a special column) on the disclosure of budgets and final accounts on their websites or on the web portals of local governments at their respective levels, and make catalogs of, and classify and grade disclosed budgets and final accounts, so as to facilitate the access and supervision by the public. However, the assessment shows that the content of the special column on budgets and final accounts set up by some assessment targets on their web portals was not classified. For example, although a special column on budgets and final accounts had been set up on the web portal of the Government of Jiangxi Province, no sub-column had been set up under this column, and the information about the budgets and final accounts of various departments of the government and the information about the completion of provincial financial revenue were all put into this column in a disorderly way and, as a result, it was very difficult to locate a specific piece of information in the column.

Secondly, multiple platforms had been set up without linkage between them. For example, information about administrative penalties was disclosed on many different platforms, such as the websites of various government departments, the special column on "double publication" (publication of information about administrative licensing and administrative penalties) on government web portals, and the enterprise credit information publicity system. The information about administrative penalties imposed by the same government department but disclosed at different platforms overlapped and were inconsistent with each other, and none of them was complete. Some platforms were not updated for a long period of time and some of them were not even known to the public. This problem was caused by the co-existence of multiple platforms of information disclosure managed by different government departments and the lack of mechanisms for coordination and synchronization between them. The credit information platform itself consisted of two systems: one was the National Enterprise Credit Information Publicity System under the State Administration for Industry and Commerce; the other was CreditChna.gov.cn under the Ministry of Industry and Information Technology. Moreover, various departments were also required by the National Development and Reform Commission to disclose information about administrative penalties in the "double publication" column of their web portals. No coordination and communication mechanism or a synchronized disclosure mechanism was established between the above three departments. This situation was not conducive to the unification of the standard of disclosure, and had led to the scattered disclosure of information and waste of administrative resources. For another example, guides to administrative approval disclosed on different platforms, such as the websites of relevant government departments, online service platforms of government web portals, and websites of government service centers, came from different sources and no linkage was established between them. As a result, it was very difficult to ensure the accuracy of such information.

2.5 Prospect of Development

The Report to the 19th National Congress of the CPC points out that the government needs to transform its functions, further streamline administration and delegate powers, develop new ways of regulation and supervision, and strengthen its credibility and administrative capacity, so as to build itself into a service-oriented government to the satisfaction of the people. The comprehensive deepening of the openness of government affairs plays an indispensable role in this process, ensuring the standardized and orderly operation of government power and enabling the people to participate in and supervise government work, and truly enjoy the dividend of the achievements of the reform.

Firstly, having a correct attitude towards the open government work. The positive attitude of relevant staff is the key to effectively carrying out the open government work. In the process of advancing the open government work, they must continuously adapt themselves to the new situation, and be clear about such questions as to why and for whom government information should be disclosed and what government information should be disclosed. Therefore, governments at various levels should pay constant attention to the training of staff on the openness of government affairs and enable them to understand that openness of government affairs is not merely the unidirectional information disclosure by the government on its own initiative and passive information disclosure upon application, but more importantly, also a process of giving full play to the role of information in administrative service, streamlining of administration, delegation of administrative power, and transition of government functions, enabling the public to participate in government decision-making and social governance, establishing a good relationship between the government and the people, and creating the social governance pattern of joint construction, joint governance, and sharing.

Secondly, rationalizing the mechanism for the disclosure of government information and strengthening the coordination and cooperation between relevant departments. The openness of government affairs should not rely only on the efforts of the government departments in charge of this work. The clear division of work and the coordination and cooperation between relevant government departments are also important safeguards for the harmonious and unified openness of government affairs. Therefore, governments should rationalize work mechanisms, strengthen the coordination between leading departments, give full play to the coordinating role of the leading group on the openness of government affairs, and, especially, unify the standard of openness of various departments, so as to avoid the disunity, inconsistency, and desynchrony in the open government work resulting from overlapping management. Meanwhile, they should give full play to the "advisory" role of the legal affairs department of the government, so as to ensure the quality of openness and eliminate potential risks.

Thirdly, attaching importance to the summarization and popularization of successful experiences. In accordance with the Plan for the Pilot Work on the Standardization of Disclosure of Government Information at the Grassroots Level, issued by the General Office of the State Council, governments at various levels throughout the country have carried out the pilot work on the standardization of the open government work at the grassroots level, which would be completed in 2018. China should take the pilot work as an opportunity to make a comprehensive summarization of the experience of open government work, and develop a set of elaborate and operable work mechanisms and standards for the open government work in various fields.

Fourthly, correctly handling the relationship between openness and non-openness. Governments at various levels should pay attention to both the public demand for information through the gradual expansion of the scope of openness in accordance with law and the limit of openness. They should draw a lesson from the incident of leakage of personal information by some government websites in Anhui Province in 2017, attach importance to the method of openness, and avoid the negative impact of inappropriate information disclosure on the parties involved and on the administrative order.

Fifthly, promoting open government work with the idea of "big openness". China should promote the open government work in accordance with the idea of integration of information disclosure, policy interpretation and response to public concerns, carry out public opinion and social risk assessment in light of the current social and public opinion situations, ensure through interpretation the accurate and comprehensive disclosure of information, eliminate the risks of misunderstanding and misinterpretation, and establish a mechanism for the rapid and appropriate response to public opinions and other social concerns.

As we all know, government websites are the primary platform for disclosure of government information and the quality of their construction has a direct impact on the effect of openness of government affairs. However, the disclosure of government information depends on the background management of the websites and information, and the latter is obviously more important than the former.

Therefore, China should strengthen the informatization of government websites, establish and improve the website background management system, set the key elements of the content of disclosure in accordance with the existing catalogs of disclosure, and ensure that administrative organs leave traces in the background management system and produce government information in every link of performance of their duties. The government information thus generated should be pushed to the external websites for disclosure after going through the internal confidentiality review procedure. Meanwhile, China should strengthen the standardization of the setup of columns on and enhance the user-friendliness of government websites.

Chapter 3
Report on the Indices of Government Transparency in China (2018)—From the Perspective of Information Disclosure on Government Websites

Innovation Project Team on the Rule of Law Index

Abstract In 2018, the Center for Studies of National Index of the Rule of Law, Chinese Academy of Social Sciences and the Innovation Project Team on the Rule of Law Indices of the Institute of Law, Chinese Academy of Social Sciences carried out the assessment of the situation of government information disclosure and openness of government affairs in 49 departments under the State Council after the institutional reform, 31 provincial-level governments, 49 governments of larger cities and 100 county-level governments, covering such aspects as the openness of decision-making, the openness of administrative services, the openness of implementation and results, policy interpretation and response to public concerns, and disclosure of government information upon application. This report analyzes the progress made and problems encountered by various assessment targets in the open government work, and puts forward corresponding countermeasure suggestions.

Keywords Openness of government affairs · Government transparency · Law-based government · Rule of law index · Government

In 2018, the Center for Studies of National Indices of the Rule of Law Chinese Academy of Social Sciences and the Innovation Project Team on Rule of Law Indices,

---

Leaders of the Project Team: Tian He, a research fellow at CASS Law Institute and the director of the Center for Studies of National Indices of the Rule of Law, Chinese Academy of Social Sciences and Lv Yanbin, a research fellow and the head of the Department of Survey and Study of National Situation of the Rule of Law of the Institute of Law, Chinese Academy of Social Sciences. Other members of the project team include: Wang Wanxiu, Wang Xiaomei, Wang Zihao, Wang Gengyu, Wang Zenan, Wang Yiming, Wang Xuxin, Bian Zejuan, Lu Yihan, Xiang Lin, Liu Yu, Liu Junxiang, Liu Haixin, Liu Yanpeng, Li Tong, Li Jiayue, Li Yancheng, Wu Junjie, Chen Dan, Wu Qianqian, Zheng Xin, Zhao Tong, Hu Changming, He Bingjie, Li Yanjie, Cai Jinge, Xu Mengya, Guo Jiayi, Huang Qing, Liang Yating, Ge Xin, Fu Tong, Liao Pei, Xiong Yushan, and Yan Huan. Final editor of the report: Lv Yanbin.

Innovation Project Team on the Rule of Law Index (✉)
Institute of Law, Chinese Academy of Social Sciences, Beijing, China
e-mail: 13263169197@163.com

H. Tian et al. (eds.), *Report on the Rule of Law Index in China 2*,
Research Series on the Chinese Dream and China's Development Path,
https://doi.org/10.1007/978-981-19-9597-2_3

the Institute of Law, Chinese Academy of Social Sciences (hereinafter referred to as the Project Team) continued to carry out a third-party assessment of the openness of government affairs of governments at various levels. This report is the summarization and analysis of the results of the assessment.

3.1 Targets, Indices and Methodology of Assessment

The assessment in 2018 covered 49 departments under the State Council having external administrative authorities after the state institutional reform, 31 provincial-level governments, 49 governments of larger cities, and 100 county-level governments. The county-level governments covered by this year's assessment were different from those covered in the 2017 assessment: the latter were county-level governments selected for the pilot program by the Notice of the General Office of the State Council on Issuing the Plan for Conducting the Pilot Program of Standardizing and Regulating Grassroots Open Government Work, which covered only some provinces, municipalities directly under the Central Government and autonomous regions. In order to increase the coverage of the 2018 assessment, the Project Team selected assessment targets from provinces covered by the pilot program randomly and from provinces not covered by the pilot program according to their GDP rankings.

The assessment indices had been set by the Project Team in accordance with the Regulations on the Disclosure of Government Information, Opinions of the General Office of the CPC Central Committee and the General Office of the State Council on Comprehensively Advancing Open Government Work, Detailed Rules on the Implementation of the Opinions on Comprehensively Promoting Open Government Work and the Key Tasks of Open Government Work in 2018, issued by the General Office of the State Council, and other relevant documents. The grade I indices for the assessment of departments under the State Council and local governments at various levels included: openness of decision-making, openness of administrative service, openness of implementation and its results, policy interpretation and response to public concerns, and disclosure of information upon application (see Tables 3.1, 3.2, 3.3, and 3.4).

The index of openness of decision-making was mainly used to examine the situation of pre-disclosure of major decision-making and the disclosure of normative documents by departments under the State Council and local governments at various levels. The index of the openness of administrative service was mainly used to examine the situation of disclosure of power lists, information about the provision of government services, the "double-random inspection" ("inspections of randomly selected entities by randomly selected inspectors"), and the imposition of administrative penalties by various departments under the State Council with corresponding authorities and governments at various levels. It is also used in the assessment of the situation of disclosure of information about the administration of compulsory education by county-level governments. The "double random" inspection information disclosed by the departments of the State Council was not used in the calculation

Table 3.1 Government transparency index system (for departments of the State Council)

Grade I indices	Grade II indices
Openness of decision-making (35%)	Pre-disclosure of major decisions (60%)
	Disclosure of normative documents (40%)
Openness of administrative service (20%)	Disclosure of power list (30%)
	Disclosure of government service information (40%)
	Disclosure of administrative penalty information (30%)
Openness of implementation and its results (25%)	Annual report on the construction of a law-based government (60%)
	Openness of the results of handling of suggestions and proposals (40%)
Policy interpretation and response to public concerns (20%)	Policy interpretation (70%)
	Response to public concerns (30%)

Table 3.2 Government transparency index system (for provincial-level governments)

Grade I indices	Grade II indices
Openness of decision-making (20%)	Pre-disclosure of major decisions (60%)
	Disclosure of normative documents (40%)
Openness of administrative service (25%)	Disclosure of power list (10%)
	Disclosure of government service information (35%)
	Disclosure of "double random" inspection information (25%)
	Disclosure of administrative penalty information (30%)
Openness of implementation and its results (25%)	Disclosure of audit results (35%)
	Annual report on the construction of a law-based government (35%)
	Openness of the results of handling of suggestions and proposals (30%)
Policy interpretation (20%)	Policy interpretation (70%)
	Response to public concerns (30%)
Information disclosure upon application (10%)	Smoothness of channels (40%)
	Standardization of responses (60%)

of assessment scores in this year's assessment. The index of openness of implementation and its results was mainly used to examine the situation of publication of annual reports on the construction of a law-based government and the disclosure of the results of the handling of suggestions and proposals; it was also used to examine

Table 3.3 Government transparency index system (for governments of larger cities)

Grade I indices	Grade II indices
Openness of decision-making (25%)	Pre-disclosure major decisions (100%)
	Disclosure of normative documents (40%)
Openness of administrative service (35%)	Disclosure of power lists (10%)
	Disclosure of government service information (35%)
	Disclosure of "double random" inspection information (25%)
	Disclosure of administrative penalty information (30%)
Openness of implementation and its results (20%)	Disclosure of audit results (35%)
	Annual report on the construction of a law-based government (35%)
	Openness of the results of handling of suggestions and proposals (30%)
	Annual report on government information disclosure (10%)
Policy interpretation and response to public concerns (20%)	Policy interpretation (70%)
	Respond to concerns (30%)

Table 3.4 Index system of government transparency index (for county-level governments)

Grade I indices	Grade II indices
Openness of decision-making (20%)	Pre-disclosure major decision-making (60%)
	Disclosure of normative documents (40%)
Openness of administrative service (30%)	Disclosure of power lists (10%)
	Disclosure of government service information (20%)
	Disclosure of "double random" inspection information (20%)
	Disclosure of administrative penalty information (25%)
	Information disclosure in the field of education (25%)
Openness of implementation and its results (25%)	Annual report on the construction of a law-based government (60%)
	Openness of the results of handling of suggestions and proposals (40%)
Policy interpretation and response to public concerns (15%)	Policy interpretation (70%)
	Response to public concerns (30%)
Disclosure upon application (10%)	Smoothness of channels (40%)
	Standardized responses (60%)

the publication of auditing results by provincial-level governments and governments of larger cities. The index of policy interpretation and response to public concerns included two grade II indices: the index of policy interpretation and the index of response to public concerns. The index of disclosure upon application was used only to examine the accessibility of the systems of online application and application by letter for disclosure of government information by the health administration departments of 31 provincial-level governments and education administration departments of 100 county-level governments and the level of standardization of their replies to such applications.

The Project Team obtained assessment data by observing the relevant information disclosed on the web portals of assessment targets and the websites of their relevant departments and analyzed the situation of implementation by assessment targets of the requirements of information disclosure. It carried out the assessment of the situation of disclosure of government information upon application by the health administration departments of 31 provincial-level governments and the education administration departments of 100 county-level governments by ways of online application (on online platforms or by email) and application by letter (registered letter) for disclosure of government information during the period of July 31-November 20, 2018. The information applied for at the provincial-level health administration departments was "statistical statements and reports containing the number of pediatric departments in the hospitals in the whole province by the end of December 2017"; and the information applied for at the 100 county (municipal or district)-level education administration departments was "information about primary schools approved by the local government to enroll children of migrant workers, including the names, addresses and enrollment scales of these schools". The time of assessment was not always the same for different assessment targets, but the overall cut-off date for assessment was December 31, 2018.

3.2 General Situation of the Assessment Results

In 2018, the departments of the State Council with the highest scores in the assessment included State Taxation Administration, Ministry of Education, Ministry of Commerce, Ministry of Transport, Ministry of Science and Technology, China Securities Regulatory Commission, State Intellectual Property Office, Ministry of Justice, Ministry of Human Resources and Social Security and Ministry of Ecology and Environment (see Table 3.5 for the assessment results); the provincial-level governments with the highest scores in the assessment included the governments of Anhui Province, Beijing Municipality, Shanghai Municipality, Guizhou Province, Sichuan Province, Shandong Province, Ningxia Hui Autonomous Region, Tianjin Municipality, Yunnan Province and Hainan Province (see Table 3.6 for the assessment results); the governments of larger cities with the highest scores in the assessment included those of Shenzhen, Qingdao, Suzhou, Chengdu, Ningbo, Hefei, Guangzhou, Fuzhou, Zibo and Yinchuan (see Table 3.7 for the assessment results); and the county-level governments with the highest scores in the assessment included those of Xicheng District of Beijing Municipality, Putuo District of Shanghai Municipality, Jiangbei District of Ningbo City in Zhejiang Province, Chancheng District of Foshan City in Guangdong Province, Hongkou District of Shanghai Municipality, Dongcheng District of Beijing Municipality, Rongcheng City of Weihai City in Shandong Province, Yiwu City of Jinhua City in Zhejiang Province, Longkou City of Yantai City in Shandong Province and Liuzhi Special District of Liupanshui City in Guizhou Province (see Table 3.8 for the assessment results).

3.3 Bright Spots Discovered in the Assessment

In 2018, which was the tenth anniversary of the promulgation of the Regulations on the Disclosure of Government Information and a key year in the process of bringing the open government work under the rule of law, the open government work in the whole country had been continuously deepened and bright spots emerged one after another in different fields of the open government work.

3.3.1 Expanding the Fields of Openness and Elaborating the Provisions on Openness

In 2018, China further expanded the fields and refined the provisions on the openness of government affairs. After issuing the Opinions on Advancing Public Disclosure of Government Information in the Field of Approval and Implementation of Major Construction Projects and the Opinions on Advancing Public Disclosure of Government Information in the Public Resource Allocation Field in 2017, the General Office of the State Council issued a series of new regulations in 2018, including the Opinions on Advancing Public Disclosure of Government Information in the Field of Social Public Interest Undertakings, the Notice on Effectively Carrying out the Gazette Work, Guiding Opinions on Comprehensively Implementing the Legality Review Mechanism for Administrative Regulatory Documents, the Notice on Strengthening the Development and Supervisory Administration of Administrative Regulatory Documents, Guiding Opinions on Comprehensively Implementing the Administrative Law Enforcement Publication System, the Recording System of Law Enforcement in the Whole Process and the Legal Review System of Major Law Enforcement Decisions, and the Notice on Focusing on Enterprises' Concerns and Further Promoting the Implementation of Business Environment Optimization Policies. The open government work in some specific fields had also been refined. For example, the Ministry of Finance issued the Measures for the Disclosure of Information about Local Government Debts (for Trial Implementation), which clarified the requirements for the disclosure of information about local government debts.

Table 3.5 Results of assessment of indices of government transparency (department of the State Council) (Unit: point)

Ranking	Departments	Openness of decision-making (35%)	Openness of administrative service (20%)	Openness of Implementation and its results (25%)	Policy interpretation and response to concerns (20%)	Total score (out of 100)
1	State Administration of Taxation	86.40	66.00	64.00	91.60	77.76
2	Ministry of Education	64.00	38.96	88.00	91.60	70.51
3	Ministry of Commerce	64.00	67.75	52.00	100.00	68.95
4	Ministry of Transport	68.80	42.16	64.00	97.90	68.09
5	Ministry of Science and Technology	40.00	60.70	100.00	84.60	68.06
6	China Securities Regulatory Commission	86.40	67.75	64.00	34.90	66.77
7	State Intellectual Property Office	54.40	41.16	82.00	87.40	65.25
8	Ministry of Justice	54.40	70.00	64.00	76.90	64.42
9	Ministry of Human Resources and Social Security	54.40	26.16	82.00	97.90	64.35
10	Ministry of Ecology and Environment	54.40	70.00	46.00	90.90	62.72
11	Ministry of Industry and Information Technology	54.40	42.16	76.00	76.90	61.85
12	Ministry of Foreign Affairs	54.40	20.16	76.00	93.70	60.81
13	General Administration of Customs	64.00	69.00	28.00	84.60	60.12

(continued)

Table 3.5 (continued)

Ranking	Departments	Openness of decision-making (35%)	Openness of administrative service (20%)	Openness of Implementation and its results (25%)	Policy interpretation and response to concerns (20%)	Total score (out of 100)
14	Ministry of Natural Resources	64.00	45.96	46.00	82.50	59.59
15	Civil Aviation Administration of China	54.40	30.96	76.00	75.50	59.33
16	State Forestry and Grassland Bureau	54.40	74.95	28.00	85.30	58.09
17	Ministry of Finance	54.40	47.00	46.00	86.70	57.28
18	National Bureau of Statistics	40.00	47.00	70.00	80.40	56.98
19	National Administration of Traditional Chinese Medicine	54.40	42.96	64.00	64.30	56.49
20	State Administration of Radio and Television	25.60	40.16	88.00	85.30	56.05
21	State Drug Administration	54.40	61.20	28.00	86.00	55.48
22	China Meteorological Administration	54.40	42.16	40.00	87.40	54.95
23	Ministry of Housing and Urban–Rural Development	40.00	42.16	58.00	89.50	54.83
24	Ministry of Civil Affairs	54.40	42.16	28.00	100.00	54.47
25	Ministry of Water Resources	54.40	41.16	28.00	93.70	53.01

(continued)

Table 3.5 (continued)

Ranking	Departments	Openness of decision-making (35%)	Openness of administrative service (20%)	Openness of Implementation and its results (25%)	Policy interpretation and response to concerns (20%)	Total score (out of 100)
26	National Health and Health Commission	54.40	41.16	40.00	76.90	52.65
27	State Sports General Administration	40.00	41.16	64.00	64.30	51.09
28	Ministry of Agriculture and Rural Affairs	54.40	42.16	70.00	30.00	50.97
29	Emergency Management Department	54.40	2.16	64.00	76.90	50.85
30	National Development and Reform Commission	54.40	42.16	28.00	72.70	49.01
31	Ministry of Culture and Tourism	40.00	42.16	28.00	97.90	49.01
32	National Energy Administration	54.40	29.36	28.00	85.30	48.97
33	State Administration of Cultural Heritage	54.40	25.16	28.00	89.50	48.97
34	State Railway Administration	40.00	62.95	28.00	74.80	48.55
35	National Bureau of Letters and Calls	54.40	41.16	40.00	51.00	47.47
36	Audit Commission	14.40	2.16	88.00	87.40	44.95
37	State Grain and Material Reserve Bureau	54.40	29.36	28.00	64.30	44.77

(continued)

Table 3.5 (continued)

Ranking	Departments	Openness of decision-making (35%)	Openness of administrative service (20%)	Openness of Implementation and its results (25%)	Policy interpretation and response to concerns (20%)	Total score (out of 100)
38	State Administration of Market Supervision	40.00	63.54	28.00	45.87	42.88
39	State Post Bureau	40.00	52.95	31.00	51.70	42.68
40	Bank of China Insurance Regulatory Commission	40.00	59.75	28.00	44.35	41.82
41	People's Bank of China	54.40	55.87	28.00	9.00	39.01
42	Ministry of Public Security	40.00	36.36	0.00	72.00	35.67
43	State-owned Assets Supervision and Administration Commission	16.80	12.56	46.00	76.90	35.27
44	National Agency for International Development Cooperation	52.00	2.16	60.00	0.00	33.63
45	State Administration of Foreign Exchange	0.00	27.76	28.00	90.90	30.73
46	State Tobacco Monopoly Bureau	0.00	29.36	40.00	63.60	28.59
47	National Ethnic Council	0.00	9.12	64.00	51.70	28.16
48	National Immigration Administration	0.00	14.16	60.00	51.00	28.03
49	National Healthcare Security Administration	0.00	2.16	60.00	0.00	15.43

Table 3.6 Results of assessment of indices of transparency (provincial-level governments) (Unit: point)

Ranking	Provincial-level Governments	Openness of decision-making (20%)	Openness of administrative service (25%)	Openness of implementation and its results (25%)	Policy interpretation and response to concerns (20%)	Information disclosure upon application (10%)	Total score (out of 100)
1	Anhui Province	88.56	64.16	77.00	100.00	97.50	82.75
2	Beijing Municipality	92.64	78.00	60.63	83.90	100.00	79.96
3	Shanghai Municipality	63.76	71.42	86.00	86.00	100.00	79.31
4	Guizhou Province	83.68	75.10	72.63	86.00	87.50	79.05
5	Sichuan Province	64.80	81.19	65.63	95.80	96.00	78.42
6	Shandong Province	61.60	81.48	73.50	83.90	100.00	77.84
7	Ningxia Hui Autonomous Region	76.00	79.89	69.13	77.60	95.00	77.47
8	Tianjin Municipality	64.80	85.63	74.13	73.40	96.00	77.18
9	Yunnan Province	47.68	83.96	78.13	83.90	87.50	75.59
10	Hainan Province	63.76	61.83	69.13	100.00	97.50	75.24
11	Hebei Province	63.76	69.48	72.63	86.00	97.50	75.23
12	Guangdong Province	82.56	70.83	54.63	86.00	100.00	75.08
13	Jiangxi Province	63.76	82.25	69.63	73.40	95.00	74.90

(continued)

Table 3.6 (continued)

Ranking	Provincial-level Governments	Openness of decision-making (20%)	Openness of administrative service (25%)	Openness of implementation and its results (25%)	Policy interpretation and response to concerns (20%)	Information disclosure upon application (10%)	Total score (out of 100)
14	Heilongjiang Province	69.76	67.90	86.63	87.40	27.50	72.81
15	Jiangsu Province	53.44	76.81	69.13	77.60	100.00	72.69
16	Chongqing	63.76	60.46	69.13	85.30	96.00	71.81
17	Liaoning Province	82.56	65.93	51.63	75.50	97.50	70.75
18	Fujian Province	41.68	74.23	52.50	100.00	95.00	69.52
19	Jilin Province	41.92	71.89	82.13	97.90	26.00	69.07
20	Inner Mongolia Autonomous Region	71.68	68.32	65.00	87.40	30.00	68.15
21	Zhejiang Province	31.20	82.00	74.13	74.80	76.00	67.83
22	Shanxi Province	45.76	62.50	53.38	91.60	97.50	66.19
23	Henan Province	81.76	72.77	21.00	77.60	100.00	65.31
24	Gansu Province	84.96	62.23	38.50	100.00	27.50	64.93
25	Qinghai Province	58.00	50.44	59.00	86.00	81.00	64.26
26	Hubei Province	45.12	60.73	68.00	77.60	67.50	63.48
27	Hunan Province	52.00	56.64	56.00	77.60	67.50	60.83
28	Xinjiang Uygur Autonomous Region	26.56	54.89	63.63	72.70	96.00	59.08

(continued)

Table 3.6 (continued)

Ranking	Provincial-level Governments	Openness of decision-making (20%)	Openness of administrative service (25%)	Openness of implementation and its results (25%)	Policy interpretation and response to concerns (20%)	Information disclosure upon application (10%)	Total score (out of 100)
29	Shaanxi Province	38.88	66.65	83.13	50.30	27.50	58.03
30	Guangxi Zhuang Autonomous Region	45.12	75.10	44.00	77.60	20.00	56.32
31	Tibet Autonomous Region	17.76	53.27	54.63	55.90	26.00	44.31

Table 3.7 Results of assessment of transparency of governments of larger cities (Unit: point)

		Openness of decision-making (25%)	Openness of administrative services (35%)	Openness of Implementation and its results (20%)	Policy interpretation and response to concerns (20%)	Total score (out of 100)
1	Shenzhen	84.40	81.55	86.63	95.80	86.13
2	Qingdao	95.44	84.73	83.13	79.70	86.08
3	Suzhou	87.44	81.33	87.50	86.00	85.03
4	Chengdu	75.76	78.79	83.13	86.00	80.34
5	Ningbo	84.40	73.50	86.63	79.70	80.09
6	Hefei	81.28	82.92	59.50	93.70	79.98
7	Guangzhou	75.76	73.22	91.00	86.00	79.97
8	Fuzhou	70.48	78.79	77.00	95.80	79.76
9	Zibo	70.48	79.29	87.50	83.90	79.65
10	Yinchuan	83.20	71.13	83.13	86.00	79.52
11	Xiamen	79.84	68.16	91.00	87.40	79.50
12	Huainan	68.48	78.24	77.00	95.80	79.06
13	Dalian	68.48	82.83	87.50	76.90	78.99
14	Wuhan	61.52	76.90	82.25	97.90	78.32
15	Jinan	78.40	74.96	78.00	83.90	78.22
16	Haikou	64.64	74.10	78.75	100.00	77.85
17	Guiyang	83.20	65.57	87.50	77.60	76.77
18	Harbin	56.00	80.65	71.13	100.00	76.45
19	Zhengzhou	59.52	79.00	74.13	83.90	74.14
20	Luoyang	52.00	83.96	73.00	76.90	72.37
21	Hangzhou	40.00	74.36	92.13	83.90	71.23
22	Zhuhai	67.20	81.04	47.00	81.10	70.78
23	Fushun	58.88	61.75	82.25	86.70	70.12
24	Shenyang	50.88	66.65	87.50	81.80	69.91
25	Shantou	48.64	57.11	82.13	100.00	68.57
26	Xi'an	60.00	71.24	52.50	86.00	67.63
27	Wuxi	48.00	72.04	55.13	95.80	67.40
28	Kunming	67.12	81.33	46.38	64.30	67.38
29	Nanning	51.52	80.55	59.50	71.30	67.23
30	Nanjing	42.88	78.83	68.63	75.50	67.14
31	Xuzhou	47.52	87.46	44.63	78.30	67.08
32	Changchun	40.00	65.48	83.13	86.00	66.74
33	Handan	71.44	36.90	78.75	97.90	66.11

(continued)

Table 3.7 (continued)

		Openness of decision-making (25%)	Openness of administrative services (35%)	Openness of Implementation and its results (20%)	Policy interpretation and response to concerns (20%)	Total score (out of 100)
34	Nanchang	60.64	65.16	52.50	77.60	63.99
35	Tangshan	40.64	67.97	74.38	75.50	63.93
36	Changsha	39.84	69.01	51.63	91.60	62.76
37	Qiqihar	68.48	77.74	10.88	72.70	61.04
38	Xining	60.00	47.75	69.13	76.90	60.92
39	Shijiazhuang	36.16	53.50	92.13	70.60	60.31
40	Hohhot	42.88	65.06	21.00	95.80	56.85
41	Jilin	44.16	66.98	24.00	64.30	52.14
42	Urumqi	33.12	59.63	35.00	77.60	51.67
43	Lanzhou	63.36	43.16	37.38	64.30	51.28
44	Benxi	46.24	42.84	38.50	79.70	50.19
45	Taiyuan	19.84	79.58	15.50	71.30	50.17
46	Datong	12.48	46.06	69.00	64.30	45.90
47	Lhasa	1.44	73.50	25.50	68.50	44.89
48	Anshan	24.48	50.44	38.50	64.30	44.33
49	Baotou	40.00	53.94	6.50	64.30	43.04

3.3.2 Making Progress in the Pre-openness of Major Decision-Making

Advancing the pre-disclosure of decision-making is an important aspect of the orderly introduction of public participation into the link of major decision-making, an important measure for implementing the strategy of modernizing the state governance system and capacity made by the CPC at its eighteenth and nineteenth national congresses, as well as an important approach to realizing the governance pattern of joint construction, joint governance, and sharing. The assessment shows that the openness of the catalog of major decision-making items had been improved in 2018. Nine governments of larger cities and 16 county-level governments disclosed the catalog of major decision-making items as compared to six and two, respectively, in 2017. Some local governments and departments under the State Council opened diversified channels for solicitation of public opinions to facilitate public participation. For example, the General Administration of Customs and the governments of Shanghai Municipality, Anhui Province, Shaanxi Province, Yunnan Province, Fujian Province, Guangzhou City, Shijiazhuang City, Changchun City and Datong City had all opened diversified channels for the solicitation of public opinions on their web

Table 3.8 Results of assessment of indices of transparency of county-level governments (Unit: point)

Ranking	County-level governments	Openness of decision-making (20%)	Openness of administrative service (30%)	Openness of implementation and its results (25%)	Policy interpretation and response to concerns (15%)	Information disclosure upon application (10%)	Total score (out of 100)
1	Xicheng District, Beijing Municipality	75.80	72.71	94.00	92.60	97.50	84.11
2	Putuo District, Shanghai Municipality	72.24	77.97	88.00	100.00	90.00	83.84
5	Jiangbei District, Ningbo City, Zhejiang Province	72.24	64.18	100.00	77.60	95.00	79.84
4	Chancheng District, Foshan City, Guangdong Province	70.80	68.46	88.00	86.00	100.00	79.60
6	Hongkou District, Shanghai Municipality	56.64	61.71	100.00	89.50	95.00	77.76
7	Dongcheng District, Beijing Municipality	58.88	70.63	88.00	81.80	97.50	76.99
3	Rongcheng City, Weihai City, Shandong Province	66.88	68.16	76.00	93.70	97.50	76.63

(continued)

Table 3.8 (continued)

Ranking	County-level governments	Openness of decision-making (20%)	Openness of administrative service (30%)	Openness of implementation and its results (25%)	Policy interpretation and response to concerns (15%)	Information disclosure upon application (10%)	Total score (out of 100)
8	Yiwu City, Jinhua City, Zhejiang Province	78.80	41.89	100.00	74.80	80.00	72.55
9	Longkou City, Yantai City, Shandong Province	46.48	56.44	88.00	97.20	95.00	72.31
10	Liuzhi Special Zone, Liupanshui City, Guizhou Province	64.32	41.19	100.00	79.70	77.50	69.93
11	Luohu District, Shenzhen City, Guangdong Province	65.20	70.63	64.00	75.50	80.00	69.56
12	Gongshu District, Hangzhou City, Zhejiang Province	72.24	59.71	88.00	86.00	10.00	68.26
13	Shanghai Municipality Pudong New Area	52.48	64.18	76.00	75.50	80.00	68.08
14	Ouhai District, Wenzhou City, Zhejiang Province	79.44	46.30	61.00	86.00	100.00	67.93

(continued)

Table 3.8 (continued)

Ranking	County-level governments	Openness of decision-making (20%)	Openness of administrative service (30%)	Openness of implementation and its results (25%)	Policy interpretation and response to concerns (15%)	Information disclosure upon application (10%)	Total score (out of 100)
15	Jinzhai county, Lu'an city, Anhui province	80.96	66.19	28.00	100.00	85.00	66.55
16	Huizhou District, Huangshan City, Anhui Province	76.88	69.32	28.00	91.60	95.00	66.41
17	Haidian District, Beijing Municipality	48.00	77.34	39.00	95.80	92.50	66.17
18	Boluo County, Huizhou City, Guangdong Province	40.88	49.70	88.00	83.90	73.50	65.02
19	Helan County, Yinchuan City, Ningxia Hui Autonomous Region	43.20	77.00	40.00	83.90	81.00	62.43
20	Daoli District, Harbin City, Heilongjiang Province	16.00	48.98	88.00	83.90	95.00	61.98

(continued)

Table 3.8 (continued)

Ranking	County-level governments	Openness of decision-making (20%)	Openness of administrative service (30%)	Openness of implementation and its results (25%)	Policy interpretation and response to concerns (15%)	Information disclosure upon application (10%)	Total score (out of 100)
21	Lingbi County, Suzhou City, Anhui Province	64.64	63.75	40.00	100.00	30.00	60.05
22	Bozhou District, Zunyi City, Guizhou Province	27.84	43.19	88.00	78.30	75.00	59.77
23	Renshou County, Meishan City, Sichuan Province	32.00	53.75	88.00	76.90	36.00	59.66
24	Xuhui District, Shanghai Municipality	66.88	46.18	34.00	93.70	97.50	59.53
25	Chaoyang District, Beijing Municipality	44.00	79.00	6.00	100.00	97.50	58.75
26	Guiping City, Guigang City, Guangxi Zhuang Autonomous Region	35.52	57.88	88.00	72.70	6.00	57.97
27	Suzhou District, Jiuquan City, Gansu Province	40.00	56.55	82.00	73.40	10.00	57.47

(continued)

Table 3.8 (continued)

Ranking	County-level governments	Openness of decision-making (20%)	Openness of administrative service (30%)	Openness of implementation and its results (25%)	Policy interpretation and response to concerns (15%)	Information disclosure upon application (10%)	Total score (out of 100)
28	Luyang District, Hefei City, Anhui Province	50.88	51.22	28.00	97.90	97.50	56.98
29	Luolong District, Luoyang City, Henan Province	15.84	35.43	88.00	87.40	75.00	56.41
30	Xincheng District, Hohhot City, Inner Mongolia Autonomous Region	36.00	44.50	88.00	66.40	20.00	54.51
31	Lixia District, Jinan City, Shandong Province	52.48	60.50	31.00	70.60	75.00	54.49
32	Jianye District, Nanjing City, Jiangsu Province	38.88	60.02	64.00	32.10	71.00	53.70
33	Nanming District, Guiyang City, Guizhou Province	44.00	51.60	34.00	86.70	77.50	53.54
34	Wafangdian City, Dalian City, Liaoning Province	32.16	44.86	88.00	30.00	71.00	53.49

(continued)

Table 3.8 (continued)

Ranking	County-level governments	Openness of decision-making (20%)	Openness of administrative service (30%)	Openness of implementation and its results (25%)	Policy interpretation and response to concerns (15%)	Information disclosure upon application (10%)	Total score (out of 100)
35	Gulou District, Fuzhou City, Fujian Province	48.00	61.83	12.00	83.90	97.50	53.49
36	Wuhua District, Kunming City, Yunnan Province	40.00	64.75	28.00	74.10	77.50	53.29
37	Tianjin Municipality Binhai New Area	24.00	54.76	40.00	81.80	95.00	53.00
38	Qianguoerluosi Mongolian Autonomous County, Songyuan City, Jilin Province	36.48	43.26	28.00	93.70	97.50	51.08
39	Qingtongxia City, Wuzhong City, Ningxia Hui Autonomous Region	40.00	44.80	64.00	83.90	10.00	51.03
40	Dongning City, Mudanjiang City, Heilongjiang Province	12.00	35.05	88.00	81.80	36.00	50.79

(continued)

Table 3.8 (continued)

Ranking	County-level governments	Openness of decision-making (20%)	Openness of administrative service (30%)	Openness of implementation and its results (25%)	Policy interpretation and response to concerns (15%)	Information disclosure upon application (10%)	Total score (out of 100)
41	Nankai District, Tianjin Municipality	12.48	54.20	40.00	76.90	96.00	49.89
42	Jinjiang City, Quanzhou City, Fujian Province	36.00	55.83	36.00	32.10	95.00	47.27
43	Longquanyi District, Chengdu City, Sichuan Province	44.00	59.78	0.00	76.90	86.00	46.87
44	Chuxiong City, Chuxiong Yi Autonomous Prefection, Yunnan Province	36.00	55.77	22.00	75.50	55.00	46.26
45	Haizhu District, Guangzhou City, Guangdong Province	52.88	45.25	28.00	83.90	20.00	45.74
46	Bobai County, Yulin City, Guangxi Zhuang Autonomous Region	59.60	47.88	13.00	76.90	27.50	43.82

(continued)

Table 3.8 (continued)

Ranking	County-level governments	Openness of decision-making (20%)	Openness of administrative service (30%)	Openness of implementation and its results (25%)	Policy interpretation and response to concerns (15%)	Information disclosure upon application (10%)	Total score (out of 100)
47	Zhenfeng County, Qianxinan Buyi and Miao Autonomous Prefecture, Guizhou Province	56.64	42.08	28.00	61.50	30.00	43.18
48	Wuqing District, Tianjin Municipality	44.64	52.41	0.00	64.30	86.00	42.89
49	Fengrun District, Tangshan City, Hebei Province	23.20	55.35	64.00	30.00	6.00	42.35
50	Ding'an County, Hainan Province	46.24	15.26	58.00	34.90	85.00	42.06
51	Pengyang County, Guyuan City, Ningxia Hui Autonomous Region	50.48	41.18	28.00	76.90	10.00	41.98
52	Xinyi City, Xuzhou City, Jiangsu Province	36.00	50.94	10.00	72.70	50.00	40.89

(continued)

Table 3.8 (continued)

Ranking	County-level governments	Openness of decision-making (20%)	Openness of administrative service (30%)	Openness of implementation and its results (25%)	Policy interpretation and response to concerns (15%)	Information disclosure upon application (10%)	Total score (out of 100)
53	Shishi City, Quanzhou City, Fujian Province	12.00	51.74	6.00	77.60	95.00	40.56
54	Jiang'an District, Wuhan City, Hubei Province	48.00	52.03	0.00	37.00	95.00	40.26
55	Suzhou Industrial Park, Jiangsu Province	27.60	50.10	0.00	79.70	76.00	40.11
56	Pingguo County, Baise City, Guangxi Zhuang Autonomous Region	36.00	40.94	28.00	86.70	6.00	40.09
57	Nong'an County, Changchun City, Jilin Province	0.00	43.79	70.00	34.90	40.00	39.87
58	Liuyang City, Changsha City, Hunan Province	43.20	47.05	4.00	86.00	27.50	39.41
59	Tengchong City, Baoshan City, Yunnan Province	24.00	30.00	28.00	72.70	75.00	39.21

(continued)

Table 3.8 (continued)

Ranking	County-level governments	Openness of decision-making (20%)	Openness of administrative service (30%)	Openness of implementation and its results (25%)	Policy interpretation and response to concerns (15%)	Information disclosure upon application (10%)	Total score (out of 100)
60	Fucheng District, Mianyang City, Sichuan Province	24.00	46.43	34.00	61.50	26.00	39.05
61	Binzhou City, Xianyang City, Shaanxi Province	23.84	31.19	28.00	75.50	65.00	38.95
62	Wanbailin District, Taiyuan City, Shanxi Province	8.00	71.15	24.00	59.40	6.00	38.45
63	Shangjie District, Zhengzhou City, Henan Province	29.76	45.05	3.00	73.40	71.00	38.33
64	Gangu County, Tianshui City, Gansu Province	38.88	37.71	16.00	84.60	20.00	37.78
65	Hengyang County, Hengyang City, Hunan Province	45.76	17.38	7.00	85.30	85.00	37.41
66	Shuyang County, Suqian City, Jiangsu Province	15.84	44.71	4.00	76.90	75.00	36.62
67	Ledong County, Hainan Province	21.60	40.15	10.00	64.30	75.00	36.01

(continued)

Table 3.8 (continued)

Ranking	County-level governments	Openness of decision-making (20%)	Openness of administrative service (30%)	Openness of implementation and its results (25%)	Policy interpretation and response to concerns (15%)	Information disclosure upon application (10%)	Total score (out of 100)
68	Meilan District, Haikou City, Hainan Province	12.00	41.69	60.00	30.00	16.00	36.01
69	Yuzhong District, Chongqing	8.00	38.44	64.00	34.90	16.00	35.97
70	Chengdong District, Xining City, Qinghai Province	0.00	27.06	60.00	34.90	75.00	35.85
71	Qian'an City, Tangshan City, Hebei Province	3.84	51.71	54.00	32.10	6.00	35.19
72	Longsha District, Qiqihar City, Heilongjiang Province	40.00	39.98	6.00	69.90	30.00	34.98
73	Ansai District, Yan'an City, Shaanxi Province	20.48	35.86	4.00	75.50	77.50	34.93
74	Jianchang County, Huludao City, Liaoning Province	12.00	23.62	28.00	72.70	75.00	34.89

(continued)

Table 3.8 (continued)

Ranking	County-level governments	Openness of decision-making (20%)	Openness of administrative service (30%)	Openness of implementation and its results (25%)	Policy interpretation and response to concerns (15%)	Information disclosure upon application (10%)	Total score (out of 100)
75	Yidu City, Yichang City, Hubei Province	8.00	46.24	16.00	34.90	95.00	34.21
76	Chang'an District, Shijiazhuang City, Hebei Province	44.16	63.90	0.00	30.00	6.00	33.10
77	Fengjie County, Chongqing	16.00	45.00	40.00	34.90	10.00	32.94
78	Xiaoyi City, Luliang City, Shanxi Province	10.08	39.44	24.00	34.90	75.00	32.58
79	Anyue County, Ziyang City, Sichuan Province	32.64	45.88	0.00	64.30	26.00	32.54
80	Weiyang district, Xi'an city, Shaanxi province	27.84	36.13	16.00	70.60	10.00	32.00
81	Xiangfu District, Kaifeng City, Henan Province	13.44	33.97	0.00	73.40	81.00	31.99

(continued)

Table 3.8 (continued)

Ranking	County-level governments	Openness of decision-making (20%)	Openness of administrative service (30%)	Openness of implementation and its results (25%)	Policy interpretation and response to concerns (15%)	Information disclosure upon application (10%)	Total score (out of 100)
82	Zhungeer Banner, Ordos City, Inner Mongolia Autonomous Region	24.00	44.32	6.00	71.30	7.50	31.04
83	Jianli County, Jingzhou City, Hubei Province	0.00	33.69	60.00	34.90	6.00	30.94
84	Tiexi District, Shenyang City, Liaoning Province	0.00	35.13	28.00	34.90	72.50	30.02
85	Baotou Rare Earth High-tech Zone, Inner Mongolia Autonomous Region	18.96	47.56	0.00	61.50	17.50	29.04
86	Qiaokou District, Zhuzhou City, Hunan Province	12.00	41.32	10.00	34.90	56.00	28.13
87	Nanchang County, Nanchang City, Jiangxi Province	13.44	24.50	10.00	34.90	95.00	27.27

(continued)

Table 3.8 (continued)

Ranking	County-level governments	Openness of decision-making (20%)	Openness of administrative service (30%)	Openness of implementation and its results (25%)	Policy interpretation and response to concerns (15%)	Information disclosure upon application (10%)	Total score (out of 100)
88	Liulin County, Luliang City, Shanxi Province	1.44	43.69	0.00	85.30	6.00	26.79
89	Tangyin County, Anyang City, Henan Province	10.08	44.30	0.00	68.50	6.00	26.18
90	Tianshan District, Urumqi City, Xinjiang Uygur Autonomous Region	12.00	21.71	4.00	87.40	26.00	25.62
91	Korla City, Bayinguoleng Prefecture, Xinjiang Uygur Autonomous Region	16.00	18.55	24.00	61.50	6.00	24.59
92	Yanji City, Yanbian Korean Autonomous Prefecture, Jilin Province	1.44	54.83	6.00	34.90	10.00	24.47

(continued)

Table 3.8 (continued)

Ranking	County-level governments	Openness of decision-making (20%)	Openness of administrative service (30%)	Openness of implementation and its results (25%)	Policy interpretation and response to concerns (15%)	Information disclosure upon application (10%)	Total score (out of 100)
93	Horqin District, Tongliao City, Inner Mongolia Autonomous Region	1.44	35.74	28.00	32.10	10.00	23.82
94	Yongdeng County, Lanzhou City, Gansu Province	32.16	35.30	0.00	30.00	6.00	22.12
95	Wanzhou District, Chongqing	0.00	44.56	4.00	34.90	7.50	20.35
96	Guixi City, Yingtan City, Jiangxi Province	13.44	31.93	0.00	32.10	30.00	20.08
97	Poyang County, Shangrao City, Jiangxi Province	1.44	35.55	0.00	32.10	6.00	16.37
98	Duilong Deqing District, Lhasa City, Tibet Autonomous Region	0.00	22.71	0.00	0.00	27.50	9.56
99	Namling County, Shigatse City, Tibet Autonomous Region	0.00	13.33	0.00	0.00	6.00	4.60

(continued)

Table 3.8 (continued)

Ranking	County-level governments	Openness of decision-making (20%)	Openness of administrative service (30%)	Openness of implementation and its results (25%)	Policy interpretation and response to concerns (15%)	Information disclosure upon application (10%)	Total score (out of 100)
100	Delingha City, Haixi Mongolian and Tibetan Autonomous Prefecture, Qinghai Province	0.00	8.00	0.00	0.00	7.50	3.15

portals while at the same time soliciting public opinions by such means as online feedback, email, telephone, fax, and letter. Many assessment targets attached importance to the interpretation of draft decisions: 29 departments under the State Council, 23 provincial-level governments, 20 governments of larger cities, and ten county-level governments disclosed the interpretations or explanations of their draft decisions. Many county-level governments, such as the governments of Xicheng District of Beijing Municipality, Putuo District of Shanghai Municipality and Rongcheng City of Shandong Province, had set up special columns on their web portals to disclose in a concentrated way the information about the adoption of the opinions solicited.

3.3.3 Markedly Improving the Disclosure of Information About the Review of Normative Documents

The Opinions of the State Council on Strengthening the Building of a Law-based Government specifically require government organs to strengthen the review of administrative regulations and rules and normative documents, establish a regular review system for administrative rules and normative documents, review normative documents every two years, and announce the results of the review to the public. The assessment shows that 39 departments under the State Council, 27 provincial-level governments, 46 governments of larger cities, and 68 county-level governments and the legal departments under them disclosed information about the review of normative documents, as compared to 17, 10, 12, and 43, respectively, in 2017.

3.3.4 Gradual Refining of the Disclosure of Government Service Information

Disclosure of government service information is a fundamental work in implementing the reform aimed at streamlining administration, delegating powers, improving regulation, and upgrading services. The assessment shows that the government service information disclosed by various assessment targets was elaborate and detailed. Firstly, the guides to government services became more detailed. Some assessment targets, on the basis of disclosing the content elements of guides to government services in strict accordance with the relevant requirements, provided more detailed and humanized government service information. For example, the guide to government service in the online service hall of the Government of Zhejiang Province not only contained the title and format texts of application materials, but also clarified the source material (the provider), form, and detailed requirements of application materials; and the guides to government services of Fujian Province and Guangdong Province contained not only clear information about the locations of services, but also transportation guide to these locations, so as to facilitate the access to the services by citizens and enterprises. Secondly, the disclosure of the results of administrative approval was refined to facilitate the access by the public. Some assessment targets made the more detailed classification of information about administrative approval according to the category and time of approval. For example, the Environmental Protection Bureau of Beijing Municipality classified the results of administrative approval into 10 categories, allowing the public to search the results by different criteria.

3.3.5 *Satisfactorily Implementing the System of "Double Random Inspection and Public Disclosure of the Results of Inspection"*

Comprehensively implementing the system of "Double Random Inspection and Public Disclosure of the Results of Inspection" (the double random system) in the field of market regulation is a major innovation of the idea and method of market regulation, as well as an important aspect of the incorporation of openness into regulatory work. The assessment shows that many assessment targets had set up special columns for the disclosure of information relating to the double random system to facilitate public access. The rate of disclosure of random inspection results in the field of market regulation was relatively high: 26 provincial-level market regulatory departments (administrative departments for industry and commerce), 37 market regulatory departments (administrative departments for industry and commerce) of larger cities, and 67 county-level market regulatory departments (administrative departments for industry and commerce) disclosed the results of random inspections they had carried out in 2018. Many assessment targets disclosed detailed content of the random inspection results for the convenience of the public. For example, the General Administration of Customs published statistical tables on the results of double random inspections, which contain such data as the number of completed inspections, and the circumstances of random inspections (including the number of randomly selected operations, percentage of randomly selected operations, and effective rate of random selection) classified by cities and categories and the 2017 List of Items Subject to Random Inspection in Customs Administrative Inspections, and labeled the previous lists that had already become invalid. Some assessment targets made integrated lists of random inspections. For example, a separate column on "disclosure of the results of double random inspection" was set up on the web portal of the Government of Haikou City to disclose in a concentrated way lists of items subject to random inspection, and the results of random inspections. The lists contained all the elements of random inspection, including items, targets, time, law enforcement personnel, and the results of inspections, enabling the public to learn about the whole process of random inspections.

3.3.6 Improving the Publication of Annual Reports on the Construction of a Law-Based Government

The Implementation Outline for Building a Law-based Government (2015–2020) requires each government department to report in the first quarter of every year the situation of the construction of a law-based government to the government at the same level and the relevant government departments at the next higher level. The reports should be disclosed to the public through newspapers and government websites. The assessment shows that the percentage of departments under the State Council publishing the reports on the construction of a law-based government had markedly increased. With increasing importance being attached to the work of construction of a law-based government, more and more departments under the State Council had prepared and published annual reports on the construction of a law-based government. In 2018, a total of 27 departments under the State Council published annual reports on the construction of a law-based government, a marked increase from the 12 in 2017. Some municipal and county governments published their reports in a timely manner: 31 governments of larger cities and 31 county-level governments met the requirements of the document on time or even ahead of the prescribed time. Moreover, the content of the reports became more standardized. Most reports were able to cover various aspects of the construction of a law-based government, including the performance of government functions, the improvement of the institutional system and the decision-making quality, law enforcement, supervision, dispute resolution, and enhancement of the quality of personnel, and give a detailed introduction to the work of construction of a law-based government in the previous year, as well as concrete explanations of relevant issues in light of local practice. Many assessment targets analyzed the main problems in their work of building a law-based government and administration by law, put forward detailed measures for improvement, and clearly pointed out the direction of future efforts.

3.3.7 Standardizing the Disclosure of Policy Interpretation Information for the Convenience of the People

Firstly, 42 departments under the State Council, 31 provincial-level governments, 49 governments of larger cities and 91 county-level governments had set up a special policy interpretation column on their web portals. Many local governments had set up special policy interpretation webpages on their web portals to disclose in a concentrated way the interpretations of the documents and policies adopted by the provincial governments and departments under them, as well as those adopted by various municipal governments, so as to facilitate the access by the public. For example, the Government of Beijing Municipality had set up special columns of textual, graphic, and video interpretations of policies under various topics, such as "securing a victory in the defense of the blue sky", "optimizing the business environment" and "prevention and control of financial risks"; the Government of Chancheng District of Foshan City in Guangdong Province had set up columns on different forms of policy interpretation, including video interpretation, illustrated interpretation, interpretation by the adopting departments, expert interpretation, and media interpretation, under the policy interpretation of its web portal, releasing more than 20 pieces of information in each column; and the Government of Guizhou Province provided a special policy interpretation search function to facilitate the direct search for policy interpretations by the public. Secondly, the content of policy interpretation was complete and standardized. Among the assessment targets that had issued policy interpretations in 2018, almost all of them had accurately explained the background, main basis, the scope of targets, key content, characteristics and highlights of the policies. Finally, the form of interpretation had become more diversified, including gif interpretation, H5 page reading, video interpretation, and animation interpretation. Multi-media interpretation is more compatible with the laws of information transmission in the era of mobile internet, gives the public a better reading experience, and enables them to better understand the relevant policies. For example, the Government of Shanghai Municipality creatively used FLASH to give an animated interpretation of the Seventh Three-year Action Plan for Environmental Protection in Shanghai Municipality.

3.3.8 Making Online Interactive Platforms an Important Channel of Response to Public Concerns

Party General Secretary Xi Jinping points out that the government should be more tolerant and patient with netizens, timely absorb constructive opinions, give timely help to those who are in difficulties, timely publicize the situation unknown to them, timely clarify their vague understandings, timely solve their complaints, and timely correct their wrong views. The assessment shows that the vast majority of assessment targets had set up reliable online government-citizen interactive platforms on which the public was able to make inquiries and put forward suggestions. 48 departments under the State Council, 31 provincial-level governments, 49 governments of larger cities, and 97 county-level governments had set up government-citizen interactive platforms on their web portals, and the setup of interactive platforms had become a common practice. Moreover, assessment targets had generally disclosed the issues raised by the public and their responses to these issues. The assessment shows that 35 departments under the State Council, 30 provincial-level governments, 49 governments of larger cities, and 97 county-level governments had responded to the issues raised by the public on interactive platforms in 2018, thereby making it convenient for the public to carry out supervision, for the government to improve the quality of feedback, and for members of the public to follow similar issues. Meanwhile, most assessment targets had given timely and effective responses to the questions submitted on the Internet interactive platforms. For example, the Government of Bozhou District of Zunyi City in Guizhou Province gave responses to most inquiries submitted through the Party secretary's mailbox within a day. To improve the quality of responses, some assessment targets attached a satisfaction evaluation questionnaire at the end of each response to a public inquiry.

3.3.9 Maintaining Unblocked Channels of Disclosure upon Application for the Convenience of the People

The assessment shows that the channels of disclosure upon application of departments under provincial-level governments were unblocked. 23 provincial-level health administration departments provided online channels of application for disclosure of government information, and the channels were unblocked; the eight provincial-level health administration departments that had not provided online channels of application for disclosure of government information had an unblocked channel of application by letters. Many assessment targets, including education departments of many county-level governments, attached importance to making disclosure upon application more convenient for the people. After receiving applications for the disclosure of government information, some assessment targets, such as the Education Department of Rongcheng City in Shandong Province, set up a special column on their websites to disclose the relevant information on their own initiatives and sent the relevant links or websites to the applicants by such means as SMS. Some, such as the Education Department of Luyang District of Hefei City in Anhui Province, published on their websites the information about concrete issues on which applications for disclosure of information had been submitted, so as to facilitate the inquiry by members of the public who needed the same information. Some county-level education administration departments notified applicants by SMS when their applications had been successfully submitted or a reply had been given to their application.

3.4 Problems Identified in the Assessment

3.4.1 The Pre-disclosure of Major Decision-Making Still Needed to Be Improved

Firstly, the information disclosure in the relevant columns of government websites was chaotic. Although some assessment targets had set up a column to solicit public opinions on major decision-making, they had disclosed no information in this column in 2018 or disclosed the relevant information somewhere else. For example, the public opinion solicitation column on the websites of the Ministry of Culture and Tourism and the Government of Taiyuan City in Shanxi Province contained only some irrelevant announcements; the Government of Wuhua District of Kunming City in Yunnan Province put the exposure drafts of relevant decisions in the "notifications and announcements" column, making them very difficult to find.

Secondly, the announcements of the solicitation of public opinions on major decision-making published by some governments, including 1 provincial-level government, 3 governments of larger cities, and 4 county-level governments, did not clearly indicate the time period of solicitation. For example, some announcements of solicitation of public opinions published by the Government of Gansu Province contained only the deadlines of the solicitation, which were earlier than the dates on which the announcements were published on the website.

Thirdly, some assessment targets, including 10 departments under the State Council, 3 provincial-level governments, 5 governments of larger cities, and 38 county-level governments, did not disclose drafts of major decisions in 2018.

Fourthly, the quality of disclosure of feedback on the public opinions solicited was low. 44 departments under the State Council, 14 provincial-level governments, 21 governments of larger cities, and 70 county-level governments did not disclose on their web portals feedback on the opinions solicited on drafts of major decisions in 2018. Some assessment targets that had disclosed the above-mentioned information failed to give an overall description of the solicitation or to disclose the number of opinions solicited or the main ideas of these opinions. Among the five departments under the State Council that had given feedback on the opinions solicited, only one disclosed the number of opinions solicited; among the 17 provincial-level governments that had given feedback on the opinions solicited, 8 only disclosed the number of opinions solicited and one only disclosed the main ideas of the opinions solicited; among the 28 governments of larger cities that had given feedback on the opinions solicited, 11 only disclosed the number of opinions solicited and 5 only disclosed the main ideas of the opinions solicited; and among the 30 county-level governments that had given feedback on the opinions solicited, 19 only disclosed the number of opinions solicited, and 2 only disclosed the main ideas of the opinions solicited.

Fifthly, the disclosure of information about the adoption of solicited opinions was not satisfactory: among the five departments under the State Council that had given feedback on the opinions solicited, two did not disclose information about the adoption of the opinions solicited; among the 17 provincial-level governments that had given feedback on the opinions solicited, one did not disclose information about the adoption of the opinions solicited; among the 28 governments of larger cities that had given feedback the opinions solicited, 3 did not disclose information about the adoption of the opinions solicited; and among the 30 county-level governments that had given feedback on the opinions solicited, one did not disclose information about the adoption of the opinions solicited. For example, the public participation column on the website of the Government of Guangzhou City only disclosed information about the number of adopted public opinions, without giving information about which opinions had been adopted, which had not, and the reasons for the non-adoption of the opinions.

3.4.2 *The Information About the Recordation and Review of Some Normative Documents Had Not Been Disclosed*

The Notice of the General Office of the State Council on Strengthening the Formulation and Supervisory Administration of Administrative Normative Documents requires relevant government organs to strengthen the recordation and review of normative documents, so as to ensure that each normative document is filed for recordation, each filed document is reviewed, and each error discovered in the review is corrected. However, the assessment shows that 13 provincial-level governments, 23 governments of larger cities, and 88 county-level governments did not disclose on their web portals or the websites of their legal departments information about the recordation and review of normative documents in 2018. Some of them, including 10 departments under the State Council, 4 provincial-level governments, 3 governments of larger cities, and 32 county-level governments, did not disclose on their web portals or the websites of their legal departments the results of the review of normative documents in recent three years. Moreover, most assessment targets did not indicate the validity status and period of validity of disclosed normative documents. 39 departments under the State Council, 15 provincial-level governments, 33 governments of larger cities, and 56 county-level governments had not set up a special sub-column for concentrated disclosure of invalidated documents under the normative document column or catalog of their web portals or the websites of their legal departments or indicated the validity status or period of validity in the specific normative documents.

3.4.3 *The Power Lists Were Not Disclosed or Updated in a Complete and Timely Manner*

Firstly, the power lists published by some local governments were incomplete: most assessment targets did not disclose the time of the compilation and issuance of power lists; the power lists of some units did not include complete "9 + X" categories of power items. For example, the 2018 version of the list of powers of various departments under the Government of Lhasa City contained only three categories of power, namely administrative licensing, administrative penalty, and administrative reward. Some government departments set the power list as an inquiry item that could be accessed only after logging into the system. The power lists disclosed by some assessment targets in the form of an attached file, such as the County-Level Power List in 2017 disclosed by the Government of Renshou County of Sichuan Province on July 14, 2017, consisted of unreadable codes.

Secondly, power lists were not adjusted in a timely manner. Article 20 of the 2017 Cultural Relics Protection Law of the People's Republic of China provides for the power of cultural relics administrative departments at and above the county level to examine and approve measures for the protection of original sites of historical and cultural relics that cannot be avoided in the choice of construction sites. However, the assessment shows that the power lists published by 4 provincial-level governments, 16 governments of larger cities, and 42 county-level governments did not contain the above-mentioned power.

Finally, the disclosure of power lists by departments under the State Council was not satisfactory. Among the departments under the State Council covered by the assessment, only 3, namely National Forestry and Grassland Administration, State Administration of Taxation, and National Medical Products Administration, disclosed their power lists. Among them, only one, namely the State Administration of Taxation, updated its power lists to the year 2018. The latest power list of the National Medical Products Administration was published in 2016. The power list published by the National Forestry and Grassland Administration did not indicate in which year it was published and contained only one category of power, namely administrative licensing. And the power list column on the website of the Ministry of Natural Resources contained only the list of administrative approval power.

3.4.4 Government Service Guides Were Incomprehensive and Inconsistent in Content

Firstly, the situation of disclosure of government service guides was unsatisfactory. The results of the spot check assessment of the disclosure of guides to three approval services, namely approval of printing of invoices by enterprises, approval and issuance of radiation safety licenses, and registration of charitable organizations, were all unsatisfactory: 14 provincial-level governments, 38 governments of larger cities, and 83 county-level governments did not publish guides to the approval of printing of invoices by enterprises; 2 provincial-level governments, 14 governments of larger cities, and 80 county-level governments did not publish guides to the approval and issuance of radiation safety licenses; and 25 provincial-level governments, 38 governments of larger cities, and 85 county-level governments did not publish guides to the registration of charitable organizations. Secondly, guides to government services were incomplete in content. The assessment shows that the government service guides provided by some assessment targets did not include such core elements as the basis, conditions, location, process and time period of application, application materials, and application fees. For example, the legal basis in the guide to the approval and issuance of radiation safety licenses published by the Government of Huainan City included only titles of laws and administrative regulations, without giving specific provisions. Thirdly, the guides for the same government service published on different platforms were inconsistent in content. The assessment shows that the guides to the same government services published by 10 provincial-level governments, 11 governments of larger cities, and 3 county-level governments on different platforms were inconsistent with each other in such contents as the titles and specific provisions of legal bases, application materials, time period of application, and subjects of application. Because the same information disclosed on different platforms often came from different sources without a unified standard of disclosure, such information cannot be updated in a synchronized way, resulting not only in a large amount of repetitive input work and the waste of administrative resources but also in the confusion among enterprises and citizens applying for government services: some of them prepared their applications according to the outdated government service guides, resulting in the use of wrong forms, incompleteness of preparation materials, visit to the wrong address, and repeated visits to government organs, which increase the time cost of applicants and reduce the public satisfaction with government services. Finally, the disclosure of the results of administrative approval by some assessment targets was chaotic. The assessment shows that some assessment targets did not disclose the results of administrative approval. For example, among the departments under the State Council, 49 did not set up a column for the disclosure of the results of administrative approval, 15 did not make classified disclosure of the results of administrative approval, and 22 did not disclose on their web portals the results of administrative approval they made in 2018. For another example, among the 31 provincial-level governments, 12 did not make classified disclosure of the results of administrative approval on the websites of their environmental protection departments, provincial-level government web portals, or the websites of provincial-level government service centers; all provincial-level governments that disclose the results of administrative approval separately in different platforms had the problems of chaotic, inconsistent and non-corresponding disclosure.

3.4.5 *Some Assessment Targets Failed to Disclose Information or Disclosed Incomplete Information About Double-Random Inspections*

Firstly, the situation of disclosure of lists of items subject to double-random inspection was not satisfactory. 16 departments under the State Council did not disclose the lists of items subject to their double-random inspection. Among the newly established departments under the State Council covered by the assessment, only the Ministry of Culture and Tourism and the Ministry of Natural Resources disclose the lists of items subject to their double-random inspection, and their times of disclosure were 2017 and 2016, respectively. Seven provincial-level governments, 6 governments of larger cities, and 52 county-level governments did not disclose on their web portals the lists of items subject to their double-random inspection. Among them, some disclosed on their web portals only the lists of items subject to the double-random inspection by some departments under them. Secondly, the lists of items subject to the double-random inspection were incomplete in content. A spot-check of the situation of disclosure of information about the double-random inspections in the field of industrial and commercial administration in various localities showed that the lists of items subject to double-random inspections published by one provincial-level government and 4 county-level governments did not include the basis for inspections; those published by 5 provincial-level governments, 1 government of larger city, and 7 county-level governments did not include the subjects of inspection; those published by 3 provincial-level governments, 3 governments of larger cities, and 8 county-level governments did not include the content of inspection; and those published by 11 provincial-level governments, 19 governments of larger cities, and 14 county-level governments did not include the method of inspection. Finally, the situation of disclosure of the results of random inspections and the related investigation and punishment was unsatisfactory. Take the field of environmental protection as an example: the environmental protection departments of 21 provincial-level governments, 19 governments of larger cities, and 62 county-level governments did not disclose the results of random inspections they had carried out in 2018 on their websites, government web portals or enterprise credit information networks; and the environmental protection departments of 20 provincial-level governments, 18 governments of larger cities, and 77 county-level governments did not disclose the results of investigations they had carried out and punishments they had imposed on violations of environmental law in 2018 on their websites, government web portals or enterprise credit information networks.

3.4.6 The Issuance of the Annual Report on the Construction of a Law-Based Government Had Not yet Been Normalized

22 departments under the State Council, 7 provincial-level governments, 12 governments of larger cities, and 63 county-level governments did not publish their annual reports on the construction of a law-based government in 2017 on their websites or the websites of their legal departments. Among the assessment targets that had published their annual reports on the construction of a law-based government, some did not publish the reports in a timely manner. The Implementation Outline for the Building of a Government under the Rule of Law (2015–2020) requires governments at various levels and the departments under them to complete and publish their annual reports on the construction of a law-based government in the first quarter of each year. By the end of March 31, 2018, however, only 12 departments under the State Council, 7 provincial-level governments, 31 governments of larger cities, and 31 county-level governments had published their annual reports on the construction of a law-based government on their websites. Some local governments even published their annual reports in the second half of the year. For example, the Government of Ouhai District of Wenzhou City in Zhejiang Province completed its annual report on the construction of a law-based government in 2017 on March 20, 2018, but did not publish the report until July 16, 2018.

3.4.7 Some Matters and Results of Administrative Penalties Were Not Disclosed in a Timely Manner

Firstly, the lists of matters of administrative penalty were incomplete in content. The lists of administrative penalty items disclosed by 2 provincial-level governments, 2 governments of larger cities, and 14 county-level governments did not include the legal bases of some administrative penalty items while those disclosed by some others did not include clear bases of administrative penalty, namely the legal bases disclosed were incomplete, without including such information as the full title of the laws or administrative regulations, the specific provisions and their content. Secondly, the level of disclosure of the results of administrative penalties was low. 34 departments under the State Council, 5 provincial-level environmental protection departments, 12 provincial-level market regulation departments, 12 market regulation departments of larger cities, 24 county-level environmental protection departments, and 38 county-level market regulation departments did not disclose the results of administrative penalties they imposed in 2018. Thirdly, the disclosure of results of administrative penalties had not been normalized. for example, although the National Cultural Heritage Administration had set up a special column on administrative penalties on its website, the column contained no information about administrative penalties, but only some notices and announcements and it had not been updated since January 2017; the column on administrative penalties on the website of Environmental Protection Bureau of Tibetan Autonomous Region contained very little information and had not been updated since 2013; the column on administrative penalties on the website of Environmental Protection Bureau of Handan City in Hebei Province had not been updated since 2017; and the website of Industrial Park Administration Committee of Suzhou City in Jiangsu Province did not disclose the information about the administrative penalties imposed by the environmental protection department of the industrial park in 2018.

3.4.8 The Audit Results of Local Governments Were Not Disclosed in a Comprehensive and Timely Manner

This year's assessment of audit results included the following four parts: "audit report on budget implementation at the local level in the year 2017/2016 and problems discovered in the audit", "special audit report in 2017", "reports on the rectification of the problems discovered in the audit in the year 2017/2016", and "website disclosure of audit information". The assessment shows that eight provincial-level governments, 29 governments of larger cities, and 75 county-level governments did not disclose the above-mentioned information in full. Moreover, it was a common phenomenon that local governments disclosed very little of their own audit information. Many local governments, such as those of Anhui Province and Tianjin Municipality, published on their web portals the audit reports of the National Audit Office, but very few of their own audit reports. Moreover, many assessment targets did not disclose audit information in a timely manner. Take the Government of Shaanxi Province as an example. The "No. 2 Audit Result in 2018" published on its web portal was actually the special audit report in 2014; and when the sample was taken for the assessment on October 20, 2018, the latest audit report on the web portal of the Government of Henan Province was published in 2016 and 25 governments of larger cities and 77 county-level governments had not published their own "audit report on budget implementation in the year 2017".

3.4.9 The Level of Disclosure of Suggestions Made by Members of People's Congresses and Proposals Made by CPPCC Members Was Still Not High

Firstly, some assessment targets did not disclose their replies to suggestions made by members of people's congresses and proposals made by CPPCC (Chinese People's Political Consultative Conference) members in 2018. The level of disclosure of suggestions and proposals by most county and district governments was relatively low. 9 departments under the State Council, 8 provincial-level governments, 13 governments of larger cities, and 49 county-level governments did not disclose their replies to the suggestions made by deputies to people's congresses in 2018 and 22 departments under the State Council, 11 provincial-level governments, 13 governments of larger cities, and 48 county-level governments did not disclose their replies to the proposals made by members of CPPCC in 2018. Although we cannot rule out the possibilities of some departments having not received any suggestions or proposals in 2018, or were not the competent authorities for dealing with the issues raised in the suggestions and proposals, or the results of the handling of suggestions and proposals were confidential or sensitive in nature, and therefore should not be made public, it is still rare for a local government to have not disclosed any reply to suggestions or proposals in a period of one year. Secondly, the replies to suggestions and proposals given by some assessment targets were not standardized. 4 departments under the State Council, 1 provincial-level government, and 2 county-level governments only disclosed the abstracts or parts of the full texts or abstracts of their official replies to the suggestions made by deputies to the National People's Congress in 2018. Thirdly, most assessment targets did not disclose information about the overall situation of their handling of suggestions and proposals in 2018. 42 departments under the State Council, 23 provincial-level governments, 43 governments of larger cities, and 77 county-level governments did not disclose information about the overall situation of their handling of suggestions made by deputies to the National People's Congress in 2018, and 41 departments under the State Council, 24 provincial-level governments, 42 governments of larger cities, and 82 county-level governments did not disclose information about the overall situation of their handling of proposals made by members of the National Committee of CPPCC in 2018.

3.4.10 *The Quality of Disclosure of Information About Policy Interpretation Still Needed to Be Improved*

Firstly, the disclosure of information about policy interpretation was chaotic. 3 departments under the State Council, 1 provincial-level government, 2 governments of larger cities, and 16 county-level governments disclosed information irrelevant to policy interpretation in the policy interpretation column on their web portals. Secondly, the disclosure of interpretations by local governments of the policies made by themselves needed to be strengthened. The policy interpretation column on the web portals of most assessment targets contained a large number of policy interpretations given by upper-level governments, but very few given by themselves. Some country-level governments disclosed dozens of policy interpretations each year, but only very few, even none of them are given by themselves. Finally, policy interpretations were not disclosed in a timely manner. The time intervals between the online disclosure of policy documents and the online disclosure of the interpretations of these policy documents by 21 departments under the State Council, 15 provincial-level governments, 25 governments of larger cities, and 38 county-level governments exceeded three working days.

3.4.11 *The Level of Disclosure of Compulsory Education Information by the Governments of Some County- and District-Level Governments Was Relatively Low*

The disclosure of information about the compulsory education enrollment policy and such information as the division of school districts, enrollment plans, enrollment conditions, schools and enrollment results by some county-level governments or the educational departments under them was not satisfactory: 40 county-level governments did not disclose the information about their documents on the work of compulsory education enrollment in 2018; 43 did not disclose the hotlines for the consultation of compulsory education enrollment policies; 40 did not disclose information about the scope of primary school enrollment in their respective administrative areas; 42 did not disclose information about the scope of secondary school enrollment in their respective administrative areas; 74 did not disclose information about the number of students to be enrolled in primary schools in their respective administrative areas in 2018; 66 did not disclose the number of students to be enrolled in high schools in their respective administrative area in 2018; 35 did not disclose the primary or secondary school admission requirements for ordinary students; 31 did not disclose the school admission requirements for children living with their migrant working parents; and 84 did not disclose the enrollment guides of ordinary public and private primary and secondary schools.

3.4.12 There Were Still Shortboards in the Disclosure of Information upon Application by Some Local Governments

In the assessment, the Project Team selected some provincial and county level government departments as targets to assess the work of disclosure of government information upon application and discovered the following problems. Firstly, online application channel was unstable and not user-friendly. For example, the online platform of the Health Administration Department of Shaanxi Province always displayed the massage "verification code error" when users tried to log into the system. After members of the Project Team submitted applications for information disclosure to the online platform of the Health Administration Department of Heilongjiang Province, they received no query code. In the telephone consultation with the platform staff, they learned that the platform had been unstable for the past year and was told to resubmit the application. And applying for disclosure of government information on the website of the Health Administration Department of Zhejiang Province was very inconvenient, requiring the applicants to go through a complicated registration procedure. The above problems were more prominent on the platforms of county-level education departments: 35 of them had such problems. Secondly, replies to applications were not given in a timely manner. During the assessment, the Project Team submitted applications for information disclosure to 100 county-level education departments through a platform or by letter, but had not received any reply from 45 of them by the end of the assessment period. Moreover, six county-level education departments exceeded the statutory time limit in replying the application. Finally, the replies to applications were non-standard. The written replies given by some county-level education departments were not affixed with official seal or failed to clearly indicate the replying organ. Many assessment targets, including three provincial-level government departments, did not clearly indicate the channels of remedy in their decisions on non-disclosure or other decisions unfavorable to applicants.

3.5 Future Prospect of Openness of Government Affairs

The Opinions on Comprehensively Advancing the Open Government Work point out that, by the year 2020, the overall open government work will enter into a new phase, the level of institutionalization, standardization and informatization will be raised significantly, and the government will win more understanding, trust and support from the people with more openness and transparency. In 2019, which is the key year in realizing the objective of all-round advancement of the open government work, China should further consolidate the previous results of the open government work, popularize the successful experiences achieved by various government organs in various fields, and raise the overall level of the open government work.

Firstly, adhering to the idea of promoting participation and administration through openness. Openness is not the objective in itself, but a means to effectively promoting orderly participation by the public and realizing joint construction, joint governance and sharing; it is not merely the display of government actions and their results, but the key to regulating the exercise of government power. Therefore, the government should scrutinize the openness work from the perspective of modernization of the governance system and governance capacity and take openness as an important means to realizing good governance at the grassroots level.

Secondly, effectively advancing the standardization of the open government work and preventing human factors from negatively affecting the level of openness. Only standardization can change the current situation of different qualities of the open government work carried out by government organs in different areas, at different levels, or under different leadership. To this end, it is necessary to strengthen the management of government information at its source, standardize the determination of the nature of the information at the link of its generation and expand the scope of openness, review the lists of government information to be disclosed, clarify the responsibilities of various departments and strengthen management through the compilation of catalogs, dynamically adjust the scope of the disclosure of government information in light of social conditions, the people's demands, and the revision of laws and administrative regulations, establish standards, clarify methods, and improve relevant operating procedures, so as to ensure that they can be easily understood and quickly mastered by persons in charge of the openness work, including new staff members.

Thirdly, relying on informatization to enhance the effect of openness. The government should rely on informatization to solidify the procedure of openness and use informatized means at various links of government administration to realize online service, online administration, and online office work, and to optimize all links of disclosure of government information, including generation of information, determination of the attribute of information, data collation, automatic information export, and foreground exhibition, and continuously reinforce the user thinking and raise the level of exhibition, so that the content and method of disclosure as well as the design of websites are based on public demands, rather than the convenience of government work.

Finally, increasing the direct adhesion between the open government work and government administrative activities. The openness of government affairs is not isolated from government administration but extends to all aspects and the whole process of government administration. Therefore, government organs should change the narrow understanding of openness, imbed openness in every link of government administration and service and, make it an indispensable part of government activity.

Chapter 4
Report on Indices of Judicial Transparency in China (2017)—From the Perspective of Information Disclosure on Court Websites

Innovation Project Team on the Rule of Law Index

Abstract In 2017, with the deepening of the reform of the judicial system and the construction and improvement of the judicial openness platform of the Supreme People's Court, judicial openness had become the consensus of courts at all levels in China. The scope of judicial information disclosure had been continuously expanded, and the disclosure of information about trial affairs had been further developed in breadth and depth. The disclosure of enforcement information had an important impact on the work of basically overcoming enforcement difficulties, and judicial reform information became more and more open and transparent. In the future, to meet the requirements of deepening the comprehensive reform of the judicial system, China still needs to further improve judicial openness in terms of details and humanization. It should optimize platform construction by relying more on information technology, deepen judicial openness from the perspective of public demand, further standardize the system of and mechanism for openness, give full play to the role of big data openness, strengthen the operation and maintenance of court websites, further improve the quality of judicial openness, and enhance judicial credibility.

Keywords Judicial openness · Judicial transparency · Rule of law index · Court informatization

---

Leaders of the Project Team: Tian He, a research fellow at CASS Law Institute and the director of the Center for Studies of National Indices of the Rule of Law, Chinese Academy of Social Sciences and Lv Yanbin, a research fellow at and the head of the Department of Survey and Study of National Situation of the Rule of Law of the Institute of Law, Chinese Academy of Social Sciences. Other members of the project team include: Wang Xiaomei, Wang Yiming, Li Yanjie, Hu Changming, Xu Bin, Liu Yanpeng, Wang Junxiu, Wang Hebin, Si Yu, Yan Wenguang, Yu Zilong, and Gao Zhenjuan. Authers of this report: Hu Changming, Assistant Research Fellow, Institute of Law, Chinese Academy of Social Sciences; Tian He.

Innovation Project Team on the Rule of Law Index (✉)
Institute of Law, Chinese Academy of Social Sciences, Beijing, China
e-mail: 13263169197@163.com

H. Tian et al. (eds.), *Report on the Rule of Law Index in China 2*,
Research Series on the Chinese Dream and China's Development Path,
https://doi.org/10.1007/978-981-19-9597-2_4

2017 was the year of the decisive battle in the current round of judicial reform, as well as the opening year of the deepening of the comprehensive supporting reform of the judicial system. According to the report to the 19th National Congress of the CPC, China will deepen the comprehensive reform of the judicial system and fully implement the judicial responsibility system. This task cannot be accomplished without the reform aimed at the continuous pursuit of fairness and justice, and even more importantly, an open and transparent judicial environment. On November 1, 2017, the Report on the Comprehensive Deepening of Judicial Reform by People's Courts, given by the Supreme People's Court at the 30th Meeting of the Standing Committee of the 12th National People's Congress, pointed out that, the concept of judicial openness had been continuously strengthened, the platform of judicial openness had been constructed, and the breadth and depth of judicial openness had been further expanded in recent years. Judicial openness had become an important part of the deepening of judicial reform in courts. On April 20, 2017, the Supreme People's Court issued the Opinions on Accelerating the Construction of Smart Courts, which pointed out that transparency is one of the three important dimensions of building smart courts. To accurately present and evaluate the effectiveness of the judicial openness in China in 2017, the Center for Studies of National Indices of the Rule of Law Chinese Academy of Social Sciences and the Innovation Project Team on Rule of Law Indices, the Institute of Law, Chinese Academy of Social Sciences (hereinafter referred to as the Project Team) continued to assess the judicial transparency of 81 courts, including the Supreme People's Court, 31 high people's courts and 49 intermediate people's courts, from the perspective of information disclosure on court websites. This was the seventh assessment conducted since 2011, and the assessment period was from September 15 to November 30, 2017.

4.1 Assessment Index System

The index system has been optimized and adjusted every year in light of the progress and changes as well as the annual characteristics of China's judicial system. In 2017, the Project Team increased the assessment of the depth and breadth of judicial openness, carried out a deep analysis of the details of openness, and focused on the assessment of the capacity for reflecting reform achievements and serving the parties through judicial openness. After adjustments, the index system included five grade I indices: "openness of trial affairs", "openness of trial", "openness of enforcement", "data openness" and "judicial reform" (see Table 4.1).

"Openness of trial affairs" mainly refers to the openness of judicial administrative affairs related to trial and enforcement, including "platform construction", "personnel information", "normative documents" and "information about disqualification for office". Since it had become the normal practice for courts to disclose their general information such as addresses, traffic maps, contact information, the scope of jurisdiction, subordinate courts, internal departments and their functions, complaint channels on their portal websites, "general information about court" was

Table 4.1 Judicial transparency index system in China (2017)

Grade I indices	Grade II indices
Openness of trial affairs (20%)	Platform construction (40%)
	Personnel information (30%)
	Normative documents (20%)
	Information about disqualification for office (10%)
Openness trial (30%)	Litigation guide (20%)
	Trial process (30%)
	Openness of court hearing (30%)
	Commutation and parole information (10%)
	Judicial documents (10%)
Openness of enforcement (20%)[a]	Guide to enforcement (40%)
	Exposure of enforcement (20%)
	Enforcement disciplinary action (10%)
	Information about cases of termination of current enforcement proceedings (10%)
	Enforcement tip-off (20%)
Data openness (20%)	Financial data (50%)
	Work report (35%)
	Judicial operational data (15%)
Judicial reform (10%)[b]	Setup of judicial reform column on court website (20%)
	Judicial reform plan (20%)
	Personnel quota system (10%)
	Registration system for the docketing of cases (20%)
	Records of external intervention in the handling of cases (20%)
	Handling of cases by leading cadres (10%)

[a]Since the openness of enforcement does not apply to the Supreme People's Court, the weights of the indices of openness of trial affairs, the openness of trial, data openness, and judicial reform of the Supreme People's Court were 30%, 30%, 30%, and 10% respectively
[b]Since the indices of the setup of judicial reform column on the website, judicial reform plan, and personnel quota system are not applicable to intermediate people's courts, the weights of indices of the registration system for the docketing of cases, records of external intervention in the handling of cases and handling of cases by leading cadres of intermediate people's courts were 70%, 20%, and 10% respectively

no longer used as an index in this assessment. The index of platform construction focused on the assessment of the effectiveness and friendliness of the court portal websites; the personnel information index was used to carry out the assessment of the following three aspects of judicial openness: the name, educational background, work experience, and main responsibilities of each leader of the court, the name, educational background, and rank of each judge, and the name of each court clerk; in addition, in 2017, a new assessment index of "information about disqualification for office" was added to the index system to assess the implementation of the system of disqualification for the appointment of judges and disclosure of related information, so as to facilitate the supervision by the public.

The openness of trial remained the focus of this year's assessment. "Openness of trial" includes openness of litigation guide, the openness of court trial, the openness of the trial process, and post-trial openness. Among them, the litigation guide is an important work of providing litigation services to the parties before the trial, and it is also one of the main purposes of visiting court websites by the parties preparing to file a lawsuit. This index was used to assess the accuracy, convenience, and comprehensiveness of the information disclosed in the litigation guide; the openness of court trials includes, in addition to observation of court trials by members of the public, live video and text broadcasting of court hearings, also live video broadcasting of trial of cases by court president; and post-trial openness mainly refers to the openness of commutation, parole, judgment documents, and judicial recommendations. Since the Supreme People's Court promulgated the judicial interpretation to make arrangements for the online publication of court judgment documents in the whole country in November 2013, online publication of judgment documents has gradually become the consensus of people's courts at all levels, but the comprehensiveness and standardization of the publication of judgment documents still need to be strengthened. The Provisions of the Supreme People's Court on the Publication of Judgments on the Internet by the People's Courts clearly require that: "For a judgment that is not published on the Internet, the case number, court of trial, date of judgment, and grounds for non-disclosure shall be published". Therefore, the index of disclosure of judicial documents in 2017 focused on evaluating the reverse disclosure of judgment documents, that is, whether the total number and case numbers of the documents that were not disclosed online and the reasons for their non-disclosure were disclosed. In 2017, a grade III index, "openness of judicial recommendations", was added to the index system to assess whether courts had disclosed the objects and main contents of judicial recommendations.

2017 was a crucial year in achieving the goal of basically overcoming the enforcement difficulties in two to three years, set by the Supreme People's Court. The openness of enforcement is very important to standardizing enforcement behavior and improving the quality and efficiency of enforcement work. "Openness of enforcement" includes the disclosure of enforcement guide, the disclosure of information about cases of termination of current enforcement proceedings,[1] exposure of enforcement actions, disclosure of information about enforcement disciplinary actions, and

[1] Termination of current enforcement proceedings refers to the temporarily suspension of enforcement proceedings in cases where there is really no property available for enforcement, until the person subject to enforcement has property available for enforcement. In practice, the procedure of termination of current enforcement proceedings is often abused. In order to improve the case closure rate, judges often terminate enforcement proceedings without exhausting the enforcement measures or when there is still property for enforcement. See "Report on Indices of Judicial Transparency in China (2016)—from the Perspective of Information Disclosure on Court Websites", in Li Lin

enforcement tip-off. In 2017, the Project Team increased the weight of the index of "information about cases of termination of current enforcement proceedings", which was set up in the previous year. In judicial practice, many courts, in order to improve their case closure rate, often deal with cases in which enforcement proceedings should not be terminated as cases of termination of current enforcement proceedings. To put a stop to this practice, the Supreme People's Court promulgated on October 29, 2016 the Notice on Issuing the Provisions on Strictly Regulating the Termination of the Enforcement Proceedings (for Trial Implementation), which not only clarifies the applicable conditions of the termination of current enforcement proceedings but also requires that the rulings on termination of current enforcement proceedings be published on the Internet. Government organs, public officials, deputies to people's congresses, and CPPCC members should serve as models of abiding by laws and regulations, and consciously implement courts' judgments. For this reason, in 2017, the Project Team carried out an assessment on the exposure of non-performance of effective judgments by the above-mentioned special subjects, so as guide courts to disclose such information.

Indices of "data openness" are divided into two categories: disclosure of financial data and disclosure of judicial operational data. The former includes the disclosure of budget and final accounts, budgetary expenditures related to official overseas visits, official vehicles, and official hospitality, and data of money and property involved in cases, while the latter refers to the disclosure of such information as annual work reports, annual reports, white papers or special reports of courts and case statistics. In 2017, the Project Team merged and simplified the similar budget and final accounts data, and on the basis of the existing indices of judicial operational data, added the grade III index of openness of bankruptcy cases, so as to guide the courts to disclose judicial operational data in a more comprehensive and refined manner.

In 2017, various measures of judicial reform were fully rolled out and implemented in courts at all levels in China, and "responsibility", "implementation" and "supervision" became the keywords of judicial reform. In 2015, the Project Team included "disclosure of judicial reform information" in the assessment index system, but did not set a weight for this index, and the results of the assessment of this index were not used in the calculation of assessment scores. In 2016, the results were used in the calculation of scores as part of the "openness of trial affairs". In 2017, the Project team increased the weight and score of disclosure of information about judicial reform information as a grade I index of judicial transparency. There are six secondary indices under this index, including the setup of the judicial reform column on court websites, judicial reform plan, personnel quota system, case docketing registration system, the record of external intervention in case handling, and handling of cases by leading cadres, among which the first three (the setup of judicial reform column on court website, judicial reform plan, and personnel quota system) were used only for the assessment of the Supreme People's Court and high people's courts.

---

and Tian He (eds.), *Development Report on the Rule Law in China: No.15 (2017)*, Beijing: Social Science Academic Press, 2017.

4.2 The Overall Result

In 2017, the average score of the judicial transparency indices of 81 courts covered by the assessment was 56.2, which was basically the same as that of the previous two years. Among all the assessment targets, 4 scored above 80 points, 18 scored between 60 and 80 points, 33 scored between 50 and 60 points and 26 scored less than 50 points. The top 20 courts in the ranking of assessment scores were the Intermediate People's Court of Guangzhou City, the Intermediate People's Court of Changchun City, the Intermediate People's Court of Ningbo City, the High People's Court of Jilin Province, the Intermediate People's Court of Jilin City, the High People's Court of Beijing Municipality, the Intermediate People's Court of Haikou City, the High People's Court of Zhejiang Province, the Intermediate People's Court of Nanjing City, the High People's Court of Shanghai Municipality, the Intermediate People's Court of Chengdu City, the Intermediate People's Court of Hangzhou City, the High People's Court of Jiangsu Province, the High People's Court of Hainan Province, the High People's Court of Hunan Province, the Intermediate People's Court of Shenzhen City, the High People's Court of Heilongjiang Province, the Intermediate People's Court of Xuzhou City and the High People's Court of Hubei Province (see Table 4.2 for assessment results).

After seven consecutive years of assessment of judicial transparency indices, the judicial transparency of courts had been improved as a whole. However, with the assessment focusing more on the effect and breadth and depth of openness, the transparency gaps between different courts were still big. Some courts had always attached importance to judicial openness, constantly innovating and deepening the contents of openness, and ranking firmly on the top in assessment results. For example, 11 courts, including the Intermediate People's Court of Guangzhou City, the Intermediate People's Court of Ningbo City, the Intermediate People's Court of Chengdu City, the High People's Court of Beijing Municipality, the High People's Court of Zhejiang Province, the Intermediate People's Court of Shenzhen City, the Intermediate People's Court of Haikou City, the Intermediate People's Court of Hangzhou City, the High People's Court of Shanghai Municipality, the High People's Court of Hunan Province and the Intermediate People's Court of Nanjing City had ranked in the top 20 for four consecutive years (2014, 2015, 2016 and 2017). Among them, the Intermediate People's Court of Guangzhou City, the Intermediate People's Court of Ningbo City, the High People's Court of Jilin Province, and the High People's Court of Zhejiang Province had ranked in the top ten for three consecutive years (2014, 2015 and 2016). The Intermediate People's Court of Guangzhou City had ranked first in the assessment of judicial transparency for three consecutive years, and its score had been continuously rising. Of course, there were also some courts that traditionally had no advantages in judicial openness, but had taken the opportunity of the four judicial openness platforms built by the Supreme People's Court to catch up and improve their rankings. In the past three years, the courts whose transparency rankings had been continuously improved included the Intermediate People's Court of Changchun City, the Intermediate People's Court of Jilin City, the

Table 4.2 Assessment results of China judicial transparency index

Ranking	Assessment targets	Openness of trial affairs (20%)	Openness of trial (30%)	Data openness (20%)	Openness of enforcement (20%)	Judicial reform (10%)	Total score
1	Intermediate People's Court of Guangzhou City	100.00	83.50	98.13	95.00	90.00	92.68
2	Intermediate People's Court of Changchun City	78.00	88.00	63.75	92.00	100.00	83.15
3	Intermediate People's Court of Ningbo City	94.00	75.50	82.50	82.00	70.00	81.35
4	High People's Court of Jilin Province	83.00	87.50	70.63	74.00	93.00	81.08
5	Intermediate People's Court of Jilin City	90.00	88.00	45.00	83.00	95.00	79.50
6	High People's Court of Beijing Municipality	67.00	81.00	83.75	79.00	70.00	77.25
7	Intermediate People's Court of Haikou City	81.00	84.50	69.38	84.00	45.50	76.78
8	High People's Court of Zhejiang Province	80.00	64.50	83.75	83.00	67.00	75.40
9	Intermediate People's Court of Nanjing City	75.00	80.50	63.75	80.00	35.00	71.40
10	High People's Court of Shanghai Municipality	55.00	85.00	61.25	74.00	72.00	70.75

(continued)

Table 4.2 (continued)

Ranking	Assessment targets	Openness of trial affairs (20%)	Openness of trial (30%)	Data openness (20%)	Openness of enforcement (20%)	Judicial reform (10%)	Total score
11	Intermediate People's Court of Chengdu City	70.50	72.00	57.50	74.00	85.00	70.50
12	Intermediate People's Court of Hangzhou City	65.00	72.00	64.38	83.00	59.50	70.03
13	The Supreme People's Court	76.00	66.00	65.63	-	70.00	69.29
14	High People's Court of Jiangsu Province	62.00	78.00	86.88	60.00	23.00	67.48
16	High People's Court of Hunan Province	66.00	69.00	75.63	62.00	46.00	66.03
17	Intermediate People's Court of Shenzhen City	60.00	73.50	63.75	44.00	70.00	62.60
18	High People's Court of Heilongjiang Province	74.00	70.50	64.38	32.00	70.00	62.23
19	Intermediate People's Court of Xuzhou City	58.00	72.00	63.75	56.00	45.50	61.70
20	High People's Court of Hubei Province	55.00	69.00	51.88	74.00	47.00	61.58

(continued)

Table 4.2 (continued)

Ranking	Assessment targets	Openness of trial affairs (20%)	Openness of trial (30%)	Data openness (20%)	Openness of enforcement (20%)	Judicial reform (10%)	Total score
21	Intermediate People's Court of Lanzhou City	69.00	67.50	48.75	52.00	70.00	61.20
22	Intermediate People's Court of Xiamen City	70.00	67.50	63.75	44.00	49.00	60.70
23	High People's Court of Jiangxi Province	74.00	66.00	51.88	52.00	46.00	59.98
24	High People's Court of Chongqing Municipality	74.00	52.50	61.25	76.00	19.00	59.90
25	High People's Court of Qinghai Province	71.00	73.50	58.13	52.00	16.00	59.88
26	Intermediate People's Court of Taiyuan City	86.50	54.00	70.00	32.00	59.50	59.85
27	Intermediate People's Court of Huainan City	72.50	64.50	41.25	52.00	70.00	59.50
28	Intermediate People's Court of Hefei City	74.00	69.00	61.25	41.00	35.00	59.45
29	High People's Court of Guangxi Zhuang Autonomous Region	66.00	70.50	48.13	60.00	33.00	59.28

(continued)

Table 4.2 (continued)

Ranking	Assessment targets	Openness of trial affairs (20%)	Openness of trial (30%)	Data openness (20%)	Openness of enforcement (20%)	Judicial reform (10%)	Total score
30	High People's Court of Sichuan Province	68.00	64.50	34.38	77.00	39.00	59.13
31	High People's Court of Inner Mongolia Autonomous Region	67.00	72.00	71.88	36.00	24.00	58.98
32	Intermediate People's Court of Shijiazhuang City	73.50	72.00	41.25	54.00	35.00	58.85
33	High People's Court of Shaanxi Province	66.50	67.50	60.63	52.00	26.00	58.68
34	Intermediate People's Court of Zibo City	71.00	64.50	46.25	56.00	45.50	58.55
35	Intermediate People's Court of Jinan City	58.00	67.50	56.25	52.00	45.50	58.05
36	Intermediate People's Court of Benxi City	67.00	69.50	45.00	44.00	59.50	58.00
37	High People's Court of Anhui Province	71.00	73.50	46.88	50.00	17.00	57.33
38	Intermediate People's Court of Handan City	65.00	75.00	46.25	40.00	35.00	56.25

(continued)

Table 4.2 (continued)

Ranking	Assessment targets	Openness of trial affairs (20%)	Openness of trial (30%)	Data openness (20%)	Openness of enforcement (20%)	Judicial reform (10%)	Total score
39	Intermediate People's Court of Zhuhai City	50.00	72.00	65.00	32.00	45.50	55.55
40	High People's Court of Fujian Province	45.00	66.00	67.50	44.00	43.00	55.40
41	Intermediate People's Court of Zhengzhou City	83.00	58.50	55.63	32.00	35.00	55.18
42	Intermediate People's Court of Wuhan City	64.00	72.00	25.63	53.00	49.00	55.03
43	High People's Court of Guangdong Province	67.00	58.50	70.00	32.00	36.00	54.95
44	High People's Court of Shandong Province	74.00	63.00	56.88	40.00	16.00	54.68
	Intermediate People's Court of Wuxi City	61.50	60.00	44.38	60.00	35.00	54.68
46	High People's Court of Hebei Province	61.00	70.50	47.50	48.00	19.00	54.35
47	High People's Court of Liaoning Province	69.00	61.50	48.13	48.00	16.00	53.08

(continued)

Table 4.2 (continued)

Ranking	Assessment targets	Openness of trial affairs (20%)	Openness of trial (30%)	Data openness (20%)	Openness of enforcement (20%)	Judicial reform (10%)	Total score
48	High People's Court of Gansu Province	43.00	66.00	36.88	68.00	36.00	52.98
49	High People's Court of Yunnan Province	61.00	67.50	41.88	42.00	36.00	52.83
50	High People's Court of Tianjin Municipality	50.00	57.00	71.88	32.00	44.00	52.28
51	Intermediate People's Court of Shantou City	54.00	61.50	61.25	32.00	35.00	51.40
52	Intermediate People's Court of Xining City	52.00	67.50	33.75	52.00	35.00	51.30
53	Intermediate People's Court of Dalian City	73.00	49.50	33.75	40.00	70.00	51.20
54	Intermediate People's Court of Xi'an City	52.00	57.00	48.75	52.00	35.00	51.15
55	Intermediate People's Court of Harbin City	39.00	67.50	56.25	40.00	35.00	50.80
56	Intermediate People's Court of Changsha City	67.50	52.50	33.75	34.00	70.00	49.80
57	Intermediate People's Court of Suzhou City	68.00	58.50	42.50	32.00	35.00	49.55

(continued)

Table 4.2 (continued)

Ranking	Assessment targets	Openness of trial affairs (20%)	Openness of trial (30%)	Data openness (20%)	Openness of enforcement (20%)	Judicial reform (10%)	Total score
58	Intermediate People's Court of Shenyang City	49.00	57.00	62.50	32.00	35.00	49.30
59	High People's Court of Xinjiang Uygur Autonomous Region	54.00	61.50	48.13	32.00	35.00	48.78
60	Intermediate People's Court of Qingdao City	43.00	64.50	31.25	44.00	45.50	47.55
61	Intermediate People's Court of Fushun City	60.00	45.00	45.00	44.00	35.00	46.80
62	Intermediate People's Court of Datong City	64.00	67.50	1.25	32.00	70.00	46.70
63	Intermediate People's Court of Nanchang City	44.50	58.50	51.25	32.00	35.00	46.60
64	High People's Court of Shanxi Province	67.00	63.00	60.63	0.00	19.00	46.33
65	Intermediate People's Court of Anshan City	63.00	52.50	38.75	32.00	35.00	46.00
66	Intermediate People's Court of Nanning City	41.00	66.00	35.00	36.00	35.00	45.70

(continued)

Table 4.2 (continued)

Ranking	Assessment targets	Openness of trial affairs (20%)	Openness of trial (30%)	Data openness (20%)	Openness of enforcement (20%)	Judicial reform (10%)	Total score
67	High People's Court of Ningxia Hui Autonomous Region	39.00	60.00	41.25	49.00	17.00	45.55
68	Intermediate People's Court of Luoyang City	54.00	63.00	33.75	16.00	56.00	45.25
69	High People's Court of Guizhou Province	60.00	70.50	50.00	0.00	19.00	45.05
70	Intermediate People's Court of Baotou City	47.00	48.00	46.25	32.00	56.00	45.05
71	High People's Court of Henan Province	24.50	60.00	52.50	40.00	36.00	45.00
72	Intermediate People's Court of Tangshan City	49.50	60.00	1.25	60.00	45.50	44.70
73	Intermediate People's Court of Kunming City	71.00	63.00	8.13	32.00	35.00	44.63
74	Intermediate People's Court of Lhasa City	51.00	72.00	1.25	36.00	49.00	44.15
75	Intermediate People's Court of Fuzhou City	60.00	46.50	41.25	32.00	35.00	44.10

(continued)

Table 4.2 (continued)

Ranking	Assessment targets	Openness of trial affairs (20%)	Openness of trial (30%)	Data openness (20%)	Openness of enforcement (20%)	Judicial reform (10%)	Total score
76	Intermediate People's Court of Qiqihar City	75.50	64.50	8.75	0.00	59.50	42.15
77	Intermediate People's Court of Urumqi City	28.00	69.00	13.75	32.00	35.00	38.95
78	High People's Court of Tibet Autonomous Region	51.00	58.00	0.00	44.00	20.00	38.40
79	Intermediate People's Court of Yinchuan City	49.00	52.50	1.25	41.00	35.00	37.50
80	Intermediate People's Court of Hohhot City	50.00	39.00	33.75	16.00	35.00	35.15
81	Intermediate People's Court of Guiyang City	40.00	48.00	31.25	1.00	45.50	33.40

High People's Court of Hainan Province, the High People's Court of Heilongjiang Province, the Intermediate People's Court of Lanzhou City, the High People's Court of Jiangxi Province, the High People's Court of Qinghai Province, the Intermediate People's Court of Benxi City, and the High People's Court of Liaoning Province. Among them, the courts whose rankings had been improved by more than 20 in the past three years included the Intermediate People's Court of Changchun City, the High People's Court of Heilongjiang Province, the Intermediate People's Court of Lanzhou City, the High People's Court of Jiangxi Province, the High People's Court of Qinghai Province and the Intermediate People's Court of Benxi City.

4.3 Bright Spots Found in the Assessment

With the advancement and deepening of judicial reform and the improvement of the judicial openness platforms of the Supreme People's Court, judicial openness has become the consensus of courts at all levels in China. In 2017, some courts, in order to improve the level of judicial openness, had learned from the leading courts in judicial openness, while others assigned special personnel to study and compare the court websites that had done a good job in judicial openness, so as to draw on their experiences and practices and improve their own level of openness. On the whole, in the field of judicial openness, a situation in which the courts compete with each other in improving the level of judicial transparency had been created, and judicial openness in the whole country had reached a new level.

4.3.1 Steadily Increasing the Transparency of Trial Affairs

4.3.1.1 Continuously Optimizing Court Websites

The assessment shows that the assessment targets had generally set up their own portal websites, which had the characteristics of high recognition and convenient search, and the phenomena of inaccessible portal websites and invalid website content clicks had been obviously reduced. The number of courts with multiple web portals had decreased from 16 in 2016 to 10, and the uniqueness of websites has improved significantly. At the same time, the friendliness of websites had been constantly improving. Firstly, the website retrieval function had become more and more complete. Providing the website retrieval function helps the parties to get the judicial information they need conveniently and quickly. Among the 81 court websites covered by the assessment, 76 (or 93.8% of the total) had retrieval function, of which 62 had comprehensive retrieval function, an increase of 4.9% points from that in 2016. Secondly, the column setting on websites became more reasonable. Some courts had set up first-level columns such as trial openness, trial affairs openness, trial process openness, and enforcement openness, so that the parties can quickly find the corresponding information. Some courts had set up three distinct sections on their portal websites: judicial service section, judicial openness section, and judicial administration section, and special sub-sections on client service, public service, and lawyer service for different objects under the judicial service section.

4.3.1.2 Disclosing Information About Judicial Personnel

The assessment shows that courts had adopted a more open attitude towards the disclosure of information about judicial personnel. In 2017, among the 81 courts covered by the assessment, those disclosing the names of their leaders, such as presidents and vice presidents, increased from 59 in 2016 to 66, accounting for 81.5% of the total. 14 disclosed the scope of responsibility of their leaders, 27 disclosed the academic qualifications of their leaders, and 23 disclosed the work experiences of their leaders, accounting for 17.3%, 33.3% and 28.4%, respectively, of the total. Among them, the Intermediate People's Court of Guangzhou City, the Intermediate People's Court of Changchun City, the Intermediate People's Court of Jilin City, the Intermediate People's Court of Ningbo City, and the Intermediate People's Court of Benxi City disclosed all the above information. The number of courts that disclose the names of judges had increased from 54 in 2016 to 58. The number of those that disclosed the tenure or the rankings of their judges had increased from 40 in 2016 to 44, and 6 courts disclosed the academic qualifications or resumes of their judges, and the Intermediate People's Court of Guangzhou City, the Intermediate People's Court of Changchun City, the Intermediate People's Court of Jilin City, the Intermediate People's Court of Ningbo City, the Intermediate People's Court of Chengdu City and the Intermediate People's Court of Hangzhou City disclosed all the above information. The number of courts that disclosed the names of court clerks (assistant judges) and other relevant information increased from 10 in 2016 to 11. In addition, 9 courts, including the High People's Court of Shandong Province, the High People's Court of Heilongjiang Province, the High People's Court of Tianjin Municipality, the Intermediate People's Court of Guangzhou City, the Intermediate People's Court of Changchun City, the Intermediate People's Court of Ningbo City, the Intermediate People's Court of Benxi City, the Intermediate People's Court of Jilin City and the Intermediate People's Court of Xining City, disclosed the scope of responsibility, educational background and work experience of all their leaders, and 10 courts disclosed the educational background and work experience of their judges. The High People's Court of Jilin Province and the Intermediate People's Court of Changchun City also disclosed the responsibilities and the names of persons-in-charge of judicial auxiliary departments such as general offices, trial administrative offices, and complaint letters and calls bureaus.

4.3.1.3 Continuously Enriching the Content of the Openness of Trial Affairs

The assessment shows that the information about trial affairs disclosed by courts was increasingly diversified. As early as in 2011, the Supreme People's Court promulgated the Provisions on Implementing the Office Disqualification of a Leader, a Trial Judge or Enforcement Judge of a Court Whose Spouse or Child Practices Law (for Trial Implementation), which stipulates that a leader or a trial or enforcement judge of a people's court whose spouse or child practices law within the jurisdiction of the court shall be subject to office disqualification. Office disqualification embodies the neutrality requirement for judges. The people are able to supervise office disqualification of judges only when courts disclose the relevant information. Otherwise, this document may become a mere scrap of paper. The assessment shows that 3 courts, namely the High People's Court of Hainan Province, the Intermediate

People's Court of Guangzhou City, and the Intermediate People's Court of Ningbo City, disclosed information about judges subject to office disqualification. The High People's Court of Hainan Province not only announced the names of spouses and children of judges but also published the situation of other close relatives, such as brothers and sisters, fathers-in-law, brothers-in-law, etc., who were in the lawyer's profession. The disclosed information was very detailed, including the judge's name, department, position, relationship with his relatives, the law firms where his relatives were working, and the work they were engaged in. In addition, it also disclosed on its own initiative the statistical information about the practice of law by former staff members of courts at three levels in Hainan Province. Moreover, among the 81 courts covered by the assessment, 62 published their own normative documents, and 53 set up a special column on their websites to publish their own normative documents, which were 6.2 and 9.9% points, respectively, higher than those of the previous year.

4.3.2 *Advancing Openness of Trial in Breadth and Depth*

4.3.2.1 Publishing Complete Litigation Guides

Publication of litigation guides is the primary litigation service provided by courts, as well as the basic requirement for judicial openness. All of the 81 courts covered by the assessment had set up a litigation guide column on their websites to publish litigation guide information in a concentrated way, showing that they attached great importance to litigation guides. The assessment shows that the publication of litigation guides by courts had the following characteristics. First, the information in the column is clearly classified and easy to find. The assessment shows that the information in the litigation guide column of 54 courts (or 66.7% of the total) was classified according to such standards as guide categories and litigation types; some, such as the High People's Court of Jiangsu Province, the Intermediate People's Court of Wuhan City and the Intermediate People's Court of Shenzhen City, published civil litigation guides, criminal litigation guides, and administrative litigation guides according to litigation types; some classified the content of the column according to the guide category. For example, the litigation guide column on the Court Litigation Service Network of Anhui Province was divided into such sub-columns as Litigation Process, Litigation Fee Charging Standard, Litigation Risk Warnings, and Notifications of Rights and Obligations; and the Intermediate People's Court of Xuzhou City disclosed information such as litigation risk warning and litigation fee-charging standard in the litigation guide column of its website. Second, the contents of litigation guides are comprehensive. Of the 81 courts covered by the assessment, 76 (or 93.8% of the total) published litigation risk warnings, 52 (or 64.2% of the total) published litigation processes, 72 (or 88.9% of the total) published samples of legal documents, 77 (or 95.1% of the total) published the fee-charging standard of litigation fees, and 48 (or 59.3% of the total) informed the parties of their rights and obligations. Third, innovating the practice to facilitate litigation by the parties. The column setting of some court websites was quite innovative. For example, the Intermediate People's Court of Wuhan City set up on its judicial openness online service platform a "Litigation Tools" column containing tools for calculating time periods for docketing and handling of cases and tools for calculating the interests for delayed performance; the Intermediate People's Court of Nanjing City set up such columns on its websites as 12,368 Service Hotline, Listening to Opinions and Suggestions, Mailbox for Deputies to People's Congresses and CPPCC Members, Judge's Work Mailbox and Mailbox of the President of the Court; and the Intermediate People's Court of Xiamen City provided risk warning information in both Chinese and English, so as to facilitate the access to information by foreign-related parties.

4.3.2.2 Substantiating the Openness of Process

The parties are the main targets of judicial openness, and the trial process is one of the main concerns of the parties. In recent years, the Supreme People's Court has taken the openness of the trial process as an important part of judicial openness. In 2017, the Project Team added such assessment items as trial process inquiry and access to electronic case files to the assessment system. The assessment shows that the general situation of openness of the court trial process was good. Among the 81 courts covered by the assessment, 68 (or 83.9% of the total) allowed parties to log into their portal websites to inquire about the processing of their cases. The column on case processing inquiry is generally set up in the party service section of court websites or litigation service websites, and parties can log into the column to view the information about the processing of their cases by using the account password given to them by courts. The High People's Court of Anhui Province also provided a brief explanation of the inquiry method to ensure the correct use of the system by the public. Moreover, the assessment shows that the announcement of court sessions was timely. Among the 81 courts covered by the assessment, only two did not publish court session announcements, while 45 (or 55.6% of the total) published court session announcements in time through the Internet. The number of courts with the court session announcement retrieval function increased to 27 (or 33.3% of the total) from 16 in 2016.

4.3.2.3 Continuously Improving the Quality of Live Video Broadcasting of Court Trials

Live video broadcasting of court trials has two aspects: the platform construction of the Supreme People's Court and the live video broadcasting of court trials by local courts on their own initiatives. As far as the platform of live video broadcasting of court trials is concerned, since the Supreme People's Court launched China Court Trial Online (http://tingshen.court.gov.cn/) in September 2016, live video broadcasting of court trials has become a normal part of the openness of trial in Chinese courts. At present, China Court Trial Online is linked not only to 32 high people's courts in China but also, through the high people's courts, to the intermediate people's courts and grass-roots people's courts under their jurisdictions, thereby achieving full coverage of courts in China. By December 2017, courts at all levels across the country had broadcast more than 580,000 court trials live through China Court Trial Online, with a total of 4.4 billion views. China Court Trial Online not only enables people to watch live broadcasting of court trials but also provides such functions as playback of court trials and ranking of hot video live broadcasts. People can also use many functions such as the retrieval of live broadcastings of court trials by such keywords as the case number and case title. In addition, in the "Advanced Notices of Court Trials" column, registered users can also subscribe to the live broadcasting of court trials announced in the notices. In the column of "Live Broadcasting of Court Trials", the public can get the basic information about court trials, express their opinions, collect and share the links, and comment on the clarity and fluency of live video broadcasts of court trials. In the "Data Disclosure" column, the public can also see the number of courts at all levels that are linked to China Court Trial Online and the cumulative number of court trials broadcasted live by each court.

The live video broadcasting of court trials by local courts had been improved to varying degrees in terms of frequency, scope, and updating rate. There were also many bright spots and innovative practices in the live broadcasting of court trials in various places. For example, the Court Trial Live Broadcast Network of the High People's Court of Shaanxi Province, on the basis of classifying court trial videos into civil, criminal, and administrative cases, further classified videos in each category into first instance cases, second instance cases and retrial cases. The Court Trial Comprehensive Service Platform of Jiangxi Province is very intuitive, indicating the live video broadcasting and review of court trials in various cities in the form of maps and facilitating the search by the public by enabling them to skip the retrieval link. The live broadcasting of court trials by the High People's Court of Heilongjiang Province was rich in content. Besides being divided into live broadcasting notices and live broadcasts, the cases were also divided into civil cases, criminal cases, administrative cases, enforcement cases, trial supervision cases, and others. The live broadcasts could also be searched by title, case type, the court of trial, and the date of trial.

4.3.2.4 Realizing Leap-forward Development of Data Openness

In 2017, the Project Team carried out the assessment of transparency of judicial statistical data of courts for the seventh consecutive year. In 2011 and 2012, when the Project Team first carried out the assessment, the disclosure of judicial statistics was very unsatisfactory, and courts generally refused to disclose such data on grounds that they were the internal information of courts. In 2017, the disclosure of judicial statistical data had become the consensus of most courts. Some courts disclosed a large number of judicial statistics in various novel forms. Some courts also provided judicial statistical reports for public reference. The progress in the disclosure of judicial data was embodied in a concentrated way in the following aspects.

Firstly, the Supreme People's Court launched the China Justice Big Data Service Platform, which integrates the functions of thematic in-depth study, judicial knowledge services, litigation-related information services, the intelligent system for similar cases, intelligent litigation assessment, and customized judicial statistical services. In the Thematic In-depth Studies column of the platform, judicial big data reports on intellectual property infringements, divorce disputes, the crime of dangerous driving, credit card fraud, and other topics are displayed; in the Customized Judicial Statistical Services column, members of the public who need relevant judicial statistical data may submit an application for information disclosure to the Supreme People's Court.

Secondly, the publication of work reports had become more and more common. In 2017, the number of courts that published their work reports increased from 38 in 2016 to 53, accounting for 65.4% of the total. Among them, 26 courts set up special columns on their websites to publish work reports in a concentrated way. It is also worth mentioning that the Gazette of the Supreme People's Court (hereinafter referred to as the Gazette) has been made accessible free of charge on the portal website of the Supreme People's Court, and the public can search the full texts of the gazettes in the previous six months by the number of issues and keywords.

Thirdly, the judicial statistical data disclosed by some courts became more and more comprehensive. For example, the Intermediate People's Court of Nanjing City and the Intermediate People's Court of Zhuhai City had set up special columns on judicial statistics on their websites, and other courts had continuously expanded the content of judicial statistics columns on their websites, and on the basis of the existing statistics of various categories of case, opened the real-time judicial statistics information disclosure function. For example, the Intermediate People's Court of Changchun City and the Intermediate People's Court of Jilin City published not only analysis reports on the trend of development of trial practice on a quarterly basis, but also real-time trial data and judicial statistical analysis reports under the column of "Trend of Development of Trial Practice" on their websites. The Intermediate People's Court of Ningbo City not only published the data of cases accepted and concluded by the court and the average number of cases concluded by judges but also allowed the parties to search relevant adjudicative data by such search criteria as the cause of action, the court of trial and time period.

Fourthly, some courts disclosed judicial recommendations. A judicial recommendation is a suggestion on improving institutions, standardizing management, and stopping loopholes put forward by a people's court in the process of trial and enforcement to the units or departments involved in a case in light of the existing problems in their work, so as to prevent disputes and crimes. Making judicial recommendations is an important duty of people's courts provided for by law, and it is also an important way for people's courts to strengthen and innovate social management, adhere to proactive justice, and serve the overall situation and the people with justice. As a part of courts' participation in social governance, the objects and content of and replies to judicial recommendations should be made public. The assessment shows that 7 courts, including the High People's Court of Shanghai Municipality, the Intermediate People's Court of Guangzhou City, the Intermediate People's Court of Changchun

City, the Intermediate People's Court of Ningbo City, the Intermediate People's Court of Benxi City, the Intermediate People's Court of Jilin City and the Intermediate People's Court of Nanjing City, published their judicial recommendations or the information about the issuance of judicial recommendations in 2017 on their websites.

4.3.3 "Basically Overcoming Difficulties in Enforcement" Through Transparent Enforcement

2017 is a crucial year for implementing the solemn commitment made by the Supreme People's Court to basically overcome enforcement difficulties in two to three years. Disclosing relevant enforcement information to the parties guarantees the parties' right to know, and also helps to put the enforcement work in the sunshine, reduce black-box operations and power rent-seeking, and strengthen the deterrence of enforcement.

4.3.3.1 Building Platforms to Expose Dishonesty

To enhance the transparency of enforcement and strengthen the supervision over the enforcement work, the Supreme People's Court stated in the Fourth Five-Year Outline of the Program for Reform of People's Courts (2014–2018) that it would "improve the information disclosure platform" by "integrating all kinds of enforcement information and promoting unified disclosure of information about enforcement on the same platform by courts nationwide, so as to make it convenient for the parties concerned to learn online about progress in the work of enforcement". China Enforcement Information Disclosure Platform (zxgk.court.gov.cn) discloses to the parties and the public all kinds of information related to enforcement cases. Using their ID numbers and passwords, the parties to cases can have access on the platform to such information as the opening of enforcement cases, enforcement personnel, change of enforcement procedure, enforcement measures, disposal of property subject to enforcement, enforcement of arbitration awards, closure of enforcement cases, distribution of money subject to enforcement, suspension of enforcement, termination of enforcement, etc. The public can also inquire about judicial auctions and other information on this website. In order to strengthen the management of money subject to enforcement and effectively safeguard the legitimate rights and interests of the parties, the Supreme People's Court opened the column of Inquiry about Announcements of Collection of Money Subject to Enforcement on the China Enforcement Information Disclosure Platform in November 2016 to enable courts to publicly announce information about money subject to enforcement in cases in which the courts are unable to get into contact with a party.

4.3.3.2 Further Improving Enforcement Guides

The openness of enforcement is firstly embodied in the disclosure of enforcement information to the parties, and the disclosure of enforcement guide is the basis of the disclosure of enforcement information. The assessment shows that, in 2017, the proportion of courts that published their enforcement guide had further increased, and the content of the enforcement guide was relatively complete. Among the 81 courts covered by the assessment, 76 (or 93.8% of the total) published their enforcement guides. The guides published by 68 courts (or 84.0% of the total) were comprehensive in contents, including both notification of rights and obligations and "instructions on enforcement". The guides published by the High People's Court of Zhejiang Province, the Intermediate People's Court of Ningbo City and the Intermediate People's Court of Qingdao City contained special classifications and were rich in content. In addition, 19 courts covered by the assessment published the enforcement flowchart, an increase of 9 (or 11.1% points) from 2016. For example, the guide published by the Intermediate People's Court of Qingdao City included the case-filing criteria, the initiation procedures, the fee-charging standards, conditions and procedures for fee reduction and exemption, workflow, and case initiation procedures of enforcement cases. The guide published by the Intermediate People's Court of Nanjing City was very rich in content, mainly including the process, jurisdiction, and time period of enforcement, materials required for the application for enforcement, the basis for enforcement, and the format of the application for enforcement.

4.3.3.3 Reaching a Consensus on the Openness of Channels for Enforcement Tip-Off

The openness of enforcement tip-off channels enables courts to get enforcement clues in time, and the parties to the enforcement cases to provide enforcement clues to the court in time, so as to fully protect their litigation rights and interests. The assessment shows that, among the 81 courts covered by the assessment, 36 (or 44.4% of the total) disclosed enforcement tip-off channels, 12.4% points higher than the previous year, and 18 (or 22.2% of the total) had set up an independent enforcement tip-off column on their websites. The enforcement tip-off columns on the websites of eight courts, including the High People's Court of Jiangxi Province, the High People's Court of Zhejiang Province, the Intermediate People's Court of Ningbo City, the Intermediate People's Court Shijiazhuang City, the Intermediate People's Court of Jilin City, the Intermediate People's Court of Hangzhou City, the Intermediate People's Court of Jinan City and the Intermediate People's Court of Tangshan City, were easy to find and provided clear tip-off methods. Especially, the websites of the High People's Court of Zhejiang Province and the Intermediate People's Court of Hangzhou City were well designed and provided comprehensive and eeasy-to-findenforcement information.

4.3.3.4 Strengthening Exposure and Deterrence of Enforcement

The Decision of the CPC Central Committee on Major Issues Pertaining to Comprehensively Promoting the Rule of Law clearly requires the "establishment of a system of law on supervision, deterrence, and punishment of parties subject to enforcement that have breached trust". The parties subject to enforcement often try to evade, even resist, enforcement by various means, and this is the direct cause of the difficulties in enforcement. To basically overcome difficulties in enforcement, it is necessary not only to improve the courts' ability to find the persons and properties subject to enforcement and standardize the court's enforcement activities but also to punish the parties subject to enforcement for dishonesty, and investigate their legal responsibilities in accordance with law if the circumstances are serious.

In 2017, the number of courts that disclosed information about penalties, such as fines and detentions, imposed on parties subject to enforcement for dishonesty increased to 13, and 7 courts disclosed the data relating to the investigation of the crime of refusal to satisfy a judgment or ruling, while 7 courts, including the High People's Court of Jilin Province, the High People's Court of Yunnan Province, the Intermediate People's Court of Guangzhou City, the Intermediate People's Court of Ningbo City, the Intermediate People's Court of Shijiazhuang City, the Intermediate People's Court of Jilin City and the Intermediate People's Court of Nanjing City, disclosed both the above-mentioned information.

In 2017, the number of courts that published the list of persons subject to restrictions on high-level spending increased to 36 (or 44.4% of the total), and the number of courts that published the list of persons subject to the restriction on leaving the country increased to 29 (or 35.8% of the total), and 25 courts (accounting for 30.9% of the total) published both lists. Ten courts published information about enforcement rewards. Among them, eight courts, including the High People's Court of Hubei Province, the High People's Court of Hunan Province, the High People's Court of Beijing Municipality, the Intermediate People's Court of Guangzhou City, the Intermediate People's Court of Changchun City, the Intermediate People's Court of Hefei City, the Intermediate People's Court of Nanjing City and the Intermediate People's Court of Haikou City, published the list of persons subject to restrictions on high-level spending, the list of persons subject to the restriction on leaving the country, and list of persons subject to enforcement by offering a reward. Among them, the Intermediate People's Court of Guangzhou City published a list of dishonest special entities subject to enforcement to disclose information about schools, hospitals, and other institutions that fail to fulfill their legal obligations and their legal representatives. The court also published in the We Media platform "Tou Tiao" such basic information as the names and ID card numbers of judgment debtors who failed to fulfill their legal obligations, so as to expand the influence and force judgment debtors to voluntarily fulfill their legal obligations.

4.3.4 Promoting Judicial Reform in a Visible Way

The report to the 18th National Congress of the CPC states that "China will further deepen the reform of the judicial system". However, the reform of the judicial system is not an internal affair of political and legal organs and people's courts, but will inevitably have an impact on the operation of judicial power and the rights and interests of the parties. This major reform concerning the whole society should not be carried out behind closed doors, but should be open and transparent. For this reason, the Project Team began to evaluate the transparency of judicial reform of courts in 2015, and the assessment results in 2017 show that the transparency of China's judicial reform had been increasing year by year.

4.3.4.1 Enriching the Content of the Judicial Reform Column on Court Websites

The judicial reform policy adopted by the Central Government needs to be implemented by local judicial organs by adopting specific implementation plans. High people's courts are the implementers and overall promoters of local judicial reform policies. Whether the judicial reform measures adopted by local judicial organs are transparent mainly depends on whether high people's courts set up judicial openness columns on their websites and adopt measures and programs for the openness of judicial reform. The assessment results show that the Supreme People's Court had taken the lead in setting up a judicial reform column in the trial affairs section of its website, in which the latest achievements and major events of judicial reform were displayed in a concentrated way. Fourteen of the 31 high people's courts had set up a judicial reform column on their websites, an increase of four from 2016. The contents of the judicial reform column also became richer. For example, in the judicial reform column of its website, the High People's Court of Jilin Province had set up the following sub-columns: judicial reform policy documents of higher-level courts, its own judicial reform plans, situation of its own judicial reform work, registration system for the docketing of cases, the judge quota system, handling of cases by court leaders, records of external intervention in the handling of cases, protection of lawyers' rights and interests, etc. Some intermediate people's courts had also set up judicial reform columns to actively disclose the information about judicial reform. For example, the judicial reform column on the website of the Intermediate People's Court of Guangzhou City covered the trends of development and documents of judicial reform, including not only the judicial reform documents issued by the Central Government and higher judicial authorities but also some documents and implementation rules formulated by the court itself. Since 2017, the court had published at irregular intervals the Special Issue on Judicial Reform of Courts in Guangzhou. A total of 53 issues had been published by July 2017. The following 11 sub-columns had been set up under the judicial reform column of its website: Trends of Development of Judicial Reform, Important News of Judicial Reform, Live Broadcasts of

Judicial Reform, Judicial Reform Policy Documents Issued by Higher-level Judicial Authorities, Overall Judicial Reform Plan of the Court, Reform of the Judicial Responsibility System, Reform of the Court Personnel Quota System, Reform of the Trial Supporting Personnel Management System, Reform of Registration System for the Docketing of Cases, Work Mechanism Reform and Protection of Lawyers' Rights and Interests.

In terms of disclosure of the judicial reform plan, 12 courts, including the High People's Court of Beijing Municipality, the High People's Court of Shaanxi Province, and the High People's Court of Heilongjiang Province, disclosed the judicial reform plans made by the Central Government. Ten courts, including the High People's Court of Jilin Province, the High People's Court of Zhejiang Province, the High People's Court of Hainan Province, the High People's Court of Hubei Province, the High People's Court of Hunan Province, and the High People's Court of Shanghai Municipality, disclosed their own judicial reform plans. The disclosure of judicial reform plans shows that the courts have the courage to accept social supervision, which is praiseworthy.

4.3.4.2 Gradually Refining the Judge Quota System and Supporting Measures

The personnel quota system is the cornerstone of the reform of the judicial responsibility system. Through the reform of this system, outstanding talents are selected to handle and be responsible for cases. The openness of the provisions on the judge quota system and the personnel selection procedure is conducive to strengthening the supervision by the whole society over the process of judicial reform of courts. In 2017, the Project Team carried out an assessment on the disclosure of the provisions relating to the personnel quota system, as well as the composition of the judge's selection committee and the selection procedure on the portal websites of high people's courts. The assessment shows that the High People's Court of Zhejiang Province, the High People's Court of Heilongjiang Province, and the High People's Court of Beijing Municipality disclosed their provisions on the judge quota system and selection procedures for quota-based judges, and the High People's Court of Zhejiang Province and the High People's Court of Heilongjiang Province also disclosed the number and name list of those selected as quota-based judges. The Intermediate People's Court of Guangzhou City also took the initiative to disclose the information about judges who had not yet become quota-based judges, but engaged in the handling of cases during the transition period, so as to facilitate public supervision.

The handling of cases by leading cadres of courts who are quota-based judges is the key to ensuring the effectiveness of the judicial personnel quota system and eliminating the drawbacks of judicial administration through judicial reform. The Opinions of the Supreme People's Court on Strengthening the Work of Case-Handling by Presidents and Chief Judges of the People's Courts at Various Levels (for Trial Implementation) stipulate that the presidents and chief judges of people's courts at various levels shall handle a certain quantity of cases as undertaking judges, and that the completion of case-handling by the presidents and chief judges of the people's courts at various levels shall be subject to public supervision: "The trial management departments of all higher people's courts shall be responsible for the calculation and verification of the annual quantity of cases handled by presidents and chief judges of people's courts under their respective jurisdictions, and circulate a notice on the completion of case-handling tasks by the presidents, vice-presidents, full-time members of the judicial committees, and other leaders within the quota of judges of the people's courts under their respective jurisdictions on a monthly basis. The notice shall include the number of cases handled, the types of cases, the trial procedures, the methods of participation, the number of court sessions, and the quality of trials." To this end, the Project Team carried out an assessment on the disclosure by courts of their provisions on and the situation of the handling of cases by leading cadres of courts in 2017. The assessment shows that two courts, namely the Intermediate People's Court of Guangzhou City and the Intermediate People's Court of Jilin City, published their provisions on the handling of cases by leading cadres. Moreover, the High People's Court of Jilin Province published an analysis report on the handling of cases by leading cadres on a quarterly basis. In the report, the proportion of leading cadres in quota-based judges, the conclusion of cases, the number of cases handled by each judge, the types of cases handled, the handling of "key cases" and the completion of case handling tasks by courts at various levels were disclosed in detail, and the number of cases handled by each leading cadre of the court was also disclosed in the report. In addition, the report also directly analyzes and comments on the handling of cases by leading cadres: "Most of the cases handled by court leaders in the province are still simple types of cases. The number of 'key cases' handled by court leaders has been only 1255, accounting for 11.36% of the total cases accepted by court leaders. The role of 'elite trial' has not been given full play to".[2] This open attitude is very commendable.

4.4 Existing Problems

In 2017, the judicial openness of courts in China had been further promoted in depth and breadth, but there was still room for improvement in the details and humanization of openness.

[2] "Analysis Report on the Handling of Cases by the Leaders of Courts in the Whole Province in the Third Quarter of 2017", available on: *Judicial Openness Network of Jilin Higher People's Court*, at http://www.jlsfygovcn/yldbafx/154304jhtml, last visited December 16, 2017.

4.4.1 The Need to Improve the Disclosure of Judgment Documents

On the one hand, with the promulgation and implementation of the Provisions of the Supreme People's Court on the Publication of Judgments on the Internet by People's Courts and the continuous upgrading and revision of China Judgments Online, the function of the platform has been strengthened continuously, classifying documents by region and type of cases, and realizing the advanced search of documents by the cause of action, case number, parties, courts, case types, judges, lawyers, legal basis and full text. The number of documents published on China Judgments Online is growing constantly. By December 31, 2017, China Judgments Online had published more than 41 million judgment documents, which is still growing at the rate of tens of thousands every day. With the number of website visits exceeding 12.5 billion times and users from more than 210 countries and regions, it has become the largest and most eye-catching open databank of judgment documents in the world. At the same time, however, there are still some problems in the disclosure of judgment documents, which are mainly reflected in the fact that the reverse disclosure has not been paid attention to by most courts. The above-mentioned judicial interpretation clearly stipulates that, for a judgment that is not published on the Internet, the case number, court of trial, date of judgment, and grounds for non-disclosure shall be published, unless the disclosure of the aforesaid information may divulge state secrets. The assessment shows that, in 2017, only seven courts, including the High People's Court of Jilin Province, the High People's Court of Shanghai Municipality, the Intermediate People's Court of Guangzhou City, the Intermediate People's Court of Nanjing City, the Intermediate People's Court of Changchun City, the Intermediate People's Court of Jilin City and the Intermediate People's Court of Haikou City, had set up a special column to disclose information about judgments not published on the Internet, including the total number, case numbers and grounds for non-disclosure, only two more than in 2016, accounting for 8.6% of the courts covered by the assessment. Moreover, since China Judgments Online collects judgment documents from all over the country, it has attracted much public attention. However, every time a user logs in on the website to inquire about the judgment documents, a dialog box will pop up, saying that "There are a lot of visits to the website at present, please enter the verification code and continue to visit wenshu.court.gov.cn". Although this setting was made out of technical considerations, it seriously affects the smoothness of public access to information, and greatly weakens the friendliness of an open platform.

4.4.2 *Unsatisfactory Disclosure of Key Information*

In 2017, some new assessment indices were created to assess the disclosure of key information about the operation of judicial power and judicial reform, but the assessment shows that the disclosure of such information was not satisfactory. For example, the assessment of the disclosure of such key information as judicial recommendations, handling of cases by the president of the court, and disclosure of special entities subject to enforcement shows that only seven courts, including the High People's Court of Shanghai Municipality and the Intermediate People's Court of Ningbo City, disclosed the information about judicial recommendations, while three courts, namely the High People's Court of Jilin Province, the Intermediate People's Court of Changchun City and the Intermediate People's Court of Jilin City, disclosed the numbers and types of cases handled by their presidents, and only one court disclosed information about special entities subject to enforcement.

Strictly implementing the procedure of termination of current enforcement is an important measure for standardizing the enforcement behavior and overcoming the difficulties in enforcement. In 2017, according to the requirements of the Notice on Issuing the Provisions on Strictly Regulating the Termination of Current Enforcement Proceedings (for Trial Implementation), the Project Team assessed the disclosure of information about cases of termination of current enforcement by various courts. The assessment shows that, among the 81 courts covered by the assessment, only 12 disclosed the information about cases of termination of current enforcement, and only 7, namely the High People's Court of Jilin Province, the High People's Court of Anhui Province, the High People's Court of Zhejiang Province, the High People's Court of Beijing Municipality, the High People's Court of Shanghai Municipality, the Intermediate People's Court of Chengdu City and the Intermediate People's Court of Hangzhou City, disclosed the complete information, including case number, the party subject to enforcement, the date on which the case is docketed case, the date of closure of the case, the final ruling and tip-offs.

4.4.3 *Insufficient Information Disclosure*

The portal websites of some people's courts were not user-friendly and the phenomenon of insufficient information disclosure on some platforms still existed. Firstly, information access was inconvenient. For example, although some courts had disclosed financial information, work reports, directories of judges, and directories of institutions, the parties could not open them directly from the webpage, but needed to download them to a local computer, and could be opened and browsed only if the corresponding software was installed. Secondly, the process of information disclosure was cumbersome and inconvenient. Take the disclosure of information about cases of termination of current enforcement proceedings on China Enforcement Information Disclosure Platform as an example. The webpage is called "Disclosure of and Inquiry about Cases of Termination of current enforcement proceedings in Courts Throughout the Country", but the webpage only provides a rotating display of information about cases of termination of current enforcement proceedings, rather than allowing users to search the list of cases of termination of current enforcement proceedings in each court, or disclose the total number of such cases in courts throughout the country. Moreover, the rotating display of cases on this website only includes three types of information: case number, the court of trial, and the date of trial, without detailed information about each case. When a user clicks on the case number, he is prompted by the system to enter the verification code, and after entering the verification code, he is required to enter the name of the party subject to enforcement. If the name of the party subject to enforcement is unknown, the information about the case cannot be viewed. Even if a case is found by the public through search, the platform only displays such simple information items as the case number, the name/title, and the ID number/organization code of the party subject to enforcement, the enforcement court, the time of docketing of the case, the date of termination of the current enforcement, the enforcement targets, and the unfulfilled amount, but not the more important information such as reasons for the termination of the current enforcement and written decisions on the termination of the current enforcement.

4.4.4 The "Matthew Effect" in Judicial Openness in Different Regions

The degree of judicial openness was uneven and the judicial transparency was polarized in various parts of the country. Some courts attached great importance to judicial openness, constantly improved website construction, enriched the content and innovated the form of openness, and basically realized the objective of disclosing all information that should be disclosed. The assessment shows that some courts in coastal regions maintained their traditional advantages and attach great importance to judicial openness. For example, the People's Court of Haishu District, the People's Court of Jiangbei District, and the People's Court of Cixi City in Ningbo City had set up columns on the reverse disclosure of judgment documents on their portal websites to regularly disclose information such as information about undisclosed judgment documents as the reason for non-disclosure, case number, the court of trial and the date of judgment. The judicial openness of courts in some regions showed a trend towards rapid progress. Some regions in Northeast China, where the judicial openness work once lagged behind other regions in the country, had made remarkable progress with more attention paid to the work by their leaders and the improvement of their websites. For example, courts in Jilin Province had made great progress in judicial openness in recent years, and the judicial openness of not only the courts covered by the assessment but also other courts in the whole province had reached a new level.

Some courts, however, had never paid sufficient attention to judicial openness, and their websites were backward with such problems as being inconvenient in retrieval, insufficient in content, slow in operation, and even inaccessible; other courts, especially grassroots courts in the central and western regions, had a weak foundation of informatization, and their software and hardware facilities were not able to meet the requirements of the construction of judicial openness platform; and some high people's courts in economically developed eastern regions did not attach importance to judicial openness, and failed to learn the successful experiences of judicial openness from their counterparts in neighboring provinces or even from intermediate people's courts in their own provinces. As a result, their rankings of information disclosure on portal websites lagged behind others. The level of judicial openness of local courts showed the Matthew effect, with the strong getting stronger and the weak getting weaker. Of the 81 courts covered by the assessment in 2017, five got less than 40 points in judicial transparency, the court ranked last in the assessment scored only 33.40 points, which was not only 2.70 points lower than the lowest score of 36.10 points in 2016, but also nearly 60 points lower than the score of 92.68 points of the court that ranked first in the assessment in 2017. In the transparency assessment, the average score of the 10 courts with the lowest scores was only 40.3 points; and seven of the 15 courts at the bottom of the 2017 ranking list had been at the bottom of the ranking list for three consecutive years.

4.4.5 Lack of Prominent Demand-Orientation of Judicial Openness

4.4.5.1 Mismatch Between the Content of Openness and the Public Demand

Some websites had an inaccurate definition of their role and used a large part of their space to report the news of the court, arrangements for court work, work schedules of court leaders, etc. For example, a high people's court had set up such columns as "court news", "activities of court leaders" and "court history display" in prominent positions on its portal website. On the portal websites of some courts, judges' cultural and sports activities and lyric poems occupied a large space. The purpose of a court website is mainly to publicize various aspects of the work of the court. Using court websites to display the routine work and daily life of judges is inconsistent with the demands of the parties and the original purpose of judicial openness of court websites.

4.4.5.2 Unreasonable Design of Website Interface

The columns on the homepages of some court websites were not reasonably designed, and the display of their contents was disorganized, making it difficult for the parties to find the information they need in time. For example, nine courts did not set up special columns for publishing normative documents, which were scattered in different parts of the website, causing great inconvenience for the parties to find these documents; although 19 courts published their work reports, they did not set up a corresponding column for publishing the reports, but put the reports in such columns as "News" or "Latest News of Court Work"; 37 courts (or 45.7% of the courts covered by the assessment) put financial information in the court the news column or did not disclose financial information. Floating windows, especially those that cannot be closed, affect the public's experience of webpage browsing and information search. The assessment shows that the websites of 12 courts still had floating windows, and the floating windows on the websites of 3 courts could not be closed.

4.4.5.3 Inconvenience in Information Retrieval and Tardiness in Information Updating

The assessment shows that retrieval functions of the websites of some courts were too simple, and some could not display search results or displayed inaccurate search results; although some courts had set up many openness columns, some of these columns could not be opened when clicked on; on the websites of some courts, the information disclosed in some columns were inconsistent with the titles of the columns. For example, some courts put news of the court into the "Rules and Regulations" column; some columns even contained no information or only titles without no text or content (this problem was more serious on the websites of some courts, with nearly half of the columns on them containing no substantive content); some courts mixed their own announcements of court session with those of lower courts. As a result, a user needs to browse these announcements one by one in order to find the information they need; in some other courts, the judicial openness had not been normalized. The contents of relevant columns on their websites were not updated in a timely manner, some did a crash job in information disclosure, uploading a large amount of information onto their websites during a short period of time, and then not updating their websites for one and a half years or even for three or five years.

4.4.6 Poor Integration of Judicial Information

The Report on Indices of Judicial Transparency in China puts forward suggestions for improving the situation of over-decentralization of judicial openness platforms of people's courts, a problem that had existed for many years. The assessment shows that, in 2017, the situation of over-decentralization of judicial openness platforms of people's courts had been improved, and the number of courts with only one accessible portal website increased to 71 from 65 in 2016. However, the problems of multiple platforms and scattered judicial information had not been fundamentally solved.

Some courts had set up a court trial live broadcasting network or a special enforcement platform in addition to their portal websites, special judicial openness networks, litigation service networks, or judicial information networks. Among the 81 courts covered by the assessment, only 13 had integrated litigation services, judicial openness, and the court portal website into one platform. The numerous platforms resulted in scattered, repetitive and contradictory judicial information, outdatedness, and a lack of timely updating of information in some channels of judicial openness. For example, a high people's court disclosed enforcement exposure information on both its portal website and the judicial information network, but the enforcement information such as the list of persons subject to the restriction on leaving the country, the list of persons subject to the restriction on high-level spending and the list of parties subject to enforcement that have breached trust was only updated on the judicial information network, and the information on its portal website had not been updated since July 2014. The double and multiple disclosures of information increase the difficulty and cost of information retrieval for the parties.

In recent years, the Supreme People's Court has vigorously promoted the construction of judicial openness platforms. A large number of special platforms of judicial openness have been set up. Over a dozen platforms of judicial openness are displayed on the homepage of the Supreme People's Court website alone, including China Judicial Process Information Online, China Court Trial Online, China Judgments Online, China Enforcement Information Disclosure Platform, Litigation Service Platform of the Supreme People's Court, National Enterprise Bankruptcy Information Disclosure Platform, Judicial Case Academy of the Supreme People's Court, National Court Litigation Activity Notification Inquiry Platform, China Justice Big Data Service Platform, Online Platform for Disclosure of Information about Cases of Sentence Commutation, Probation and Serving a Sentence out of Prison, and many sub-platforms have been set up under some these platforms. The construction of a large number of these websites and platforms is indeed helpful in improving the coverage of judicial openness. However, the Supreme People's Court has not attached importance to the integration of various platforms, and the interconnection among these platforms is insufficient. After a user enters a sub-platform, it is often impossible for him to return to the upper-level platform or enter other platforms. It is extremely inconvenient for the parties to search for relevant information on different websites. More importantly, the data on different platforms cannot be shared. For example, more than half of the provinces in China directly use the Enforcement Case Process Information Management System of the Supreme People's Court, but the judgment documents of enforcement cases in this system still need to be returned to local courts and uploaded to the judgment document network from local courts.

4.4.7 *Questionable Fees for the Live Broadcast of Court Trials*

The assessment shows that local courts encountered the problem of paid service when uploading live videos of court trials to China Court Trial Online, that is, local courts needed to pay expensive platform usage fees and infrastructure rental fees to the platform construction enterprises of China Court Trial Online. As a national judicial openness platform, this practice is questionable. Firstly, it increases the burden of judicial openness of local courts. As a court trial live broadcast platform designated by the Supreme People's Court, China Court Trial Online covers a wide range. More than 3000 courts in China have to sign contracts with and pay fees to the platform constructors, which increases the burden of judicial openness of local courts. Secondly, it hinders the popularization and openness of live broadcast of court trials to a certain extent. Because the number and efficiency of live videos of court trials uploaded by local courts are related to the amount of fee paid to the third party, the work of live broadcast of court trials of local courts is dependent on the ability to pay the fee, and this practice has an adverse effect on the work of judicial openness of courts in economically underdeveloped areas and those with weak ability to pay. Thirdly, because platform builders monopolize the channel of the live broadcast of court trials, when the Supreme People's Court assesses the openness of local courts according to the situation of openness of platform, platform builders become the deciders of the work of live broadcast of court trials in a certain sense, and such assessment results are likely to be unfair.

4.5 Suggestions for Improvement and Prospect of Future Development

The Report on Deepening Judicial Openness and Promoting Judicial Justice, adopted by the Supreme People's Court on November 5, 2016, points out that deepening judicial openness and promoting judicial justice are the long-term tasks of people's courts. The report to the 19th National Congress of the CPC points out that China will further promote judicial reform and deepen the comprehensive supporting reform of the judicial system, and puts forward clearer directions and requirements for judicial reform and judicial openness.

4.5.1 *Optimizing Platform Construction by Relying on Information Technology*

The court informatization system version 3.0 not only raises higher requirements but also provides a platform for judicial openness to expand its breadth and depth.

However, the problems existing in informatization itself will also restrict the in-depth development of judicial openness. Therefore, China should speed up the informatization of courts, improve and optimize court websites and solve the prominent problems in judicial openness work, such as invalid search column setting, inconsistent multi-platform data release, inaccurate and incomplete information about the case handling process, and imperfect function of one-click Internet access to judgment documents, so as to enable court informatization to fully and effectively serve judicial openness, promote the optimization of court websites and judicial openness platforms, use information technology to promote judicial transparency and protect the parties and the public's right to know.

4.5.2 Deepening Judicial Openness from the Perspective of Public Demand

The objective of enabling the people to feel fairness and justice in every judicial case embodies higher demand for judicial openness. In the future, China should continuously expand the breadth and depth of judicial openness, be parties- and the public-oriented, and strive to meet the diverse judicial needs of the masses of the people. Some courts need to change their judicial ideas and open their judicial information to the public, take the vital interests of the people as the starting point, solicit more opinions and suggestions from the public, and enable the public to supervise and promote the judicial openness of courts, so as to truly serve the people and provide convenience to the people.

4.5.3 Further Standardizing the System of and Mechanism for Openness

Due to the lack of clear institutional norms, there are some problems in the process of judicial openness, such as inconsistency in content and form, irregularity, and randomness, which should be dealt with by standardizing and strengthening the coercive force of judicial openness. In recent years, the Supreme People's Court has issued judicial interpretations to make clear demands for the online disclosure of judgment documents and openness of cases of termination of current enforcement proceedings. In the future, it should gradually formulate rules on the disclosure of information about the judicial process, trial affairs, and enforcement disciplinary actions, further refine the standards and scope of judicial openness, strictly perform the duties of open trial stipulated by the Constitution and laws, and effectively protect the lawful rights of the parties to participate in trial activities and to have access to trial information. At the same time, attention should be paid to the scope of disclosure stipulated by law, strictly guarding state secrets and trial secrets while disclosing relevant information in accordance with law.

4.5.4 Raising the Level of the Openness of Judicial Big Data

On December 8, 2017, the Political Bureau of the CPC Central Committee conducted the second collective study on the implementation of the national big data strategy. At the study session, General Secretary Xi Jinping emphasized that big data is changing and developing with each passing day. We should assess the situation, draw up plans carefully, make arrangements in advance, strive to take the initiatives, have a deep understanding of the current situation and trend of big data development and its impact on economic and social development, analyze the achievements and existing problems in the development of big data in China, and promote the implementation of the national big data strategy. In the judicial field, open and shared services are an important concept in the construction of smart courts in China, an important means to achieve judicial justice, meet the demands of the masses of the people and promote judicial reform and judicial management, as well as important nourishment for the academic development in the field of law. Obtaining research results from data is currently one of the most important ways of making progress in legal research, as well as an important direction for future development. Big data can help academic circles realize the transition from theoretical exploration to empirical analysis, and reach conclusions that are more scientific, more well-founded, and more in line with practical needs. However, currently it is still very difficult for scholars to obtain judicial data. Courts with a large amount of judicial data, especially the Supreme People's Court, should disclose judicial information such as judgment documents and guiding cases with a more open mind, and not set obstacles such as verification codes to the browsing and downloading of relevant materials and documents by the public. Meanwhile, they should rely on the newly-launched China Justice Big Data Service Platform to strengthen the research and utilization of judicial information resources, so as to better serve judges, the people, and economic and social development.

4.5.5 Strengthening the Operation and Maintenance of Court Websites

Judicial openness requires the input of not only technology but also human resources. Take the website judicial information disclosure as an example. The judicial information within a court is changing all the time. The lack of a special website maintenance personnel will inevitably lead to the delay in updating and even the erroneous release of judicial information. Therefore, to strengthen judicial openness, special network technicians and professionals who are familiar with judicial work should be assigned for the daily operation and maintenance of online platforms. Judicial information should not only be disclosed but also be disclosed effectively and in a correct way. Timely review and adjustment of disclosed information should also be carried out to ensure the standardization of judicial information release.

Chapter 5
Report on Indices of Judicial Transparency in China (2018)—From the Perspective of Information Disclosure on Court Websites

Innovation Project Team on the Rule of Law Index

Abstract In 2018, with the deepening of the reform of the judicial system and the improvement of the judicial openness platforms of the Supreme People's Court, judicial openness had become the consensus of courts at all levels in China, the scope of openness of trial affairs had been continuously expanded, the disclosure of trial information had been further developed in both breadth and depth, the disclosure of enforcement information had exerted an important impact on the realizing of the goal of "basically overcoming the difficulties in enforcement", and judicial reform became more and more open and transparent. In the future, in order to meet the requirements for deepening the comprehensive reform of the judicial system, China still needs to further improve the details and humanization of judicial openness, optimize the platform construction by relying on information technology, deepen judicial openness from the perspective of public demand, further standardize the system of and mechanism for openness, give full play to the role of big data openness, strengthen the operation and maintenance of court websites, and further improve the quality of judicial openness and enhance judicial credibility.

Keywords Judicial openness · Judicial transparency · Justice in the sunshine · Judicial reform

---

Leaders of the Project Team: Tian He, a research fellow at CASS Law Institute and the director of the Center for Studies of National Indices of the Rule of Law, Chinese Academy of Social Sciences and Lv Yanbin, a research fellow at and the head of the Department of Survey and Study of National Situation of the Rule of Law of the Institute of Law, Chinese Academy of Social Sciences. Other members of the project team include: Ma Xiaoling, Wang Xiaomei, Wang Yiming, Liu Yanpeng, Ruan Yuqing, Yang Xinlan, Song Junjie, Pang Yue, Zhao Yiming, Hu Changming, Li Dongsheng, Li Yanjie, En He, Cai Hanchan and Xiong Yushan. Authors of this report: Hu Changming, Assistant Research Fellow, Institute of Law, Chinese Academy of Social Sciences.

Innovation Project Team on the Rule of Law Index (✉)
Institute of Law, Chinese Academy of Social Sciences, Beijing, China
e-mail: 13263169197@163.com

H. Tian et al. (eds.), *Report on the Rule of Law Index in China 2*,
Research Series on the Chinese Dream and China's Development Path,
https://doi.org/10.1007/978-981-19-9597-2_5

2018 was the first year of deepening the comprehensive reform of the judicial system by people's courts. Strengthening judicial openness is an important measure for implementing constitutional and legal principles and ensuring the people's participation in the administration of justice, an important content of the work of deepening the comprehensive reform of the judicial system and improving the mechanism for the operation of judicial power, and an inevitable requirement for promoting the comprehensive law-based governance and building a socialist state under the rule of law. In March 2018, the Supreme People's Court mentioned "openness" 18 times in its work report made at the first session of the 13th National People's Congress. While affirming that China had made great progress in judicial openness, it put forward further requirements for judicial openness, emphasizing that people's courts should "actively disclose judicial information so that judicial justice can be seen, evaluated and supervised".

To present and evaluate the achievements made by China in judicial openness in 2018, the Center for Studies of National Indices of the Rule of Law of the Chinese Academy of Social Sciences and the Innovation Project Team on Rule of Law Indices of the Institute of Law, Chinese Academy of Social Sciences (hereinafter referred to as the Project Team) continued to assess the judicial transparency of 81 courts, including the Supreme People's Court, 31 high people's courts and 49 intermediate people's courts, from the perspective of information disclosure on court websites. This was the eighth assessment of judicial transparency in China conducted by the Project Team since 2011, and the assessment period was from September 15 to November 30, 2018.

5.1 Assessment Index System

The index system of judicial transparency in China has been optimized and adjusted every year since its establishment in light of the progress and changes as well as the annual characteristics of China's judicial system. In 2018, the index system strengthened the assessment of the actual results of judicial openness, focusing on the openness of enforcement and the openness of judicial reform. After adjustments, the index system included five grade I indices: "openness of trial affairs", "openness of trial", "openness of enforcement", "data openness" and "openness of judicial reform". "Openness of trial affairs" mainly refers to the openness of judicial administrative affairs related to trial and enforcement, including platform construction, personnel information, normative documents, and information about disqualification for office. Since it had become the normal practice for courts to disclose their general information such as address, traffic map, contact information, the scope of jurisdiction, subordinate courts, internal departments and their functions, and complaint channels on their portal websites, it was no longer used as a content of assessment this year.

The index of platform construction focused on the assessment of the effectiveness and friendliness of court portal websites; in this year, the barrier-free function of the court websites was added as a part of the assessment of the user-friendliness of court websites; the personnel information index was used to assess the disclosure of the following two aspects of judicial information: the name, educational background, work experience, and main responsibilities of each leader of a court, and the name, educational background and rank of each judge in a court. In this year's assessment, we also used this index to assess the disclosure of information about auxiliary judicial personnel, namely assistant judges and court clerks and we continued to assess the situation of implementation and openness of the system of disqualification for the appointment of judges.

The openness of trial includes the openness of the litigation guide, the openness of the trial process, the openness of court trial, the openness of commutation of sentence and parole, and the openness of judicial documents. Among them, the index of openness of litigation guides assessed the accuracy, convenience, and comprehensiveness of the information disclosed in litigation guides on portal websites of courts. The openness of court trials, in addition to the disclosure of information about the rules on the observation of court trials by members of the public, reservation for the observation of court trials, and live video broadcasting of court trials, also stressed the live text broadcasting of court trial because this form of live broadcasting is more conducive to enabling the parties to learn about the whole process of court trials in a quicker and more convenient way than live video broadcasting. The index of disclosure of commutation and parole information emphasizes the assessment of whether the portal websites of courts provided the link to the National Online Platform for Disclosure of Information about Cases of Sentence Commutation, Probation and Serving a Sentence out of Prison to enable the parties to directly browse the relevant information; the focus of the assessment of openness of judicial documents was still the reverse disclosure of judgment documents, that is, whether the courts had disclosed on their websites the total number, case numbers, judgment dates of judicial documents that had not been disclosed on the Internet and reasons for the non-disclosure.

The openness of enforcement remained the focus of this year's assessment. 2018 was the decisive year for achieving the goal of basically overcoming enforcement difficulties in two to three years, set by the Supreme People's Court. The openness of enforcement is very important to standardizing enforcement behavior, improving the quality and efficiency of enforcement work, and enhancing the satisfaction of the parties. It includes enforcement inquiry, the disclosure of information about cases of the termination of current enforcement proceedings, enforcement exposure, disclosure of information about enforcement disciplinary actions, and enforcement tip-off. In 2018, the Project Team adjusted the index of openness of enforcement and added the inquiry index; in the enforcement exposure index, two assessment items had been added: the disclosure of information about dishonest judgment debtors and inquiry about enforcement exposure; in the enforcement disciplinary action index, the assessment item of disciplinary action inquiry was added to guide the court to actively disclose the enforcement information, and facilitate the timely and accurate inquiry about the enforcement by the parties.

The data openness index includes the openness of financial data, work reports and judicial affairs data. Financial data include budgets and final accounts, budgetary expenditures related to official overseas visits, official vehicles, and official hospitality, and data on the money and property involved in cases; work reports refer to the annual work reports, annual reports, white papers, judicial recommendations and special report of courts; and judicial affairs data includes the disclosure of case statistics and other information. This year, the Project Team increased the weight of the assessment of the columns on the publication of work reports and the disclosure of financial openness on court websites, further merged and simplified similar budget and final accounts data, and added the new assessment item of disclosure of statistics of judicial recommendations. At the same time, it also added the new assessment item of the timeliness of the publication of annual reports and white papers to guide the courts to disclose judicial data in a timely and effective manner.

In recent years, the Project Team has attached great importance to the disclosure of judicial reform information. Since 2015, the Project Team has incorporated the disclosure of judicial reform information into the assessment system. In 2016, the Project Team used it in the calculation of scores as a grade II index under "openness of trial affairs". In 2017, judicial reform information was taken as a grade I index of judicial transparency, and its weight and score were increased. In 2018, five grade II indices were set up under the index of disclosure of judicial reform information: the setup of judicial reform column on court websites, judicial reform plan, reform of the judge quota system, registration system for the docketing of cases, and handling of cases by leading cadres, among which the index of judicial reform plan was used only for the assessment of the Supreme People's Court and high people's courts. On the basis of the assessment in 2017, the Project Team adjusted the index according to the new situation of judicial reform, added the assessment items of comprehensive supporting reform of judicial system under the index of judicial reform, the assessment items of the provisions and standards on the appointment and withdrawal of quota-based judges and the guarantee mechanism for judges under the judicial reform plan index, and the assessment item of the number of cases handled by quota-based judges under the index of reform of the judge quota system (Table 5.1).

5.2 The Overall Result

In 2018, the average score of the judicial transparency indices of 81 courts covered by the assessment was 56.58, which was basically the same as those of the previous two years. Of the 81 assessment targets, the number of those that scored above 80 points was 6, 2 more than 2017, the number of those that scored between 60 and 80 points (including 60 points) was 19, one more than 2017, the number of those that scored between 50 and 60 points was 31, and the number of those that scored less than 50 points was 25. The top 20 courts in the ranking of assessment scores were the Intermediate People's Court of Guangzhou City, the Intermediate People's Court of Haikou City, the High People's Court of Zhejiang Province, the Intermediate People's Court of Nanjing City, the Intermediate People's Court of Ningbo City, the High People's Court of Jilin Province, the Intermediate People's Court of Changchun City,

Table 5.1 Judicial transparency index system in China in 2018

Grade I indices	Grade II indices
Openness of trial affairs (20%)	Platform construction (40%)
	Personnel information (30%)
	Normative documents (20%)
	Information about disqualification for office (10%)
Openness of trial (30%)	Litigation guide (20%)
	Trial process (30%)
	Openness of court hearing (30%)
	Commutation and parole information (5%)
	Judicial documents (10%)
Openness of enforcement (20%)[a]	Guide to enforcement (15%)
	Enforcement inquiry (15%)
	Enforcement exposure (30%)
	Enforcement disciplinary action (15%)
	Information about cases of termination of current enforcement proceedings (10%)
	Enforcement tip-off (15%)
Data openness (20%)	Financial data (40%)
	Work report (30%)
	Judicial affairs data (30%)
Openness of judicial reform (10%)[b]	Setup of judicial reform column on court website (20%)
	Judicial reform plan (20%)[b]
	Registration system for the docketing of cases (20%)
	Reform of the personnel quota system (20%)
	Handling of cases by leading cadres (20%)

[a]Since the openness of enforcement does not apply to the Supreme People's Court, the weights of indices of openness of trial affairs, openness of trial and data openness, and openness of judicial reform of the Supreme People's Court were 30%, 30%, 30%, and 10% respectively
[b]Since the index of judicial reform plan is not applicable to the assessment of intermediate people's courts, the weights of indices of the registration system for the docketing of cases, reform of the judge quota system, and leading cadres' handling of cases in intermediate courts were 30%, 30%, 20%, and 20% respectively

the Intermediate People's Court of Chengdu City, the Intermediate People's Court of Jilin City, the High People's Court of Sichuan Province, the High People's Court of Jiangsu Province, the High People's Court of Shanghai Municipality, the High People's Court of Beijing Municipality, the Intermediate People's Court of Hangzhou City, the Intermediate People's Court of Hefei City, the High People's Court of Hubei Province, the Intermediate People's Court of Xuzhou City, the Intermediate People's Court of Shenzhen City, the Supreme People's Court and the High People's Court of Hunan Province (see Table 5.2).

Table 5.2 Assessment results of judicial transparency indices in China in 2018 (Unit: point)

Ranking	Courts	Openness of trial affairs	Openness of trial	Openness of enforcement	Data openness	Openness of judicial reform	Total score (out of 100)
1	Intermediate People's Court of Guangzhou City	96.00	100.00	81.50	96.00	70.00	91.70
2	Intermediate People's Court of Haikou City	78.00	95.00	88.00	93.60	95.00	89.92
3	High People's Court of Zhejiang Province	90.00	90.50	85.50	84.60	57.00	84.87
4	Intermediate People's Court of Nanjing City	90.00	83.00	80.00	89.00	75.00	84.20
5	Intermediate People's Court of Ningbo City	85.00	74.00	87.00	95.20	70.00	82.64
6	High People's Court of Jilin Province	78.00	93.50	81.50	74.00	74.00	82.15
7	Intermediate People's Court of Changchun City	83.00	91.50	64.00	72.20	68.00	78.09
8	Intermediate People's Court of Chengdu City	85.00	76.00	79.00	69.60	75.00	77.02
9	Intermediate People's Court of Jilin City	86.50	79.00	60.00	79.00	80.00	76.80

(continued)

Table 5.2 (continued)

Ranking	Courts	Openness of trial affairs	Openness of trial	Openness of enforcement	Data openness	Openness of judicial reform	Total score (out of 100)
10	High People's Court of Sichuan Province	85.00	68.00	81.50	75.00	66.00	75.30
11	High People's Court of Jiangsu Province	62.00	67.00	75.00	84.00	38.00	68.10
12	High People's Court of Shanghai Municipality	51.00	79.00	76.00	57.60	67.00	67.32
13	High People's Court of Beijing Municipality	63.00	62.00	76.00	76.00	57.00	67.30
14	Intermediate People's Court of Hangzhou City	58.00	64.00	83.00	74.00	38.00	66.00
15	Intermediate People's Court of Hefei City	70.00	59.00	69.00	72.00	45.00	64.40
16	High People's Court of Hubei Province	59.00	69.00	68.00	69.00	42.00	64.10
17	Intermediate People's Court of Xuzhou City	61.00	79.50	49.50	69.00	40.00	63.75

(continued)

Table 5.2 (continued)

Ranking	Courts	Openness of trial affairs	Openness of trial	Openness of enforcement	Data openness	Openness of judicial reform	Total score (out of 100)
18	Intermediate People's Court of Shenzhen City	57.00	60.00	64.50	76.00	60.00	63.50
	The Supreme People's Court	82.00	54.00	–	54.00	65.00	63.50
20	High People's Court of Hunan Province	68.00	66.50	55.50	74.00	38.00	63.25
21	High People's Court of Tianjin Municipality	72.00	70.50	52.00	53.00	57.00	62.25
22	High People's Court of Hainan Province	53.00	49.00	56.50	92.00	67.00	61.70
23	High People's Court of Heilongjiang Province	71.00	64.50	39.00	70.00	59.00	61.25
24	Intermediate People's Court of Xiamen City	60.00	58.00	65.00	72.00	40.00	60.80
25	High People's Court of Jiangxi Province	72.00	59.00	62.50	53.00	48.00	60.00
26	High People's Court of Anhui Province	59.00	60.00	78.00	55.00	25.00	58.90

(continued)

Table 5.2 (continued)

Ranking	Courts	Openness of trial affairs	Openness of trial	Openness of enforcement	Data openness	Openness of judicial reform	Total score (out of 100)
27	High People's Court of Hebei Province	57.00	63.50	63.00	55.00	36.00	57.65
28	High People's Court of Guangxi Zhuang Autonomous Region	64.00	59.00	56.00	60.00	38.00	57.50
29	Intermediate People's Court of Shijiazhuang City	60.00	64.50	55.00	52.00	40.00	56.75
30	High People's Court of Fujian Province	63.00	47.00	30.00	98.00	40.00	56.30
31	Intermediate People's Court of Dalian City	56.00	70.00	43.00	50.00	45.00	55.30
32	High People's Court of Chongqing Municipality	73.00	56.00	55.00	51.00	25.00	55.10
35	High People's Court of Henan Province	43.50	62.00	52.50	62.60	43.00	54.62
36	High People's Court of Liaoning Province	54.00	46.00	71.00	62.00	33.00	54.50

(continued)

Table 5.2 (continued)

Ranking	Courts	Openness of trial affairs	Openness of trial	Openness of enforcement	Data openness	Openness of judicial reform	Total score (out of 100)
37	High People's Court of Guangdong Province	59.00	61.50	35.00	67.00	38.00	54.45
38	Intermediate People's Court of Huainan City	69.00	59.00	49.50	45.00	40.00	54.40
39	High People's Court of Gansu Province	52.00	61.50	60.50	40.00	51.00	54.05
40	High People's Court of Shaanxi Province	60.50	57.00	45.00	62.00	33.00	53.90
41	Intermediate People's Court of Nanchang City	54.00	59.00	52.00	53.00	43.00	53.80
	Intermediate People's Court of Zhuhai City	53.00	53.00	54.00	66.00	33.00	53.80
43	Intermediate People's Court of Shenyang City	68.00	54.00	43.00	54.00	45.00	53.70
44	High People's Court of Yunnan Province	52.00	54.00	61.50	50.60	43.00	53.32
45	Intermediate People's Court of Xi'an City	47.50	62.00	45.00	61.00	40.00	53.30

(continued)

Table 5.2 (continued)

Ranking	Courts	Openness of trial affairs	Openness of trial	Openness of enforcement	Data openness	Openness of judicial reform	Total score (out of 100)
46	Intermediate People's Court of Benxi City	60.00	54.00	52.00	47.60	50.00	53.12
47	Intermediate People's Court of Xining City	37.00	51.50	62.00	68.00	40.00	52.85
48	Intermediate People's Court of Tangshan City	60.00	53.50	53.50	55.00	30.00	52.75
49	High People's Court of Ningxia Hui Autonomous Region	60.00	59.00	36.00	60.00	38.00	52.70
50	Intermediate People's Court of Changsha City	58.00	66.50	36.50	50.00	38.00	52.65
51	Intermediate People's Court of Jinan City	55.00	47.00	71.00	48.00	25.00	51.40
52	Intermediate People's Court of Handan City	59.00	63.00	38.50	47.00	30.00	50.80
53	Intermediate People's Court of Kunming City	64.00	49.50	34.50	66.00	30.00	50.75
54	Intermediate People's Court of Zhengzhou City	71.00	56.50	30.00	52.00	30.00	50.55

(continued)

Table 5.2 (continued)

Ranking	Courts	Openness of trial affairs	Openness of trial	Openness of enforcement	Data openness	Openness of judicial reform	Total score (out of 100)
55	Intermediate People's Court of Qingdao City	55.00	39.50	56.00	69.00	25.00	50.35
56	Intermediate People's Court of Lanzhou City	61.00	51.00	47.50	46.00	40.00	50.20
57	Intermediate People's Court of Baotou City	42.00	66.50	30.00	55.00	45.00	49.85
58	High People's Court of Guizhou Province	59.00	65.00	24.50	47.00	41.00	49.70
	Intermediate People's Court of Taiyuan City	51.00	53.00	30.00	63.00	50.00	49.70
	Intermediate People's Court of Suzhou City	48.00	51.00	44.00	55.00	50.00	49.70
61	High People's Court of Shandong Province	47.00	63.00	40.50	52.00	28.00	49.60
62	Intermediate People's Court of Urumqi City	51.00	65.00	30.00	55.00	25.00	49.20
63	Intermediate People's Court of Zibo City	49.00	38.00	67.00	56.00	25.00	48.30

(continued)

Table 5.2 (continued)

Ranking	Courts	Openness of trial affairs	Openness of trial	Openness of enforcement	Data openness	Openness of judicial reform	Total score (out of 100)
64	Intermediate People's Court of Datong City	72.00	54.00	30.00	35.00	45.00	48.10
	High People's Court of Xinjiang Uygur Autonomous Region	50.00	51.00	30.00	65.00	38.00	48.10
	Intermediate People's Court of Wuxi City	56.00	41.00	54.00	54.00	30.00	48.10
67	Intermediate People's Court of Harbin City	41.00	57.00	38.50	62.00	25.00	47.90
68	Intermediate People's Court of Yinchuan City	47.00	59.00	30.00	60.00	25.00	47.60
69	High People's Court of Inner Mongolia Autonomous Region	65.00	34.00	30.00	69.00	41.00	47.10
70	Intermediate People's Court of Guiyang City	39.00	43.00	40.00	70.00	35.00	46.20
71	Intermediate People's Court of Wuhan City	62.00	56.00	52.50	17.00	30.00	46.10

(continued)

Table 5.2 (continued)

Ranking	Courts	Openness of trial affairs	Openness of trial	Openness of enforcement	Data openness	Openness of judicial reform	Total score (out of 100)
72	Intermediate People's Court of Qiqihar City	72.00	49.50	2.50	61.00	38.00	45.75
73	Intermediate People's Court of Hohhot City	51.00	64.00	15.00	45.00	25.00	43.90
74	Intermediate People's Court of Nanning City	40.00	46.00	34.50	60.00	30.00	43.70
75	High People's Court of Shanxi Province	42.00	57.00	0.00	69.00	36.00	42.90
76	High People's Court of Tibet Autonomous Region	47.00	30.00	41.00	60.00	33.00	41.90
77	Intermediate People's Court of Fushun City	58.00	35.50	41.00	41.00	25.00	41.15
78	Intermediate People's Court of Anshan City	65.00	22.00	30.00	60.00	25.00	40.10
79	Intermediate People's Court of Luoyang City	54.00	37.50	17.50	46.00	50.00	39.75
80	Intermediate People's Court of Fuzhou City	38.00	31.00	36.50	47.00	25.00	36.10

(continued)

Table 5.2 (continued)

Ranking	Courts	Openness of trial affairs	Openness of trial	Openness of enforcement	Data openness	Openness of judicial reform	Total score (out of 100)
81	Intermediate People's Court of Lhasa City	69.00	35.00	30.00	6.00	25.00	34.00

The eight consecutive years of assessment of judicial transparency indices show that the judicial transparency of assessment targets had been continuously improving, especially the scores of advanced courts in judicial openness had been continuously rising, the score gaps among courts had narrowed, and the competition had become increasingly intense: by increasing its total score by 5 points, a court might increase its ranking by more than 20. However, the assessment also shows that some courts had always failed to attach importance to judicial openness, disclosing little information or outdated information on their websites, and staying at low-ranking positions for many years. As a result, the transparency gap between courts continues to widen. Some courts had always attached importance to judicial openness, constantly innovating and deepening the content of openness, and ranking firmly at the forefront of assessment results. For example, 16 courts, including the Intermediate People's Court of Guangzhou City, the Intermediate People's Court of Haikou City, the High People's Court of Zhejiang Province, the Intermediate People's Court of Nanjing City, the Intermediate People's Court of Ningbo City, the High People's Court of Jilin Province, the Intermediate People's Court of Changchun City, the Intermediate People's Court of Chengdu City, the Intermediate People's Court of Jilin City, the High People's Court of Shanghai Municipality, the High People's Court of Beijing Municipality, the Intermediate People's Court of Hangzhou City, the Supreme People's Court, the Intermediate People's Court of Xuzhou City, the Intermediate People's Court of Shenzhen City, and the High People's Court of Hunan Province had ranked in the top 20 for three consecutive years (2016, 2017, and 2018). Among them, seven courts, including the Intermediate People's Court of Guangzhou City, the High People's Court of Zhejiang Province, the Intermediate People's Court of Nanjing City, the Intermediate People's Court of Ningbo City, the High People's Court of Jilin Province, the Intermediate People's Court of Changchun City, and the Intermediate People's Court of Jilin City, had ranked in the top ten for three consecutive years (2016, 2017 and 2018).

In 2018, some courts began to attach importance to judicial openness, drew on the experience of advanced courts, revised their portal websites, carried out the work of judicial openness brilliantly, and improved their rankings in the assessment. Among them, the following courts had continuously improved their rankings in the transparency index assessment in the past three years: the High People's Court of

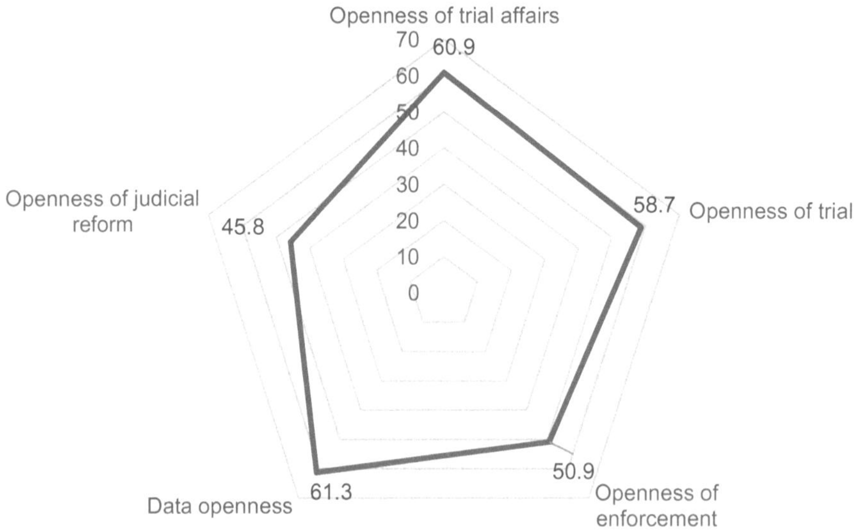

Fig. 5.1 Average score of each section of the China judicial transparency index system

Sichuan Province, the Intermediate People's Court of Haikou City, the High People's Court of Hubei Province, the High People's Court of Tianjin Municipality, the Intermediate People's Court of Xi'an City and the High People's Court of Ningxia Hui Autonomous Region. Especially, the High People's Court of Sichuan Province raised its ranking from the 40th in 2016, to the 30th in 2017, and to the top ten in 2018, the High People's Court of Ningxia Hui Autonomous Region rose from the bottom in 2016 to the 49th in 2018, and the High People's Court of Hubei Province, the High People's Court of Tianjin Municipality, and the Intermediate People's Court of Xi'an City raised their rankings by more than 20.

Among the five sections of the index system, data openness had the highest average score (61.3), followed by the openness of trial affairs (60.9), the openness of trial (58.7), and the openness of enforcement (50.9), with the openness of judicial reform having the lowest score of only 45.8 (see Fig. 5.1).

5.3 Bright Spots Found in Assessment

With the deepening of judicial reform and the improvement of the judicial openness platforms of the Supreme People's Court, judicial openness has become the consensus of courts at all levels in China. In 2018, the Supreme People's Court, for the first time, commissioned a third-party institution, the Institute of Law of Chinese Academy of Social Sciences, to assess the judicial openness in China. At the level of local courts, courts in some regions had achieved leap-forward development as a whole, and made uniform arrangements for the work of judicial openness in the whole province, autonomous region, or municipality directly under the Central Government, leading the whole country in judicial transparency, while some other courts had been constantly innovating the form and content of openness. Generally speaking, there were many bright spots in the work of judicial openness carried out by courts across the country, and big progress had been made in judicial transparency in some fields.

5.3.1 Strengthening the Top-Level Design

In 2018, the Supreme People's Court issued a number of normative documents on promoting and standardizing judicial openness. The Opinions of the Supreme People's Court on Further Deepening Judicial Openness, issued on November 20th, raise judicial openness to the height of strengthening the restraint on the operation of power, safeguarding the people's right to know and their rights of participation, expression and supervision, carrying forward the socialist core values, and enhancing the people's awareness of the rule of law, not only establishing the principles of active openness, law-based openness, timely openness, comprehensive openness, and substantive openness, but also clarifying the nine main scopes and contents of judicial openness, and raising further demands on the procedures, platform carrier construction, and management and organizational guarantee of judicial openness. These opinions are not only a programmatic document of the Supreme People's Court on judicial openness but also implementation requirements for the specific operation of judicial openness.

On February 12th, the Supreme People's Court issued the Provisions on the Disclosure of Trial Process Information on the Internet by People's Courts, which became the first normative document requiring the disclosure of information about the court trial process on the Internet. It requires that people's courts should disclose trial process information on the Internet in a legal, standardized, timely, and facilitative manner, and that, beginning from September 1, 2018, the trial process information of all courts in the country should be uniformly disclosed on the platform China Judicial Process Information Online.

5.3.2 Strengthening the Construction of Unified Platforms of Openness

Since the 18th National Congress of the Communist Party of China, the Supreme People's Court has vigorously promoted the judicial openness of people's courts, and successively built four major platforms of judicial openness, namely the platforms for the openness of judgment documents, the openness of the trial process, the openness of enforcement and the openness of trial. China Judgments Online, as the largest judgment document website in the world, had published nearly 60 million effective judgment documents of courts at all levels in China, with more than 21.2 billion visits by December 31, 2018. With its search function gradually improved, it is visited by people from more than 210 countries and regions around the world. It publishes judgment documents in five categories, namely judgments in criminal, civil, administrative, enforcement and compensation cases, and in six languages, namely Han language and five minority languages: Mongolian, Tibetan, Uygur, Korean and Kazakh.

On the platform China Court Trial Online, special columns such as Live Broadcasts of Court Trials, Advance Notices of Court Trials, Review of Live Broadcasts, Broadcasting of Recorded Court Trials, Major Cases, Hot Spot Ranking, Court Navigation, and Data Openness had been set up to meet different levels of need of the parties and the public for watching court trial videos. By December 31, 2018, the platform had released live broadcasts and recorded videos of court trials of more than 2.3 million cases, and had received more than 13.9 billion visits.

Disclosing enforcement information to the parties is conducive to safeguarding the parties' right to know, increasing the transparency of enforcement work, reducing black-box operation and power rent-seeking, and strengthening the deterrent of enforcement. Since the launching of China Enforcement Information Disclosure Platform (zxgk.court.gov.cn), its contents had been continuously enriched. At present, the platform enables its users to inquire about such information as enforcement cases, parties subject to enforcement, consumption restriction, termination of current enforcement proceedings, legal documents and announcements of enforcement, and guides to enforcement of all courts in the country, and provides rotating display of information about dishonest judgment debtors, persons subject to the restriction on high-level spending and the openness of enforcement on its homepage, thus enhancing the deterrent of the openness of enforcement. By December 31, 2018, the platform had released information about more than 35.98 million enforcement cases, over 51.89 million pieces of information about parties subject to enforcement, and more than 12.88 million pieces of information about dishonest judgment debtors.

China Judicial Process Information Online is a unified platform for judicial openness created by the Supreme People's Court in recent years. At present, the platform has achieved complete coverage of courts at all levels in China. Through this platform, parties can contact judges of the Supreme People's Court, sign for documents, and inquire about the progress of the handling of cases in courts throughout the country. Moreover, the public can also inquire about the institutional setup, guides to judicial openness, lists of judges, the opening of court trials, rosters of judges, litigation guides, and other information of most courts in China, and put forward opinions and suggestions through this platform, which has become another bright spot and hallmark of judicial openness in China.

The practice of building platforms of openness by the Supreme People's Court and high people's courts is conducive to unifying the standards on the openness of trial and enforcement, facilitating the access by the public and parties to court information through a unified website or a unified entrance, avoiding the problems and difficulties encountered in the information search on the website platforms of different courts, enabling users to search information about courts in the whole country or in the whole province, autonomous region, or municipality directly under the Central Government by visiting just one website, improving the level of intensiveness of judicial openness, and raising the efficiency of information search by the public.

5.3.3 Constantly Innovating the Form of Judicial Openness

In recent years, with the vigorous development of new media, China has been constantly making breakthroughs and innovations in the form of judicial openness, with traditional portal websites remaining the main form of judicial openness. Moreover, local courts have been actively exploring innovative forms of judicial openness and combining them with traditional websites to form an all-round and three-dimensional form of openness. For example, the High People's Court of Shanghai Municipality, the Intermediate People's Court of Zhengzhou City, the Intermediate People's Court of Fuzhou City, and the Intermediate People's Court of Xiamen City provided QR codes and links to official Weibo and WeChat accounts and mobile phone clients on the homepage of their portal websites to enable visitors to subscribe to their Weibo and WeChat accounts by scanning the codes, thereby broadening the channels for the public to obtain judicial information. Courts in Zhejiang Province have taken the lead in the whole country in developing the WeChat applet "Zhejiang Mobile Micro Court", which takes advantage of WeChat's powerful user base to expand the users of the applet, and extends judicial openness from the portal website to the mobile phones of the parties, enables the parties to see and feel fairness and justice in the synchronous openness of the whole process of cases handling, greatly reduces the problems of complaint letters and visits and distrust resulting from information asymmetry, insufficient openness and poor communication, and makes judicial openness closer to the people and more popular with the parties. The High People's Court of Gansu Province has set up a new media matrix column on its website to disclose the QR codes of official Weibo and WeChat accounts of courts at all levels in the province. The Enforcement Information Disclosure Platform of the People's Court of Shishi City in Fujian Province not only enables users to have access to such information about enforcement as enforcement cases, the list of dishonest judgment debtors, the list of persons subject to the restriction on high-level spending, the list of persons subjected to restriction on leaving the country, detention, seizure, property disposal, legal documents, and enforcement judges but also copy all these contents to its WeChat official account, so that the parties can easily search and obtain this information on their mobile phones.

Moreover, with the increasing frequency of foreign exchanges, some courts have also taken the initiative to disclose the litigation service information in multiple languages. For example, Beijing Trial Information Network (bjcourt.gov.cn) translated the guidance documents of the Supreme People's Court, the documents on the openness of docketing of cases, bankruptcy cases, and litigation services into English, and publishes these documents in both Chinese and English. The Intermediate People's Court of Xiamen City also provided both Chinese and English versions of the guides to the filing of civil and administrative cases, so as to facilitate the consultation by foreign parties.

5.3.4 Achieving Remarkable Results in the Disclosure of Judgment Documents

Since the Supreme People's Court promulgated a judicial interpretation to make arrangements for the online publication of court judgment documents in the whole in November 2013, online publication of judgment documents has gradually become the consensus of people's courts at all levels. In 2018, new progress was made in the disclosure of judgment documents. First, the reverse disclosure of judgment documents had been paid more and more attention to. Among the 81 courts covered by the assessment, 18 published the number of documents not disclosed online, and the case number and the reasons for the non-disclosure of each of these documents, an increase of 11 from that in 2017. Among the above-mentioned 18 courts, there were 6 high courts and 12 intermediate courts, a significant increase as compared with 2 and 5, respectively, in the previous year. Second, most courts published rules and regulations on the work of judgment documents on their portal websites. Article 13 of the Provisions of the Supreme People's Court on the Publication of Judgments on the Internet by the People's Courts stipulates that high people's courts and intermediate people's courts shall supervise and guide the publication of judgments on the Internet by the people's courts within their respective jurisdictions. The systems of disclosure of judgment documents are important means for courts to organize and guide the publication of judgment documents on the Internet, which can ensure the orderly implementation and promote the standardized development of the disclosure of judgment documents. Third, publishing analysis reports on the online disclosure of judgment documents. Some courts covered by the assessment regularly analyzed the disclosure of judgment documents by courts in their respective jurisdictions, and publish the analysis results on their websites for public supervision. For example, in Jilin Province, the High People's Court of Jilin Province, Intermediate People's Court of Changchun City and the Intermediate People's Court of Jilin City published on a quarterly basis analysis reports on the disclosure of judgment documents on the Internet, covering the online disclosure of judgment documents, judgment documents in minority languages and withdrawal and revision of judgment documents, etc. by intermediate courts and grass-roots courts in their respective jurisdictions, and put forward clear requirements for the online disclosure of judgment documents after that. The publication of these analysis reports made the disclosure of local judgment documents more transparent, and also exerted certain pressure on and motivated local courts to disclose judgment documents. Fourth, new achievements in the disclosure of judgment documents had been constantly made. A search on CNKI database with "judgment documents" as the keyword shows that there were less than 50 results before 2012. The number began to increase steadily since 2013, when judgments documents were uploaded to the Internet on a large scale, increasing by 63 in 2013, 89 in 2014, and more than 100 every year after 2015. The increase in the number of papers taking judgment documents as the research object shows that the openness of judgment documents promotes legal research. Moreover, in 2018, after hot cases such as the cases of murder by Didi ride-sharing drivers and the case of justifiable defense by "Longge" in Kunshan City, many scholars searched for relevant cases on China Judgments Online for case analysis.

5.3.5 Humanizing the Methods of Information Disclosure

Judicial information should not only be disclosed but also be disclosed in a way easily visible to relevant parties. The assessment shows that, in 2018, the construction of court websites throughout the country had become increasingly people-centered and the parties need-oriented. Firstly, facilitating the parties' participation in litigation. Litigation fees are a cost that every litigation participant will have to consider. If a court website only lists the provisions on the payment of litigation fees, the parties may still be unable to calculate the litigation cost correctly in the face of complicated calculation methods. Therefore, some courts directly provided the calculation formula of litigation fees on their portal websites. For example, the Court Openness Network of Zhejiang Province and the Judicial Openness Online Service Platform of the Intermediate People's Court of Wuhan City provided litigation fee calculators, which enable the parties to calculate their litigation fees by entering the type of case and the amount claimed in litigation. Moreover, these websites also provided applets for the calculation of late fees for deferred performance and interest rates to facilitate the calculation and verification by the parties. Secondly, providing more practical information on websites. Some courts disclosed on their own initiative some practical information to the parties in light of their needs in judicial practice. For example, the Intermediate People's Court of Ningbo City disclosed information about major cases, judicial authentication documents, and judicial auction announcements on its website, while the Intermediate People's Court of Haikou City provided online application channels, channels for contacting judges and online petition channels for litigation participants on the homepage of its website and actively solicited the assessment opinions of the parties on judges. Thirdly, providing convenience for special parties. In 2018, the Project Team added the assessment of barrier-free function to the website user-friendliness index. Among the 81 courts covered by the assessment, 56, or 69.14% of the total, provided the function of font enlargement or voice playback to assist the visually impaired to browse their websites, and 2 of them provided both of the above two functions, which greatly facilitated the access to judicial information by the visually impaired. Moreover, the website of the Intermediate People's Court of Hangzhou City provided visitors with vision protection colors for them to choose from on its homepage, which is a truly people-oriented and innovative approach worthy of praise. And Xinjiang Court Litigation Service Platform published judgment documents in three languages: Chinese, Uygur and

Kazakh. Fourthly, adopting forms of openness that are closer to the people. Financial information disclosure is an important part of judicial openness, but financial information is highly professional, diversified in form and complex in classification, which makes it difficult for ordinary people to understand and supervise. The High People's Court of Sichuan Province supplemented the disclosure of budget and final accounts information with charts, which are more vivid and closer to the people, so as to achieve comprehensive and substantive disclosure. The Intermediate People's Court of Ningbo City disclosed the number of cases closed by all courts in the city in the form of histogram, and allowed the public to customize the scope of their inquiry according to their needs.

5.3.6 Continuously Enhancing the Awareness of Active Openness

The assessment shows that, in 2018, the awareness of active openness of courts in the whole country had been continuously enhanced. Firstly, actively expanding the scope of disclosure of personnel information. The assessment shows that some courts not only disclosed the information about court leaders, judges and judicial assistants, but also took the initiative to expand the scope of disclosure to cover members of adjudicative committees, supervisors against corruption, leaders and cadres of functional departments, people's assessors and the roster of judicial authentication institution, which were the focus of attention of the parties. For example, the High People's Court of Beijing Municipality actively disclosed not only the names, genders, units and other detailed information of people's assessors in courts at all levels in the municipality but also the lists of organizations of specially invited mediators and rosters of specially invited mediators of courts in the municipality, the list of institutions selected for appraisal, assessment and auction, and the list of credit guarantee companies. The High People's Court of Guangdong Province disclosed the names of the principal responsible persons of internal functional institutions, members of various professional adjudicative committees, and spokespersons of all courts in the province and their contact information. Secondly, actively disclosing information about judicial reform, including relevant policies, latest practices and achievements of judicial reform. For example, the Intermediate People's Court of Jilin City disclosed on its own initiative the information about the latest progress in judicial reform, including the construction of the trial team and the establishment of professional trial collegial panels, and published the Report on the Implementation and Rectification Measures for the Reform of the Judicial Responsibility System. The Intermediate People's Court of Haikou City had set up a sub-column on comprehensive supporting reform of the judicial system under the column of judicial reform of its website, disclosing information about the flat management of cases in the court and the exercise of trial supervision power by the president and division chiefs of the court. The Intermediate People's Court of Nanjing City updated the list of quota-based judges in a timely manner every year, and actively published the list of judges who had left their posts and the list of members of the judge selection committee. The High People's Court of Jilin Province and the Intermediate People's Court of Guangzhou City disclosed on their own initiative information about the protection of lawyers' rights and interests. Thirdly, actively disclosing information about the enforcement of judgments, which is the focus of public concern. Beijing Trial Information Network regularly disclosed the results of evaluation and auction cases randomly selected by lottery, and information about bankruptcy administrator of relevant cases, the number of cases in the enforcement proceedings and the number of cases of termination of current enforcement proceedings handled by each court in the city, the case number, the ruling on the termination of current enforcement proceedings and other detailed information about each of such cases. The Intermediate People's Court of Nanjing City and the Intermediate People's Court of Changchun City provided analysis and prediction on the changes in the number of closed cases in the data disclosure column of their websites, so as to help judicial decision-making. Fourthly, providing functions of application for and complaint about information disclosure. For example, the Intermediate People's Court of Guangzhou City drew on the practice of government information disclosure, actively provided guide and application forms for judicial information disclosure, and issued implementation measures for handling applications for judicial information disclosure.

5.4 Existing Problems

5.4.1 The Details of the Disclosure of Judgment Documents Still Need to Be Improved

After the promulgation and implementation of the Provisions of the Supreme People's Court on the Publication of Judgments on the Internet by the People's Courts, courts throughout the country have fully recognized the importance of the disclosure of judgment documents, and with the continuous upgrading and revision of China Judgments Online, made great progress in this field of work. Nevertheless, they still have a long way to go in meeting the demand of the public and the requirements in the Provisions. The existing problems include: First, China Judgments Online still needs to be improved. Although it has realized the function of advanced search by such items as the cause of action, case number, party, court, case type, judge, lawyer, legal basis and full text, it is still not humanized enough and has such shortcomings as inaccurate search results, artificial obstacles to search, and the need to delete the existing search conditions before conducting a new search. For example, after the Project Team entered two search conditions of "intermediate people's court" and "criminal judgment documents", the website showed "no data meeting the search conditions". After the Project Team searched the website three times in a row, it was required by the website to enter the verification code before it could continue to browse the web page. Especially, the website run very slowly, and its response time was unbearably long. The insufficient website construction prevented the powerful database and functions of the judgment document platform from giving full play to their roles. Second, the disclosure of judgment documents does not meet the legal requirements. The judgment documents uploaded by some courts are just a fixed template without any substantive content. For example, in the First-instance Civil Judgment Document No.2555 (2016) (Yu 1681), published on October 11, 2016, only the information about the plaintiff and defendant is relatively complete. All other contents of the judgment document, such as the plaintiff's claim, the defendant's response, the fact ascertained by the court, the opinions of the court, and the judgment, were replaced by ellipsis, and the judgment document was only a formality without substantive content. This phenomenon is not uncommon on the platform. For another example, Article 17 Paragraph 2 of the Provisions of the Supreme People's Court on the Publication of Judgments on the Internet by the People's Courts stipulates that "China Judgments Online shall adopt a system of case numbers subject to different trial procedures according to cases, so as to realize the correlation of judgments." However, at present, most of the documents on China's Judgment Online have not yet realized the correlation between cases with different trial procedures, which is not convenient for the public to find related cases and search for relevant information. Thirdly, the reverse disclosure of judgment documents needs to be further improved. The assessment shows that, in 2018, the implementation of the system of reverse disclosure of judgment documents was still poor: among the 81 courts covered by the assessment, only 18 (or 22.2% of the total), including the High People's Court of Tianjin Municipality, the High People's Court of Jilin Province, the High People's Court of Qinghai Province, the Intermediate People's Court of Dalian City, the Intermediate People's Court of Chengdu City, the Intermediate People's Court of Xi'an City and the Intermediate People's Court of Xuzhou City, disclosed the number of judgment documents not disclosed online and their case numbers and reasons for non-disclosure. Moreover, the assessment also shows that the reasons given by some courts for not disclosing judgment documents online were unclear, vaguely expressed as "other"; some courts gave far-fetched reasons for not disclosing judgment documents online, such as system failure or rejection by the platform; and the contents of judgment documents published by some courts were inconsistent with the legal requirements.

5.4.2 The User-Friendliness of Websites Needs to Be Further Improved

The user-friendliness of a court portal website directly shows whether the website builders implement the user-oriented thinking, whether the public and the parties are the objects of judicial openness, and whether the portal website is treated as an important window of judicial openness. The assessment shows that the user-friendliness of many court websites was still not satisfactory, and there were even setbacks in some aspects. Firstly, the number of floating windows on websites had increased. In 2018, there was a significant increase in court portal websites with floating windows throughout the country. The contents of these floating windows included the internal work of the court, such as Party-building work, court publicity work, selection of top ten police officers, recent key work tasks of the court (such as cracking down on organized crimes and basically overcoming difficulties in enforcement), introduction to website columns, etc. The assessment shows that the number of courts with floating windows on their websites was 29, accounting for 35.8% of all courts covered by the assessment, 18 more than that in 2017, with the increase rate exceeding 160%. Of the floating windows on the websites of the above-mentioned 29 courts, those of 10 courts were located on the two sides of the webpage in a way that did not affect the browsing of the webpage by the users. Among those of the remaining 19 courts, those of 11 courts could be closed and those of 8 could not be closed, 2 and 5 more than in 2017, and there were even as many as 4 floating windows on the homepage of one court, which seriously affects the website browsing experience. Secondly, there were artificially set browsing obstacles. In addition to China Judgments Online, some local courts had also set up browsing barriers in the columns of judgment documents: after a user carries out a search more than three times in a row, he or she is required to enter the verification code. Although this practice can prevent some companies from using crawler technology to crawl court judgment documents, it brings great inconvenience to the general public in searching, browsing and downloading judgment documents, resulting in poor website experience. Thirdly, some information plug-in links could not be browsed directly. Some courts did not directly disclose information on their website, but put information files on the web page in the form of plug-ins, which must be downloaded to local computers, and can be opened and browsed only if the corresponding software is installed on the local computers. This practice creates unnecessary obstacles to information disclosure.

5.4.3 There is Still Room for Improvement in the Openness of Enforcement

In recent years, the Central Government has attached great importance to overcoming difficulties in enforcement. In June 2016, The 18th Central Leading Group for Comprehensively Deepening Reform reviewed and approved at its 25th meeting the Opinions of the General Office of the CPC Central Committee and the General Office of the State Council on Accelerating the Advancement of the Development of a Credit Supervision, Warning and Punishment System of Dishonest Persons Subject to Enforcement, which clearly state that China will "further improve the capacity of people's courts for the enforcement work" and "uphold judicial authority". By relying on the strong leadership of the Party, an overall pattern of basically overcoming difficulties in enforcement work had been developed. A research team of the

Standing Committee of the National People's Congress and the National Committee of the Chinese People's Political Consultative Conference had repeatedly investigated enforcement difficulties in the whole country and identified the problems and difficulties in the enforcement work of courts. "Basically overcoming enforcement difficulties" is not only the main task in comprehensively deepening the reform of the national court system but also one of the top priorities of local political and legal departments at all levels. The openness of enforcement is of great significance for enhancing the deterrence of enforcement and standardizing enforcement behavior. However, the assessment shows that the situation of openness of court enforcement in China was still not optimistic. Among the six grade II indices, namely enforcement guide, enforcement inquiry, information about termination of current enforcement proceedings, enforcement exposure, enforcement disciplinary actions, and enforcement tip-off, only two, namely enforcement guide and enforcement tip-off, had an average score rate of over 50%, while other indices showing that the phenomena of lack of openness and incompleteness in the content of openness were common among assessment targets. Firstly, the rate of openness of the enforcement process was not high. The assessment of the openness of the court enforcement process shows that only 19 out of 80 courts[1] disclosed the enforcement process or flowchart, accounting for 23.75% of the total, and this situation was not conducive to the understanding of the enforcement process by parties. Secondly, the termination of current enforcement proceedings was still not transparent. "Termination of current enforcement proceedings" refers to the temporary suspension of enforcement proceedings in cases where there is really no property available for enforcement, until the person subject to enforcement has property available for enforcement. In practice, the procedure of termination of current enforcement proceedings is often abused. In order to improve the case closure rate, judges often terminate enforcement proceedings without exhausting the enforcement measures or when there is still property for enforcement.[2] The disclosure of information about the termination of current enforcement proceedings is conducive to standardizing the handling of cases of termination of current enforcement proceedings, and to the supervision by the applicants for enforcement and the public. The assessment shows that, among all the courts covered by the assessment, only 11, including the High People's Court of Gansu Province, the High People's Court of Zhejiang Province, the High People's Court of Beijing Municipality, the Intermediate People's Court of Chengdu City, the Intermediate People's Court of Hangzhou City, the Intermediate People's Court of Nanjing City and the Intermediate People's Court of Haikou City, disclosed the complete information about cases of termination of current enforcement proceedings, including the case number, the person subject to enforcement, the date of docketing of the case, the date of closing of the case, the ruling on the termination

[1] Since the openness of enforcement does not apply to the Supreme People's Court, the assessment of this index was carried out on 80 courts.

[2] "Report on Indices of Judicial Transparency in China (2016)—from the Perspective of Information Disclosure on Court Websites", in Li Lin and Tian He (eds.), *Development Report on the Rule Law in China: No.15 (2017)*, Beijing: Social Science Academic Press, 2017.

of current enforcement proceedings, the total number of cases and tip-offs, and 3 other courts disclosed partial information. Together they accounted for 17.50% of all the assessment targets. Although this was a significant improvement from 2017, it was still far from meeting the expectation of the public. Thirdly, the disclosure of information about enforcement disciplinary actions was insufficient. In 2015, a new index on the disclosure of information about "enforcement disciplinary actions" was added to the index system, so as to facilitate social supervision, force courts to strengthen the application of enforcement disciplinary measures, and at the same time create an environment in which "those who evade enforcement will certainly be punished".[3] After the assessment for four consecutive years, the situation of disclosure of information about "enforcement disciplinary actions" by courts at all levels was still not optimistic. In 2018, 14 courts, or 17.50% of all those covered by the assessment, disclosed information about cases of fines, detention and other sanctions, only 7 courts, or 8.75% of the total, disclosed information about enforcement cases in which criminal responsibility was investigated, and only 5 courts, or 6.25% of the total, provided channels for the inquiry about enforcement disciplinary actions. Fourthly, the situation of enforcement exposure still needed to be further improved. The assessment shows that, in 2018, among all the courts covered by the assessment, 47, or 58.75% of the total, published the list of dishonest judgment debtors, 35, or 43.75% of the total, published the list of persons subject to the restriction on high-level spending, 30, or 37.50% of the total, published the list of persons subjected to restriction on leaving the country, 21, or 26.25% of the total, published the announcements of reward for enforcement tip-offs, 10, or 12.50% of the total, published the list of special entities subject to enforcement, and 13, or 16.25% of the total, provided the functions of enforcement expose and inquiry on their websites. Among the courts that disclosed the above information, some had not updated such information in the past six months or even three or five years, so there was still room for further improvement in enforcement exposure.

5.4.4 The Disclosure of Judicial Reform Information is Still Faced with Many Difficulties

The reform of the judicial system is one of the key points of the work of courts and even the whole political and legal system since the 18th National Congress of the Communist Party of China. Disclosing information about the process, contents and achievements of the reform is conducive to building social consensus. The assessment shows that, although the awareness of disclosure of judicial reform information

[3] Innovation Project Team on Rule of Law Indices of the Law Institute of Chinese Academy of Social Sciences, "Report on Indices of Judicial Transparency in China (2015)—from the Perspective of Information Disclosure on Court Websites", in Li Lin and Tian He (eds.), *Development Report on the Rule Law in China: No.14 (2016)*, Beijing: Social Science Academic Press, 2016.

among local courts had gradually increased and more and more courts had set up judicial reform columns on their websites, the disclosure of judicial reform information as a whole, and especially disclosure of the key information, was inadequate.

Firstly, the judicial reform columns on most court websites were poorly constructed and not updated in a timely manner. The assessment shows that, although the current round of judicial reform had been carried out vigorously for many years, a considerable part of judicial reform information had not been made public. Of the 81 courts covered by the assessment, only 35, or 43.21% of the total, had set up a judicial reform column on their websites and disclosed information about supporting reforms of the judicial system; among them, only 18, or 22.22%, updated the content of these columns in a timely manner. This shows that most courts still had not realized the importance of the openness of judicial reform. In terms of the disclosure of judicial reform plan,[4] 8 courts published the judicial reform plan adopted by the Central Government or their own implementation rules for judicial reform, accounting for 25% of the total, while only the Supreme People's Court, the High People's Court of Jiangsu Province and the High People's Court of Hainan Province published the judge guarantee mechanism and its implementation rules, accounting for 9.38% of the total. Secondly, the disclosure of measures for the reform of the judicial personnel quota system was inadequate. The reform of the judicial personnel quota system is one of the important tasks as well as the key to the success of this round of judicial reform. As such, it is a matter of great concern both inside and outside the court system. The assessment shows that the level of openness of the reform of the judicial personnel quota system, including the disclosure of information about the implementation process of the reform, selection criteria for quota-based judges and completion of reform tasks, was not high. Among the Supreme People's Court and 31 high people's courts, only 9 disclosed the rules and selection criteria for judges, accounting for 28.13% of the total; 6 disclosed selection procedures for quota-based judges, accounting for 18.75% of the total; 2 disclosed members of the judge selection committee, accounting for 6.25% of the total; and none of them disclosed provisions on judges' withdrawal from the quota system. Of the 81 courts covered by the assessment, only 26, or 32.10% of the total, including the High People's Court of Sichuan Province, the High People's Court of Hunan Province, the Intermediate People's Court of Guangzhou City, the Intermediate People's Court of Hefei City and the Intermediate People's Court of Wuhan City, disclosed the number of cases handled by quota-based judges, the numbers of courts that disclosed the number of cases handled by quota-based judges, the withdrawal of judges from the quota system and actual cases of guarantee for judges were 3, 2 and 2, accounting for only 3.70%, 2.47% and 2.47%, respectively, of the total. China still has much to do and a long way to go in the openness of the reform of the judicial personnel quota system. Thirdly, the handling of cases by leading cadres was not open and transparent. The Opinions of the Supreme People's Court on Strengthening the Work of Case-Handling by Presidents and Chief Judges of the People's Courts at Various Levels (for Trial

[4] This index was used for the assessment of only the Supreme People's Court and 31 high people's courts.

Implementation), issued on April 10, 2017, not only require presidents, vice presidents, full-time members of adjudicative committees, chief judges and deputy chief judges who have entered the judge quota system to handle cases but also clarify the number and types of cases to be handled by the president of a court. The Opinions also require the trial management department of each court to calculate, verify, and issue periodical notification on the number of cases handled by the presidents and chief judges of the court. The assessment shows that the number of courts that disclosed the provisions on the handling of cases by the president of the court and the number of cases handled by the president of the court was still too small: only 7 courts, or 8.64% of the total, including the Supreme People's Court, the High People's Court of Jilin Province, the Intermediate People's Court of Guangzhou City, the Intermediate People's Court of Ningbo City, the Intermediate People's Court of Jilin City, the Intermediate People's Court of Chengdu City and the Intermediate People's Court of Haikou City, disclosed the provisions on the handling of cases by the president of the court, 11 courts, or 13.58% of the total, disclosed the number of cases handled by the president of the court, and only 5 courts, or 6.17% of the total, disclosed the types of cases handled by the president of the court.

5.4.5 *The Level of Openness of Courts Varies from Region to Region*

The assessment in 2017 revealed the Matthew effect in judicial openness in various parts of the country. The assessment in 2018 shows that there was no apparent change in the uneven levels of judicial openness of courts in different parts of the country, and there was even a trend toward intensification of polarization, with the widening of the gap between the top ten courts and the bottom ten courts in the ranking of assessment scores. The judicial openness work carried out by advanced courts had become more and more solid. For example, in light of the latest progress in judicial openness and the judicial transparency report of the previous year, the Intermediate People's Court of Guangzhou City especially prepared a plan for judicial transparency index self-assessment and rectification, which included the current situation of judicial openness, the results of self-assessment and responsible departments, and courts from which advance experience had been drawn on. In recent years, although the Intermediate People's Court of Shenzhen City had ranked high in the assessment of judicial transparency, it was not satisfied with the *status quo*, but continued to expand the scope of judicial openness, and constantly improved its portal website, so as to continuously raise the level of judicial openness.

In contrast, some courts did not attach sufficient importance to judicial openness. As a result, their websites were poorly managed, and their judicial openness work was at a standstill. Firstly, the accessibility to their portal websites was intermittent. The assessment shows that the accessibility to the portal websites of some courts was intermittent during the two-month assessment period, sometimes these websites could be viewed normally, and sometimes they became inaccessible, which seriously affected user experience. Some court websites had a large number of information vacancies during the maintenance and upgrading period, and the maintenance and upgrading time was too long, which affected the effect of judicial openness. Secondly, the updating of website contents was slow. To achieve good results, judicial openness work must be done in a persistent way. Some courts had the practice of uploading all information onto their websites at the same time, then not updating the contents of their websites for half a year or even several years afterward. The assessment shows that some courts had not updated the contents on their websites since 2012. On the websites of some courts, contents such as a brief introduction to the court and institutional setup had not been updated for more than ten years, the work reports were those of six years ago, and the introductions to the previous and current presidents of the court were still those of 2007. The trial information disclosed by many courts did not indicate the dates on which they were put online, so it was impossible to judge whether the information has been outdated. In the assessment of administrative litigation guides, it was found out that only 13 courts, or 16.05% of the total, had published and updated administrative litigation guides. Thirdly, some of the disclosed information was incorrect or incomplete. Compared with non-disclosure and tardiness in disclosure or updating, errors in disclosed information can more easily mislead the public. For example, the trial information network of a court informed the parties that they had two options of non-litigation dispute resolution: enforcement reconciliation by the parties and mediation by people's mediation organizations, which are of the nature of social organizations. In fact, there are at least two more non-litigation dispute resolution options: arbitration and administrative mediation. Moreover, although the law stipulates that social organizations can set up people's mediation committees, the statement that "people's mediation organizations are of the nature of social organization" is not accurate and rigorous enough.

5.5 Suggestions and Prospects of Improvement

In 2018, courts in the whole country had made great progress in promoting judicial openness, but there were also many fields in which improvements still urgently needed to be made. On the whole, courts at all levels need to implement the requirements of the Opinions of the Supreme People's Court on Further Deepening Judicial Openness, continue to broaden and deepen judicial openness, improve the relevant institutions and systems, optimize and upgrade platform carriers of judicial openness, raise the level of refinement, standardization and informatization of judicial openness, promote the construction of a more open, dynamic, transparent and convenient judicial mechanism, create a new pattern of comprehensive deepening of judicial openness, and realize the modernization of trial system and trial capacity.

5.5.1 *Attaching Importance to Judicial Openness*

The Opinions of the Supreme People's Court on Further Deepening Judicial Openness take judicial openness as an important starting point for realizing the modernization of the trial system and trial capacity and promoting the new development of people's court work in a new era and raise high demand on the work of judicial openness. Promoting judicial openness is not an expedient measure or an image project, but a popular project that serves the overall interest of the Party and the country, economic and social development, and the practical interests of the broad masses of the people, and enables the people to feel fairness and justice in every judicial case. Therefore, first of all, courts at all levels need to attach great importance to judicial openness. Firstly, court leaders need to attach great importance to the work. Courts in which the leaders, especially the "top leaders", attach importance to judicial openness, often rank high in the assessment of judicial transparency. Judicial openness is a systematic project. Only when leaders attach importance to this work, can they form synergy, persevere, and continuously deepen judicial openness. Secondly, judicial openness should be combined with the supporting reform of the judicial system. Courts should have the awareness that promoting judicial openness is a basic work of deepening the supporting reform of the judicial system, promote judicial openness in the process of implementing the supporting reform of the judicial system, and further deepen the reform of the judicial system through judicial openness.

5.5.2 *Refining the Standards of Judicial Openness as Soon as Possible*

Compared with the openness of government affairs, judicial openness has such problems as lack of uniformity and standardization and arbitrariness in content and form. In the process of judicial openness, courts in different parts of the country have attached different levels of importance to the work, resulting in uneven levels of judicial openness in different regions. In regions with a high level of judicial openness, courts disclose all kinds of judicial information on their websites, while in regions with a low level of judicial openness, courts have not yet completely solved the basic problems of accessibility to and information updating on their websites. In some regions, court websites stay at the level of publicizing the work arrangements made by court leaders, court culture construction, judges' personal thoughts and feelings, and so on. These problems existed because, although the Supreme People's Court had attached great importance to judicial openness and issued many normative documents in recent years to clarify the principles and requirements of judicial openness, due to the absence of supporting implementation rules, there was a lack of unity and compulsion in judicial openness, and courts had no clear ideas about such questions as which information can be made public, which must be made public, what are the scope and key fields of openness, and information in which fields should not be disclosed. Take the live broadcast of court trials as an example. On the one hand, the live broadcasts of the trials of a large number of cases had extremely low views; on the other hand, the trials of some cases of great social concern were not broadcast live. Therefore, it is suggested that the Supreme People's Court carry out relevant studies and issue normative documents on compulsory judicial openness as soon as possible, so as to unify standards and channels of openness and bring judicial openness into the scope of assessment of courts.

5.5.3 Properly Handling the Relationship Between Openness on Unified Platforms and Innovative Openness

In 2018, Chinese courts, led by the Supreme People's Court, began to construct a unified platform of judicial openness and disclose the information of all courts on this platform. Meanwhile, some high people's courts also actively built their own judicial openness platforms, unified the standards and channels of information disclosure, and uniformly disclosed all the information of the courts at three levels in the whole province, autonomous region or municipality directly under the Central Government on the platform. Unified platforms are conducive to unifying standards of openness, making judicial information more open, transparent and convenient for the people, conducting special analyses, and serving judicial decision-making by making full use of big data. However, some questions relating to the construction of openness platforms, such as how to deal with the relationship between the construction of uniform openness platforms and the construction by courts at various levels of their own platforms, still need to be answered. Therefore, we suggest that China raise the awareness of courts at all levels of the importance of centralized information disclosure through publicity and training, take the release of information in accordance with regulations on a unified platform as the basic requirement of judicial information disclosure, supplemented by the disclosure by various courts of their own individualized information, and while disclosing judicial information on a centralized and unified platform, encourage courts at all levels to innovate the form and content of their own information disclosure.

5.5.4 Designating Special Departments to Be Responsible for Judicial Openness

At present, there are such problems in judicial openness as inadequate maintenance of portal websites, insufficient disclosure of key information, lack of unity in columns and contents of court portal websites in various regions, and multiple platforms of openness, which are partially caused by the fact that people's courts have too many tasks and have not designated a competent department to be responsible for the work of judicial openness. In addition to the four major platforms of openness, the Supreme People's Court has also constructed the National Enterprise Bankruptcy Information Disclosure Platform, Judicial Case Academy of the Supreme People's Court and China Justice Big Data Service Platform, which are not under the administration of a unified competent department. The department in charge of judicial openness is also different in different local courts: it could be the trial administration office, the information office, or the general office of a court. In the work of judicial openness, as a routine work of a court, it is necessary to review and maintain information on a regular basis, and the lack of a unified competent department responsible for the work leads to the lack of a unified policy. Therefore, we suggest that China establish a unified department in courts to be responsible for judicial openness work, and assign special personnel to maintain the portal websites, so as to ensure the accuracy and timeliness of information release.

5.5.5 Expanding Channels of Judicial Openness Through the Application of Information Technology

In the information age, the continuous development of informatization is forcing courts to disclose more trial information, and the construction of Version 3 of the Smart Court System also provides powerful technical support for judicial openness. In recent years, local courts have tried various ways to be close to the people, broadened judicial openness channels through Weibo, WeChat, App, WeChat applets and other channels, and achieved good results. We suggest that courts at all levels continue to make good use of information tools, assist openness through SMS, WeChat, telephone voice system, e-mail, client-side and other media, expand judicial service capacity, and continuously broaden the channels through which parties can obtain trial information. Of course, in using various new media platforms, attention should be paid to protecting the information security of the parties and ensuring that their privacy and information autonomy are not infringed upon while protecting the right to know of parties and the public. Moreover, while expanding new channels of judicial openness, it is necessary to make it clear that portal websites are the basic platforms of judicial openness, and promote the positive interaction between court websites and new media such as Weibo, WeChat, and client-side.

Chapter 6
Report on Indices of Procuratorial Transparency in China (2017)—From the Perspective of Information Disclosure on the Websites of Procuratorates

Innovation Project Team on the Rule of Law Index

Abstract In 2017, the Innovation Project Team on Rule of Law Indices of Institute of Law of Chinese Academy of Social Sciences, based on previous five consecutive years' assessment, fine-tuned the assessment indices, and carried out a quantitative assessment of the openness of procuratorial affairs of the Supreme People's Procuratorate, the procuratorates of 31 provinces, autonomous regions and municipalities directly under the Central government, and the procuratorates of 49 larger cities by taking information disclosure on portal websites as the mainline. This report reviews and analyzes the current situation, achievements and problems of the openness of procuratorial affairs in China in 2017 from four perspectives: basic information, guide to procuratorial affairs, procuratorial activities, and statistics and reports, and puts forward suggestions on the continuous improvement of openness of procuratorial affairs in such aspects as content, channel platform, process and mechanism.

Keywords The openness of procuratorial affairs · Portal website · Quantitative assessment

In 2017, the Innovation Project Team on Rule of Law Indices of Institute of Law of Chinese Academy of Social Sciences (hereinafter referred to as the "Project Team") carried out the assessment of the transparency of procuratorial work in China for the sixth consecutive year.

Leaders of the Project Team: Tian He, a research fellow at CASS Law Institute and the director of the Center for Studies of National Indices of the Rule of Law, Chinese Academy of Social Sciences, and Lv Yanbin, a research fellow at and the head of the Department of Survey and Study of National Situation of the Rule of Law of the Institute of Law, Chinese Academy of Social Sciences. Other members of the Project Team include: Wang Xiaomei, Li Yanjie, Hu Changming, Xu Bin, Liu Yanpeng, Wang Yiming, Zhu Xuefei, Liu Ying, Li Chenlong, Di Xingsi, Song Junjie, Shao Yuwen, Qing Wubang, Gao Jieran, and Guo Rui. Authors of this report: Li Yanjie, an assistant research fellow at Institute of Law, Chinese Academy of Social Sciences, Tian He, and Lv Yanbing.

Innovation Project Team on the Rule of Law Index (✉)
Institute of Law, Chinese Academy of Social Sciences, Beijing, China
e-mail: 13263169197@163.com

H. Tian et al. (eds.), *Report on the Rule of Law Index in China 2*,
Research Series on the Chinese Dream and China's Development Path,
https://doi.org/10.1007/978-981-19-9597-2_6

6.1 Targets, Indices and Methods of Assessment

In the assessment in 2017, the Project Team, on the basis of the assessment carried out in the previous five years, in accordance with the spirit of the relevant documents issued by the Central Government, and in light of the result of the survey of the actual situation, adopted the index system used in the assessment of the previous year, with only additions and deletions of some indices below the grade II level and corresponding fine-tuning of weights.

The targets of assessment of procuratorial transparency in 2017 were the same as those in 2016, including the Supreme People's Procuratorate, the procuratorates of 31 provinces, autonomous regions and municipalities directly under the Central Government, and the procuratorates of 49 larger cities.

The content of the assessment was still divided into four sections: basic information, guides to procuratorial affairs, procuratorial activities, and statistics and reports, with the weight of 20%, 30%, 30% and 20%, respectively (see Table 6.1).

In 2017, the Project Team fine-tuned some specific indices. On June 27, 2017, the Standing Committee of the 12th National People's Congress adopted at its 28th meeting the Decision on Amending the Civil Procedure Law of the People's Republic of China and the Administrative Procedure Law of the People's Republic of China, which came into effect on July 1, 2017. As a result, civil public interest litigation and administrative public interest litigation have become important duties of procuratorates at all levels. In view of this new development, contents related to public

Table 6.1 Assessment index system for procuratorial transparency and weight of indices (2017)

Grade I indices	Grade II Indices
Basic information (20%)	Setup of websites (20%)
	Micro-platform (20%)
	Institutional structure (30%)
	Personnel information (30%)
Guide to procuratorial affairs (30%)	Workflow (20%)
	Instructions on procuratorial affairs (30%)
	Press conferences (20%)
	Online consultation (30%)
Procuratorial activities (30%)	Legal documents (40%)
	Public examination of criminal petitions (30%)
	Investigation and handling of major cases (30%)
Statistics and reports (20%)	Work report (40%)
	Budget and final accounts (30%)
	Budgetary expenditures related to three kinds of official spending (official overseas visits, official vehicles, and official hospitality) (30%)

interest litigation were included in the guides to procuratorial affairs and procuratorial activities in the assessment in 2017. In November 2017, the Standing Committee of the 12th National People's Congress adopted at its 30th meeting the Decision on Promoting the Pilot Program on the National Supervisory System Reform All Over the Country and the (Draft) Supervision Law was also published for solicitation of public opinions. According to the decision and the new law, the functions of investigation of corruption and bribery, and dereliction of duty and prevention of duty crime of the supervision departments (bureaus) and corruption prevention bureaus of local people's governments and people's procuratorates at or above the county level were integrated into the functions of supervisory committees. In view of this new development, the assessment contents of self-investigation cases and duty crime prevention in the indices of guides to procuratorial affairs and procuratorial activities were deleted, integrated, or reduced in weight.

With respect to the channels of acquisition of assessment data, the Project Team continued to take portal websites as the main channel, supplemented by verification by telephone, Weibo and WeChat. Six assessment targets had no portal website or had portal websites that could not be opened during the assessment period. They included two provincial-level procuratorates, namely the People's Procuratorate of the Xinjiang Uygur Autonomous Region and the People's Procuratorate of the Tibet Autonomous Region, and four municipal-level people's procuratorates, namely those of Benxi, Qingdao, Xining and Lhasa. The portal websites of the People's Procuratorates of Guangzhou City[1] and Shenzhen City[2] in Guangdong Province, and Luoyang City[3] in Henan Province had been inaccessible for several days or even a longer period time during the assessment and verification period.

The assessment officially commenced on 10 August 2017 and was completed on 15 November 2017. Website contents uploaded and achievements and innovations discovered after the verification were mentioned in the report, but not used in the calculation of assessment scores.

---

[1] The homepage of the portal website of the People's Procuratorate of Guangzhou City (http://wsjcy.qyw.gov.cn/) used 3D display technology, which requires the installation of a plug-in named Silverlight. Although the performance of this website in previous years' assessment was unstable, it could be opened most of the time and even achieved good results in the assessment. However, during the 2017 assessment period after the installation of the plug-in, members of the Project Team tried to open the website using different browsers, such as Sogou, 360 and IE, but without success. During the verification period, the website became accessible and assessment and verification were carried out.

[2] The portal website of the People's Procuratorate of Shenzhen City (http://www.shenzhen.jcy.gov.cn/) showed the message "The website is under revision. Please wait!" and only three sections of the website, namely "Inquiry about Bribery Case Files", "Disclosure of Budget and Final Accounts in 2016" and "Disclosure of Budget and Final Accounts Disclosure in 2017", were accessible during the assessment and verification period. At the end of the verification period, the website became accessible, and assessment and verification were carried out.

[3] During most of the assessment and verification period, the portal website of the People's Procuratorate of Luoyang City (http://www.luoyang.jcy.gov.cn/) showed the message "This page cannot be visited normally due to unstable service!" But sometimes it functioned normally. The Project Team kept trying to visit the website on a daily basis and ultimately succeeded in completing the assessment and verification of this website.

6.2 Overall Assessment Results

The assessment shows that the transparency of procuratorial work had steadily increased in 2017. On the whole, after years of construction of institutions and improvement of practice, remarkable results had been achieved in the openness of procuratorial affairs, which had been continuously extended to judicial case handling, and positive results had also been achieved in satisfying the public's right to know, facilitating the handling of affairs by the public and the parties, and promoting the standardization of procuratorial activities. The top ten procuratorates in the ranking of assessment scores of procuratorial transparency in 2017 were: the People's Procuratorate of Jiangsu Province, the Supreme People's Procuratorate, the People's Procuratorate of Nanjing City, the People's Procuratorate of Suzhou City, the People's Procuratorate of Shanghai Municipality, the People's Procuratorate of Shandong Province, the People's Procuratorate of Xuzhou City, the People's Procuratorate of Hubei Province, the People's Procuratorate of Anhui Province and the People's Procuratorate of Guangdong Province; at the provincial level, the top five procuratorates in the ranking of assessment scores were: the People's Procuratorate of Jiangsu Province, the People's Procuratorate of Shanghai Municipality, the People's Procuratorate of Shandong Province, the People's Procuratorate of Hubei Province and the People's Procuratorate of Anhui Province; and at the level of larger cities, the top five people's procuratorates in the ranking of assessment scores were: the People's Procuratorate of Nanjing City, the People's Procuratorate of Suzhou City, the People's Procuratorate of Xuzhou City, the People's Procuratorate of Nanchang City and the People's Procuratorate of Shantou City (see Table 6.2).

As far as the regional dimension is concerned, the situation of openness of procuratorial affairs in economically developed regions was better than that in economically under-developed regions. For example, the assessment targets in Jiangsu Province performed well in the assessment in 2017. But there were exceptions. Some assessment targets in relatively underdeveloped areas had also performed well in the assessment. Take the index on statistics and reports as an example. Procuratorates in Guangxi Zhuang Autonomous Region, Henan Province, Inner Mongolia Autonomous Region, Liaoning Province, Heilongjiang Province, and Shenyang City had performed well while some procuratorates in economically developed regions failed to achieve satisfactory results in the assessment of this index. This was obviously related to the importance attached to the openness of procuratorial affairs and the differences in institution building. The failure to do a good job in the openness of procuratorial work results not from a lack of ability to do so, but from a lack of willingness to do so. Moreover, as far as the hierarchical dimension is concerned, generally speaking, higher-level procuratorial organs attached more importance to the openness of procuratorial affairs, while the importance attached to the work varied greatly among lower-level procuratorial organs.

Table 6.2 Overall Assessment Results of Procuratorial Transparency in China in 2017 (full score: 100 points)[4]

Ranking	Procuratorates	Total scores	Basic information	Guide to procuratorial affairs	Procuratorial activities	Statistics and reports
1	People's Procuratorate of Jiangsu Province	72.10	86.50	86.00	30.00	100.00
2	The Supreme People's Court	71.78	87.00	84.60	30.00	100.00
3	People's Procuratorate of Nanjing City	71.05	83.50	74.50	40.00	100.00
4	People's Procuratorate of Suzhou City	64.58	73.50	55.60	44.00	100.00
5	People's Procuratorate of Shanghai Municipality	64.40	69.00	72.00	30.00	100.00
6	People's Procuratorate of Shandong Province	62.78	57.00	74.60	30.00	100.00
7	People's Procuratorate of Xuzhou City	62.65	73.50	59.50	42.00	87.50
8	People's Procuratorate of Hubei Province	62.18	84.00	54.60	30.00	100.00
9	People's Procuratorate of Anhui Province	61.98	87.00	68.60	30.00	75.00
10	People's Procuratorate of Guangdong Province	61.58	79.50	55.60	30.00	100.00
11	People's Procuratorate of Hunan Province	61.00	94.00	44.00	30.00	100.00

(continued)

[4] *The statistics in the assessment were accurate to two decimal places.

Table 6.2 (continued)

Ranking	Procuratorates	Total scores	Basic information	Guide to procuratorial affairs	Procuratorial activities	Statistics and reports
12	People's Procuratorate of Nanchang City	59.00	69.00	44.00	40.00	100.00
13	People's Procuratorate of Shantou City	58.58	72.00	42.60	38.00	100.00
14	People's Procuratorate of Guangzhou City	58.08	73.50	56.60	38.00	75.00
15	People's Procuratorate of Jilin Province	57.18	69.00	64.60	30.00	75.00
16	People's Procuratorate of Guangxi Zhuang Autonomous Region	57.08	69.00	47.60	30.00	100.00
17	People's Procuratorate of Liaoning Province	56.78	72.00	44.60	30.00	100.00
18	People's Procuratorate of Tianjin Municipality	56.18	69.00	44.60	30.00	100.00
19	People's Procuratorate of Inner Mongolia Autonomous Region	55.58	84.00	32.60	30.00	100.00
20	People's Procuratorate of Beijing Municipality	54.78	69.00	56.60	30.00	75.00

(continued)

Table 6.2 (continued)

Ranking	Procuratorates	Total scores	Basic information	Guide to procuratorial affairs	Procuratorial activities	Statistics and reports
21	People's Procuratorate of Sichuan Province	53.00	69.00	34.00	30.00	100.00
22	People's Procuratorate of Shenzhen City	52.98	68.50	38.60	34.00	87.50
23	People's Procuratorate of Zhengzhou City	52.58	73.50	46.60	38.00	62.50
24	People's Procuratorate of Changsha City	51.48	52.00	46.60	32.00	87.50
25	People's Procuratorate of Hebei Province	50.68	69.00	59.60	30.00	50.00
26	People's Procuratorate of Zhejiang Province	49.98	72.00	38.60	30.00	75.00
27	People's Procuratorate of Shijiazhuang City	49.88	69.00	39.60	34.00	70.00
28	People's Procuratorate of Henan Province	49.28	66.00	23.60	30.00	100.00
29	People's Procuratorate of Baotou City	49.10	69.00	31.00	40.00	70.00
30	People's Procuratorate of Heilongjiang Province	48.98	60.00	26.60	30.00	100.00
31	People's Procuratorate of Wuhan City	48.58	87.00	52.60	38.00	20.00

(continued)

Table 6.2 (continued)

Ranking	Procuratorates	Total scores	Basic information	Guide to procuratorial affairs	Procuratorial activities	Statistics and reports
32	People's Procuratorate of Wuxi City	48.20	47.00	30.00	46.00	80.00
33	People's Procuratorate of Shanxi Province	48.18	79.50	27.60	30.00	75.00
34	People's Procuratorate of Chongqing Municipality	47.58	62.00	50.60	0.00	100.00
35	People's Procuratorate of Ningbo City	46.88	72.00	15.60	36.00	85.00
36	People's Procuratorate of Zhuhai City	46.50	45.00	49.00	36.00	60.00
37	People's Procuratorate of Shenyang City	46.45	64.00	11.50	34.00	100.00
38	People's Procuratorate of Jiangxi Province	46.08	57.00	35.60	30.00	75.00
39	People's Procuratorate of Jinan City	44.83	63.00	42.10	32.00	50.00
40	People's Procuratorate of Yunnan Province	44.58	57.00	30.60	30.00	75.00
41	People's Procuratorate of Hohhot City	44.08	66.00	12.60	42.00	72.50
42	People's Procuratorate of Chengdu City	43.28	54.00	46.60	40.00	32.50

(continued)

Table 6.2 (continued)

Ranking	Procuratorates	Total scores	Basic information	Guide to procuratorial affairs	Procuratorial activities	Statistics and reports
43	People's Procuratorate of Nanning City	42.48	79.00	18.60	32.00	57.50
44	People's Procuratorate of Datong City	41.98	69.00	56.60	4.00	50.00
45	People's Procuratorate of Kunming City	41.43	39.00	51.10	36.00	37.50
46	People's Procuratorate of Hainan Province	41.38	57.00	36.60	30.00	50.00
47	People's Procuratorate of Guizhou Province	41.20	69.00	28.00	30.00	50.00
48	People's Procuratorate of Zibo City	40.98	44.00	23.60	32.00	77.50
49	People's Procuratorate of Lanzhou City	39.98	39.00	24.60	36.00	70.00
50	People's Procuratorate of Xiamen City	39.70	79.50	32.00	4.00	65.00
51	People's Procuratorate of Hangzhou City	39.48	32.00	17.60	36.00	85.00
52	People's Procuratorate of Shaanxi Province	39.28	57.00	29.60	30.00	50.00
53	People's Procuratorate of Dalian City	38.48	72.00	28.60	30.00	32.50

(continued)

Table 6.2 (continued)

Ranking	Procuratorates	Total scores	Basic information	Guide to procuratorial affairs	Procuratorial activities	Statistics and reports
54	People's Procuratorate of Fujian Province	37.78	69.00	16.60	30.00	50.00
55	People's Procuratorate of Gansu Province	35.68	42.00	27.60	30.00	50.00
56	People's Procuratorate of Fuzhou City	34.78	24.00	25.60	36.00	57.50
57	People's Procuratorate of Guiyang City	34.58	42.00	11.60	34.00	62.50
58	People's Procuratorate of Xi'an City	33.68	54.50	38.60	4.00	50.00
59	People's Procuratorate of Harbin City	31.98	50.00	18.60	38.00	25.00
60	People's Procuratorate of Urumqi City	30.40	47.00	7.00	38.00	37.50
61	People's Procuratorate of Tangshan City	30.10	41.00	27.00	46.00	0.00
62	People's Procuratorate of Huainan City	29.28	42.00	8.60	36.00	37.50
63	People's Procuratorate of Handan City	28.68	60.00	21.60	34.00	0.00
64	People's Procuratorate of Ningxia Hui Autonomous Region	28.48	54.00	20.60	30.00	12.50

(continued)

Table 6.2 (continued)

Ranking	Procuratorates	Total scores	Basic information	Guide to procuratorial affairs	Procuratorial activities	Statistics and reports
65	People's Procuratorate of Jilin City	27.28	51.00	5.60	38.00	20.00
66	People's Procuratorate of Taiyuan City	26.00	14.00	6.00	38.00	50.00
67	People's Procuratorate of Luoyang City	25.58	69.00	18.60	4.00	25.00
68	People's Procuratorate of Haikou City	24.68	24.00	23.60	6.00	55.00
69	People's Procuratorate of Changchun City	23.20	54.00	20.00	8.00	20.00
70	People's Procuratorate of Yinchuan City	21.60	21.00	24.00	34.00	0.00
71	People's Procuratorate of Qinghai Province	18.70	50.00	4.00	0.00	37.50
72	People's Procuratorate of Hefei City	18.60	30.00	11.00	6.00	37.50
73	People's Procuratorate of Qiqihar City	17.78	30.00	22.60	0.00	25.00
74	People's Procuratorate of Fushun City	16.78	14.00	5.60	6.00	52.50
75	Anshan	9.18	17.00	12.60	0.00	10.00
–	People's Procuratorate of Xinjiang Uygur Autonomous Region	–	–	–	–	–

(continued)

Table 6.2 (continued)

Ranking	Procuratorates	Total scores	Basic information	Guide to procuratorial affairs	Procuratorial activities	Statistics and reports
–	People's Procuratorate of Xining City	–	–	–	–	–
–	People's Procuratorate of Tibet Autonomous Region	–	–	–	–	–
–	People's Procuratorate of Qingdao City	–	–	–	–	–
–	People's Procuratorate of Lhasa City	–	–	–	–	–
–	People's Procuratorate of Benxi City	–	–	–	–	–

Unit: points

6.3 Summarization of Achievements and Experiences

The assessment shows that the situation of openness of procuratorial affairs in 2017 was stable, with the continuous implementation of the policies of the Central Government and documents of the Supreme People's Procuratorate, the promotion of existing innovative explorations, and the emergence of new types and forms of "optional exercises". On the whole, the implementation of the work was stable, and the procuratorial organs were gradually opening up.

6.3.1 Making the Openness of Procuratorial Affairs the Focus of Reform

In 2017, the Report on the Comprehensive Deepening of Judicial Reform by the People'tgcys Procuratorates, submitted by the Supreme People's Procuratorate to the Standing Committee of the National People's Congress, used a relatively large space to report the work of "Building a Transparent Judicial Mechanism", indicating that procuratorates throughout the country had achieved full coverage of the case information disclosure system, the electronic case file system, whole-process video reception, Weibo, WeChat and news client-side, the spokesperson system and procuratorial open day activities.[5] At the local level, the openness of procuratorial affairs had become an important part of the work reports of local procuratorates. Some procuratorates also published special reports on the openness of procuratorial affairs. For example, the People's Procuratorate of Jiujiang City in Jiangxi Province published a systematic report on the main practices of, shortcomings in, and future plans for the work of openness of procuratorial affairs of procuratorial organs in the whole city.[6]

This shows that the openness of procuratorial affairs, as an important part of procuratorial reform, had been attached importance by the Supreme People's Procuratorate and local people's procuratorates at all levels. Meanwhile, the Supreme People's Procuratorate had issued the Opinions on Further Strengthening the Construction of Portal Websites of Procuratorial Organs and other institutional documents, and made use of informatization to promote the openness of procuratorial affairs, especially the organic combined the openness of procuratorial affairs and online case handling and online service, thereby making continuous progress and forming a positive interaction between different mechanisms.

6.3.2 *Initially Forming a Synergy Through Multiple Channels*

The practice of promoting the openness of procuratorial affairs with the help of new media is noteworthy. On the basis of the comprehensive opening of Weibo and WeChat accounts by the procuratorates covered by the assessment, other platforms of openness had surfaced. For example, more and more procuratorates had opened procuratorial accounts in *Toutiao*, which had become a new channel for the openness of procuratorial affairs. Meanwhile, the functions of new media, such as openness and service, had become increasingly rich. For example, the WeChat official account of the People's Procuratorate of Baotou City in Inner Mongolia Autonomous Region (bt-jcy) integrated a number of columns on the openness of procuratorial affairs and interactive columns, with such functions as online tip-off, online complaint, case information disclosure, and access to archives of the crime of offering bribes, thus providing a convenient new channel for the public to obtain procuratorial information and even handle their affairs online. Such practices had become increasingly widespread.

The websites of procuratorates were well connected with new platforms such as Weibo and WeChat. Against the background of full coverage of Weibo and

[5] See the Report on the Comprehensive Deepening of Judicial Reform by People's Procuratorates—Submitted by the Supreme People's Procuratorate to the 30th Meeting of the Standing Committee of the 12th National People's Congress on November 1, 2017. Available at: http://www.spp.gov.cn/zdgz/201711/t20171102_204.013.shtml, last visited on December 24, 2017.

[6] See the Report of the People's Procuratorate of Jiujiang City on Promoting Judicial Openness, available at: http://www.jxjjrd.gov.cn/dyxc/201705/t20170526_1729652.htm, last visited date on December 23, 2017.

WeChat accounts of procuratorates, more and more procuratorial organs were attaching importance to the connection both in form and in content between the openness through traditional portal websites and the openness through new media. 28 provincial-level procuratorates and 30 procuratorates of larger cities, or 90.32% and 61.22% of the totals respectively, provided Weibo links or QR codes on their own web portals through which users could log in to the official Weibo accounts of the procuratorates; and 27 provincial-level procuratorates and 28 procuratorates of larger cities, or 87.10% and 57.14% of the totals respectively, provided WeChat QR code on their own portal websites which enabled users to scan and log in to the WeChat official accounts of the procuratorates by mobile phone. Through the above measures, a diversified and multi-level procuratorial information disclosure pattern with both concentration and division of disclosure had taken shape and the communication power, guiding power, influence and credibility of the openness of procuratorial affairs had been significantly improved.

6.3.3 Increasing the Convenience of Information Access

The search function has gradually become the standard of websites of procuratorates. Search engines of websites play an important role in the public's rapid access to procuratorial information. The assessment shows that 25 provincial-level procuratorates and 29 procuratorates of larger cities, or 80.65% and 59.18% of the totals respectively, provided retrieval functions that had been proven to be effective; among them, 6 provincial-level procuratorates and 13 procuratorates of larger cities, or 19.35% and 26.53% of the totals respectively, provided advanced retrieval functions.

Remarkable achievements had been made in the centralized and unified openness. On the one hand, since the launching of the national unified platform for the openness of procuratorial affairs, the functions of this platform had become increasingly diversified, and the effect of the centralized disclosure was obvious. After more than three years of operation of the Online Case Information Disclosure Platform of People's Procuratorates (http://www.ajxxgk.jcy.gov.cn) since its launching in 2014, the contents of centralized disclosure had become increasingly rich, and information updates had been timely on this platform. With respect to the disclosure of legal documents, this platform currently classifies the documents into such categories as indictments, protests, non-prosecution decisions, criminal petition re-examination decisions, and other legal documents.[7] With respect to information about important cases, the information was divided into duty crime cases, hot criminal cases, typical cases and other cases. Another important discovery in the 2017 annual assessment was that the platforms for the access to archives of the crime of offering bribes were

[7] It should be pointed out here that, by the end of the 2017 assessment, although classifications had been made of the case information on the website, many categories still contained no information. Against the background that the construction of the framework of the platform has basically completed, local procuratorial organs should be more active in filling in the contents of the platform as soon as possible, and move towards institutionalized and normalized operation of the system.

gradually centralized. The homepage of the website of the Supreme People's Procuratorate provides the icon of "Access to archives of the crime of offering bribes". By clicking on this icon, one can find not only work introductions, work instructions and workflows, but also relevant laws and administrative regulations, information releases, work trends and industry trends, as well as an "Inquiry Navigation" column, which integrates links to platforms or special web pages on the access to archives of the crime of offering bribes in Sichuan Province, Hunan Province, Guangdong Province, Inner Mongolia Autonomous Region, and Shandong Province. On the other hand, relatively centralized openness of local procuratorial affairs has become a common practice of many procuratorial organs. A typical example is the portal website of the People's Procuratorate of Heilongjiang Province, which provides links to "Provincial Procuratorial Weibo Group", "Provincial Procuratorial WeChat Group" and "Provincial Procuratorial News Client Group" on its homepage, thereby not only enriching the content of the openness of procuratorial affairs and producing a matrix cluster effect but also facilitating the inquiry and utilization by the public. For another example, the People's Procuratorate of Qinghai Province disclosed the departmental budgetary expenditures of procuratorial organs at three levels in the province and summarized them into a table, which is convenient for browsing, comparison, and social supervision.[8]

Press conferences had become more and more common. The assessment of portal websites shows that 17 provincial-level procuratorates and 15 procuratorates of larger cities, or 54.84% and 30.61% of the totals respectively, had held press conferences since January 1, 2017. Two provincial-level procuratorates and three procuratorates of larger cities, or 6.45% and 6.12% of the totals respectively, disclosed complete information, including pictures, texts and videos, about the press conferences they had held. Among them, the Procuratorate of Shandong Province put the complete video recordings of press conferences on its portal website.[9] This kind of video disclosure is highly intuitive and live, and retains the contents and details of press conferences in an original way. As such, it will become one of the important directions of development of the openness of procuratorial affairs in the future.

Floating windows could be closed. Floating windows on websites can serve as reminders. However, if they cannot be closed, they will hinder browsing and be disliked by users. The assessment shows that 9 provincial-level procuratorates and 5 procuratorates of larger cities, or 29.03% and 10.20% of the totals respectively, had floating windows that could be closed on their web portals; no provincial-level procuratorates and only 3 procuratorates of larger cities had floating windows that could not be closed on their portal websites. This shows that, in the utilization of floating windows, the mainstream practice of procuratorates at all levels had been

[8] See the Annex to Explanations of Departmental Budgets of Procuratorial Organs in the Whole Province in 2016: Table of Departmental Budgets of Procuratorial Organs in the Whole Province. XLS, http://www.qh.jcy.gov.cn/jwgk/308.jhtml, last visited on December 25, 2017.

[9] For example, "Press Conference on Juvenile Procuratorial Work of Procuratorial Organs in Shandong Province in 2017", http://www.sdjcy.gov.cn/html/2017/xwfb_0808/15775.html, last visited on December 22, 2017.

trying to give full play to their role of attracting the audience's attention while not hindering the normal browsing and access to information by users.

6.3.4 *Diversifying the Openness of Legal Documents*

By the end of the assessment, 38 procuratorates of larger cities, or 77.55% of the total, had disclosed indictment documents on their own portals or information disclosure platforms. On the basis of the increasing popularization of disclosure of indictments, the disclosure of other legal documents had also been normalized. 10 procuratorates of larger cities, or 20.41% of the total, disclosed protest documents on their own portal websites or information disclosure platforms; 27 procuratorates of larger cities, or 55.10% of the total, disclosed decisions on the re-examination of criminal petitions on their own portal websites or information disclosure platforms.[10] Moreover, the People's Procuratorate of Beijing Municipality also normalized the disclosure of information about victims' rights and obligations.[11] Obviously, on the premise of not involving confidentiality, this practice of continuously and actively disclosing all kinds of procuratorial documents on the Internet deserves attention and popularization.

6.3.5 *Extending the Function of Openness of Procuratorial Affairs*

Some procuratorates had strengthened the online service function through the openness of procuratorial affairs. With respect to the access to archives of the crime of offering bribes, 20 provincial-level procuratorates and 30 procuratorates of larger cities, or 64.52% and 61.22% of the totals respectively, provided inquiry guides or links to inquiry platforms and contact information. During the assessment period, although the main section of the website of the People's Procuratorate of Shenzhen City could not be opened due to website revision, the column "Access to Archives of the Crime of Offering Bribes" still could be opened, not only disclosing the office addresses and telephone numbers of procuratorial organs in the whole city, materials required for the application for the access to archives of the crime of offering bribes, application method and operation tips, result collection method and application for the review of objections but also allowing users to log in to the "System of Application for Access to Archives of the Crime of Offering Bribes of Shenzhen City"

[10] It should be noted that, after the assessment, the Project Team found out that the number of procuratorial organs publishing such legal documents in a concentrated way on information disclosure networks continued to increase.

[11] See the "Public Announcements" column of its website at http://www.bjjc.gov.cn/bjoweb/gsgg/index.jhtml, last visited on 9 December 2017.

by clicking on the "Entrance to the System of Access to Archives of the Crime of Offering Bribes" icon or directly log in to the system and submit the application for online access. Some procuratorates had endeavored to cultivate the rule of law thinking among enterprises and the public and promote the universal observance of law through the openness of procuratorial affairs. The non-public economy is an important engine for reform and innovation, economic growth and employment promotion, and various legal risks faced by non-public enterprises should not be underestimated. For this reason, the People's Procuratorate of Wuxi City in Jiangsu Province published the Guide to the Prevention of Common Legal Problems for Non-public Enterprises,[12] which clarifies the rights and obligations of enterprises themselves and related subjects with respect to production and business operation, contract management, labor and employment, intellectual property rights, and violations of law and crimes, so as to enhance their capacity for carrying out the business operation and defending their rights in accordance with law. The WeChat official account of the People's Procuratorate of Shanghai Municipality provided the function of legal Q&A, which enables users to quickly get the information and guidance they need.

6.3.6 *Making Remarkable Achievements in the Disclosure of Statistics and Reports*

Nineteen provincial-level procuratorates and 14 procuratorates of larger cities, or 61.29% and 28.57% of the totals respectively, published their annual work reports in 2016. Among them, 4 provincial-level procuratorates and 4 procuratorates of larger cities clearly indicated "summary" or similar expressions on their reports. Twenty-one provincial-level procuratorates and 16 procuratorates of larger cities, or 67.74% and 32.65% of the totals respectively, published their work reports in 2015. With respect to the disclosure of budget and final accounts, 26 provincial-level procuratorates and 19 procuratorates of larger cities, or 83.87% and 38.78% of the totals respectively, simultaneously disclosed the budget and final accounts for 2016 and the budget for 2017. Among them, some procuratorates used Excel forms to disclose their budget and final accounts in a deep and systematic way, which is praiseworthy. It is worth mentioning that some procuratorates explored the disclosure of procuratorial data by drawing on the experience of the disclosure of government and court data. For example, the People's Procuratorate of Jiangsu Province published the main data of judicial cases handled by procuratorial organs in the whole province.[13] The People's Procuratorate of Shanghai Municipality published the White Paper on

[12] Guide to the Prevention of Common Legal Problems for Non-public Enterprises, http://www.wuxi.jcy.gov.cn/doc/2017/10/13/1540908.shtml, last visited on December 14, 2017.

[13] Disclosure of Main Data of Judicial Cases Handled by Procuratorial Organs in Jiangsu Province from January to September, 2017 (with Attached Tables), http://www.jsjc.gov.cn/xinwenfabu_34003/201711/t20171108_186775.shtml. Last visited on December 25, 2017.

Financial Procuratorial Work in Shanghai every year, which systematically analyzed financial crime cases. This kind of data disclosure will lay the foundation for the application of big data, and should be paid attention to and promoted in a timely manner.

6.3.7 Achieving Remarkable Results in Barrier-Free Access to Information

It is estimated that currently there are more than 85.02 million people with disability in China, of which 12.63 million have visual disabilities.[14] Therefore, strengthening the construction of barrier-free portal websites of procuratorial organs plays a positive role in eliminating the digital divide, better safeguarding the rights of people with disabilities and other special groups to know and participate, and enabling them to enjoy social fairness and justice, and has become an important symbol of civilization in modern society. In recent years, some procuratorial organs have attached importance to the barrier-free construction and transformation of portal websites, and this practice deserves attention and promotion. The website of the People's Procuratorate of Hainan Province provides its own voice prompt system, which is convenient for blind and amblyopia people to get and use the information they need, thereby taking a solid step toward barrier-free information accessibility. The portal website of the People's Procuratorate of Guangdong Province has made a big step forward toward barrier-free information accessibility by providing such auxiliary functions as "big-character screen display", "tools for the elderly", "screen reading" and "tools for the blind people" on its homepage and other webpages, and set up corresponding shortcut keys, thus providing great convenience for groups with physical dysfunction to obtain procuratorial information.

6.4 Existing Problems and Shortcomings

After years of development, the achievements in openness of procuratorial affairs need to be reviewed and summarized, but attention should also be paid to the existing problems, especially some chronic problems that have existed for many years, common problems that widely exist in many regions, and stagnation and even retrogression in certain fields.

First, the phenomenon of nonfeasance in the openness of procuratorial affairs was prominent among some procuratorates. (1) The construction of portal websites

[14] See "The total number of disabled people in China at the end of 2010 and the number of people with various disabilities and various levels of disability", in the portal website of China Disabled Persons' Federation, http://www.cdpf.org.cn/sjzx/cjrgk/201206/t20120626_387581.html, last visited on December 24, 2017.

had still not been popularized. Against the background that Weibo and WeChat had achieved full coverage, many procuratorates still had not set up their own websites or their websites were still inaccessible, which showed that local procuratorial organs had not attached sufficient importance to the work of website construction. Among them, the website of the People's Procuratorate of Xining City in Qinghai Province had remained inaccessible for two consecutive years.[15] (2) The websites of some procuratorates lacked necessary maintenance. The assessment shows that the web portals of many procuratorates, including those of Anshan City in Liaoning Province and Handan City in Hebei Province, were rudimentary and provided little information. The phenomenon of empty columns in portal websites still existed to varying degrees. For example, the column "Introduction to the Leaders of the Procuratorate" on the portal website of the People's Procuratorate of Xi'an City in Shaanxi Province had been empty for two consecutive years in 2016 and 2017.

Second, lack of continuity in openness. The openness of procuratorial affairs is like a boat sailing against the current: it will be pushed backward if it does not move forward. Procuratorial work involves a large number of activities and their results, the information of which needs to be continuously disclosed, or disclosed at regular intervals. Take the disclosure of budget, final accounts and "budgetary expenditures related to three kinds of official spending" as an example. Such information should be continuously disclosed on an annual basis. The assessment shows, that under strong supervision, the disclosure of this information was once popularized, but became stagnated or even regressed in recent years. Although procuratorates of Hebei Province, Changchun City, and Jilin Province disclosed the information in previous years, they did not do so in 2016 and 2017. The contents of "Legal Documents" and "Work Report" columns on the website of the People's Procuratorate of Gansu Province had not been updated since 2014. The "Legal Consultation" column on the website of the People's Procuratorate of Lanzhou City in Gansu Province was last updated on January 1, 2012. The latest piece of information disclosed in the "Notices and Announcements" column on the website of the People's Procuratorate of Jilin City in Jilin Province was "Final Accounts of Various Departments under the People's Procuratorate of Jilin City in 2015", which was posted in September 2016, and the column had not been updated since then.[16]

There were similar problems in the online disclosure of work reports by people's procuratorates of Jilin Province, Hubei Province and Beijing Municipality. The standards on the docketing of cases, rights and obligations, and instructions disclosed on the website of the People's Procuratorate of Hangzhou City in Zhejiang Province were posted in 2005[17] and had obviously already become obsolete.

---

[15] In 2017, although the website of the People's Procuratorate of Qinghai Province (http://www.qh.jcy.gov.cn/) provided on its homepage a link to the website of the People's Procuratorate of Xining City, the link was actually not to the website of the People's Procuratorate of Xining City, but to the homepage of the website of the People's Procuratorate of Qinghai Province itself.

[16] Homepage—Notices and Announcements, http://www.jilin.jcy.gov.cn/tzgg/, last visited on 14 December 2017.

[17] http://www.hzjcy.gov.cn/website/directorycontent.aspx? SEL = 786, last visit on December 14, 2017.

Third, the disclosure of the basic information about procuratorates was still not timely. (1) The disclosure of institutional structure had not kept up with actual changes. Disclosing information about the institutional structure and functions of procuratorial organs is the most basic content of the openness of procuratorial affairs, but the performance of assessment targets in this aspect of work in 2017 was unsatisfactory. The assessment shows that only three provincial-level procuratorates and five procuratorates of larger cities, or 9.68% and 10.20% of the totals respectively, provided complete information about their setup of departments, division of functions and contact telephone numbers. (2) No substantial breakthrough had been made in the disclosure of personnel information. In sharp contrast to the comprehensive disclosure of judges' information by courts, the disclosure of procurators' information had not yet been popularized. Only four provincial-level procuratorates and one people's procuratorate of larger city, or 12.90% and 2.04% of the totals respectively, provided complete information about the names, positions, responsibilities, educational background and work experience of their leaders. Among them, the People's Procuratorate of Inner Mongolia Autonomous Region did an especially good job. Eight provincial-level procuratorates and ten people's procuratorates of larger cities, or 25.81% and 20.41% of the totals respectively, provided partial or complete information about the names, positions, responsibilities, and educational background of procurators.[18] Among them, the People's Procuratorate of Jiangsu Province announced the persons in charge and the personnel of the various departments under it, and specially indicated procurators that had entered the quota system.

Fourthly, the disclosure of guides to procuratorial affairs was far from meeting the demand. As the "compulsory exercises" of openness of procuratorial affairs, the publication of guides to procuratorial affairs should be given priority and widely carried out. However, the results of the assessment of this work are not satisfactory. (1) The assessment score of the guide to procuratorial affairs section was far lower than the average level. Statistical analysis of the assessment results shows that only the People's Procuratorate of Jiangsu Province, the Supreme People's Procuratorate, the People's Procuratorate of Shanghai Municipality, the People's Procuratorate of Shandong Province, the People's Procuratorate of Nanjing City, the People's Procuratorate of Anhui Province and the People's Procuratorate of Jilin Province scored higher than 60 points in this section of the assessment, which was far lower than the average total score. (2) Many procuratorates still had not fully disclosed their guides to procuratorial affairs. For example, 11 provincial-level procuratorates and 31 procuratorates of larger cities, or 35.48% and 63.27% of the totals respectively, did not disclose the guide to criminal petition on their web portals, 15 provincial-level procuratorates and 32 procuratorates of larger cities, or 48.39% and 65.31% of the totals respectively, did not disclose the guide to civil and administrative petitions on their web portals, and 26 provincial-level procuratorates and 44 procuratorates of

[18] It should be noted here that none of the procuratorial organs covered by the assessment had disclosed the complete information about the names and tenure of all procurators. Therefore, the Project Team lowered the standard in the assessment, so that those disclosed part of above information about procurators were counted. Even so, the assessment results were still not optimistic.

larger cities, or 83.87% and 89.80% of the totals respectively, did not disclose the guide to procuratorial work at prisons and reformatories. (3) The disclosed guides were not updated in a timely manner. A basic requirement for the openness of procuratorial affairs is to revise and improve the guide to procuratorial affairs and the list of procuratorial powers and responsibilities in a timely manner with the promulgation and revision of relevant laws and policies, so as to enable the parties and the public to understand the operational mode of public power and their own rights and obligations. In the field of openness of government affairs, a dynamic adjustment mechanism for the list of powers and responsibilities of government agencies had been generally established. In contrast, the dynamic updating of guides to procuratorial affairs was far from being popularized. With the implementation of the Decision on Amending the Civil Procedure Law of the People's Republic of China and the Administrative Procedure Law of the People's Republic of China on July 1, 2017, civil public interest litigation and administrative public interest litigation have become important duties of procuratorates at all levels. The Supreme People's Procuratorate held a press conference on "fully implementing the system of institution of public interest litigation by procuratorial organs and protecting national interests and public interests from infringement in accordance with law" on June 30, 2017, and the Supreme People's Procuratorate also formulated and issued the Opinions on Issues Related to Deepening the Pilot Work of Public Interest Litigation in 2016. However, the disclosure of information about public interest litigation by local procuratorates was not satisfactory. The assessment shows that only five provincial-level procuratorates and three procuratorates of larger cities, or 16.13% and 6.12% of the totals respectively, published the latest guides to public interest litigation in accordance with the revised law in 2017. A noteworthy phenomenon here was that some procuratorates were able to update in a timely manner news reports and publicity materials on their websites, but not guides to procuratorial affairs. Still take public interest litigation as an example. Although many procuratorates claimed in their publicity materials that they had attached importance to and promoted public interest litigation, most of them failed to update their guides to procuratorial affairs on their websites in a timely manner. If they had failed to even disclose and update in a timely manner the information about public interest litigation work, their implementation effect of this work was questionable. Obviously, this had a negative impact on the implementation and functioning of the newly introduced legal system.

Fifthly, the user-friendliness of the openness of procuratorial affairs needed to be improved. Take the publication of guides to procuratorial affairs as an example. Although many assessment targets had published the guides, the guides they published were not user-friendly, namely, they were not convenient for users to get, understand and apply. The manifestations of this problem included: First, the lack of necessary classification. Most of them were just a simple list of different kinds of information without any classification. Although some classified the content of their guides, the setup of the columns on their websites needed to be improved. For example, although the People's Procuratorate of Wuxi City in Jiangsu Province published the Online Notice of Litigation Rights and Obligations of Victims of Crimes, the notice was placed in the column of "Special Focus" and mixed with other news and publicity materials. For another example, the so-called "Legal Consultation" column on the website of the People's Procuratorate of Lanzhou City in Gansu Province contained a hotch-potch of information, including judicial interpretation documents, news reports and typical cases, without a clear positioning.[19] Second, the lack of integrity. For example, the column of "Inquiry about Laws and Regulations" on the website of the People's Procuratorate of Jilin Province consisted of two sections: "Judicial Interpretations" and "Rules and Regulations".[20] However, the contents of the column was seriously incomplete and the laws formulated by the National People's Congress and its Standing Committee and the administrative regulations formulated by the State Council were nowhere to be found. Third, the lack of readability. The contents of the guides published by many procuratorial organs were directly copied from legal documents. Although they had no problem in terms of preciseness, they are difficult for the general public to understand. Fourth, the lack of interactivity. Providing information through online platform consultation is an important channel of the openness of government affairs and judicial openness and it is also conducive to the development of interactive and demand-oriented openness. Among the assessment targets, 10 provincial-level procuratorates and 19 procuratorates of larger cities, or 32.26% and 38.78% of the totals respectively, had established an effective online consultation platform. Fifth, the lack of unity. In terms of external portal websites, two provincial-level procuratorates and the people's procuratorate of one larger city still had two or more portal websites, without indicating which one was new and which one was old. It should be made clear here that portal websites, as the primary and authoritative online openness platforms, should be unique. In terms of information disclosure by new media, the problem of lack of synchronization and consistency among multiple platforms had also emerged. For example, the People's Procuratorate of Anhui Province opened two Weibo platforms, but only its Sina Weibo (https://weibo.com/anhuijiancha) was updated in time, while its Tencent Weibo (http://e.t.qq.com/anhuijiancha) was relatively lagging behind in updating.

Sixthly, the stability of the platform of openness had become a prominent problem. During the assessment in 2017, the portal websites of the people's procuratorates of Qinghai Province, Hangzhou City, Zhejiang Province, Luoyang City, Henan Province, Guangzhou City, Guangdong Province, etc., had shown such problems as page failure and temporary website failure. This may be related to the fact that some leaders of procuratorates focused too much attention on new openness platforms such as Weibo, WeChat and client-side, while ignoring the construction of portal websites, or the compatibility and security of website construction.

Seventhly, the problem of a serious imbalance in the development of procuratorial openness. (1) Imbalance in content. For example, the people's procuratorates of Taiyuan City, Shanxi Province, Tangshan City, and Hebei Province still focused

---

[19] People's Procuratorate of Lanzhou City in Gansu Province >> Legal Consultation >> Channel Home Page, http://www.lzsrmjcy.gov.cn/html/list_1240.html, last visited on December 14, 2017.

[20] See "Home Page >> Sunshine Procuratorial Affairs >> Convenience Service >> Inquiry about Laws and Regulations", http://www.jl.jcy.gov.cn/ygjw/bmfw/flfgcx/, last visited on December 14, 2017.

on news and publicity information, while not attaching enough importance to the disclosure of information that the public are more concerned about, such as guides to the handling of affairs, and notices of rights and obligations. (2) Imbalance in the types of disclosed documents. More attention needs to be paid to the disclosure of such procuratorial legal documents as sentencing recommendations, procuratorial suggestions and procuratorial opinions. The root cause of this problem was the common phenomenon of valuing procuratorial work over disclosure of procuratorial information. The investigation of some procuratorates by the Project Team also shows that the focus of grass-roots procuratorates was often on public prosecution, supervision over investigation, arrest approval and other procuratorial work, and the openness of procuratorial affairs was often not paid enough attention to, and far from being institutionalized and normalized.

6.5 Prospects and Suggestions

For a long time, procuratorates, as state organs with a strong "mystique" color, have been little known by ordinary people. At present, when the openness of legislative, government, judicial and police affairs has become a common practice, the mystique of procuratorates still lingers. In order to meet the needs of rights protection and in view of the problems identified in the assessment, China needs to deepen the openness of procuratorial affairs by being demand-oriented, strengthening interactive response, continuously expanding procuratorial functions, and paying attention to the following aspects of the work.

Comprehensive disclosure. (1) The publication of guides to procuratorial affairs should be strengthened. Through the unified arrangement of the Central Government and the strong promotion by the Supreme People's Procuratorate, China has achieved unprecedented results in the openness of procuratorial affairs, such as the disclosure of procuratorial legal documents and information about the investigation of major cases. However, it should also be noted that the disclosure of the guides to and instructions on procuratorial work is lagging behind. In the future, China should pay more attention to the comprehensive and balanced advancement of openness of procuratorial affairs. Against the background of comprehensive law-based state governance, especially with the advancement of judicial reform and the reform of the national supervision system, the revision of a series of laws such as the Organic Law of People's Procuratorates and the Procurator Law will be put on the agenda of the Chinese legislature. Therefore, it is necessary for procuratorates to make advance preparations, adjust the functions, guides and procedures as soon as possible before the revision of the laws, and disclose the relevant information on their websites as soon as the laws come into effect. (2) On the premise of not violating the confidentiality requirements of national laws and administrative regulations, methods of routine disclosure of procuratorial legal documents such as sentencing recommendations, procuratorial suggestions and procuratorial opinions need to be actively explored and a corresponding system should be established. (3) The publication of statistics and data should become the focus of the openness of procuratorial affairs. Against the background of the deepening of big data application and the generalization and normalization of disclosure of procuratorial documents, the disclosure of relevant statistics should begin as soon as possible, so as to better serve the judicial reform and the needs of enterprises and citizens.

Integrating channels of openness at various levels to form a synergy. (1) Attention should be paid to the function of procuratorate portal websites as the primary platform of openness. We should be soberly aware that, although the openness on new media platforms has the advantages of easy access and strong communication, the fundamental importance of portal websites should not be underestimated. First of all, we should ensure that the portal websites are smoothly accessible at any time and place 24 h a day. Procuratorates at all levels should enhance their awareness of the importance of website construction, clarify the main responsibility for portal website construction and management, strengthen cooperation with departments responsible for cyberspace administration, industrial information technology, public security, protection of state secrets and other relevant departments, intensify the construction of technical facilities, improve the daily monitoring mechanism, identify and solve the outstanding problems in their own portal website and those of lower-level procuratorates in a timely manner, and strive to ensure the stability of the carriers of platforms of openness. (2) Important and formal procuratorial information should be disclosed through multiple channels. It is necessary to highlight the advantages of portal websites, such as authority and formality, and give full play to their orientation and tone-setting functions. Meanwhile, efforts should be made in giving full play to the role of WeChat and Weibo in posting, publicizing and interpreting the information released on portal websites, and in the demassified and objectified transmission, so as to combine different platforms to form a synergy and maximize the effect, transmissibility and influence of openness. (3) Procuratorial organs at different levels should have different emphases in the openness of procuratorial affairs. For example, laws and regulations, judicial documents and service guides at the general level can be uniformly disclosed by provincial-level procuratorates; people's procuratorates of cities divided into districts and counties and districts are responsible for the openness of procuratorial affairs with local characteristics and particularities, such as information about the changes in organizational structure, office location and contact information resulting from procuratorial reform. This is conducive to ensuring not only the unified implementation of legal supervision but also the rapid access to localized and personalized procuratorial information by the public. Take the disclosure of information about major cases for another example. In addition to the centralized platform of the Supreme People's Procuratorate, it is more appropriate for local procuratorates at various levels to make targeted disclosure on their own websites, so as to highlight local characteristics and local demands. The People's Procuratorate of Shandong Province has set up the "Authoritative Release" column on its website, and clearly marked "taking out tigers" or "swatting flies" in the title of each piece of information, thereby not only enhancing the vividness and readability of the contents of the column but also distinguished its function from that of "Information about Important Cases" column on the Online Case Information

Disclosure Platform of People's Procuratorates, as well as enhancing the deterrent effect on crimes.

Embedding the openness of procuratorial affairs into the work process of procuratorial organs. The assessment in many consecutive years shows that some procuratorial organs that have started early and achieved outstanding results in the openness of procuratorial affairs in the past have failed to make continuous progress in recent years. The reason behind this phenomenon is that the openness of procuratorial affairs is a time-consuming and laborious work. If it relies only on the importance attached to it by a certain leader, then the work will inevitably suffer when the leader leaves his post, or no longer attaches importance to the work. The openness of procuratorial affairs outside the scope of traditional procuratorial work is inevitably considered by the leaders and business departments of procuratorates as something that increases the workload and aggravates the dilemma of insufficient personnel. The way out of this dilemma is to draw on the successful experience of openness of government and judicial affairs and embed the openness of procuratorial affairs into the daily work process of procuratorial organs. Take cases of civil and administrative petitions as an example. The decision on whether or not to disclose the relevant legal documents online should be taken as an essential link in the handling of such cases. Before making the decision of not to disclose such documents, the staff should submit the matter to the leaders of relevant organs for approval. This is conducive not only to the implementation of the concept of "taking openness as the norm and non-openness as the exception", but also to the institutionalization and normalization of openness of procuratorial affairs.

Building the capacity for barrier-free information services. According to the requirements of the Law on the Protection of Disabled Persons and the Regulations on the Construction of Barrier-free Environment, procuratorial organs should take the lead to build the capacity for barrier-free services on websites, and carry out the barrier-free transformation of such openness platforms as web portals, Weibo, WeChat, clients, etc., so as to create a barrier-free service environment on online platforms, and enable special groups such as the disabled and the elderly to obtain procuratorial information in a convenient and speedy way.

Chapter 7
Report on Indices of Procuratorial Transparency in China (2018)—From the Perspective of Information Disclosure on the Websites of Procuratorates

Innovation Project Team on the Rule of Law Index

Abstract In 2018, the Innovation Project Team on Rule of Law Indices of Institute of Law of Chinese Academy of Social Sciences, on the basis of the previous six consecutive years' assessment, fine-tuned the assessment indices, and carried out a quantitative assessment of the openness of procuratorial affairs of the Supreme People's Procuratorate, the procuratorates of 31 provinces, autonomous regions and municipalities directly under the Central government, and the procuratorates of 49 larger cities by taking information disclosure on portal websites as the mainline. In 2018, procuratorates in China had achieved remarkable results in the openness of procuratorial affairs, normalizing the disclosure of case information and legal documents and becoming increasingly skillful in the use of new media. Some procuratorates in the central and western regions distinguished themselves with outstanding performance, and many bright spots emerged in the exploration of providing convenience to the people and benefiting enterprises. Meanwhile, the problems existing in the openness of procuratorial affairs should not be underestimated. Meanwhile, some assessment targets had failed to make any new progress in their work, a unified standard had not yet been adopted for the de-identification of documents, some website platforms were unstable, and the problem of unbalanced development of procuratorial work was still prominent. China is still faced with the tough task of developing procuratorial work in depth and width.

Leaders of the Project Team: Tian He, a research fellow at CASS Law Institute and the director of the Center for Studies of National Indices of the Rule of Law, Chinese Academy of Social Sciences, and Lv Yanbin, a research fellow at and the head of the Department of Survey and Study of National Situation of the Rule of Law of the Institute of Law, Chinese Academy of Social Sciences. Other members of the Project Team include: Wang Xiaomei, Wang Yiming, Liu Yanpeng, Liu Ying, Li Tong, Wu Haomin, Song Junjie, Zhang Xiyue, Hu Changming, Li Yanjie, and Guo Shasha. Authors of this report: Li Yanjie, an associate research fellow at Institute of Law, Chinese Academy of Social Sciences, Tian He, and Lv Yanbing. Li Tong, Guo Shasha and Zhang Xiyue participated in the writing of some parts of this report.

Innovation Project Team on the Rule of Law Index (✉)
Institute of Law, Chinese Academy of Social Sciences, Beijing, China
e-mail: 13263169197@163.com

H. Tian et al. (eds.), *Report on the Rule of Law Index in China 2*,
Research Series on the Chinese Dream and China's Development Path,
https://doi.org/10.1007/978-981-19-9597-2_7

Keywords The openness of procuratorial affairs · Portal website · Quantitative assessment

In 2018, the Innovation Project Team on Rule of Law Indices of the Law Institute of Chinese Academy of Social Sciences (hereinafter referred to as the "Project Team") carried out the assessment of the transparency of procuratorial work in China for the seventh consecutive year.

7.1 An Overview of the Assessment

In the assessment of procuratorial transparency in 2018, the Project Team, based on the practice in the past six years, continued to use the assessment index system of 2017, but made additions and deletions to grade III and grade IV indices, and corresponding adjustments to the weights of relevant indices. The assessment targets were also the same as those since 2013, including the Supreme People's Procuratorate, the procuratorates of 31 provinces, autonomous regions and municipalities directly under the Central Government, and 49 procuratorates of larger cities. The explorations of the openness of procuratorial affairs made some procuratorates not covered by the assessment were also mentioned in the report, but not used in the calculation of scores or in the ranking of assessment results.

Firstly, the assessment indices were still divided into four sections: basic information, guides to procuratorial affairs, procuratorial activities and statistics and reports (see Table 7.1).

Secondly, with regard to the specific assessment indices and assessment methods, considering that the disclosure of legal documents on the Online Case Information Disclosure Platform of People's Procuratorates had gradually become normalized, in this year's assessment, the Project Team had taken the Online Case Information Disclosure Platform of People's Procuratorates as the main source and the portal websites of procuratorates covered by the assessment as the supplement sources of legal documents.

Thirdly, the specific assessment indices and their weights had been appropriately adjusted in light of the revision and improvement of relevant laws, the development of openness of procuratorial affairs in 2017 and the pre-assessment. With respect to the disclosure of indictments and important case information that had already become a common practice of procuratorates, its weight was moderately reduced, and more importance was attached to the disclosure of other types of documents. In view of the fact that the disclosure of work reports was increasingly becoming a required routine, the assessment of the disclosure of special reports and white papers was introduced and the weight of statistics on the disclosure of documents was moderately increased. At the level of law, the Constitution, the Organic Law of the People's Procuratorates and the Criminal Procedure Law were revised and the Supervision Law was passed in 2018. Moreover, the Procurator Law was in the process of being revised, and the

Table 7.1 Assessment index system for procuratorial transparency in China (2018)

Grade I indices	Grade II indices
1. Basic information (20%)	1.1 Setup of websites (20%)
	1.2 Micro-platform clients (30%)
	1.3 Institutional structure (20%)
	1.4 Personnel information (30%)
2. Guide to procuratorial affairs (30%)	2.1 Workflow (8%)
	2.2 Instructions on rights and obligations (60%)
	2.3 Online consultation platforms (8%)
	2.4 Public interest litigation (16%)
	2.5 Press conferences (8%)
3. Procuratorial activities (30%)	3.1 Legal documents (70%)
	3.2 Examination of petitions (20%)
	3.3 Information about major cases (10%)
4. Statistics and reports (20%)	4.1 Procuratorial report (40%)
	4.2 Financial information (40%)
	4.3 Document statistics (20%)

revision and improvement of relevant laws had brought new opportunities and challenges to the openness of procuratorial affairs. In particular, on October 26, 2018, the Standing Committee of the National People's Congress passed a decision on amending the Criminal Procedure Law, which improves the systems of and mechanisms for procuratorial proposals, sentencing recommendations, and imposition of lenient punishments on those confessing to their crimes and accepting punishments. These new developments became important indices for measuring the openness of procuratorial affairs, especially the openness of guides to procuratorial affairs.

At the level of judicial interpretation, the Supreme People's Court and the Supreme People's Procuratorate jointly issued Interpretation on Several Issues concerning the Application of Law in Cases Relating to Procuratorial Public Interest Litigation in February 2018. Article 13 of the Interpretation clearly stipulates that where a procuratorial organ decides to file civil public interest litigation, it should make a public announcement in accordance with law. Where, after the expiration of the public announcement period, the organ prescribed by law or the relevant organization does not file a lawsuit, a people's procuratorate may file a lawsuit with a people's court. This pre-litigation announcement procedure has also raised new requirements for the openness of procuratorial affairs.

With respect to data acquisition channels, the Project Team still took portal websites of procuratorates as the main channel, supplemented by Weibo and WeChat.

The assessment time was from October 15th to December 1st, 2018. Information released online and practices and explorations made by assessment targets after the expiration of the assessment period were mentioned in the report, but not used in the calculation of assessment scores.

7.2 General Situation

In 2018, the Supreme People's Procuratorate and local procuratorates attached high importance to the openness of procuratorial affairs, and openness had increasingly become the consensus of procuratorates at all levels. A landmark event was the issuance in July 2018 by the Supreme People's Procuratorate of the Action Guide to Smart Procuratorial Work in China (2018–2020), which clarifies the development direction of procuratorial informatization and proposes to make procuratorial work more scientific, intelligent and people-oriented. This will provide more stable and advanced technical support and more possibilities for adopting new methods and making new achievements in the openness of procuratorial affairs. For example, the establishment and improvement of procuratorial knowledge bases, case bases and document bases provides more convenience in the access to procuratorial information. In 2018, the Supreme People's Procuratorate mentioned the openness of procuratorial affairs in several procuratorial documents. In the Opinions on Giving Full Play to Procuratorial Functions to Provide Judicial Guarantee for Winning the "Three Critical Battles", issued by the Supreme People's Procuratorate in June 2018, it is stated that procuratorates should turn "the handling of judicial cases into a vivid classroom for popularizing law", "carefully select and timely publish typical cases in the fields of finance, poverty alleviation and environmental protection with high social concern, with accurate application of laws, a good grasp of policies and good case handling effect, and make full use of newspapers, radio, television, portal websites, WeChat, Weibo, news clients and other platforms to publicize and interpret the principles, policies and relevant laws and administrative regulations relating to the 'Three Critical Battles'". The Notice on Maximizing Functions and Roles of Procuratorates to Create a Rule-of-Law Environment for the Protection of the Lawful Rights and Interests of Entrepreneurs and Support the Innovation and Entrepreneurship of Entrepreneurs points out that "Media publicity platforms shall be made full use to promptly publicize procuratorates' working arrangements, measures, progress and effect, analyze cases of infringement on property rights, and summarize and publicize good practices, experiences and cases of effectively protecting property rights in accordance with the law." As a result, legal documents, major cases and typical cases in these fields have become new growth points of openness of procuratorial affairs.

In June 2018, the physical hall of 12,309 Procuratorial Service Center was officially launched. The 12,309 Procuratorial Service Center consists of an online platform (website: www.12309.gov.cn/) and a physical hall. The public can obtain the "one-stop service" provided by procuratorates at all levels through web portals, service hotlines and mobile terminals. The Report of the Supreme People's Procuratorate on Strengthening Legal Supervision over Civil Litigation and Enforcement Activities by People's Procuratorates specifically mentions "continuing to deepen judicial openness" as an important measure for enhancing social awareness and influence of procuratorial work.[1]

The 2018 assessment shows that 31 provincial-level procuratorates and 49 procuratorates of larger cities all had opened their own portal websites, and all of these websites were accessible.[2] This was a qualitative leap compared with the situation in 2012 when the first assessment was carried out and even with that in 2017. However, it should also be pointed out that during the assessment and verification period, the web portals of several procuratorates of larger cities, such as that of Ningbo City in Zhejiang Province, had been inaccessible for several days or even a longer period of time.

The top ten in the ranking of all assessment targets in the 2018 assessment of procuratorial transparency were the People's Procuratorate of Anhui Province, the People's Procuratorate of Jiangsu Province, the People's Procuratorate of Changsha City, the Supreme People's Procuratorate, the People's Procuratorate of Jiangxi Province, the People's Procuratorate of Hunan Province, the People's Procuratorate of Guangdong Province, the People's Procuratorate of Baotou City, the People's Procuratorate of Hebei Province and the People's Procuratorate of Tianjin Municipality; the top five in the ranking of provincial-level procuratorates were the People's Procuratorate of Anhui Province, the People's Procuratorate of Jiangsu Province, the People's Procuratorate of Jiangxi Province, the People's Procuratorate of Hunan Province, and the People's Procuratorate of Guangdong Province; and the top five in the ranking of procuratorates of larger cities were the People's Procuratorate of Changsha City, the People's Procuratorate of Baotou City, the People's Procuratorate of Xiamen City, the People's Procuratorate of Tangshan City and the People's Procuratorate of Hefei City.

Generally speaking, the websites of provincial-level procuratorates were slightly better than those of procuratorates of larger cities, with richer content and more exquisite and user-friendly page design. The websites of some procuratorates had strong customizability and relatively user-friendly interfaces. For example, the official website of the People's Procuratorate of Hubei Province had adopted the barrier-free reading mode, which enables the users to select their own font size and color of display. Some websites actively responded to the call for the transformation of the functions of procuratorates by setting up public interest litigation columns, while

[1] See the Report of the Supreme People's Procuratorate on Strengthening Legal Supervision over Civil Litigation and Enforcement Activities by People's Procuratorates, delivered by Mr. Zhang Jun, the Procurator-General of the Supreme People's Procuratorate, at the sixth meeting of the Standing Committee of the 13th National People's Congress on October 24, 2018.

[2] Among them, the People's Procuratorate of Shaanxi Province also had an old version of its website (website: www.sn.jcy.gov.cn:8084/), which was marked with "old version", at the time of assessment.

others set up case interpretation columns to interpret laws with real cases, supplemented by videos or animation; and the websites of most procuratorates provided links to the 12,309 Center for Procuratorial Affairs (Table 7.2).

7.3 Achievements and Innovations

The assessment results show that, in 2018, China had achieved some results in the openness of procuratorial affairs, including the continued implementation of the "compulsory exercises" required by the Central Government and innovations and explorations of "optional exercises" by local procuratorates, and had been deepening the openness of the procuratorial system day by day.

7.3.1 Significant Progress Had Been Made in the Disclosure of Basic Information

With respect to the disclosure of institutional information, 7 provincial-level procuratorates and 12 procuratorates of larger cities, or 22.58% and 24.49% of the totals respectively, provided complete information about the setup, functions and contact telephone numbers of various departments under them; 23 provincial-level procuratorates and 30 procuratorates of larger cities, or 74.19% and 61.22% of the totals respectively, provided part of such information. The reason for this result is that most of the assessment targets failed to provide complete information, especially contact telephone numbers of the departments under them, which was closely related to their understanding of openness. Once this bottleneck of understanding is broken through, the complete disclosure of departmental information will be rapidly popularized.

Outstanding results had also been achieved in the disclosure of personnel information. With respect to the disclosure of information about leaders of procuratorates, 29 provincial-level procuratorates and 42 procuratorates of larger cities, or 93.55% and 85.71% of the totals respectively, provided all or part of the information about the names, positions, scope of responsibility, educational background and work experience of their leaders; 10 provincial-level procuratorates and 28 procuratorates of larger cities, or 32.26% and 57.14% of the totals respectively, provided part of or all information about the names, tenure and identity of their procurators. The practices of some procuratorates were more eye-catching. For example, the People's Procuratorate of Jiangsu Province disclosed the information about the organizational structure and personnel information, including department responsibilities, names and administrative rankings of staff members, personnel quota, department contact telephone numbers, etc., together in one column of its website. For another example, the People's Procuratorate of Haikou City had set up two sub-columns,

Table 7.2 Results of assessment of procuratorial transparency indices in China (2018) (full score: 100 points)

Ranking	Procuratorates	Total score	Basic information	Guide to procuratorial affairs	Procuratorial activities	Statistics and reports
1	The People's Procuratorate of Anhui Province	78.80	100.00	76.00	60.00	90.00
2	The People's Procuratorate of Jiangsu Province	78.00	100.00	70.00	60.00	95.00
3	The People's Procuratorate of Changsha City	76.60	79.00	70.00	86.00	70.00
4	The Supreme People's Procuratorate	70.60	65.00	72.00	60.00	90.00
5	The People's Procuratorate of Jiangxi Province	69.80	97.00	48.00	60.00	90.00
6	The People's Procuratorate of Hunan Province	68.50	65.00	65.00	60.00	90.00
7	The People's Procuratorate of Guangdong Province	68.00	87.00	62.00	60.00	70.00
8	The People's Procuratorate of Baotou City	67.20	87.00	54.00	52.00	90.00
9	The People's Procuratorate of Hebei Province	66.90	77.00	65.00	80.00	40.00
10	The People's Procuratorate of Tianjin Municipality	66.10	77.00	49.00	60.00	90.00
11	The People's Procuratorate of Xiamen City	65.70	65.00	65.00	64.00	70.00

(continued)

Table 7.2 (continued)

Ranking	Procuratorates	Total score	Basic information	Guide to procuratorial affairs	Procuratorial activities	Statistics and reports
11	The People's Procuratorate of Tangshan City	65.70	66.00	57.00	78.00	60.00
13	The People's Procuratorate of Hefei City	65.40	82.00	56.00	64.00	65.00
14	The People's Procuratorate of Changchun City	64.10	77.00	45.00	64.00	80.00
15	The People's Procuratorate of Shantou City	63.90	62.00	69.00	56.00	70.00
16	The People's Procuratorate of Nanjing City	63.60	90.00	50.00	42.00	90.00
17	The People's Procuratorate of Fujian Province	63.30	77.00	53.00	60.00	70.00
17	The People's Procuratorate of Zhejiang Province	63.30	75.00	41.00	60.00	90.00
19	The People's Procuratorate of Shanxi Province	63.10	42.00	59.08	0.00	65.00
20	The People's Procuratorate of Wuxi City	62.90	75.00	49.00	64.00	70.00
21	The People's Procuratorate of Inner Mongolia Autonomous Region	62.10	62.00	59.00	60.00	70.00
22	The People's Procuratorate of Chengdu City	62.00	80.00	58.00	52.00	65.00

(continued)

Table 7.2 (continued)

Ranking	Procuratorates	Total score	Basic information	Guide to procuratorial affairs	Procuratorial activities	Statistics and reports
23	The People's Procuratorate of Beijing Municipality	61.90	77.00	67.00	40.00	72.00
24	The People's Procuratorate of Datong City	61.70	52.00	59.00	52.00	90.00
25	The People's Procuratorate of Xinjiang Uygur Autonomous Region	61.50	77.00	67.00	40.00	70.00
26	The People's Procuratorate of Hangzhou City	61.10	82.00	47.00	42.00	90.00
27	The People's Procuratorate of Hainan Province	61.00	97.00	42.00	50.00	70.00
28	The People's Procuratorate of Henan Province	60.90	74.00	47.00	60.00	70.00
29	The People's Procuratorate of Harbin City	60.70	67.00	57.00	54.00	70.00
30	The People's Procuratorate of Ningxia Hui Autonomous Region	60.50	54.00	59.00	60.00	70.00
31	The People's Procuratorate of Hohhot City	60.40	67.00	46.00	54.00	85.00
32	The People's Procuratorate of Xuzhou City	60.10	65.00	45.00	52.00	90.00

(continued)

Table 7.2 (continued)

Ranking	Procuratorates	Total score	Basic information	Guide to procuratorial affairs	Procuratorial activities	Statistics and reports
33	The People's Procuratorate of Jilin Province	59.40	67.00	52.00	60.00	62.00
34	The People's Procuratorate of Shanghai Municipality	59.20	77.00	68.00	30.00	72.00
35	The People's Procuratorate of Chongqing Municipality	58.70	61.00	55.00	60.00	60.00
36	The People's Procuratorate of Hubei Province	58.40	67.00	42.00	60.00	72.00
37	The People's Procuratorate of Shijiazhuang City	58.10	72.00	37.00	64.00	67.00
38	The People's Procuratorate of Shandong Province	57.90	62.00	45.00	60.00	70.00
39	The People's Procuratorate of Jilin City	57.50	62.00	45.00	52.00	80.00
39	The People's Procuratorate of Lanzhou City	57.50	57.00	43.00	64.00	70.00
39	The People's Procuratorate of Guangzhou City	57.50	72.00	45.00	52.00	70.00
42	The People's Procuratorate of Zhengzhou City	56.40	65.00	46.00	52.00	70.00

(continued)

Table 7.2 (continued)

Ranking	Procuratorates	Total score	Basic information	Guide to procuratorial affairs	Procuratorial activities	Statistics and reports
43	The People's Procuratorate of Huainan City	56.30	77.00	41.00	52.00	65.00
44	The People's Procuratorate of Nanchang City	55.70	72.00	47.00	64.00	40.00
45	The People's Procuratorate of Luoyang City	55.50	57.00	45.00	52.00	75.00
46	The People's Procuratorate of Shenzhen City	55.20	39.00	44.00	64.00	75.00
47	The People's Procuratorate of Dalian City	54.90	62.00	43.00	52.00	70.00
48	The People's Procuratorate of Guangxi Zhuang Autonomous Region	54.20	67.00	36.00	60.00	60.00
49	The People's Procuratorate of Suzhou City	53.70	75.00	17.00	52.00	90.00
50	The People's Procuratorate of Handan City	53.60	77.00	32.00	42.00	80.00
51	The People's Procuratorate of Guiyang City	53.50	72.00	35.00	52.00	65.00
52	The People's Procuratorate of Sichuan Province	53.40	67.00	50.00	60.00	35.00
53	The People's Procuratorate of Haikou City	53.00	54.00	40.00	54.00	70.00

(continued)

Table 7.2 (continued)

Ranking	Procuratorates	Total score	Basic information	Guide to procuratorial affairs	Procuratorial activities	Statistics and reports
54	The People's Procuratorate of Liaoning Province	52.60	65.00	32.00	60.00	60.00
54	The People's Procuratorate of Zhuhai City	52.60	57.00	32.00	52.00	80.00
56	The People's Procuratorate of Shaanxi Province	52.30	52.00	13.00	80.00	70.00
57	The People's Procuratorate of Heilongjiang Province	51.90	48.00	41.00	60.00	60.00
58	The People's Procuratorate of Ningbo City	51.40	54.00	42.00	52.00	62.00
59	The People's Procuratorate of Gansu Province	51.20	57.00	36.00	60.00	55.00
60	The People's Procuratorate of Benxi City	51.00	69.00	32.00	52.00	60.00
61	The People's Procuratorate of Yinchuan City	50.90	69.00	45.00	52.00	40.00
62	The People's Procuratorate of Jinan City	50.40	61.00	42.00	52.00	50.00
63	The People's Procuratorate of Shenyang City	50.30	67.00	21.00	62.00	60.00
64	The People's Procuratorate of Fuzhou City	49.90	67.00	23.00	52.00	70.00
65	The People's Procuratorate of Xi'an City	49.80	52.00	46.00	52.00	50.00

(continued)

Table 7.2 (continued)

Ranking	Procuratorates	Total score	Basic information	Guide to procuratorial affairs	Procuratorial activities	Statistics and reports
66	The People's Procuratorate of Zibo City	47.90	54.00	35.00	42.00	70.00
67	The People's Procuratorate of Qiqihar City	46.20	47.00	22.00	54.00	70.00
68	The People's Procuratorate of Taiyuan City	45.80	22.00	36.00	64.00	57.00
69	The People's Procuratorate of Guizhou Province	44.90	67.00	45.00	20.00	60.00
70	The People's Procuratorate of Nanning City	44.20	42.00	34.00	42.00	65.00
71	The People's Procuratorate of Fushun City	43.70	39.00	21.00	64.00	52.00
72	The People's Procuratorate of Anshan City	43.20	65.00	22.00	52.00	40.00
73	The People's Procuratorate of Yunnan Province	39.10	64.00	21.00	60.00	10.00
74	The People's Procuratorate of Qinghai Province	38.30	32.00	13.00	60.00	50.00
75	The People's Procuratorate of Wuhan City	37.00	57.00	30.00	42.00	20.00
76	The People's Procuratorate of Qingdao City	35.90	44.00	25.00	52.00	20.00

(continued)

Table 7.2 (continued)

Ranking	Procuratorates	Total score	Basic information	Guide to procuratorial affairs	Procuratorial activities	Statistics and reports
77	The People's Procuratorate of Tibet Autonomous Region	35.40	62.00	30.00	30.00	25.00
78	The People's Procuratorate of Urumqi City	34.10	37.00	17.00	52.00	30.00
79	The People's Procuratorate of Kunming City	29.90	26.00	17.00	52.00	20.00
80	The People's Procuratorate of Lhasa City	24.40	47.00	18.00	32.00	0.00
81	The People's Procuratorate of Xining City	18.10	14.00	9.00	42.00	0.00

Unit: points

"Brief Introductions to Leaders of the Procuratorate" and "Information about Procurators", under the column of "Openness of Procuratorial Affairs" on its website. The former discloses the complete information about each leader of the procuratorate, including name, gender, date of birth, native place, educational background, date of starting work, current position, ranking and responsibilities, while the latter discloses the basic information about ordinary procurators in the procuratorate. Moreover, the People's Procuratorate of Haikou City also disclosed the names, positions and rankings of the heads of various departments within the procuratorate in the column of "Organizational Structure". The People's Procuratorate of Henan Province disclosed the information about leaders of the procuratorate, members of the procuratorial committee, quota-based procurators, people's supervisors, special procurators and other personnel in different categories. The Supreme People's Procuratorate also disclosed the information about candidates for legal interns.

7.3.2 The Disclosure of Case Information Had Been Developing Towards Normalization

Since the Procuratorial Case Information Disclosure System (www.ajxxgk.jcy.gov.cn/) was put into operation in 2014, case information such as case-handling process, case handling results, legal documents and service channels have been uniformly disclosed on this platform, which has become an important window platform for the openness of procuratorial affairs, facilitating and even satisfying the need for the exercise of the right to know, the right of supervision and litigation rights of the general public, parties and their agents and defenders.

The popularization of disclosure of information about major cases. 30 provincial-level procuratorates and 48 procuratorates of larger cities, accounting for 96.77% and 97.96% of the totals respectively, disclosed information about major cases through their portal websites or the Procuratorial Case Information Disclosure System. Now the question had changed from whether the information about major cases should be disclosed or not to whether the disclosure of such information should be normalized and how effective the disclosure of such information is.

The disclosure of legal documents had increasingly become a "compulsory exercise". On the one hand, disclosing indictments had gradually become a common practice among procuratorates; on the other hand, the disclosure of such procuratorial documents as non-prosecution decisions and criminal petition reexamination decisions had become more and more common. With regard to the disclosure of criminal petition reexamination decisions, 27 provincial-level procuratorates and 37 procuratorates of larger cities, accounting for 87.10% and 75.51% of the totals respectively, published criminal petition reexamination decisions through their own web portals or the Procuratorial Case Information Disclosure System. Obviously, the publication of criminal petition reexamination decisions had gradually developed from the practice of some individual procuratorates to an extensive and normalized practice of most procuratorates. The reason for this was that, on the one hand, the Supreme People's Procuratorate published the procuratorial opinion on the Nie Shubin Case and the criminal petition reexamination decision on the Lin XX Case on the Procuratorial Case Information Disclosure Network, thereby setting a good example of disclosing legal documents for procuratorates at all levels. On the other hand, in the "Disclosure of Legal Documents" column of the Procuratorial Case Information Disclosure Network, legal documents were classified into protests, non-prosecution decisions and criminal petition reexamination decisions, and this practice had played an important role in promoting openness.[3]

7.3.3 *Remarkable Results Have Been Achieved in the Openness Through New Media*

The results of the 2018 assessment show that all the assessment targets had not only achieved full coverage of official Weibo and WeChat accounts and client-sides

[3] However, it should also be noted that a sub-column of "Other Legal Documents" was set up under the "Disclosure of Legal Documents" column of the Procuratorial Case Information Disclosure Network, but the Project Team found that, by the end of the assessment, this sub-column contained no information about most assessment targets.

but also made great progress in the seamless connection between new media and traditional portal websites. 30 provincial-level procuratorates and 42 procuratorates of larger cities, accounting for 96.77% and 85.71% of the totals respectively, provided links to or QR codes of their official Weibo accounts on the homepages of their official websites. 27 provincial-level procuratorates and 40 procuratorates of larger cities, accounting for 87.10% and 81.63% of the totals respectively, provided links to or QR codes of their WeChat official accounts on the homepages of their official websites. The assessment results also show that the assessment targets had made a qualitative leap in the updating rate of their official Weibo accounts and the expansion of the functions of their WeChat official accounts. The Project Team used the newly revised Organic Law of People's Procuratorates, adopted on October 26, 2018, to test the rate of updating of the official Weibo and WeChat accounts of procuratorates, and found out that, by the end of October 2018, 29 provincial-level procuratorates and 42 procuratorates of larger cities, accounting for 93.55% and 85.71% of the totals respectively, had posted the relevant provisions, interpretations or news reports of the newly revised law in their official Weibo accounts; 28 provincial-level procuratorates and 22 procuratorates of larger cities, accounting for 90.32% and 44.90% of the totals respectively, provided consultation through their WeChat official accounts; and 17 provincial-level procuratorates and 20 procuratorates of larger cities, accounting for 54.84% and 40.82% of the totals respectively, allowed the public to handle some procuratorial business through their WeChat official accounts.

7.3.4 *The Openness of Data and Reports Was Effective*

In 2018, procuratorates in China achieved commendable results in the publication of their work reports. 29 provincial-level procuratorates and 37 procuratorates of larger cities, accounting for 93.55% and 75.51% of the totals respectively, had set up a work report columns or similar columns with corresponding contents on their websites; 28 provincial-level procuratorates and 38 procuratorates of larger cities, accounting for 90.32% and 77.55% of the totals respectively, published their annual reports on procuratorial work in 2017 on their websites. Moreover, since 2017, the People's Procuratorate of Jiangsu Province had been publishing the Announcements of the People's Procuratorate of Jiangsu Province on its portal website, covering such information as institutional norms, important documents, reference cases, appointments and dismissals, etc., thereby greatly enhancing the seriousness and authority of the openness of procuratorial affairs.

The People's Procuratorate of Jiangsu Province and the People's Procuratorate of Xuzhou City in Jiangsu Province had set up special columns of "Disclosure of Case Handling Data" on their websites.[4] The contents of the columns included "Disclosure of Main Case Handling Data", which was updated on a quarterly basis, and

[4] http://xz.jsjc.gov.cn/jianwu/baxiang/, last visited on 26 December 2018.

"Disclosure of Discipline Inspection, Supervision and Procuratorial Data", which was updated on an annual basis. This was a valuable step forwards in data openness.

In May 2018, the Procuratorate of Guangdong Province issued the White Paper on Juvenile Procuratorial Work in Guangdong Province, which used a series of statistical data to show the changes in the situation of juvenile delinquency and the protection of juvenile rights and interests in the province. In December 2018, the People's Procuratorate Hunan Province held a press conference on the White Paper on Procuratorial Public Interest Litigation and released the White Paper on Procuratorial Public Interest Litigation in Hunan Province, which made statistical analysis on the collection of clues, filing of cases, procuratorial suggestions, public interest litigation, court judgments and effects of procuratorates in Hunan Province. This was of positive significance to the deepening of public interest litigation by procuratorates.

The openness of financial budgets had gradually become a common practice. 28 provincial-level procuratorates and 40 procuratorates of larger cities, accounting for 90.32% and 81.63% of the totals respectively, disclosed their budgets in 2018 before the end of the assessment period; 27 provincial-level procuratorates and 40 procuratorates of larger cities, accounting for 87.10% and 81.63% of the totals respectively, disclosed their final accounts in 2018 before the end of the assessment period; and 27 provincial-level procuratorates and 40 procuratorates of larger cities disclosed their budgetary expenditures related to "three kinds of official spending" (official overseas visits, official vehicles, and official hospitality) in 2018. Today, it has become the normal practice for procuratorates to disclose their budgets and final accounts and their budgetary expenditures related to "three kinds of official spending", while non-disclosure of such information has become an exception.

7.3.5 The Performance of Some Procuratorates in Central and Western Provinces Was Eye-Catching

Generally speaking, the level of openness of procuratorial affairs in economically developed coastal cities was much higher than that in economically underdeveloped areas and border areas. For example, the official website of the People's Procuratorate of Xining City in Qinghai Province was a mere ornament, without disclosing any information. However, some procuratorates in the central and western regions had made rapid progress in the openness of procuratorial affairs. For example, the procuratorates of Anhui Province, Jiangxi Province, Hunan Province, Hebei Province, Tianjin Municipality, Changsha City, Hunan Province, Baotou City, Inner Mongolia Autonomous Region had achieved good results in their overall performance or in some fields and some indices. On the whole, the People's Procuratorate of Anhui Province won the championship and became the biggest "dark horse" in the assessment. As far as the section indices are concerned, the portal website of Handan People's Procuratorate had set up a personnel information column, which disclosed in an Excel table the complete information about each procurator in the procuratorate, including the name, gender, date of birth, administrative post and tenure, legal post and time of appointment, place of birth and other information, thereby making a big step forward in personnel information disclosure.

7.3.6 Active Explorations Had Been Made into the Convenience and User-Friendliness of Websites

The retrieval function had become more and more common. Among the 31 provincial-level procuratorates, 27, or 87.10% of the total, provided retrieval functions that had been proven to be effective on their websites; and among the 49 procuratorates of larger cities, 41, or 83.67% of the total, provided retrieval functions that had been proven to be effective on their websites. Among them, the retrieval functions provided by the Supreme People's Procuratorate and the People's Procuratorate of Jiangsu Province allow users to select search location, set time and other elements for screening, select sorting method, and provide relevant "intelligent recommendations", which was great progress compared with those in the past. What's more worth mentioning is that, after the assessment, the Project Team found out that the web portals of more procuratorates provided new retrieval functions.

Intensive openness had developed in width and depth. The Supreme People's Procuratorate had opened the 12,309 Procuratorial Service Center, which is a unified and comprehensive external public service network platform of procuratorates across the country. By combining four channels, namely the 12,309 Platform (www.12309.gov.cn/), the 12,309 procuratorial service hotline, the 12,309 mobile client-side mobile app and the 12,309 WeChat official account, it integrates the functions of procuratorial service, the openness of procuratorial affairs, supervision and consultation, and provides one-stop service to people from all sectors of society.

Attention had been paid to facilitating public use in the openness of procuratorial affairs. (1) Gradually standardizing the expressions of titles of legal documents. In the beginning, it was common for legal documents to take "Indictment (Applicable to Cases of Crimes Committed by Natural Persons) (Public Edition)" as the title, which did not provide readers with relevant information, and was not conducive to the access and use by the public. By 2018, it became more and more common for legal documents to provide such information as defendants and causes of action. (2) Disclosing document templates to facilitate their use. For example, the People's Procuratorate of Shaanxi Province provided templates of such legal documents as indictments, protests, criminal indictments with incidental civil action, and petitions in civil administrative cases, which can guide the public to write their own legal documents. (3) Placing information of public concern in a conspicuous position. For example, the Procuratorial Network of Jiangsu Province put "The Guide to Procuratorial Affairs" in the first column on the homepage of its website, and divided its contents into "Procuratorial Instructions" and "Case Handling Process", so as to facilitate the search and use by the public.

Significant achievements had been made in information barrier-free construction. In 2018, many procuratorates carried out whole or partial information accessibility reconstruction of their portal websites. Among them, the procuratorates of Xuzhou City and Nanjing City in Jiangsu Province provide the functions of "listening to the news" and "magnifying glass" on their portal websites in the form of text and icons in conspicuous positions, so as to facilitate the access to information by visually impaired people. The People's Procuratorate of Anhui Province set up a "barrier-free website" and a barrier-free client-side at the same time. The former provides convenience for users by such means as sound, speech pacing, reading, color matching, increase or reduction of font size, large subtitles and screen reading, while the latter can be installed and used by clicking on the "Install" button.

Press conference has become an important method of openness. Two or three years ago, holding a press conference to publicize procuratorial affairs was considered a good performance by a procuratorate in the openness of procuratorial affairs. Until 2017, only two provincial-level procuratorates and three procuratorates of larger cities disclosed the contents of press conferences in a complete and comprehensive manner by means of pictures and texts.[5] The 2018 assessment shows that 25 provincial-level procuratorates and 18 procuratorates of larger cities, or 80.65% and 36.73% of the totals respectively, disclosed information about press conferences in a complete and comprehensive manner, indicating that the disclosure of information about press conferences had become a common practice of procuratorates throughout the country. Moreover, procuratorates in Jiangsu Province, Anhui Province and some other regions released press conference notices in advance on their websites, which played a positive role in keeping the public informed about press conferences and improving the effect of press conferences.

7.4 Problems and Prospects

After many years of implementation, procuratorial reform will inevitably enter the deep-water area and encounter bottlenecks in terms of idea, inertia and institution. Some problems in the openness of procuratorial affairs have not been solved for many years, and the deep-seated causes and even the "genetic factors" behind them are worth exploring. Only by solving these problems can the openness of procuratorial affairs be steadily advanced and new breakthroughs and new achievements made in a new era.

[5] See "Report on Indices of Procuratorial Transparency in China (2017)", in *Development Report on the Rule of Law in China No.16 (2018)*, Beijing: Social Science Academic Press, 2018.

7.4.1 There Are Prominent Problems in Some Fields that Urgently Need to Be Solved

Neither provincial-level procuratorates nor people's procuratorates of larger cities had done a satisfactory job in the disclosure of personnel information in the basic information column of their websites and in the convenience of their WeChat official accounts. Especially, they performed poorly in the disclosure of basic information about the procuratorate not because they were unable to do the job well, but because they had not made an effort to do the job well. Compared with courts, which had generally disclosed the complete information about judges and quota-based judges on the Internet, procuratorates still needed to strengthen the disclosure of information about procurators. The retrieval function provided by the websites of some procuratorates was totally useless. For example, no matter what keywords were used in the site search on the website of the People's Procuratorate of Yunnan Province, the search results were always exactly the same.

With respect to the disclosure of procuratorial legal documents, the disclosure of sentencing recommendations, procuratorial proposals, procuratorial opinions and other types of documents were in serious stagnation, and few relevant legal documents had been disclosed. The disclosure of advance notices and results of public examination of criminal petitions had basically not yet started.

The development of openness of procuratorial affairs had been hindered by self-restriction. The Procuratorate of Dongcheng District of Beijing Municipality submitted to the court a legal document of sentencing recommendation in as early as 1999. The sentencing recommendation system began to be fully implemented in Beijing in 2008, and, with the issuance of the Opinions on Several Issues Concerning the Regulation of Sentencing Procedures (for Trial Implementation) in 2010, began to be implemented on a trial basis in the whole country, and gradually became a part of China's criminal justice system. Therefore, on the one hand, the disclosure of sentencing recommendations is not directly prohibited by law; on the other hand, against the background of increasing popularization and normalization of disclosure of indictments, protests, non-prosecution decisions and criminal petition reexamination decisions, it is logical and natural to explore the disclosure of sentencing recommendations. However, some procuratorates have directly rejected the openness of sentencing recommendations by stating that it does not belong to the scope of openness of case documents, thereby preventing lower-level procuratorates from making their own explorations in this field.

To solve this problem, it is necessary to emancipate the mind, carry out top-level design and institutional implementation of openness of procuratorial affairs in the new era in accordance with the principle of "taking openness as the norm and non-openness as the exception" and the idea of negative list.

7.4.2 The User-Friendliness and Convenience of Openness of Procuratorial Affairs Need to Be Improved

After the content of openness of procuratorial affairs has been greatly improved, the issue of how to improve the effect of the disclosed content and enhance the friendliness of user experience and convenience of information acquisition has quickly been put on the table.

The chaotic placement of website contents has become a prominent problem. The basic requirements of openness of procuratorial affairs include the diversity of contents, classification of website contents into different sections, and consistency between the name and content of each section. The problem of chaotic placement of website contents was very prominent when the assessment of procuratorial transparency was first carried out six years ago and remained so in the 2018 assessment. For example, the "Organizational Structure of the Procuratorate" sub-column is placed in the "Introduction to the Procuratorate" column, the "Openness of Procuratorial Affairs" column, or the "Basic Information" column of the websites of different procuratorates. The "Personnel Information" column on the websites of some procuratorates actually contains institutional information, such as organization structure, responsibilities and contact information. Some procuratorates have set up columns on specific topics on their websites, but these columns are empty, and their contents are put in other columns. As a result, although some information has been disclosed online, they are very difficult to find because of misplacement.

The websites of some procuratorates have floating windows that cannot be closed, which hinders the browsing by users. For example, the portal websites of five provincial-level procuratorates and two procuratorates of larger cities still have floating windows that cannot be closed on their homepages. It should be said that floating windows have the advantage of being eye-catching, and bringing specific information to the attention of website visitors, but those that cannot be closed hinder the normal browsing of the website by visitors and prevent them from obtaining other procuratorial information.

Some information is disclosed in uncommon file formats that are inconvenient to use. For example, the budget and final accounts information of some procuratorates is disclosed not in the commonly used pdf or doc format, but in the ceb format, which creates unnecessary difficulties for the public in the access to such information. Moreover, the web portals of some procuratorates require users to register first and then log in before they can use their services, even for the consultation on some simple legal issues, thereby raising the threshold of openness of procuratorial affairs.

Poor readability of disclosed information. For example, the information about major cases disclosed by procuratorates of Susong County in Anhui Province and Fucheng County in Hebei Province is very brief, which does not reflect the importance of such information. As a result, such information has a low page view and fails to achieve the expected effect of disclosure.

Lack of necessary interaction. The WeChat official accounts of some assessment targets provided a "consultation" button. However, after the Project Team clicked on the button and submitted consultation questions, it did not receive any response for several days or even more than ten days.

Procuratorates at all levels should proceed from public demand and constantly push forward the openness of procuratorial affairs in width and depth in light of the need of safeguarding the right to know, the right of participation, the right of expression, and the right of supervision. Special attention should be paid to (1) Raising the intelligence level of site search, and improving the accuracy of search by drawing on the effective search technologies of commercial websites, databases and other fields; (2) Improving the layout and design and reasonably classifying the contents of websites as soon as possible, so as to enable the public to quickly obtain the information they need; (3) Enhancing the readability and transmissibility of openness of procuratorial affairs, respecting and making good use of the law of communication, disclosing information in a way easily acceptable to the people, and organically unifying the openness and publicity of procuratorial affairs; and (4) Drawing on the experience of openness of government affairs and judicial openness, and utilizing technical means to realize the searchability, verifiability and applicability of disclosed procuratorial information.

7.4.3 The Need to Change the Current Situation of Being Stagnant and Doing a Crash Job in the Openness of Procuratorial Affairs and to Move Towards the Normalization of the Work

The openness of procuratorial affairs is like sailing against the current, if you don't advance, you will retreat. Stagnation and doing a crash job have become two common problems of some assessment targets in the openness of procuratorial affairs.

Dynamic updating of website contents needs to be strengthened. The work report column on the websites of some procuratorates has not been updated for a long time. A typical example is that of the People's Procuratorate of Gansu Province: the latest annual work report disclosed in the column was that of 2014. After the revision of the Criminal Procedure Law in October 2018, many procuratorates failed to update such information as the rights and obligations of criminal suspects in their guides to procuratorial affairs in light of the revision of the law. For another example, according to the unified arrangement made by the Supreme People's Procuratorate, procuratorates across the country should stop the inquiry about bribery crime files beginning from August 1, 2018. However, by the end of the assessment, the "Bribery Crime File Inquiry" column was still in a prominent position on the homepages of the websites of many procuratorates, with its content remaining the same, which could easily lead to misunderstanding. After the promulgation of the Supervision Law and the amendment of the Criminal Procedure Law, many assessment targets had not updated the guides to procuratorial affairs accordingly. By the end of the assessment, many of them still had not updated the Criminal Procedure Law or related guides on their websites in accordance with the amendment. This problem also existed in Jiangsu Province, Anhui Province and other provinces where the situation of openness of procuratorial affairs was relatively good.

The phenomenon of doing a crash job in the openness of procuratorial affairs was prominent. For example, the work reports of the People's Procuratorate of Hainan Province from 2012 to 2018 were all disclosed on July 9, 2018, and all the work reports of the People's Procuratorate of Guizhou Province were disclosed on its website on July 10, 2018.

Although the problems of doing a crash job and being stagnation are two different problems in the openness of procuratorial affairs, they are caused by the same deep-seated factor, that is, the lack of necessary mandatory and operable legal basis, technical standards, and reward and punishment mechanism, which leads to short-term actions like passing winds in the openness of procuratorial affairs: a little progress is made in the work every time a push is given by the leaders, and the work becomes stagnant whenever the focus of the leaders is shifted away from it. Whenever a document is issued by higher authorities or the Supreme People's Procuratorate, a crash job is done to implement it; but after a while, the momentum is lost and there is no more sustained motivation to continue the work. In view of this situation, China should consider adopting legislation at the central level, introduce operational unified standards for the openness of judicial documents, strengthen rewards and punishments, and enhance the endogenous driving force of openness of procuratorial affairs.

7.4.4 There Are a Wide Variety of Practices of Openness of Procuratorial Affairs Which Need to Be Standardized and Unified Through Institutional Construction

The development of openness of procuratorial affairs once showed a tendency towards "barbaric growth". The enthusiasm of procuratorates in various regions for exploration had been brought into full play, but after several years of development, problems such as lack of standardization, unity and sustainability had also emerged. There are a wide variety of practices in various parts of the country. A typical example in this respect is the de-identification of information about parties in procuratorial legal documents. In the disclosure of indictments, different procuratorates and even different departments within the same procuratorate have widely divergent practices relating to partial anonymization of the parties and de-identification of their places of origin, current residences, case information and evidence. Take the disclosure of information about major cases for another example. The information released by procuratorates of Nanhai District of Foshan City in Guangdong Province and Xingtai City in Hebei Province on the case information disclosure network has been de-identified; the information released by the procuratorates of Beijing Municipality, Zunyi City in Guizhou Province, and Jilin City in Jilin Province contains the real names of the parties; while the Procuratorate of Jiangsu Province and some other procuratorates do not follow a unified rule, but decide whether or not to de-identify the information in light of the circumstances of each case.

In view of the above problems, China should strengthen the top-level design, and strike a balance between the protection of personal information and the openness of procuratorial affairs and between promoting the publicity of the rule of law and avoiding the spread of crime craft, and adopt a unified standard of openness and de-identification.

7.4.5 *The Lack of Sufficient Embodiment of Local Characteristics and the Need to Ensure that Each Unit Performs Its Own Functions*

Against the background that unified and intensive national platforms, such as the Online Case Information Disclosure Platform of People's Procuratorates and the 12,309 Procuratorial Service Center, are becoming increasingly powerful and functional, the web portals of procuratorates at various levels still have great potential. Take guides to procuratorial affairs for example. The contents, including the workflow of procuratorates (such as the instructions on petitions), in this section of the portal websites of many procuratorates are directly copied from the website or documents of the Supreme People's Procuratorate, which are not specific enough to provide clear guidance for ordinary people. Procuratorates should list in their work flowcharts the specific units responsible for this work in the province or city, rather than giving very general information about relevant units.

The content of portal websites should be updated in time to ensure that people are not misled by outdated website information. Procuratorates should improve the construction of online consultation platforms, reduce unnecessary thresholds and advance procedures for consultation, and respond to relevant consultations in a timely and accurate manner. If the consultation content is general and not confidential in nature, the replies can be made public, so as reduce the consultation workload.

7.4.6 *The Instability of Platforms is a Prominent Problem, and It is Necessary to Strengthen Operation Guarantee and Maintenance Support*

Informatization is the foundation of the modern openness of procuratorial affairs. On the one hand, informatization can greatly facilitate the access to procuratorial information by the public; on the other hand, it can greatly reduce the workload of the staff of procuratorates in the openness of procuratorial affairs. However, the assessment shows that China still has a long way to go in combining procuratorial openness and informatization. For example, the websites of people's procuratorates of Qinghai Province, Ningbo City, Zhuhai City, Chengdu City, and Xining City were not stable enough and could rarely be opened during the assessment verification period. The assessment also shows that the official Weibo and WeChat accounts of some procuratorates could not be opened, which greatly undermined the credibility and authority of these official platforms. To solve this problem, China should, firstly, give full play to the role of portal websites and intensive platforms as the primary platforms of openness of procuratorial affairs, and enhance the functions of information release, responding to public concerns, and handling procuratorial affairs; secondly, attach importance to the communication effect and service effect of openness of procuratorial affairs, promote service through openness, and improve the image and enhance the credibility of procuratorates through openness; and thirdly, strengthen interaction and communication on the basis of openness.

Chapter 8
Report on Indices of Transparency of Police Affairs in China (2017)—From the Perspective of Information Disclosure on the Websites of Public Security Organs

Innovation Project Team on the Rule of Law Index

Abstract In China, the openness of police affairs has the dual attributes of the openness of government affairs and judicial openness, as well as special values in the dimensions of people's livelihood, the rule of law, justice, and honesty. In 2017, the Innovation Project Team on Rule of Law Indices of Law Institute of Chinese Academy of Social Sciences developed the index system of transparency of police affairs in China and carried out an assessment of the openness of police affairs of public security organs of 4 municipalities directly under the Central Government and the capital cities of 27 provinces and autonomous regions from the perspective of information disclosure on the websites of public security organs. The assessment results show that transparency of police affairs has become a benchmark and model of openness of government affairs, which is mainly manifested in the networking and transparency of services, local intensification of openness of police affairs, improvement of openness of institutional information, normalization of openness of budget and final accounts, the obvious trend towards data openness, and gradual scale-openness of administrative penalties. In the future, China should further strengthen personnel openness, improve financial openness, integrate platforms of openness, standardize document openness, and establish big data of police affairs, so as to meet the needs for comprehensively deepening the public security reform.

Leaders of the Project Team: Tian He, a research fellow at CASS Law Institute and the director of the Center for Studies of National Indices of the Rule of Law, Chinese Academy of Social Sciences, and Lv Yanbin, a research fellow at and the head of the Department of Survey and Study of National Situation of the Rule of Law of the Institute of Law, Chinese Academy of Social Sciences. Other members of the Project Team: Wang Xiaomei and Li Yan Yanjie, Hu Changming, Xu Bin, Liu Yanpeng, Wang Yiming, Gao Zhenjuan, Song Shuang etc. Author of this report: Wang Xiaomei, Associate Research Fellow, Institute of Law, Chinese Academy of Social Sciences.

Innovation Project Team on the Rule of Law Index (✉)
Institute of Law, Chinese Academy of Social Sciences, Beijing, China
e-mail: 13263169197@163.com

H. Tian et al. (eds.), *Report on the Rule of Law Index in China 2*,
Research Series on the Chinese Dream and China's Development Path,
https://doi.org/10.1007/978-981-19-9597-2_8

Keywords Transparency of police affairs · Openness of police affairs · Openness of law enforcement · Big data of police affairs

Openness and transparency are the essential requirements and prominent features of modern rule of law. With the implementation of the Regulations on the Disclosure of Government Information since 2008, especially the development of the Internet and information technology and the establishment of the national big data strategy, openness of government affairs, which is highly integrated with informatization, has reached a new level in both breadth and depth, and completed the leap from one-way openness to two-way interaction and from e-government to smart government. In the development process of openness of government affairs, the openness of police affairs was first extended to the whole country. In 1999, the Ministry of Public Security issued the Notice on Implementing the System of Openness of Police Affairs in Public Security Organs in the Whole Country (No. 43 [1999] of the Ministry of Public Security) and made arrangements for the openness of police affairs in the whole country. In the construction of e-government, public security organs have also been the departments that have made the largest investment and achieved the fastest development in informatization. Informatization continuously expands the scope of openness of police affairs, innovates the way of openness, and promotes the transparency of police affairs in all directions.

Public security organs are responsible for not only administrative law enforcement, but also the investigation of criminal cases, so the openness of police affairs has the dual attributes of the openness of government affairs and judicial openness. The Decision of the CPC Central Committee on Major Issues Pertaining to Comprehensively Promoting the Rule of Law, adopted at the Fourth Plenary Session of the 18th Central Committee of the Communist Party of China, clearly stated that China will promote the openness of political and legal affairs, including the openness of trial, the openness of procuratorial affairs, the openness of police affairs and the openness of prison affairs. In order to objectively and accurately measure the openness of police affairs in China, the Innovation Project Team on Rule of Law Indices of Law Institute of Chinese Academy of Social Sciences (hereinafter referred to as the "Project Team") developed the index system of transparency of police affairs in China and selected public security organs at certain levels to conduct the assessment of transparency of police affairs in China from the perspective of website information disclosure.

8.1 The Special Values of Openness of Police Affairs in China

According to the People's Police Law, the people's police consist of police working in public security organs, state security organs, and prisons, as well as judicial police working in people's courts and people's procuratorates. Compared with those of other state organs, the responsibilities of public security organs have the widest coverage and are most representative. The openness of police affairs here only refers to the openness of police affairs of public security organs. Public security organs are the functional departments of the government. The Regulations on the Disclosure of Government Information and other documents on the openness of government affairs issued by the Central Committee of the Communist Party of China and the State Council are all applicable to the openness of police affairs, and the values of the openness of government affairs, such as guaranteeing citizens' right to know, supervising the operation of power and preventing corruption of power, are also applicable to the openness of police affairs. The decision of the Project Team to develop the independent Index System of Transparency of Police Affairs in China in addition to the Index of Transparency of Government Affairs in China is mainly based on the special values of the openness of police affairs in China in the following dimensions.

8.1.1 The People's-Livelihood Dimension of Openness of Police Affairs in China

The function orientation of modern government is to provide public administration and service. Compared with other government functional departments, public security organs have the most extensive functions, which are closely related to the work and life of the people. According to the People's Police Law, the functions of public security organs cover household registration, entry and exit, public security, traffic safety, cyber-security, economic and cultural security, criminal investigation, drug control, security service and fire protection. It can be said that, in China's institutional structure, no organ can have such a profound impact on all aspects of people's lives as public security organs, ranging from national security, public safety and social order at the macro level to individual citizens' travel and accommodation at the micro level. The openness of police affairs requires the people's police to adhere to the principle of openness and bring convenience to the people when providing public administration and services, and to disclose information about the locations and work procedures of police services for the convenience of the people, so as to embody the idea of law enforcement for the people, and better serve and improve people's livelihood.

8.1.2 The Rule-of-Law Dimension of the Openness of Police Affairs in China

Law-based and transparent law enforcement is the objective need of standardizing and perfecting public security law enforcement work and building a law-based public security system. Public security organs not only have extensive powers in such fields as public security, fire control, household registration and traffic management but also can take compulsory and punitive measures that directly affect the personal rights and property rights of citizens. Therefore, public security administrative law enforcement is the key field of law-based government and the epitome of government law enforcement. In a society under the rule of law, the greater the power, the bigger the restriction it will be subject to. Public security organs can have an extensive and profound impact on the rights of citizens, and consequently, they should exercise their powers in strict accordance with law. Police officers are the law enforcement teams that pay the most and sacrifice the most in peacetime and have made great contributions to national security and social stability. However, some public security personnel has been criticized for their crude and rude law enforcement behaviors. In 2016 and 2017, the Lei Yang case in Beijing, the rude law enforcement case in Lanzhou, and the child-throwing law enforcement incident in Shanghai were all related to the irregular law enforcement by public security personnel, which constantly hurts the feeling of the public and pushes the law enforcement of public security organs to the cusp of public opinion. In order to promote the standardization of public security law enforcement, the General Office of the CPC Central Committee and the General Office of the State Council issued the Opinions on Deepening the Standardization of Public Security Law Enforcement in September 2016. To standardize law enforcement, in addition to clarifying law enforcement norms, China should also take openness as the entry point to create "transparent police affairs", disclose the basis, process and results of law enforcement, accept social supervision, and promote standardization through openness, so as to increase legalization of public security law enforcement.

8.1.3 The Judicial Dimension of the Openness of Police Affairs in China

Law enforcement by public security organs includes administrative law enforcement and criminal law enforcement. As far as the criminal investigation is concerned, the openness of police affairs belongs to the category of judicial openness, so it is different from the openness of government affairs in terms of standard and application of law. In judicial practice, even within the scope of judicial openness, compared with procuratorial and adjudicative activities, criminal investigation activities are mostly carried out in secret, so the openness of criminal investigation has a logic different from those of openness of procuratorial affairs and openness of trial. In order to promote the openness and transparency of criminal law enforcement, the Criminal Investigation Department of the Ministry of Public Security issued the Notice on Implementing the Case-handling Openness System on July 26, 2005 (No.1228 [2005] of the Criminal Investigation Department of the Ministry of Public Security), and decided to implement the case-handling openness system in the criminal investigation departments of public security organs throughout the country beginning from August 1, 2005.

On November 25, 2013, the People's Daily published an article entitled Deepening the Reform of the Judicial System, which listed the openness of police affairs as one of the major issues in the reform of the judicial system, and stated that China will continue to promote the openness of police affairs and prison affairs. On February 15, 2015, the Central Committee of the Communist Party of China deliberated on and approved the Framework Opinions on Several Major Issues Concerning Comprehensively Deepening the Public Security Reform, which stated that China will improve the operation mechanism for law enforcement power and push forward the reform of the system of openness police affairs in breadth and depth.

8.1.4 *The Integrity Dimension of the Openness of Police Affairs in China*

Transparency of police affairs and openness of law enforcement are the objective needs of a credible society. At a certain stage of economic and social development, it becomes urgent to build an honest society. Public security law enforcement involves traffic safety, entry and exit, public security, fire protection, and so on. The information about the violations of law and crimes at the disposal of public security organs is an important data source for building a social honesty system. In order to implement the Notice of the State Council on Issuing the Outline of the Plan for Building the Social Credit System (2014–2020) (No. 21 [2014] of the State Council) and the Guiding Opinions of the State Council on Establishing and Improving the System of Joint Incentive for Keeping Faith and Joint Punishment for Losing Faith and Accelerating the Development of Social Honesty (No. 33 [2016] of the State Council), the National Development and Reform Commission, the Ministry of Transport, the Ministry of Public Security, the Civil Aviation Administration of China, and China Railway Corporation jointly issued the Guiding Opinions on Strengthening Credit Construction in the Field of Transportation and Travel (No.10 [2017] of the National Development and Reform Commission) on January 3, 2017, requiring public security and traffic administrative departments to disclose to the public information about persons and enterprises responsible for 13 kinds of serious traffic violations through local news media, web portals and other channels beginning from the Spring Festival travel rush in 2017. The Traffic Management Bureau of the Ministry of Public Security regularly discloses this kind of information through the "122 Transportation Network", and simultaneously on Credit China Network, providing references for financial, insurance, credit and other institutions in the evaluation and determination of relevant qualifications (such as market access, financing credit, determination of insurance rates, tax credit rating and credit rating) of the parties. Linking the serious traffic violation records of citizens and enterprises with personal credit, industry access, financial and insurance interests, etc. is conducive to promoting self-discipline and conscious observance of law by citizens, and the clarification of the subject responsibility for safety, and conscious strengthening of road transport safety management by enterprises. The disclosure of the above information also helps the full development of social supervision, provides real cases for traffic safety publicity and education, and opens up a new path for continuously enhancing the people's awareness of observance of traffic law, safety and public morality. Furthermore, disclosing information about serious traffic violations by citizens and enterprises is one of the important steps to establishing a unified social credit code system based on citizen ID numbers and organization codes of enterprises, and a system linking criminal records with credit. It is conducive to effectively supervising and restraining in accordance with law those who break laws and promises, gives full play to the role of credit punishment, supervision and deterrence, and becomes an inevitable requirement for deepening public security reform in the new era.

8.2 The Index System and Assessment Targets and Methods

Since establishing a scientific and reasonable index system is the precondition of and the key to index assessment, the Project Team, on the basis of a careful review of the relevant legal documents, a full investigation of the actual practices of public security organs in various parts of China as well as those of police in other countries, and extensive solicitation the opinions of the police, lawyers and scholars, developed the index system of transparency of police affairs in China from the perspective of the information needs of the public and the parties and in light of the key issues of the comprehensive police reform.

8.2.1 The Principles of the Design of the Index System

Like those of other rule of law indices, the design of indices of transparency of police affairs in China follows the principles of being based on law, objectivity and neutrality, highlighting key points, and being appropriately proactive.

8.2.1.1 Being Based on Law

The index system of transparency of police affairs in China was designed in strict accordance with the requirements provided for in the Constitution, laws, administrative regulations and rules on the openness of police affairs. The Constitutional provision that "all power belongs to the people" is the logical starting point of openness of all powers, including the openness of police affairs. The process and results of the operation of powers given by people should be open to the people and subject to their supervision. Article 44 of the People's Police Law stipulates that: "The people's policemen, in performing their duties, must conscientiously subject themselves to the supervision by society and citizens. The rules and regulations formulated by the people's police organs that have a direct bearing on the interests of the public shall be made known to the public." The Regulations on the Disclosure of Government Information promulgated in 2008 provide a legal basis for the openness of police affairs. To promote the openness of police affairs, the Ministry of Public Security has successively formulated three normative documents, namely, the Notice on Implementing the System of Openness of Police Affairs in the Whole Country, adopted in 1999, the Notice of the Criminal Investigation Department of the Ministry of Public Security on Implementing the System of Openness of Handling of Cases, adopted in 2005, and the Provisions on Openness of Law Enforcement by Public Security Organs, implemented on January 1, 2013. Among them, the Provisions on Openness of Law Enforcement by Public Security Organs integrate the requirements of openness of law enforcement scattered in some laws, administrative regulations and normative documents, and constitute the direct basis for the design of the index system of transparency of police affairs in China.

8.2.1.2 Objectivity and Neutrality

Different from the usual empirical research by questionnaire survey, the assessment of indices of transparency of police affairs in China does not include a satisfaction questionnaire survey, but emphasizes the objectivity of empirical research through the design of a relatively objective index system. In the design of the index system for the third-party assessment, the Project Team adhered to the principle of objectivity and neutrality, and tried to transform the subjective and arbitrary judgment criteria of "good" and "bad" into objective and operational assessment indices. The design of any index was completely based on such considerations as to whether it conforms to the law and reason and whether it is helpful for the public to obtain information. Once the index system was determined, it allowed members of the Project Team only to make "yes" or "no" judgments, rather than subjective "good" or "bad" judgments, on the assessment items, thereby minimizing their discretionary space.

8.2.1.3 Highlighting the Key Points

As mentioned above, public security organs have very extensive functions. An operable index system cannot cover all these functions, but can only set up indices on some selected key fields or aspects that are closest to the people's lives. For the first annual assessment of indices of transparency of police affairs in China, the design of assessment indices follows the principle of starting with the easier tasks before moving on to the more difficult ones, and constantly adjusting and enriching the assessment content with the progress of assessment year by year. In 2017, the index system of transparency of police affairs in China focused on three functions: household registration, entry and exit administration, and traffic safety administration.

8.2.1.4 Being Appropriately Proactive

The design of the index system embodied the principle of basing on the present situation and being appropriately proactive. The index system must not only reflect the actual situation of public security organs in promoting the transparency of police affairs, but also point out the future direction of openness of police affairs through investigation and assessment, and provide countermeasures and suggestions for public security organs to further improve the transparency of police affairs. Of course, the guiding indices consisted only a small part of the index system, and their weights were also low.

8.2.2 The Construction and Interpretation of the Index System

According to the provisions of the Notice on Implementing the System of Openness of Police Affairs in Public Security Organs in the Whole Country, promulgated in 1999, the law enforcement case handling and administrative work of public security organs should be open to the public, except for those that cannot be made public according to laws and administrative regulations. In view of the fact that public security organs are not only government functional departments that provide public administration and services, but also law enforcement agencies, the Project Team set up indices of transparency of police affairs in two dimensions: service and law enforcement. In addition, basic information about personnel, finance and materials involved in the provision of services and enforcement of law should also be disclosed to the public. Generally speaking, the index system of transparency of police affairs in China consists of three grade I indices: "disclosure of basic information", "openness of service" and "openness of law enforcement" (see Table 8.1).

8.2.2.1 Disclosure of Basic Information

Basic information mainly refers to the functions, institutional structure, personnel, finance, and material resources of public security organs. Five grade II indices had been set up under the index of disclosure of basic information: "website construction", "functional structure", "personnel information", "financial information" and "annual report or work summaries".

"Website construction" mainly assesses the friendliness of websites, that is, whether there is a floating window on the homepage. Floating windows are set up to remind visitors to pay attention to a certain piece of information, but they often interfere with webpage reading, and the reminders of important information can be placed at the top of the webpage for rolling display.

Table 8.1 Index system of transparency of police affairs in China (2017)

Grade I indices and their weights	Grade II indices and their weights
Disclosure of basic information (40%)	Website construction (10%)
	Functional structure (30%)
	Personnel information (20%)
	Financial information (20%)
	Annual report or work summaries (20%)
Openness of service (20%)	Household registration service (40%)
	Traffic control services (30%)
	Entry and exit services (30%)
Openness of law enforcement (40%)	Case inquiry (30%)
	Openness of documents (40%)
	Release of information about major cases (10%)
	Police notification (10%)
	Supervision and complaint (10%)

The index of "functional structure" aims to enable the public to know the responsibilities and institutional setup of public security organs, including the responsibilities of public security organs, the rights and obligations of the people's police, internal structure and functions, window units, police substations, etc. Although, compared with other institutions, public security organs are no strangers to the public–people of all ages know that they can ask the police for help when they encounter difficulties, few people really know the functions of public security organs. Therefore, it is necessary to publicize the functions and structure of public security organs and the powers of the police, and disclose the contact information of window units and police stations for the convenience of the people. The Provisions on Openness of Law Enforcement by Public Security Organs also provide for clear requirements on openness.

In addition to the disclosure of institutional information, disclosure of personnel information is also an important part of the disclosure of basic information. Questions such as what kind of people are leading the police force, how many police officers are providing services, and what the quality structure of law enforcement personnel is are all related to the quality of service and law enforcement. There are three grade III indices under the index of "personnel information": "leadership information", "number of police officers" and "police structure", among which "leadership information" assesses the disclosure of information such as the name, position, responsibilities, work experience and educational background of leaders of public security organs.

The index of "financial information" mainly assesses the disclosure of information about the budget and final accounts, budgetary expenditures related to official overseas visits, official vehicles, and official hospitality, salaries and allowances of police officers, and fines and other fees collected by public security organs. After years of practice of openness of government affairs, the disclosure of budget and final accounts and budgetary expenditures related to official overseas visits, official vehicles, and official hospitality has become a consensus of society. In contrast, the disclosure of the income of public officials is still a forbidden zone. The salary and allowance of police officers, as public officials, should be open and transparent. Moreover, although the collection of administrative fines and fees follow the principle of separating revenue from expenditure, the amounts of fines and fees collected by public security organs within a certain period of time should be made open to the public.

Data openness is the focus of the openness of police affairs. For the first assessment of transparency of police affairs in China, the Project Team decided to construct the index of data openness by starting with annual reports or work summaries. Through the publication of annual reports or work summaries, public security organs can show the public their performance and effectiveness of work, and accept the supervision of the public.

8.2.2.2 Openness of Service

The openness of service mainly refers to the disclosure by public security organs to the public of information about the legal basis, conditions, processing procedures and time limits, channels and methods of application for public security administrative licenses, non-administrative licenses, recordation items, as well as the catalog of materials to be submitted with the application, and related model texts, standard documents and format requirements. Three grade II indices have been set up under the "service openness" index: "household registration service", "traffic control service" and "entry and exit service".

The "household registration service" index mainly assesses whether public security organs provide guides to the applications for household registrations, resident ID cards, residence permits and other documents. The "traffic control service" index mainly assesses whether public security organs provide the public with the general knowledge of handling of traffic accidents, guides to the application for driver's licenses and motor vehicle licenses, and information about traffic conditions on expressways and traffic control information. Article 39 of the Road Traffic Safety Law stipulates that, if the traffic administrative department of a public security organ needs to take measures to restrict traffic or make a decision directly relating to the road traffic activities of the public, it shall announce such measures to the public in advance. The Provisions on the Openness of Law Enforcement by Public Security Organs also require the disclosure of information about traffic restriction measures, traffic control measures and on-site control measures taken by public security organs. The "entry-exit service" index mainly assesses whether public security organs disclose the guides to the application for electronic ordinary passports for going abroad for private reasons, the application for and endorsement of travel passes for Mainland residents to travel to or from Taiwan, and travel passes for Mainland residents to travel to and from Hong Kong and Macao.

8.2.2.3 Openness of Law Enforcement

The Provisions on the Openness of Law Enforcement by Public Security Organs define the openness of law enforcement as disclosing by public security organs of such information as the basis, process, progress and results of criminal and administrative law enforcement to the public or specific targets in accordance with laws, administrative regulations and rules, or other normative documents, and handling police affairs openly online. The openness of law enforcement is conducive to standardizing the law enforcement behavior of public security organs, protecting citizens' right to know, participate, express and supervise, and realizing fair and honest law enforcement. Under the index of "openness of law enforcement", the Project Team has set up five secondary indices: "case inquiry", "document openness", "information release about major cases", "police notifications" and "supervision and complaint", which cover the openness of both administrative law enforcement cases and criminal law enforcement cases, both openness of process and openness of results, both static information disclosure and dynamic information release, and both publication to the general public, and notifications to specific targets.

"Case inquiry" refers to the provision by public security organs to specific targets of information about the process and result of the handling of administrative and criminal cases on information platforms. According to the Regulations on the Openness of Law Enforcement by Public Security Organs, when public security organs accept applications for administrative licenses, non-administrative licenses, and recordation items online or in window units, they can provide inquiry numbers to the applicants, so as to facilitate the inquiry by the applicants of the acceptance, progress and results of their applications. In addition to providing case inquiry function to specific targets, the openness of law enforcement includes another important function, that is, the openness of documents. According to Article 5 of the Law on Public Security Administration Penalties, the implementation of public security administration penalties should be made public. "Openness of documents" mainly refers to the disclosure of administrative penalty decisions and administrative reconsideration decisions, which can be the disclosure of original texts or summaries, or the provision of document retrieval function to enable the public to find the target information accurately. "Release of information about major cases" requires public security organs to release in a timely manner information about major cases with wide influence, so as to respond to public concerns and prevent panic and rumors. Article 9 of the Provisions on Openness of Law Enforcement by Public Security Organs stipulates that "public security organs shall disclose to the public the progress of the investigation and results of the handling of major cases involving public interests and of great concern to the society" and that public security organs can regularly disclose to the public the social security situation, fire and road traffic safety situation, safety precautions and early warning information, etc. In order to implement this advocatory stipulation, the Project Team set up the index of "police notification", which requires public security organs to regularly publish police information, so as to keep the public informed about the public security and environmental safety situations around them. According to Article 46 of the People's Police Law, a citizen or an organization has the right to make exposure of or accusation against the violation of laws or disciplines by a policeman. The Provisions on Openness of Law Enforcement by Public Security Organs also clearly provide that public security organs should disclose the methods and channels of reporting or making complaints about violations of laws or disciplines by police officers. For this reason, the Project Team has set up the index of "supervision and complaints", which requires public security organs to provide instructions on complaints and reports of violations of laws or disciplines by police officers and disclose information about the handling of non-confidential cases of complaints and reports of violations of laws or disciplines by police officers.

8.2.3 Assessment Targets and Methods

The assessment targets of the index system of transparency of police affairs in China include the municipal-level public security organs in 27 cities where the people's governments of provinces or autonomous regions are located and public security organs of 4 municipalities directly under the Central Government. As far as the administrative level is concerned, the reason why the Project Team selects the public security bureaus at a specific administrative level as assessment targets is that the municipal-level public security organs have the function of connecting upper-level and lower-level public security organs, not only undertaking and implementing the tasks and arrangements made by higher-level public security organs but also leading and making overall plans for the police work of public security sub-bureaus and county-level public security bureaus. As far as the region is concerned, public security organs in cities where provincial-level people's governments are located are more representative and, generally speaking, can reflect the local level of the openness of police affairs.

In the assessment of indices of transparency of police affairs in China, the Project Team mainly adopted the method of website observation, whereby members of the Project Team assessed the online openness of police affairs of the assessment targets using the index system as reference. The assessment method was adapted to the continuous expansion and renewal of openness of police affairs. Traditionally, the channels of openness of police affairs include bulletin boards, plaques, manuals, newspapers, radio stations, and television stations. In order to adapt to the development of social informatization, the Regulations on the Openness of Law Enforcement by Public Security Organs clearly take government websites as a main channel of openness in addition to traditional channels.

When carrying out the assessment, members of the Project Team took the official websites of the assessment targets as the main source of information, supplemented by the websites of public security organs at higher levels and unified special information disclosure platforms. The government information disclosure platforms and credit information platforms at the corresponding level were also taken as references. After the assessment, assessment results were verified by some other members of the Project Team, focusing on checking the index items for which points were deducted from assessment scores. Both assessors and verifiers took and preserved screenshots as evidence during the assessment and verification. In addition to the website observation method, the Project Team also adopted the telephone verification method to verify the telephone numbers disclosed on websites. The time period for the collection of assessment data was from December 1, 2017 to December 31, 2017.

8.3 Assessment Results: Transparency of Police Affairs Has Become a Model of Openness of Government Affairs

In the assessment in 2017, the 31 public security organs covered by the assessment of transparency of police affairs indices got an average score of 67. 3 points. Among them, 25 public security organs scored above 60 points, with a passing rate of 80. 6%. The top ten public security organs in the ranking of assessment scores were the Public Security Bureau of Hangzhou City, the Public Security Bureau of Nanning City, the Public Security Bureau of Hefei City, the Public Security Bureau of Wuhan City, the Public Security Bureau of Fuzhou City, the Public Security Bureau of Guiyang City, the Public Security Bureau of Shanghai Municipality, the Public Security Bureau of Nanjing City, the Public Security Bureau of Xi'an City and the Public Security Bureau of Changsha City. Among them, the Public Security Bureau of Guiyang City and the Public Security Bureau of Shanghai Municipality tied for the sixth place, and the Public Security Bureau of Xi'an City and the Public Security Bureau of Changsha City tied for the ninth place (see Table 8.2). Compared with the results of the assessments of government transparency indices in China, judicial transparency indices in China, procuratorial transparency indices in China, and legislative transparency indices in China conducted by the Project Team, the results of the assessment of transparency of police affairs indices were better in terms of the highest score, average score, and passing rate, thereby becoming a benchmark and model of the openness of government affairs in China.

Table 8.2 Assessment results of transparency of police affairs in China

Ranking	Assessment targets	Disclosure of basic information (40%)	Openness of service (20%)	Openness of Law enforcement (40%)	Total scores
1	Public Security Bureau of Hangzhou City	62	100	95	82.8
2	Public Security Bureau of Nanning City	78	100	74	80.8
3	Public Security Bureau of Hefei City	66	100	84	80
4	Public Security Bureau of Wuhan City	80	100	66	78.4
5	Public Security Bureau of Fuzhou City	66	100	79	78
6	Public Security Bureau of Guiyang City	72	100	71	77.2
	Public Security Bureau of Shanghai Municipality	64	100	79	77.2
8	Public Security Bureau of Nanjing City	42	100	95	74.8
9	Public Security Bureau of Xi'an City	52	100	84	74.4
	Public Security Bureau of Changsha City	62	100	74	74.4
11	Public Security Bureau of Lanzhou City	72	100	60	72.8
12	Public Security Bureau of Jinan City	52	100	79	72.4
	Public Security Bureau of Shijiazhuang City	36	100	95	72.4

(continued)

Table 8.2 (continued)

Ranking	Assessment targets	Disclosure of basic information (40%)	Openness of service (20%)	Openness of Law enforcement (40%)	Total scores
14	Public Security Bureau of Guangzhou City	76	100	54	72
15	Public Security Bureau of Hohhot City	50	100	79	71.6
16	Public Security Bureau of Chongqing Municipality	64	100	60	69.6
17	Public Security Bureau of Zhengzhou City	72	100	50	68.8
	Public Security Bureau of Kunming City	72	100	50	68.8
19	Public Security Bureau of Chengdu City	68	100	45	65.2
20	Public Security Bureau of Taiyuan City	58	100	50	63.2
	Public Security Bureau of Yinchuan City	58	100	50	63.2
22	Public Security Bureau of Changchun City	52	100	55	62.8
	Public Security Bureau of Harbin City	52	100	55	62.8
24	Public Security Bureau of Tianjin Municipality	42	100	61	61.2
25	Public Security Bureau of Chongqing Municipality	30	100	71	60.4

(continued)

Table 8.2 (continued)

Ranking	Assessment targets	Disclosure of basic information (40%)	Openness of service (20%)	Openness of Law enforcement (40%)	Total scores
26	Public Security Bureau of Nanchang City	42	100	45	54.8
27	Public Security Bureau of Haikou City	66	100	20	54.4
28	Public Security Bureau of Shenyang City	60	100	20	52
29	Public Security Bureau of Urumqi City	34	100	40	49.6
30	Public Security Bureau of Xining City	46	100	18	45.6
31	Public Security Bureau of Lhasa City	34	94	30	44.4

8.4 Bright Spots Discovered in the Assessment

Among government departments, public security organs had made a larger investment in informatization, and their level of informatization was correspondingly high. Promoted by "Internet plus Police affairs", the openness of police affairs had become a benchmark and model of openness of government affairs, the manifestations of which are the followings.

8.4.1 Services Had Become Networked and Transparent

With respect to government service, public security administration is closely related to people's work and life, and the openness and convenience of its service directly affect the level of security of people's livelihood. In 2017, the Project Team selected three government services, namely household registration, traffic control, and entry and exit, for the assessment of openness of service. The results show that, with the exception of the Public Security Bureau of Lhasa City, which did not provide information about the openness of traffic control service, all the assessment targets got full scores in the assessment of transparency of service by disclosing all information that should be disclosed. Public security organs provided through their websites all the information in the guide category, which is used to guide citizens in the application of registered permanent residence, ID cards, driver's licenses, motor vehicle licenses, entry and exit documents, etc., general knowledge about the handling of traffic accidents and traffic control information, and inquiry about the traffic conditions on expressways.

The openness of police service has benefited from the mature practice of public security organs in providing services online for a long period of time. In 2012, the Ministry of Public Security introduced 14 measures for the convenience and benefit of the people, including improving the "online public security bureaus, online police stations and online police offices", and promoting online application, online processing, and online examination and approval of public security administrative affairs. Online service involves not only information disclosure in advance, that is, disclosing to the public information about the legal basis, conditions, procedures, and other information about the application for administrative licenses, non-administrative licenses, and recordation items as well as related legal rights and obligations enjoyed by applicants and supervision and remedy channels, but also information disclosure during and after the event, that is, disclosing to specific targets information about the acceptance and the results of processing of applications for administrative licenses, non-administrative licenses, and recordation items. Promoting online information disclosure and online handling of service matters by public security organs embodies the idea of attaching equal importance to administration and service and unifying the maintenance of order and safeguarding of rights. It is an inevitable requirement for safeguarding people's livelihood and building a service-oriented government, and a key step toward intelligent police affairs.

8.4.2 Local Intensification Had Been Realized for the Openness of Police Affairs

The local intensification of openness of police affairs refers to the intensified openness of police affairs in some fields and some regions. First, intensification of the disclosure of entry and exit information. There are two platforms for the intensive disclosure of entry-exit information: one is the official website of the Exit-entry Administration of the Ministry of Public Security, which discloses laws and regulations, dynamic information, service guides, and other information related to entry and exit; the other one is the Public Security Entry and Exit Online Service Platform, which provides online service guidance related to entry and exit, online booking of entry and exit documents and border inspection business in various parts of the country, and online office inquiry service. Second, intensification of the disclosure of traffic administration information. According to Article 5 of the Road Traffic Safety Law, the public security department under the State Council is responsible for the administration of road traffic safety nationwide. The Traffic Management Bureau of the Ministry of Public Security has constructed a unified national Internet

Traffic Safety Comprehensive Service Management Platform (122.gov.cn), with 31 local channels (among them, the local channels of Jiangsu Province and Zhejiang Province cover prefectural-level cities under them) to provide local traffic safety management information and online business processing. Third, the realization of one-stop openness of police affairs in some areas. The Public Security Bureau of Shanghai Municipality has set up "Sunshine Police Hall" as an all-round comprehensive online police service platform, providing the public with one-window disclosure of police information and public inquiry of handling of cases, one-network administrative approval, one-stop interaction between the police and the people, and services for the convenience and benefit of the people. "One-window openness" refers to providing specific subjects with information about such services as inquiry about case handling progress, appointment for meeting with lawyers, and video meeting with relatives, and disclosing to the public of information about administrative penalties, administrative reconsideration, criminal reconsideration and review, and return of stolen goods. "One-network handling of affairs" refers to the provision of guides to the handling of affairs relating to public security, entry and exit, traffic police, border defense, fire protection, cybersecurity, safety on the water, airport, population, criminal investigation and other affairs and online handling of some businesses by Shanghai Public Security Government Service Hall to individuals and legal persons. And "one-stop service" refers to the interactive communications between the police and the public such as online consultation, petition hall, hot issues, police appointment, opinion solicitation, and mobile police affairs, convenience services such as transportation and travel, and online "110" services such as reporting clues of various illegal and criminal activities and "110" mailbox.

8.4.3 The Disclosure of Institutional Information Was Satisfactory

As the main providers of public services, public security organs should disclose to the public information about their functions, rights and obligations of the police, institutional setup and contact information of window units and police stations. The assessment results show that, except for the information about the rights and obligations of the police, the disclosure of information about the functional structure of public security organs was generally good. All 31 public security organs had disclosed information about their institutional functions and internal institutions on their websites, with the openness rate reaching 100%; 29 public security organs disclosed the contact telephone numbers of their window units, with the openness rate reaching 93. 5%; and 19 public security organs disclosed the contact information of police stations under them, with the openness rate reaching 61. 3%.

In some places, telephone numbers of public security organs were disclosed in an intensive way. For example, the Public Security Department of Shaanxi Province built a platform of openness of police law enforcement and handling of cases by public security organs, and set up a special column on the platform to disclose in an intensive way the telephone numbers of window units and police stations; and the Public Security Bureau of Shijiazhuang City disclosed in an intensive way in the convenience service column of its website the addresses and contact information of police stations, criminal police squadrons and window service units under its administration. In comparison, the openness of the rights and obligations of the people's police was low. Among the 31 public security organs, only these of Beijing, Tianjin, Shanghai, Taiyuan and Yinchuan had disclosed the information, with a disclosure rate of only 16.1%.

In order to verify the disclosed telephone numbers, members of the Project Team randomly selected two police stations located in different districts and counties from the public security bureaus that disclosed the contact telephone numbers of the police stations under them and dialed the telephone numbers disclosed on the Internet. The results show that most telephone numbers were valid. However, the telephone numbers of the following four police stations were invalid, always busy or unable to be connected at different time periods (during and after working hours): the Xincheng Police Station in Changqing District of Jinan City, the Zhongdong Police Station of Public Security Sub-bureau of Economic and Technological Development Zone of Changchun City, Zhaozhou Town Police Station in Zhao County of Shijiazhuang City, and Jinshui Road Public Security Sub-bureau (Police Station) of Zhengzhou City. Moreover, the staff member of Wenji Road Police Station in Lantian County of Xi'an City who answered the phone call made by members of the Project Team was stiff in his manner.

8.4.4 The Openness of Budget and Final Accounts Had Become the Norm

After the implementation of the government information disclosure system in recent years, the openness of budget and final accounts, as important government information, had become the norm, and the disclosure of budget and final accounts information in the public security system was no exception. The assessment results show that all public security organs covered by the assessment, with the exception of that of Lhasa City, had disclosed their budget and final accounts and budgetary expenditures related to official overseas visits, official vehicles, and official hospitality. Some of them also disclosed the financial information of their subordinate organs. For example, the Public Security Bureau of Kunming City disclosed the information about disclosure of self-assessment of fiscal expenditure performance of each branch and detention center under it in 2016 in the "Publicity of Fiscal Budget and Final Accounts" column on its website.

8.4.5 *The Trend Towards Data Openness Was Obvious*

Public security organs gather a large amount of data in the process of providing public administration and services. The openness of public security data, with the exception of those that are confidential, is of great significance for improving the social credit system and promoting scientific decision-making and precise administration by the government. Although the Project Team had not set up a separate data openness index in the assessment in 2017, it assessed the disclosure of work summaries and statistical information of public security organs. The assessment results show that some public security organs consciously disclosed all kinds of statistical data, and the trend toward the openness of public security data was obvious. The data disclosed by public security organs included comprehensive work summaries, case-handling results, service statistics, and so on. For example, the Public Security Bureau of Kunming City periodically disclosed the results of the investigation and punishment of traffic violations and public security violations in the motor vehicle passenger transport industry. The Public Security Bureau of Hangzhou City published its work summaries over the years in the column of "Statistical Analysis" on its website, and disclosed fire information and traffic accident information, including data reviews and analysis reports, on a monthly and quarterly basis respectively. The Public Security Bureau of Changsha City published a series of analysis reports, including Entry: Data Analysis of Persons Going Abroad in the Whole City in November 2017, Public Announcements of Serious Traffic Violations of Key Vehicles in 2017, and Analysis of Traffic Accidents in Changsha City in the First Half of 2017. The Public Security Bureau of Chongqing Municipality published reports on analyses of "110" data and data of persons going abroad. And the Public Security Bureau of Guiyang City published its own work summaries and those of compulsory drug rehabilitation centers.

8.4.6 *The Openness of Penalties Had Gradually Become a Common Practice*

The openness of penalties consists of two levels: one is the disclosure by public security organs of information about violations of law, and the other is the online publication by public security organs of written decisions on administrative penalties. The assessment shows that, to deter illegal activities and build social integrity, public security organs had intensified the disclosure of penalty information. Take "publication and public disclosure of information about serious traffic violations" as an example. Local channels of the Internet Traffic Safety Comprehensive Service Management Platform of the Ministry of Public Security had set up the column of "publication and public disclosure of information about serious traffic violations" to disclose information about "serious violations by key vehicles", "cheatings in the examination for motor vehicle drivers", "drivers who had their driving licenses degraded for being deducted a total of 12 points in an assignment period" and "drivers responsible for fatal traffic accidents". By December 23, 2017, with the exception of the Channel of Hainan Province, which could not be opened, among the 30 local channels, only those of 9 provinces, namely Jilin, Jiangxi, Shandong, Henan, Hubei, Hunan, Guizhou, Yunnan and Qinghai, had not disclosed information about serious traffic violations, while those of 21 provinces, autonomous regions, or municipalities directly under the Central Government, or 67.7% of all the assessment targets, had disclosed such information. Among them, that of Tibet Autonomous Region clearly stated that no serious traffic violation had occurred in the autonomous region in the current year.

In order to meet the requirements of double disclosure of credit information, public security organs, while intensifying the disclosure of license information, had also strengthened the disclosure of administrative penalty information. The assessment results show that, among the 31 public security organs, 13 published administrative penalty decisions, and some also provided the retrieval function for the decisions. Some local public security organs (such as that of Nanning City), disclosed the information about criminal cases, administrative cases, administrative reconsideration cases and state compensation cases in the public security law enforcement disclosure column of their websites.

8.5 Problems and Prospects

On the whole, China has achieved good results in the openness of police affairs. Meanwhile, there are also some problems in the work that need to be solved in the future.

8.5.1 Strengthening the Disclosure of Personnel Information

Personnel is the basic guarantee for the provision of public services and enforcement of laws. The disclosure of police personnel information includes the disclosure of information about the leaders of public security organs and the number and structure of police personnel. The assessment results show that most public security organs disclosed only the information about their leaders, but not the information about the number and structure of police personnel. Among the 31 public security organs, although 26 disclosed information about their leaders, only 13 disclosed complete information about their leaders, including the names, responsibilities, educational background and work experience of their directors and deputy directors, with the remaining 13 disclosing only incomplete information. Among the 31 public security organs, only five disclosed the number of police officers. Among them, the Public Security Bureau of Hohhot City and the Public Security Bureau of City Shenyang provided the list of administrative law enforcement personnel, the Public Security

Bureau of Taiyuan City disclosed its personnel quota, the Public Security Bureau of Haikou City disclosed the number of police officers, and the Public Security Bureau of Wuhan City disclosed more detailed information, including not only the list and details of in-service personnel but also the numbers of quota and in-service members of administrative staff in the organization establishment table. As for the structure of the police personnel, only the Public Security Bureau of Wuhan City enabled the public to get such information from the list of in-service personnel it disclosed. In the future, public security organs should strengthen the disclosure of personnel information by disclosing not only detailed information about members of their leading groups but also the list of law enforcement personnel and the number and structure of the police force.

8.5.2 *Improving Financial Openness*

In addition to the disclosure of information about budget, final accounts and budgetary expenditures related to official overseas visits, official vehicles, and official hospitality, financial openness also includes the disclosure of information about the income of public officials and the collection of fees and fines. The assessment results show that public security organs, while generally disclosing information about their budget, final accounts and budgetary expenditures related to official overseas visits, official vehicles, and official hospitality, were very unwilling to disclose information about the salaries and allowances of police officers, and the fines and the fees they had collected. The assessment shows that, among the 31 public security organs, none disclosed information about salaries and allowances of their staff, two disclosed information about the fees they had collected, one, namely the Public Security Bureau of Guangzhou City, published the Income of Exit-Entry Administration Detachment of Guangzhou City from Collection of Fees in 2016, and one, namely the Public Security Bureau of Changsha City, disclosed the data of the collection of administrative fees in 2013. In the future, public security organs should strengthen the disclosure of information about the income of public officials, and bring the information about the collection of fines and fees into the scope of financial openness, so as to truly realize financial transparency.

8.5.3 *Integrating Platforms of Openness*

The assessment shows that platforms of openness of police affairs were scattered. Public security organs disclosed information not only on their official websites but also on the information disclosure websites of the government at the same level, and those of public security organs at the next higher level. Even the official websites of public security organs had many special platforms, such as separate platforms for entry and exit and traffic administration. Scattered platforms not only increase the cost of disclosure, but also cause data fragmentation, and prevent the public from obtaining complete information. For example, the Public Security Bureau of Jinan City had set up a public inquiry system for the handling law enforcement cases on the Minsheng Police Platform of Shandong Province (sponsored by the Public Security Department of Shandong Province) to publish administrative penalty decisions, but disclosed no information in the administrative penalty publication column of Jinan site of Shandong Government Service Platform. Currently, China is integrating government affairs openness platforms throughout the country. The Opinions of the General Office of the CPC Central Committee and the General Office of the State Council on Comprehensively Promoting the Openness of Government Affairs (No. 6 [2016] of the General Office of the CPC Central Committee), the Detailed Rules of the General Office of the State Council for the Implementation of the Opinions on Comprehensively Promoting the Openness of Government Affairs (No. 80 [2016] of the General Office of the CPC Central Committee), and the Opinions of the General Office of the State Council on Strengthening the Development of Contents of Information on Government Websites (No. 57 [2014] of the General Office of the CPC Central Committee) all require the promotion of the intensive construction of openness platforms. In the future, with the trend of intensive construction of government websites and on the precondition of ensuring technical security, China should further integrate platforms, so as to realize the intensive openness of police affairs.

8.5.4 Standardizing the Openness of Documents

For law enforcement agencies, the openness of documents mainly refers to the disclosure of administrative penalty decisions and administrative reconsideration decisions. The assessment shows that, because the disclosure of documents involves the protection of personal information, many public security organs de-identified the contents of documents before disclosing them. For example, the public security bureaus of Shijiazhuang, Jinan, Hefei, Guiyang, Xi'an, Xining and other cities de-identified such information as names, ID numbers, dates of birth and home addresses of violators of law or applicants when disclosing relevant documents. Whether a document should be de-identified before disclosure depends on the purpose of the disclosure of the document. Administrative penalty decisions, as credit information, are unable to achieve their purpose of disclosing credit information if de-identified. The purpose of publishing administrative reconsideration decisions is to supervise the reconsideration organs. Although it has nothing to do with the disclosure of credit information, there is no need to hide the applicants' names. In order to protect the privacy of individual citizens, it is only necessary to de-identify the dates of birth, ID numbers, detailed addresses and other information of natural persons when publishing the documents. In the future, when standardizing the disclosure of documents, China should establish information processing standards, including the standards on the de-identification of such personal information as home addresses, contact information, ID numbers, bank account numbers and health status of natural persons, as well as the names of natural persons other than the punished persons or applicants.

8.5.5 Opening up Public Security Data

Against the background of the implementation of the national big data strategy, it is particularly important for public security organs to keep their data open, because they have obtained a large amount of accurate information, from basic identification information to accurate movement track data, in the process of provision of administrative services and enforcement of laws. By relying on information technology, police information is highly digitized, and the development of openness of police affairs at an advanced stage inevitably requires data openness and the establishment of public security big data shared by society. Public security organs are both administrative law enforcement organs and criminal investigation organs. In the process of promoting the opening up of public security data, they should properly handle the relationship between openness and confidentiality, neither disclosing law enforcement information that involves state secrets, may hinder normal law enforcement activities or affect social stability, nor refusing to disclose any information that should be disclosed under the pretext of confidentiality. Article 28 of the Provisions on Openness of Law Enforcement by Public Security Organs stipulates that public security organs should establish and improve the examination and approval procedures and confidentiality review mechanism for the openness of law enforcement. Take the publication of the work plans of public security organs as an example. The assessment shows that public security organs had adopted inconsistent standards on the boundaries between openness and confidentiality when disclosing such information. Some public security organs, such as the Public Security Bureau of Hefei City, had set up a special column on the disclosure of annual work plans on their websites, but stated in the column that "The work plans of this bureau involve police secrets and are not suitable for disclosure to the public". However, many local public security organs had published their work plans. For example, the Public Security Bureau of Kunming City disclosed information about the key points of work, plan for the division of work and work priorities in 2017; the Public Security Bureau of Guiyang City published its annual audit work report in 2017; and the Public Security Bureau of Xi'an City published its work plan in 2017.

In the future, a screening mechanism for confidential matters should be established. If confidential matters in a piece of information can be identified, public security organs should disclose the information after removing the confidential matters, rather than refusing to disclose the whole information on the grounds of partial confidentiality. Otherwise, public security big data will not be constructed, and the credibility and affinity of public security organs will be undermined.

Chapter 9
Report on Indices of Transparency of Police Affairs in China (2018)—From the Perspective of Information Disclosure on the Websites of Public Security Organs

Innovation Project Team on the Rule of Law Index

Abstract The openness of police affairs, as an important aspect of the deepening police reform, is of great significance for standardizing public security law enforcement, increasing police credibility, and enhancing people's sense of security and gain. In 2018, the Innovation Project Team on Rule of Law Indices of the Law Institute of the Chinese Academy of Social Sciences adjusted and optimized the index system of police transparency in China to further meet the new demands of society for the openness of police affairs and reflect the characteristics of police work in the new era. The assessment of indices of police transparency in China in 2018 shows that, through a series of openness activities, such as convenience service, sunshine law enforcement, the openness of penalties and data openness, public security organs in China had achieved practical results in improving people's livelihood, highlighting the rule of law, and promoting honesty and intelligent decision-making. Meanwhile, they had also encountered selection dilemmas between publicity and openness, openness and confidentiality, real name and anonymity, decentralization and intensification, etc. Desensitization, intensification and standardization will eventually become China's path choice in enhancing the transparency of police affairs.

Keywords Police transparency · Openness of police affairs · Sunshine law enforcement · Big data of police affairs · Rule of law index

---

Leaders of the Project Team: Tian He, a research fellow at CASS Law Institute and the director of the Center for Studies of National Indices of the Rule of Law, Chinese Academy of Social Sciences, and Lv Yanbin, a research fellow at and the head of the Department of Survey and Study of National Situation of the Rule of Law of the Institute of Law, Chinese Academy of Social Sciences. Other members of the Project Team: Ma Fanjun, Wang Xiaomei, Wang Yiming, Wang Na, Wang Ying, Liu Yanpeng, Gu Jingxuan, Hu Changming, Li Yanjie, Chai Jinge, Xu Haitong, Gao Zhenjuan, etc. Author of this report: Wang Xiaomei, Associate Research Fellow, Institute of Law, Chinese Academy of Social Sciences.

Innovation Project Team on the Rule of Law Index (✉)
Institute of Law, Chinese Academy of Social Sciences, Beijing, China
e-mail: 13263169197@163.com

H. Tian et al. (eds.), *Report on the Rule of Law Index in China 2*,
Research Series on the Chinese Dream and China's Development Path,
https://doi.org/10.1007/978-981-19-9597-2_9

"Transparency" is an important dimension of modern rule of law, as well as the inherent requirement for the supervision aimed at ensuring the standardized and clean operation of public power. Although China started late in the information disclosure work, it has the late-mover advantage because it started the work in the era of highly developed information technology and the popularization of Internet applications. The breadth of information disclosure, the interactivity between the supply side and the demand side of information, and the convenience of information access have been amplified exponentially with the help of Internet platforms. As both government departments responsible for the administration of household registration, entry and exit, transportation and public security, and criminal investigation departments, public security organs not only provide public services but also have the dual functions of administrative law enforcement and criminal law enforcement, which directly affect citizens' daily activities such as living and traveling, as well as the people's livelihood. The standardization and transparency of the operation of their power concern citizens' personal safety and property safety, the realization of social fairness and justice, and the enhancement of the people's sense of security and gain. 2018 was the 10th anniversary of the implementation of the Regulations on the Disclosure of Government Information. As the organs in control of a large amount of government information, public security organs are the best observation points to track the implementation of the government information disclosure system in China and the breadth and depth of openness of police affairs are also important aspects of transparency of the Chinese government. Since public security organs are also criminal investigation departments, the openness of police affairs, together with the openness of trial, the openness of procuratorial affairs, and the openness prison affairs, constitute a complete system of openness of political and legal affairs, which belongs to the category of judicial openness in a broad sense.

To review and summarize the achievements of information disclosure work in China, explore and analyze the deep-seated problems in the process of building a transparent China, and promote the improvement of the information disclosure system, the Center for Studies of National Indices of the Rule of Law of Chinese Academy of Social Sciences and the Innovation Project Team of Rule of Law Index of Institute of Law (hereinafter referred to as the "Project Team") continue to assess the indices of police transparency in China from the perspective of website information disclosure. This was the second annual assessment since the first one in 2017.

9.1 The Index System and Targets and Methods of Assessment

9.1.1 Optimization of the Index System

A scientific index system is a precondition and guarantee for the success of index assessment. In order to ensure the continuity of index assessment, the index system should maintain certain stability, and its framework and important indexes should be maintained over the years. A scientific index system should be fine-tuned and optimized in a timely manner to adapt to institutional changes and practical needs. In the process of research and development of the index system of police transparency in China, the Project Team based itself on the institutional regulations and work practice of openness of police affairs, as well as the needs of the public and the parties, extensively solicited opinions from the legal community, and took into full consideration and integrated the key issues of the comprehensive police reform in China. In 2018, in accordance with the latest documents on the system of openness of police affairs, the Project Team optimized the index system of police transparency in China in terms of comprehensiveness, timeliness, convenience, and accuracy of information disclosure, so as to further highlight the characteristics of the times, and better serve the needs of improving the people's livelihood, standardizing police law enforcement and deepening the reform of the police system.

9.1.1.1 Adapting to the New Situation of Openness of Law Enforcement

The openness of police affairs originates from the Constitution. The Constitutional stipulation that "all powers belong to the people" reveals the source and attribute of powers. Powers that originate from the people and have public attributes should operate in a way that can be seen and supervised by the people. Article 44 of the People's Police Law stipulates that: "The people's policemen, in performing their duties, must conscientiously subject themselves to the supervision by society and citizens. The rules and regulations formulated by the people's police organs that have a direct bearing on the interests of the public shall be made known to the public." As early as 1999, the Ministry of Public Security issued the Notice on Implementing the System of Openness of Police Affairs in Public Security Organs Throughout the Country (No.43 [1999] of the Ministry of Public Security). However, at that time, the openness of police affairs was mainly the openness of police-related documents, such as those relating to law enforcement basis, procedural provisions, rights and obligations, police disciplines, etc., which belong to static openness and flat openness. In 2005, the Criminal Investigation Bureau of the Ministry of Public Security issued the Notice on Implementing the System of Openness of Handling of Cases (No.1228 [2005] of the Ministry of Public Security), which required the criminal investigation departments of public security organs throughout the country to implement the system of openness of handling of cases and disclose information about the filing, and progress and results of handling of criminal cases. The targets of openness were limited to the parties and stakeholders of relevant cases. In 2012, the Ministry of Public Security promulgated the Provisions on Openness of Law Enforcement by Public Security Organs (No.38 [2012] of the Ministry of Public Security), which integrate the requirements of openness of law enforcement scattered in some laws, administrative regulations and normative documents, and constitute the direct basis for the design of the index system of transparency of police affairs in China. In August 2018, the Ministry of Public Security revised this document and promulgated the new Provisions on the Openness of Law Enforcement by Public Security Organs (No.26 [2018] of the Ministry of Public Security) to meet the new requirements for deepening the practice of law-based governance and the reforms of "simplification of administrative procedures, decentralization of powers, combination of decentralization with appropriate control, and optimization of services". Article 35 of the Provisions stipulates that: "Public security organs may entrust third-party institutions to assess the openness of law enforcement and improve their work by taking the assessment results as a reference." Although this document has only been implemented since December 1, 2018, it also provides an important reference for optimizing the index system. In the 2018 index system of openness of police affairs in China, the Project Team increased the weight and further enriched the content of the index of the openness of law enforcement.

9.1.1.2 Responding to the People's Concerns and Demands

The well-known saying "Ask the police for help whenever you encounter difficulties" reflects the unlimited trust of the people in the government and public security organs. However, in the process of promoting administration by law and building a law-based government, a precondition for standardizing public security law enforcement is to "slim down" police affairs by stripping out non-police matters. To this end, public security organs reviewed and published their lists of powers and responsibilities. For matters within the scope of their powers and responsibilities, public authorities should exercise their powers and fulfill their responsibilities in strict accordance with law. For example, an important duty of public security organs is to crack down on the crime of abduction of and traffic in children. Upon receiving a report of a missing child, public security organs should file a case in time after verification, and initiate corresponding search measures. It is a basic human right for children to be searched and rescued in a timely and effective way by the public authorities after their disappearance, which concerns the safety of children, the happiness of families and the stability of society, and embodies the active fulfillment state responsibilities by relevant organs. In 2018, in response to the common concern of the whole society, the Project Team added the index of information disclosure upon application to the police transparency index system to assess the disclosure upon application of information about the protection of the rights and interests of children by public security organs.

9.1.1.3 Responding to the Needs of the Big Data Era

In the process of providing administrative services and enforcing the law, public security organs have obtained massive data, such as newborn population, migrant population, car ownership, traffic accidents, traffic flow on roads, emergency situation, public security, and crime situation. The aggregation and mining of these data are of great significance for improving government administration, assisting scientific decision-making, and accurately predicting social situations. In the recommendation part of the 2017 Assessment Report on Indices of Transparency of Police Affairs in China, the Project Team pointed out that the openness of police affairs at an advanced stage of development will inevitably demand data openness and the establishment of public security big data shared by the whole society. The 2018 Provisions on Law Enforcement Openness of Public Security Organs also contain suggestive provisions on data openness. For example, articles 11 and 17 of the Provisions stipulate that public security organs may regularly disclose such information as public security situations, road traffic safety situations, and safety precautions to the public. In order to meet the needs of the national big data strategy, "police affairs big data" is set as a grade I index in the index system of transparency of police affairs in 2018.

9.1.1.4 Responding to the Construction of Social Credit System

In the information age, the core competition will eventually be manifested in the effective possession of information. This is true for individuals, organizations, as well as society. Faced with an increasingly complex market and society, it is difficult for the government to sustain itself by only relying on traditional regulatory means. Therefore, establishing a new regulatory system with credit as the core has become an inevitable choice as well as the only way to realize the modernization of the state governance system and capacity. The Communist Party of China emphasized the construction of a social integrity system at its 18th National Congress and the third and fourth plenary sessions of its 18th Central Committee. In 2014 and 2016, the State Council successively issued the Outline of the Plan for Building the Social Credit System (2014–2020) and the Guiding Opinions on Establishing and Improving the System of Joint Incentive for Keeping Faith and Joint Punishment for Losing Faith and Accelerating the Development of Social Honesty, which stipulate that local governments should promote the integration and application of credit information of various departments and units in their respective regions. Disclosure of law enforcement information by public security organs to the public helps law enforcement subjects accept social supervision on the one hand, and puts law enforcement counterparts, especially those who are subject to administrative penalties, under the supervision of public opinion on the other hand, thus promoting the construction and perfection of the social credit system. It was for this reason that, in 2018, the Project Team strengthened and improved the designs and weights of the index of openness of law enforcement results and the index of openness of law enforcement documents under the grade I index of "law enforcement openness" in the index system, so as to promote the openness of the results of administrative licensing, administrative penalty and administrative reconsideration by public security organs and the realization of the sharing, integration, and application of credit information.

9.1.2 *The Construction and Interpretation of the Index System*

The index system of transparency of police affairs in China in 2018 consists of four grade I indices: "disclosure of basic information", "convenience service", "openness of law enforcement" and "data openness" (see Table 9.1).

Table 9.1 Index system of transparency of police affairs in China (2018)

Grade I indices and their weights	Grade II indices and their weights
Disclosure of basic information (25%)	Website construction (10%)
	Functional structure (30%)
	Personnel information (30%)
	Financial information (30%)
Convenience services (20%)	Household registration services (40%)
	Traffic control services (30%)
	Entry and exit services (30%)
Openness of law enforcement (30%)	Law enforcement basis (5%)
	Process and time limit of law enforcement (10%)
	Rights and obligations of parties (5%)
	Openness of process (20%)
	Openness of results (20%)
	Openness of documents (20%)
	Supervision and complaints (20%)
Data openness (25%)	Annual reports (5%)
	Annual work summaries (10%)
	Traffic statistics (10%)
	Statistics of administrative law enforcement (20%)
	Statistics of criminal cases (10%)
	Statistics of complaints against police officers (5%)
	Release of information about major cases (5%)
	Police alerts (5%)
	Data disclosure upon application (30%)

9.1.2.1 Disclosure of Basic Information

Basic information mainly refers to the functions, institutional structure, personnel, finance, and material resources of public security organs. Four grade II indices have been set up under this index: "website construction", "functional structure", "personnel information" and "financial information".

The friendliness of websites, as the carriers of the openness of police affairs, directly affects the effect of openness. An important principle of website friendliness is not forcing the audience to read anything on the website. On an ideal website, the setup of the home page columns or directories should be scientific and eye-catching, allowing the public to read the target information by clicking on the corresponding columns. Of course, this raises higher demands on information integration and classification. At the current stage, the index of website friendliness is used to assess whether there is a floating window on the homepage of a website. A floating window is set up to draw the attention of visitors to a certain piece of information, but it often interferes with webpage reading. Moreover, the important or latest information can be placed on the top of the webpage for rolling display, which can also draw the visitors' attention to the information.

The index of "functional structure" aims to enable the public to know the responsibilities and institutional setup of public security organs, including the responsibilities of public security organs, the rights and obligations of the people's police, internal structure and functions, window units, police substations, etc. Public security organs are familiar "strangers" to the people—although people of all ages know that they can ask the police for help when they encounter difficulties, few really know exactly what police affairs are. Therefore, it is necessary to publicize the functions and structure of public security organs and the powers and responsibilities of the police, and disclose the contact information of police stations for the convenience of the people.

As a public authority, public security organs should keep a certain degree of social openness of the number, structure and quality of their personnel, who are supported by public finance. The assessment results in 2017 show that personnel openness was a weak link, and the reason for that given by public security organs was that information such as the number of police officers in a police bureau belonged to classified information and could not be disclosed. It is undeniable that some functions of public security organs, such as anti-drug work, are sensitive. However, the information required to be disclosed in the index system is only the general quantitative and structural information of public security organs, which does not involve sensitive information, and does not belong to secrets of criminal investigation. Therefore, the 2018 index system retained the "personnel information" index, which consisted of three grade III indices: "leadership information", "number of police officers" and "police structure", because issues such as what kind of people are leading the police force, how many police officers are providing services, and what the quality structure of law enforcement personnel is will inevitably have an impact on the level of police service and the quality of law enforcement.

Since public security organs are supported by public finances, it is an inherent requirement of a law-based government for them to disclose their financial information, including information about the budget and final accounts, budgetary expenditures related to official overseas visits, official vehicles, and official hospitality, and salaries and allowances of police officers. Moreover, although public security organs, as the main collectors of administrative fees and administrative penalties, follow the principle of separating revenue from expenditure, the amounts of fines and fees they collected should be disclosed to the public.

9.1.2.2 Convenience Services

The public administration and services provided by public security organs cover household registration, entry and exit, public security, traffic safety, cyber-security, economic and cultural security, and security guard service, the efficiency and convenience of which have a profound impact on the work and life of citizens. Article 27 of the 2018 Provisions on the Openness of Law Enforcement by Public Security Organs requires public security organs to disclose on the Internet information about items of police affairs and administrative fees, and provide online consultation, online booking of police services, online applications, and other online services. The 2018 index system still assessed "convenience service" from three aspects: "household registration service", "entry and exit service" and "traffic control service". Compared with that of 2017, the index item of "online inquiry about the progress of the processing of application" was added to each service in the 2018 index system. "Household registration service" mainly assessed the disclosure by public security organs of addresses and contact telephone numbers of the household registration offices in each district, the guides to the application of residence permits, online application service, and online inquiry about the progress of the processing of applications. "Entry and exit service" mainly assessed the convenience for mainland residents to apply for electronic ordinary passports, travel passes for Mainland residents to travel to and from Hong Kong and Macao and travel passes for Mainland residents to travel to or from Taiwan, including the disclosure of the addresses and contact telephone numbers of the reception halls in each district, the disclosure of the addresses and contact telephone numbers of the reception halls where foreigners could apply for visas or Taiwan compatriots could apply for residence permits and the publication of related guides, and provision of online inquiry about the progress of the processing of applications. "Traffic control service" mainly assessed the handling of traffic violations, the disclosure of the addresses and contact telephone numbers of service halls for the application of motor vehicle licenses and driver's licenses, and the provision of online inquiry about the progress of the processing of applications.

9.1.2.3 Openness of Law Enforcement

The openness of law enforcement can be divided into static openness and dynamic openness. Static openness refers to the disclosure of law enforcement guide information, such as classified disclosure of information about the basis, process, and time limit of law enforcement, rights and obligations of the parties, instructions on supervision and complaint, etc. Dynamic openness refers to the openness of handling of cases, including the progress and results of handling of cases, the disclosure of documents, and the disclosure of contents of supervision and complaints. In the 2018 index system, seven grade II indices were set up under the "openness of law enforcement" index: "law enforcement basis", "law enforcement process and time limit", "rights and obligations of the parties", "openness of process", "openness of results", "openness of documents " and "supervision and complaints". The "law enforcement basis" index was used mainly to assess whether public security organs disclosed the basis of administrative law enforcement and criminal law enforcement. The "law enforcement process and time limit" index was used mainly to assess whether public security organs disclosed such information as the flowcharts and time limits for accepting and handling reported cases, and the flowcharts and time limits for handling administrative cases, criminal cases, administrative reconsideration cases, and state compensation cases. The "rights and obligations of the parties" index was used mainly to assess whether public security organs disclosed the notices of rights and obligations to criminal suspects, suspected violators of law, victims, and witnesses. Article 27 of the 2018 Provisions on Law Enforcement Openness of Public Security Organs requires public security organs to provide online inquiries about law enforcement information such as the acceptance, the progress and results of handling of cases. The "openness of process" index was used to assess the disclosure of information to specific targets, and whether the progress of the handling of cases can be inquired about online. The "openness of results" index was used to assess whether public security organs disclosed on their own initiative the results of administrative penalties and administrative licensing. The "openness of documents" index was used to assess whether public security organs published administrative penalty decisions and administrative reconsideration decisions on the Internet, and provided the document retrieval function. The "supervision and complaints" index was used to assess whether public security organs provided instructions on complaints and disclosed the contents of supervision and complaints online.

9.1.2.4 Data Openness

Data openness is the emphasis of openness of police affairs. The data openness index in the 2017 index system was established by taking annual reports or work summaries as the starting points. To further promote the data openness of public security organs, "data openness" was set up as a grade I index in the 2018 index system. It consisted of nine grade II indices: "annual reports", "annual work summaries", "traffic statistics", "administrative law enforcement statistics", "criminal case statistics", "statistics of complaints against police officers", "release of information about major cases", "police alerts" and "data disclosure upon application".

Annual reports and annual work summaries are a unit's review of the work in the past year, including achievements, existing problems, and plans for future work. Compared with annual work summaries, annual reports contain richer and more detailed information. Annual reports on police work originated from the annual comprehensive reports of business activities and financial status provided by enterprises to shareholders and other interest groups. The annual reports of listed companies must be open to the public. Now, not only enterprises but also more and more public institutions and organizations have begun to prepare and publish annual reports to introduce and show their achievements to society. As units supported by public finance, public security organs should prepare detailed annual reports on their functions, composition, documents, activities, main achievements, and important data. Through the publication of annual reports or work summaries, public security organs can show their work performance and achievement in the previous year in a concentrated way and accept the supervision of the public.

The openness of "traffic statistics" refers to the disclosure by public security organs of statistical data of traffic conditions in a certain region and a certain period, including situations of traffic congestion, traffic control, traffic accident rate, and other related statistical data. The openness of "administrative law enforcement statistics" refers to the disclosure by public security organs of statistical data of administrative penalties, administrative licensing, or other law enforcement statistics. The disclosure of "criminal case statistics" refers to the disclosure by public security organs of statistical data of criminal cases according to the type of crimes. The disclosure of these statistical data helps the public have an overall understanding and judgment of urban traffic situation, public security situation, and the comprehensive social situation, and also provides data support for relevant researchers and policymakers to make scientific decisions.

Supervision and complaint are basic constitutional rights of citizens. In order to prevent supervision and complaint from becoming a mere formality and effectively promote the substantive handling of complaints, the Project Team designed the index of "statistics of complaints against police officers", which was used to assess the disclosure by public security organs of the situation of classified handling of complaints. The index of "release of information about major cases" was used to assess the disclosure by public security organs of information about the progress of investigation and results of handling of major cases/incidents involving public interests and of great concern to society, as well as major decisions and actions taken to crack down on illegal and criminal activities. The "police alerts" index was used to assess whether public security organs regularly issue police alert information. The index of "disclosure upon application of the number of docketed cases of missing children" was used to assess whether the channels of disclosure of information by public security organs upon application were unimpeded on the one hand, and whether public security organs make substantial disclosure of such information on the other hand.

9.1.3 Targets and Methods of Assessment

The assessment targets in the assessment of indices of transparency of police affairs in China in 2017 included the municipal-level public security organs of 27 cities where the people's governments of provinces or autonomous regions are located and 4 municipalities directly under the Central Government. In the 2018 assessment, the Project Team further expanded the scope of assessment targets to cover the public security organs of five cities specifically designated in the state plan, including Dalian, Qingdao, Ningbo, Xiamen, and Shenzhen, thereby increasing the total number of assessment targets to 36. Municipal-level public security organs have the function of connecting upper-level and lower-level public security organs, not only undertaking and implementing the tasks and arrangements made by higher-level public security organs but also leading and making overall plans for the police work of public security sub-bureaus and county-level public security bureaus. Public security organs in cities where provincial-level people's governments are located are more representative and, generally speaking, can reflect the local level of openness of police affairs. In China, the five cities specifically designated in the state plan, namely Dalian, Qingdao, Ningbo, Xiamen, and Shenzhen, are the leading cities in terms of economic development and social environment construction and have made some innovations in the openness of police affairs, which should provide better references for other cities.

The channels for the openness of police affairs are diversified, including on-site modes such as setting up bulletin boards and plaques and distributing manuals, traditional media such as newspapers, radio stations and television stations, and online platforms such as websites, mobile clients and self-service terminals. To adapt to the development of social informatization, articles 18, 24 and 29 of the 2018 Provisions on the Openness of Law Enforcement by Public Security Organs clearly take government websites as the primary platforms for the openness of police affairs and stipulate that the disclosure of law enforcement information to the public, provision of law enforcement information inquiry services to specific targets, and even the online handling of affairs should be carried out through government websites, with mobile client-sides, self-service terminals and traditional media as auxiliary platforms. This stipulation completely agrees with the idea that "websites are the primary platforms of information disclosure" consistently adhered to by the Project Team. In the assessment of indices of police transparency in China, the Project Team adopted the method of website assessment. When assessing websites, members of the Project Team took the official websites of the assessment targets as the main source of information, supplemented by the websites of public security organs at higher levels, unified local platforms for the openness of special police affairs, information disclosure platforms of local government at the same level, credit information platforms, as well as mobile phone terminals such as WeChat official accounts.

After the assessment, assessment results were verified by some other members of the Project Team, focusing on checking the index items for which points were deducted from assessment scores. Both assessors and verifiers took and preserved screenshots as evidence during the assessment and verification. In addition to the website observation method, the Project Team also adopted the telephone verification method to verify the telephone numbers disclosed on websites. In the 2018 assessment, the Project Team added the assessment method of "disclosure upon application" by directly applying to public security organs for information disclosure. The time period for the collection of assessment data was between December 1, 2018 and December 31, 2018.

9.2 Assessment Results

In 2018, the average score of the assessment of police transparency indices of 36 assessment targets was 66.53 points. Among them, 26 scored above 60 points, with a passing rate of 72.22%. The top ten public security organs in the ranking of assessment scores were the Public Security Bureau of Nanjing City, the Public Security Bureau of Shenzhen City, the Public Security Bureau of Guiyang City, the Public Security Bureau of Wuhan City, the Public Security Bureau of Guangzhou City, the Public Security Bureau of Ningbo City, the Public Security Bureau of Xi'an City, the Public Security Bureau of Xiamen City, the Public Security Bureau of Fuzhou City, and the Public Security Bureau of Shijiazhuang City. (See Table 9.2). Among the public security organs of 31 municipalities directly under the Central Government and provincial capitals (or capitals of autonomous regions), fifteen rose in ranking in the 2018 assessment as compared with the 2017 assessment. Among them, the Public Security Bureau of Shenyang City, the Public Security Bureau Guangzhou City, the Public Security Bureau of Zhengzhou City, the Public Security Bureau of Nanjing City, and the Public Security Bureau of Shijiazhuang City had risen significantly in the ranking. The Public Security Bureau of Nanjing City, the Public Security Bureau of Guiyang City, the Public Security Bureau of Wuhan City, the Public Security Bureau of Xi'an City, and the Public Security Bureau of Fuzhou City had ranked in the top ten in the assessment of the 31 public security organs of municipalities directly under the Central Government and provincial capitals (or capitals autonomous region) for two consecutive years. The average score of public security organs in the five cities specifically designated in the state plan was 70.92 points. Among them, the Public Security Bureau of Shenzhen City, the Public Security Bureau of Ningbo City, and the Public Security Bureau of Xiamen City were among the top ten of all 36 assessment targets, indicating that the overall level of openness of police affairs in cities specifically designated in the state plan was relatively high, but the differences among these cities were big.

In order to verify the actual effect of disclosure of police affairs data by public security organs and the smoothness of channels of information disclosure upon application, the Project Team sent applications for government information disclosure to the 36 public security organs covered by the assessment by mail in the name of the Project Team on January 9, 2019. By February 20, 2019, the Project Team had

Table 9.2 Results of assessment of indices of police transparency in China (2018)

1	Public Security Bureau of Nanjing City	82.00	100.00	89.00	90.00	89.70
2	Public Security Bureau of Shenzhen City	86.00	100.00	94.00	72.65	87.86
3	Public Security Bureau of Guiyang City	97.00	100.00	89.00	44.50	82.06
4	Public Security Bureau of Wuhan City	89.50	100.00	73.00	60.80	79.48
5	Public Security Bureau of Guangzhou City	82.00	100.00	86.00	48.15	78.34
6	Public Security Bureau of Ningbo City	73.00	100.00	80.50	62.50	78.03
7	Public Security Bureau of Xi'an City	80.00	100.00	84.00	50.00	77.70
8	Public Security Bureau of Xiamen City	73.00	100.00	82.50	55.80	76.95
9	Public Security Bureau of Fuzhou City	73.00	100.00	64.50	70.80	75.30
10	Public Security Bureau of Shijiazhuang City	68.00	100.00	89.00	39.75	73.64
11	Public Security Bureau of Hangzhou City	60.50	100.00	78.00	60.00	73.53
12	Public Security Bureau of Zhengzhou City	77.50	100.00	85.00	32.65	73.04
13	Public Security Bureau of Changsha City	62.50	100.00	67.00	65.15	72.01
14	Public Security Bureau of Hefei City	60.50	100.00	82.00	43.30	70.55
15	Public Security Bureau of Shanghai Municipality	76.00	100.00	65.00	40.00	68.50
16	Public Security Bureau of Beijing Municipality	68.50	100.00	74.00	36.30	68.40
17	Public Security Bureau of Yinchuan City	75.50	100.00	68.50	33.30	67.75
18	Public Security Bureau of Changchun City	77.50	100.00	64.00	29.50	65.95
19	Public Security Bureau of Jinan City	60.50	100.00	71.50	35.80	65.53
20	Public Security Bureau of Shenyang City	75.50	100.00	50.50	39.00	63.78
21	Public Security Bureau of Kunming City	53.50	100.00	42.50	64.90	62.35
22	Public Security Bureau of Tianjin Municipality	56.00	100.00	67.50	30.80	61.95
23	Public Security Bureau of Chengdu City	68.00	100.00	45.50	45.00	61.90
24	Public Security Bureau of Lanzhou City	77.50	100.00	60.00	16.50	61.50
25	Public Security Bureau of Haikou City	68.00	100.00	30.00	57.00	60.25
26	Public Security Bureau of Qingdao City	53.50	100.00	51.00	45.80	60.13
27	Public Security Bureau of Hohhot City	61.00	100.00	48.50	40.00	59.80
28	Public Security Bureau of Harbin City	75.50	100.00	51.00	19.00	58.93
29	Public Security Bureau of Nanning City	73.00	100.00	34.00	35.50	57.33
30	Public Security Bureau of Nanchang City	68.00	100.00	47.50	21.15	56.54
31	Public Security Bureau of Lhasa City	58.00	100.00	40.00	32.50	54.63
32	Public Security Bureau of Urumqi City	64.00	100.00	32.50	28.50	52.88
33	Public Security Bureau of Dalian City	68.00	100.00	25.50	28.00	51.65
34	Public Security Bureau of Taiyuan City	63.50	100.00	46.00	5.00	50.93
35	Public Security Bureau of Chongqing Municipality	41.00	100.00	38.00	28.15	48.69
36	Public Security Bureau of Xining City	46.00	100.00	45.50	10.00	47.65

Unit: point

received replies from a total of 27 public security organs, and the channel smoothness rate was 75%. The assessment shows that 31 public security organs published their own information disclosure guides on their own websites or the websites of the governments at the same level, among which 23, or 63. 89% of all the assessment targets, provided clear information about the departments that accept applications for information disclosure and the electronic version of the information disclosure application form. Of the 27 public security organs that replied to the applications, 25, or 69.44% of all the assessment targets, replied within the statutory time limit (15 working days); 20 provided in their replies the information about the remedy channels for those who refuse to accept the decisions on their applications, among which 10, or 27.78% of all assessment targets, provided clear information about the time limit and accepting organs of complaints or appeals against the decisions. The assessment also shows that, among the 27 public security organs that responded to the application, only 2 provided the data applied for by members of the Project Team in their replies, while most of the others refused to disclose them on the grounds that "the applied information is classified", "the applied information does not belong to government information" or "this organ does not have the information applied for", indicating the problems in police data disclosure work of some public security organs.

9.3 The Effect of Openness of Police Affairs: A System of Intelligent Police Affairs is Beginning to Take Shape

The assessment results in 2018 show that public security organs actively constructed online comprehensive service platforms, carried out a series of activities of openness, such as convenience service, sunshine law enforcement, the openness of punishment, and data openness, and achieved practical results in improving people's livelihood, highlighting the rule of law, promoting honesty and integrity, and facilitating intelligent decision-making. As a result, a system of intelligent police affairs began to take shape in China.

9.3.1 Providing Convenient Services to Improve People's Livelihood

Public security organs are not only law enforcement departments responsible for maintaining social order and stability, but also service management departments closely related to people's livelihood. The openness of police affairs requires the people's police to adhere to the principle of openness and convenience when providing public administration and services such as household registration, entry and exit, public security, traffic safety, cybersecurity, economic and cultural security,

security guard service, etc., disclosing information about not only the offices where people can apply for various certificates and licenses and procedure of application but also online application channels, so as to provide convenience for the people, embody the concept of law enforcement for the people, and improve the people's livelihood. In as early as 2012, in order to safeguard the people's livelihood and build a service-oriented government, the Ministry of Public Security launched 14 measures for the convenience and benefit of the people, including improving the "online public security bureaus, online police stations, and online police offices", and promoting online application, online processing and online examination and approval of matters of public security administration. In 2015, the Framework Opinions on Several Major Issues Concerning Comprehensively Deepening Public Security Reform also put forward a series of policy measures and institutional arrangements for servicing the reform and opening up, promoting economic development, and providing convenience to and benefiting the people, including deepening the reform of the administrative approval system, solidly promoting the reform of the household registration system, innovating population service management, improving the system of foreigners' permanent residence in China, and reforming the system of border defense, entry and exit, transportation, and fire control supervision and management. The assessment results in 2018 show that, to implement the requirements of providing convenience to and benefiting the people put forward in the Framework Opinions on Several Major Issues Concerning Comprehensively Deepening Public Security Reform, local public security organs had published service guides, and set up comprehensive service platforms and mobile terminals to facilitate the consultation, handling of affairs, inquiry and supervision by the people, thus taking a key step towards intelligent police affairs. All the 36 public security organs covered by the assessment had published the list of materials needed for handling the relevant affairs, and provided guidance on the handling of relevant affairs, online booking service, online application service, and online inquiry service; and 25, or 69. 44% of the total, disclosed the telephone numbers of all police stations under them. For example, the Public Security Bureau of Shenzhen City had made great efforts to build a one-stop police affairs platform, promising "zero distance service" and "one-stop service", providing the handling of 165 affairs and the online handling of 137 affairs. It not only provided inquiries about the progress and results of the handling of affairs but also disclosed to the public the progress and results of the handling of affairs in the past 30 days. The Public Security Bureau of Jilin Province constructed the "Internet plus Public Security" comprehensive service platform to provide online services in the fields of household registration, entry and exit, traffic control, public security, supervision, border defense, fire protection, cybersecurity, drug control and economic and cultural protection, the "appointment and application" service and inquiry about service guides. In addition, the platform also provides online consultation services, and discloses the questions asked and answers given in the consultations, and sorts out the hot issues of household registration, traffic police, entry and exit, legal system, and public security in the consultation, so as to provide references for more people. Some public security organs had made innovations in providing precision services.

For example, the website of the Public Security Bureau of Guangzhou City organically combined business consultation with service guide to enable users to enter the corresponding web pages and read the target information after answering several simple "yes" and "no" questions. In addition to providing PC terminal services, public security organs also followed the development trend of mobile communication by providing mobile terminal services through apps, WeChat official accounts, and WeChat applets. This kind of "handheld police affairs" and " police affairs at fingertips" provides the public with more convenient inquiries and online services. Moreover, some public security organs had also connected PC terminals and mobile terminals to provide interactive services. For example, the Public Security Bureau of Guangzhou City provided at the bottom of the homepage of its PC terminal website the QR code or WeChat share to enable users to read the relevant information on mobile terminals anytime and anywhere, thus realizing the interaction between PC terminals and mobile terminals.

9.3.2 Highlighting the Rule of Law Through Sunshine Law Enforcement

In a country under the rule of law, the greater a power, the greater the supervision and restriction it is subject to. When public security organs exercise the law enforcement power in such fields as public security, fire control, household registration and traffic management, they often take compulsory and punishment measures against citizens' person and property. Therefore, as the epitome of government law enforcement, public security administrative law enforcement should be strictly regulated. Apart from administrative law enforcement, public security organs are also responsible for the investigation of criminal cases, so public security law enforcement is also a power in the judicial category. In order to standardize public security law enforcement, the General Office of the CPC Central Committee and the General Office of the State Council issued the Opinions on Deepening the Standardization Construction of Public Security Law Enforcement in September 2016. In addition to putting law enforcement power into an "iron cage" through institutionalization and informatization, China should also increase the openness of the law enforcement process and law enforcement results, promote standardization through openness, create "sunshine police affairs" and accept social supervision, so as to increase the level of legalization of public security law enforcement. The 2015 Framework Opinions on Several Major Issues Concerning Comprehensively Deepening Public Security Reform stated that China would improve the operation mechanism of law enforcement power and push forward the reform of the system of openness of police affairs in width and depth. The Guiding Opinions on Comprehensively Implementing the Administrative Law Enforcement Publication System, the Recording System of Law Enforcement in the Whole Process and the Legal Review System of Major Law Enforcement Decisions, adopted by the Central Commission for Comprehensively Deepening Reform on

November 14, 2018, provide that "An administrative law enforcement agency shall, within 20 working days from the date of an enforcement decision, disclose the information about law enforcement agency, object of law enforcement, classification of law enforcement, and law enforcement conclusion to the public, and accept social supervision. Information about a law enforcement decision such as administrative licensing and administrative penalty should be disclosed to the public within seven working days from the date of the law enforcement decision unless otherwise required by any law or administrative regulations."

Complete openness of law enforcement refers to the openness of the whole process of law enforcement, including the disclosure of law enforcement basis, law enforcement flowchart, rights and obligations of the parties, process nodes, results, documents, supervision, etc., covering both static and dynamic openness, both *ex-ante* openness and in-process and *ex-post* openness, both openness of process and openness of results, and both openness to the parties and openness to society. The 2018 assessment shows that, among the 36 public security organs covered by the assessment, 31, or 86.11% of the total, provided inquiries about the law enforcement process, enabling the parties to inquire about the progress of the handling of their cases online with case numbers and passwords; 21, or 58.33% of the total, disclosed the results of administrative licensing to the public; 18, or 50% of the total, disclosed administrative reconsideration documents online; and 21, or 58.33% of the total, provided the document retrieval function. The Public Security Bureau of Shenzhen City had done a particularly good job in the openness of law enforcement, dividing the openness into *ex-ante* openness, in-process openness and *ex-post* openness, and disclosing the names, positions, main responsibilities and tasks of the personnel in administrative law enforcement post windows of each department of the Bureau. The Public Security Bureau of Changsha City set up a financial information catalog in the openness of police affairs column of its website to disclose the amount of administrative fees it collected each month.

The openness of supervision was a bright spot in the openness of law enforcement in 2018. Openness supervision means that the public security organs should not only provide complaint channels but also disclose information about complaints received and their handling. As the saying goes, "complaints are gold". The public chooses to supervise the government by raising their personal demands or exposing social problems through the channels of complaints, opinions, and suggestions because they have trust in the government. Citizens' right to criticize and supervise the government is specifically provided for and guaranteed by the Constitution. In practice, however, although many government departments have opened online complaint channels, problems such as insufficient importance attached to public complaints and lack of feedback or timely feedback still exist. As a result, supervision and communication between the government and the people become a mere formality. In order to force public authorities to actively handle and feedback on complaints, the Project Team carried out the assessment of the openness of supervision over public security organs. The assessment result shows that, among the 36 public security organs covered by the assessment, 33 or 91. 67% of the total, provided guidance or channels for supervision and complaint, and 26, or 72. 22% of the total, published their feedback on complaints online. Public security organs of some cities (such as Shenzhen, Lanzhou, Qingdao, and Dalian) disclosed all complaints, suggestions and the results of their handling on the Internet, so as to enable the people to experience the smoothness of communication channels between them and the government and see the sincerity of the government in listening to their demands.

The Public Security Bureau of Shenzhen City had published a guide to the system of tipoffs with rewards, accepted online tipoffs, and published typical cases of tipoffs with rewards to guide citizens to actively provide effective clues about crimes. The Public Security Bureau of Lanzhou City published in the "Messages to the Department" column of the website of the Government of Lanzhou City the list of replies to complaints from the public, listing such information as the number, type, title, processing status and acceptance time of each complaint. By clicking on a piece of information in the list, readers could also see the detailed content of the complaint and reply to it. From the disclosed information, we can see that the public had raised many sharp questions in this column. For example, some citizens asked: "Why do the vehicles of urban management and law enforcement department we see on the road have no registration plates? What impression does it give to the public as a law enforcer? Who gave them this power?" To this question, the public security organ gave the following answer: "After verification, we confirm that the vehicles of urban management and law enforcement department should have local vehicle license plates on them. A penalty will be imposed on them if they do not display their license plates in accordance with regulations. The traffic police detachment of our bureau has already instructed the traffic police brigades in various precincts to strengthen road patrol and intensify the investigation and punishment of vehicles involved in the violations of regulations on vehicle license plates. At the same time, a letter will be sent to the Urban Management and Law Enforcement Department, demanding it to use its vehicles in a reasonable and lawful way, and put an end to the illegal practice of driving a vehicle without a license plate on it." From the content of the reply, we can see that the law enforcement department had faced up to the problems and indicated that it would strengthen the standardization of law enforcement. The Public Security Bureau of Dalian City published letters from the public and replies to them in the "Serving the People" column on its official website. If government organs try to cover up the problems reported by the public, or even retaliate against those who criticize them, they will lose the support of the people. On the other hand, if they face up and positively responded to criticisms and openly accepted supervision by public opinion, they will win the support and understanding of the people.

9.3.3 *Disclosing Information About Administrative Penalties to Encourage Honesty*

When economic and social development reaches a certain stage, it becomes urgent to build a credible society. Sunshine police affairs and openness of law enforcement are not only the essential requirements of the operation of public powers but also the objective needs of building a credible society. Public security law enforcement involves traffic safety, entry and exit, public security and other matters. The information about illegal and criminal activities acquired by public security organs is an important data source for building a social credit system. In the construction of credit systems in various places, it is particularly important for public security organs to push information about punishment for the violations of law to credit platforms. In January 2017, the Ministry of Public Security, the Civil Aviation Administration of China and other departments jointly issued the Guiding Opinions on Strengthening the Construction of the Credit System in the Field of Transportation and Travel (No.10 [2017] of the National Development and Reform Commission), requiring public security and traffic administration departments to publish information about individuals and enterprises with serious traffic violations. In order to meet the requirements of deepening public security reform in the new era, the Framework Opinions on Several Major Issues Concerning Comprehensively Deepening Public Security Reform put forward the plan to speed up the construction of a unified social credit code system for citizens based on citizen ID card numbers, and promote the establishment of a system linking criminal records with credit and related occupational access. The openness of administrative penalties has two levels, at the first level is the disclosure of information about violations of law, and at the second level is the online publication of administrative penalty decisions made by public security organs. Article 12 of the 2018 Provisions on Openness of Law Enforcement by Public Security Organs stipulates that "public security organs shall gradually disclose to the public the effective legal documents of administrative penalty decisions and administrative reconsideration results". The assessment shows that, to deter violations of law and build social integrity, public security organs strengthened the disclosure of administrative penalty information. Of the 36 public security organs covered by the assessment, 26, or 72. 22% of the total, disclosed information about administrative penalties, and 21, or 58.33% of the total, published administrative penalty documents on their websites. Some public security organs did not directly publish such documents on the Internet, but accepted inquiries by non-anonymous citizens. Citizens who want to inquire about the penalty decisions in administrative cases only need to enter their ID numbers on the login page of the Case Information Inquiry Platform, and then search for relevant legal documents according to such conditions as case name, case type, time of imposition of penalty and the organ imposing the penalty. Some other public security departments (such as that of Nanning City), disclosed the information about criminal cases, administrative cases, administrative reconsideration cases, and state compensation cases in the public security law enforcement information disclosure column of their websites.

9.3.4 Promoting Intelligent Decision-Making Through the Openness of Data

In the information age, those who control data control the world, and data openness has become an irresistible trend. The openness of data has two aspects, one is data sharing among public authorities, and the other is the openness of data by public authorities to society. From the perspective of data sources, the data obtained by public authorities in the process of administration and service come from administrative counterparts, which are public data, not the private assets of public authorities, and therefore should be open to the public with the exception of those that should be kept confidential in accordance with law. However, many departments still take public data as their private property and refuse to share it with other departments and society. For this reason, the Project Team carried out the assessment of data openness as the focus of openness of government affairs and judicial openness, so as to promote the social sharing of data resources and the establishment of a big database for the people. The openness of data is the precondition of intelligent decision-making. Analysis and mining of open data can provide effective support for scientific and accurate decision-making by the government, and data governance will become an inevitable choice in the modernization of the state governance system and capacity.

Public security organs have the most extensive scope of administration and service, as well as the power to enforce the law. Therefore, public security data are not only massive, but also highly accurate, and, as such, are rich mines worth exploring. To promote the opening up of data by public security organs and the establishment of public security big data for the people, the Project Team put forward requirements for data disclosure in such aspects as annual report, annual work summary, traffic statistics, administrative law enforcement statistics, statistics of criminal cases, statistics of complaints against police officers, the release of information about major cases, and police alert. The assessment results show that, in 2018, public security organs had raised their awareness of data openness, and set up special columns on annual work plans, data releases, and statistical information on their websites.

As far as the publication of annual reports and annual work summaries is concerned, although none of the 36 public security organs covered by the assessment had published their annual reports, 15 had directly or indirectly published their work summaries or work plans. There were several ways of publishing work summaries. First, direct publication. For example, the Public Security Bureau of Shenzhen City discloses the work summary of the previous year and the work plan of the current year in March every year; the Public Security Bureau of Ningbo City discloses the (relatively brief) work summary of the previous year and the work arrangement for the current year from February to March every year, and discloses the work summary of the current month and the work arrangement for the next month in the end of each month; the Public Security Bureau of Changsha City, the Public Security Bureau of Hangzhou City, the Public Security Bureau of Haikou City, the Public Security Bureau of Xi'an City, the Public Security Bureau of Guiyang City, the Public Security Bureau of Qingdao City and the Public Security Bureau of

Fuzhou City had disclosed their key points of work, work reports, work summaries and work plans; and the Public Security Bureau of Shenyang City published the Summary of Public Security Work in Shenyang City in 2017 as the key points of the work of openness of government affairs. Second, the inclusion of the work of the previous year in departmental final accounts. For example, the 2017 departmental final accounts of the Vehicle Management Department of Kunming Public Security Bureau included an "Introduction to Key Tasks of Work in 2017", which was equivalent to its work summary in 2017; and the public security bureaus of Nanjing City and Xi'an disclosed a detailed work summary in 2017 in their final accounts for 2017. Thirdly, publication of special work reports. For example, the public security bureaus of Kunming City and Hangzhou City published reports on the construction of a law-based government; the Public Security Bureau of Qingdao City published its reports on the construction of a law-based government in 2016 and 2017; the Public Security Bureau of Chengdu City published the Report on the Completion of Main Work Objectives in 2016; the Public Security Bureau of Shenzhen City publishes its work report on the construction of a law-based government in late December of each year in the "Annual Information Disclosure Report" column of its website; the Public Security Bureau of Beijing Municipality publishes the summary of the work of construction of a law-based government and the reports on performance tasks of the bureau and their completion; the Public Security Bureau of Guiyang City publishes its audit work reports in previous years; and the Public Security Bureau of Haikou City publishes various implementation opinions and special work summaries in the "Meeting Minutes" column of its website.

As far as the disclosure of public security statistics is concerned, of the 36 public security organs covered by the assessment, 12 provided traffic statistics, among which 10 disclosed traffic statistics in each district in detail on a monthly basis; and 9 of the 36 public security bureaus disclosed the statistical data of administrative penalty and administrative licensing (or other law enforcement activities). The most typical practices of publication of statistics were those of the public security bureaus of Shenzhen City, Guangzhou City, Hangzhou City and Kunming City. The Public Security Bureau of Shenzhen City had set up a special "Statistical Data" column on its website to publish statistics on vehicle administration, traffic administration, public security administration and anti-cyber fraud work on a monthly basis. It had also set up the "Data Openness" column in the openness of police affairs directory of its website to allow users to click on the link to go straight to the Data Openness Platform of Shenzhen Municipal Government. The Public Security Bureau of Guangzhou City published on the website of Guangzhou Municipal Government the Administrative Law Enforcement Data of Guangzhou Public Security Bureau in 2017, which provided statistical tables on the implementation of administrative penalties, administrative licensing, administrative enforcement, and other administrative law enforcement activities, and gave a detailed explanation of its administrative law enforcement situation in 2017. It also published the analysis of the situation of the public security hotline on a monthly basis, disclosing the number of 12,345 government service hotline items (calls to the public security hotline), and analyzing the top five items, quantity and proportion of citizens' demands, and items with rising and falling demands. The Public Security Bureau of Hangzhou City disclosed traffic accident situation by district on a monthly basis, and regularly published fire analysis reports. The Public Security Bureau of Kunming City disclosed information about various administrative cases. For example, it disclosed on a monthly basis the results of administrative approval items of Kunming Exit-Entry Administration in the first half of 2018, including the number of overseas business consultations, the numbers of various kinds of application form issued, the numbers of issuance and endorsement of exit documents, and the acceptance and approval of application for entry documents submitted by various overseas personnel, information about the handling of public security registration in the motor vehicle passenger transport industry in Kunming, including the number of registration, information about the investigation and punishment of violations of law in business premises for Internet access services, information about the investigation and punishment of public security violations in motor vehicle passenger transport industry in Kunming, information about investigation and punishment of traffic violations in Kunming, including the number and reasons of administrative detentions, the number and reasons of revocations of driver's licenses, and investigation and punishment of all kinds of serious traffic violations.

9.4 The Dilemma of Choice Faced by China in the Openness of Police Affairs

In 2018, public security organs in China achieved practical results in improving people's livelihood, highlighting the rule of law, encouraging honesty, and promoting intelligent decision-making by carrying out a series of openness activities such as convenience service, sunshine law enforcement, openness punishment and data openness. However, in the process of promoting openness of police affairs, public security organs are faced with the dilemmas of choice between publicity and openness, between openness and confidentiality, between real name and anonymity, and between dispersion and intensification, in addition to the common problems in openness of government affairs, such as not timely and incomplete information updating.

9.4.1 Publicity and Openness

At the beginning of their establishment, government websites were used as a new media platform to release news, publicize the activities of leaders and show the exemplary deeds of the unit. With the advancement of openness of government affairs, more and more government departments choose to disclose information on websites, and the openness function of websites is becoming more and more prominent. However, due to the publicity mindset formed over a long period of time, many government websites are still publicity-oriented, with a distinct color of publicity in page setting and directory structure. News pictures, media reports and leaders' activities occupied a prominent position on the homepages of the websites of most public security organs covered by the assessment. For example, on the homepage of the website of the Public Security Bureau of Hefei City, news pictures and news catalogs occupy half of the page, and there were four news and publicity columns alone, namely, "Public Security Highlights", "Press Release", "Trends in Police Work" and "Police Showcase". Once publicity is given priority over openness, the effect of openness will be greatly reduced, and there will be no timeliness, comprehensiveness, accuracy and convenience of information disclosure to talk about. In fact, official websites of government organs should be platforms for serving the people, realizing their right to know, and enabling them to handle their affairs conveniently. And if they do well in openness, they can attract more people's attention, which is the best publicity, and the publicity work itself should be given to the media. In the future, public security organs should establish the ideas that their official websites are the primary platforms for the openness of government affairs and that openness is the best publicity, as well as the public demand-orientation of government websites.

9.4.2 Openness and Confidentiality

Because the functions of public security organs involve sensitive matters such as drug control and criminal investigation, some police information is confidential and cannot be made public. In practice, however, local public security organs have different standards on whether some categories of information are confidential. Take the staffing quota of public security organs as an example. The assessment shows that the public security bureaus of Guiyang City, Shenyang City and Hohhot City disclosed the name list of administrative law enforcement personnel. Those of Taiyuan City and Haikou City disclosed the number of policemen, while the Public Security Bureau of Wuhan City disclosed more detailed information, including not only the list and details of on-the-job staff members but also the number of administrative staffing quota and the number of on-the-job administrative personnel in the Table of Institutional Staffing of the Public Security Bureau of Wuhan City. Some other public security bureaus, such as those of Lanzhou, Xiamen, Hefei, Yinchuan, Harbin, and Nanchang, although did not directly disclose the number of their personnel, listed the number of their staffing quota or number of on-the-job staff members in their disclosed budgets and final accounts. The Public Security Bureau of Harbin City also lists the number of staff members in each unit under its jurisdiction and their administrative levels. In sharp contrast to the above-mentioned public security organs, the public security bureaus of Kunming, Nanning and other cities specifically stated in their public budgets for 2018 that the quota and the actual number of staff members were confidential information and would not be disclosed according to law. Among the 36 public security organs covered by the assessment, 19, or 52.78% of the total, did not disclose information about the number of their staff members. Even different departments in the same public security bureau had different standards on the disclosure of the same kind of information. Take disclosure of the number of staff members and vehicles as an example. The Public Security Bureau, the Department of Motor Vehicles and the Detention Center of Kunming City had all disclosed their quotas and actual numbers of administrative staff members and vehicles in their public budgets and final accounts. However, the Traffic Police Detachment of Kunming Public Security Bureau clearly stated in its final accounts for 2017 that "the specific quotas and actual numbers of staff members and vehicles are confidential information and, according to relevant confidentiality regulations, cannot be disclosed to the public". Even Kunming People's Police School of Yunnan Province, a public institution without much sensitive information, made it clear in its final accounts for 2017 that "the specific numbers of personnel and vehicles of this school are confidential information according to relevant confidentiality regulations". The Drug Rehabilitation Management Office of Kunming City had a similar practice. In view of this situation, the Project Team carried out a special investigation on the practice of the Ministry of Public Security in the disclosure of similar information. The Ministry of Public Security disclosed the information about motor vehicles of the Ministry and its subordinate units in its public departmental final accounts in 2017, including the total number of vehicles, the number of vehicles used by leading cadres at the ministerial level, the number of ordinary official vehicles, the number of vehicles used for the performance of ordinary law enforcement duty, the number of special professional and technical vehicles, and the number of other vehicles (large and medium-sized buses used for transporting police, prison vehicles and ambulances used for escorting important criminals, police dog transport vehicles and teaching vehicles for students to learn driving skills, etc.).

In addition to the numbers of police officers and official vehicles, public security organs had different views on whether their work summaries and work plans should be considered confidential. With the exception of the above-mentioned public security organs in Shenzhen, Qingdao, Shenyang, and Xi'an, which disclosed their work summaries, key points of work, and work plans, most public security organs covered by the assessment did not disclose such information on grounds that they involved police secrets. For example, the Public Security Bureau of Dalian City clearly stated on its website that "In accordance with the Law of the People's Republic of China on Guarding State Secrets and the Provisions of the Ministry of Public Security on Secrecy Work of Public Security Organs and after examination and approval by the Secrecy Committee of the Public Security Bureau of Dalian City, we decide that the work summaries and key points of work of public security organs are information involving police secrets, and therefore are not disclosed to the public in accordance with law". The Public Security Bureau of Hefei City published its work plan for 2018, but did not publish its work plans in previous years on the grounds that they involved police secrets.

In addition to the disclosure of budget, final accounts and budgetary expenditures related to official overseas visits, official vehicles, and official hospitality, financial openness also includes the disclosure of public officials' income and the collection of fines and fees. The assessment results show that the personnel expenses mentioned by public security organs in their disclosed budget and final accounts included salaries, allowances and subsidies. Two assessment targets disclosed information about the collection of fees: one was the Public Security Bureau of Guangzhou City, which published the 2016 Revenue of Guangzhou Exit-Entry Administration Detachment from Collection of Fees, and listed the amounts of various fees and fines and confiscations collected by security organs in Guangzhou City in its final accounts table in 2017; the other one was the Public Security Bureau of Changsha City, which disclosed the data of the collection of administrative fees in 2013. In the future, public security organs should strengthen the disclosure of the income of their staff members, and bring the information about the collection of fines and fees into the scope of financial openness, so as to truly realize financial transparency.

9.4.3 Real Name and Anonymity

The 2018 Provisions on Openness of Law Enforcement by Public Security Organs contain specific provisions on the openness of administrative penalty decisions, requiring the anonymization of natural persons subject to an administrative penalty. The assessment results show that, among the 21 public security organs that published administrative penalty decisions online, 13, or more than 60% of the total, anonymized natural persons subject to an administrative penalty. For example, the public security bureaus of the cities of Shijiazhuang, Jinan, Hefei, Guiyang, Xi'an, and Xining also deidentified violators of law or applicants when disclosing their ID numbers, date of birth, home addresses, and other information. The documents of the Ministry of Public Security provide for the anonymized disclosure of administrative penalty decisions for the sake of protecting the privacy of natural persons. However, the issue of whether to choose real name disclosure or anonymous disclosure should be determined by the purpose of document disclosure. The purpose of publishing administrative penalty decisions is to facilitate supervision, which includes both the social supervision over the result of the exercise of the power of administrative penalty and the public opinion supervision over persons subject to administrative penalties. Anonymous disclosure excludes the second kind of supervision mentioned above and is not conducive to the construction of the social credit system. In horizontal comparison, it has become the norm for courts to publish judgment documents on the Internet. The Supreme People's Court repeatedly revised the regulations on the publication of documents on the Internet, and finally chose the real name disclosure. In a law-based society, citizens' privacy should be respected and protected. However, for the purpose of accepting social supervision and protecting greater public interests, some rights relating to privacy can be appropriately derogated. The Framework Opinions on Several Major Issues Concerning Comprehensively Deepening Public Security Reform put forward the plan to speed up the construction of a unified social credit code system for citizens based on citizen ID card numbers and promote the establishment of a system linking criminal records with credit and access to certain occupations. In the future, in order to improve the construction of the social credit system, it is necessary to strengthen the association analysis and deepen the application of administrative law enforcement big data. Anonymization in the publication of law enforcement documents will impede data association.

9.4.4 Decentralization and Intensification

Too many platforms with too scattered information is a common problem in the openness of government affairs, including judicial openness, especially in the openness of police affairs. The assessment shows that some assessment targets had up to seven or eight platforms of openness of police affairs, including the official website of the public security bureau (some public security bureaus had two official websites. For example, the Public Security Bureau of Lanzhou City had two official websites: http://gaj.lanzhou.gov.cn and http://www.lzsgaj.gov.cn), websites of functional departments of a public security bureau (for example, the website of the Traffic Administration Department of the Public Security Bureau of Beijing Municipality: http://www.bjjtgl.gov.cn), the websites of higher-level public security organs, and a unified platform for the openness of law enforcement (such as the website of the Public Security Law Enforcement Information Disclosure and Inquiry System of Yunnan Province http://220.163.12.25), intelligent police affairs platforms (such as the Internet plus Public Security Government Service Platform of Yunnan Province), and special police affairs platforms (such as the Public Security Entry and Exit Online Service Platform: http://219.136.255.192, Traffic Safety Integrated Service Management Platform: http://www.122.gov.cn). Some websites, such as government websites at the same level and Credit China local channels, although not platforms for the openness of police affairs, also publish some or some categories of police affairs information. The information released by different platforms is inconsistent in quantity and content, and there is also a lack of effective linkage between different platforms.

The numerous platforms not only increase the cost of openness but also result in data fragmentation and create obstacles to the access to complete information by the public. Article 32 of the 2018 Provisions on Openness of Law Enforcement by Public Security Organs requires public security organs to build an Internet open government platform to uniformly disclose law enforcement information of public security organs. Meanwhile, it stipulates that law enforcement openness can be realized through the unified Internet openness platform of a higher-level public security organ or the people's government at the same level. In the future, China should follow the trend towards intensive construction of government websites and, on the precondition of ensuring technical security, integrate platforms of openness of police affairs to realize the intensive disclosure of police information. Moreover, the friendliness of platforms needs to be further improved, and the floating windows on web pages should be closed. The assessment results show that, among the 36 public security organs covered by the assessment, 16 had floating windows on the homepages of their websites, which impeded information access by visitors.

9.5 Choosing the Path of Improving the Transparency of Police Affairs in China

Attitude determines standards, standards determine transparency, and transparency determines trust. In view of the problems such as the conservative attitude toward openness, too many platforms, and the lack of standards in the openness of police affairs, China should choose desensitization, intensification, and standardization as its path to enhancing the transparency of police affairs.

9.5.1 Desensitization

Public security organs are both administrative law enforcement organs and criminal investigation organs. In the process of promoting the opening up of public security data, they should properly handle the relationship between openness and confidentiality, neither disclosing law enforcement information that involves state secrets, hinders normal investigation activities, or affects social stability, nor refusing to disclose any information under the pretext of confidentiality. As to which public security affairs belong to the category of confidential information, contain clear stipulations should be made in the Provisions on the Specific Scope and Security Classification of State Secrets in Public Security Work and the Provisions on the Specific Scope of Police Secrets in Public Security Work. However, these two documents themselves are also classified, so the public has no way of knowing which public security affairs belong to confidential information. In practice, local public security organs have different standards on whether a specific affair belongs to the scope of confidential information, and it is difficult for outsiders to know which standard is correct and which one is wrong. With the continuous improvement of the rule of law and the substantiation of the openness of government affairs, some police affairs should undergo a desensitization process. Take the work plans of public security organs as an example. Many public security organs refuse to disclose them on the grounds that "they involve police secrets". However, the assessment also shows that many public security organs published their work plans after desensitization treatment. For example, the final accounts of the Beijing Municipal Public Security Bureau in 2017 contained a "description of confidential matters", that is, "information that has been confirmed by the National Administration for Protection of State Secrets as involving state secrets and removed from the budget information disclosure in accordance with relevant provisions of state laws and administrative regulations and the provisions on the scope of confidential information". In the future, if confidential information in a document can be separated from the document, a public security organ should publish the document after removing the confidential information, rather than refusing to disclose the whole document on the grounds of partial confidentiality. Otherwise, public security big data will not be constructed, and the credibility and affinity of public security organs will be damaged.

9.5.2 *Intensification*

The intensive construction of government websites is an inevitable trend of development. Therefore, on the premise of ensuring technical security, China should also integrate platforms of openness of police affairs to realize the intensification of disclosure of police information. Some public security organs began to intentionally develop their websites in the direction of intensification. For example, the Public Security Bureau of Qingdao City moved the Qingdao Public Security Traffic Information Service Platform to Qingdao Public Security Network from April to May 2018; the Public Security Bureau of Xiamen City moved its official website (Xiamen Public Security Public Service Network) to the unified technological platform of the website of Xiamen Municipal Government, which was launched on September 20, 2018, with a new domain name: http://ga.xm.gov.cn. The Public Security Bureau of Shenzhen City provided a transitional mode for the intensification of openness of police affairs by setting up a unified directory of openness on its official website, with most of the information disclosed on its official website and some of the information moved to the corresponding intensive platforms, and provided linkages to such information on the official website. For example, it moved online inquiry about administrative penalty decisions and progress of the handling of cases to the Guangdong Public Security Law Enforcement Information Disclosure Platform, the openness of information about law enforcement subjects to Shenzhen Government Online, and the list of powers and responsibilities to Guangdong Government Service Network (Shenzhen), and provided corresponding links on its official website. In the future, when the openness of government affairs develops to an advanced stage, "one-stop" openness will become the inevitable choice, and "the disclosure of all police information on one website" will be realized.

9.5.3 *Standardization*

Standardization is an indicator of the maturity of the industry. The deep-seated reason for the existence of some chaotic phenomena in the openness of police affairs is the absence of a standard resulting from the lack of a unified understanding. In the future, China should standardize the openness of police affairs and gradually develop the industrial standard on the openness of all government affairs. Of course, the standardization of openness of police affairs is a systematic project, requiring the further change of ideas, the unification of understandings, the digital management of police affairs, and the screening, refinement, scientific classification, and effective integration of data and information.

Chapter 10
Report on Indices of Maritime Judicial Transparency in China (2017)—From the Perspective of Information Disclosure on the Websites of Maritime Courts

Innovation Project Team on the Rule of Law Index

Abstract In 2017, the Innovation Project Team on Rule of Law Indices of Law Institute of Chinese Academy of Social Sciences conducted the fifth assessment of the judicial openness of 10 maritime courts in China. In order to increase comparability, the Project Team also conducted an assessment and comparative study of the judicial openness of the higher/intermediate people's courts where 10 maritime courts were located. The assessment results show that the maritime judicial transparency in China had steadily improved, with the overall situation of judicial openness of maritime courts slightly better than that of ordinary courts, and remarkable progress made in the publication of typical maritime cases and white papers on maritime trials. Meanwhile, some problems identified in previous assessments remained, the situations of "zombie columns" and scattered information release platforms had not been improved, and the polarization pattern continued. In order to better serve and guarantee the construction of "the Belt and Road" and the strategy of building China into a major maritime power, maritime judicial openness should develop in the direction of institutionalization, normalization and internationalization. China should continue to enhance the transparency of maritime justice, improve the institutions of and the working mechanism for openness, unify information release platforms, and publish typical cases, guiding cases and white papers on maritime trials on a regular basis.

Keywords Maritime justice · Transparency · Judicial openness · Rule of law index

Leaders of the Project Team: Tian He, a research fellow at CASS Law Institute and the director of the Center for Studies of National Indices of the Rule of Law, Chinese Academy of Social Sciences, and Lv Yanbin, a research fellow at and the head of the Department of Survey and Study of National Situation of the Rule of Law of the Institute of Law, Chinese Academy of Social Sciences. Other members of the Project Team include: Zhang Wenguang, Wang Xiaomei, Li Yanjie, Wang Junxiu, Wang Shan, etc. Author of this report: Zhang Wenguang, an associate research fellow at the Institute of International Law, Chinese Academy of Social Sciences. This report has received support and help from many experts, scholars, judges, and lawyers in the design of indices, investigation, research and preparation of the report, to who we would like express our deep appreciation.

Innovation Project Team on the Rule of Law Index (✉)
Institute of Law, Chinese Academy of Social Sciences, Beijing, China
e-mail: 13263169197@163.com

H. Tian et al. (eds.), *Report on the Rule of Law Index in China 2*,
Research Series on the Chinese Dream and China's Development Path,
https://doi.org/10.1007/978-981-19-9597-2_10

In 2017, in order to assess the development of maritime judicial transparency in China, the Innovation Project Team on Rule of Law Indices of Law Institute of Chinese Academy of Social Sciences (hereinafter referred to as the "Project Team") conducted the fifth investigation and assessment of maritime judicial transparency in China from the perspective of information disclosure on the websites of maritime courts.

10.1 A Review of Important Events of Maritime Judicial Openness in China in 2017

In 2017, the 10 maritime courts in the country continued to disclose information about court trials and enforcement through their official websites, provincial-level judicial openness platforms, national judicial openness platforms, China Foreign-related Commercial and Maritime Trial Network and various other media, thereby continuously improving the transparency, credibility and international influence of Chinese maritime justice.

10.1.1 The Importance Attached to Judicial Openness by the Work Report of the Supreme People's Court

On March 12, 2017, the Supreme People's Court stated in its work report that China would "Improve the four major platforms for the openness of the trial process, trial activities, judgment documents and enforcement information, and further increase the breadth and depth of judicial openness, so that the people can see and feel fairness and justice", "improve the system of and mechanism for, and enhance the effect of openness, and enable the people to feel more fairness and justice", and "strengthen international judicial exchanges, tell the story of China's rule of law well, and contribute more Chinese judicial wisdom to the advancement of global governance".[1]

[1] The Supreme People's Court, "Report on the Work of the Supreme People's Court", http://news.xinhouanet.com/politics/2017lh/2017-03/19/c_1120653949.htm, last visited on December 26, 2017.

10.1.2 The Release of the Top Ten Typical Maritime Cases of the Year for the First Time by the Supreme People's Court

In April 2017, the Supreme People's Court released ten typical cases of maritime trials in 2016, which demonstrated the role of maritime justice in safeguarding national maritime rights and interests, guiding international maritime rule-making, unifying maritime adjudication standards, and enhancing the credibility of maritime justice.[2] This was the first time that the Supreme People's Court issued the top ten typical maritime cases of the year, which had attracted wide attention from the maritime and legal circles.

10.1.3 The Second Batch of Ten Typical Cases Involving "the Belt and Road Initiative" Issued by the Supreme People's Court

On May 15, 2017, the Supreme People's Court released the second batch of typical cases involving the construction of "the Belt and Road". Among them, there are four cases related to maritime justice, which involve the nature of the rights of the holder of a bill of lading, compensation for pollution damage in sea areas, contract of carriage of goods by sea, expenses for overdue use of containers, and so on.

10.1.4 The First Maritime Criminal Case in China Tried by a Chinese Maritime Court

On June 5, 2017, the Maritime Court of Ningbo City, as a pilot court with jurisdiction over maritime criminal cases, accepted the case of a foreign-related maritime traffic accident involving Allan Mendoza Tablate. This was the first maritime criminal case accepted and tried by a Chinese maritime court, as well as one of the maritime cases with the highest social attention this year. During the trial of the case, the Maritime Court of Ningbo City released information in a timely manner through the Internet, and the judgment document was made public on the Internet after it came into effect, with good results.

---

[2] The Supreme People's Court, "Ten Typical Cases of Maritime Trials in China in 2016", *People's Court News*, April 29, 2017, pp. 3–4.

10.1.5 New Breakthroughs in the Informatization of Maritime Courts

On April 19, 2017, Shanghai Maritime Court held the launching ceremony of the Joint Maritime Command Center. On June 28th, the Smart Maritime Court (Shanghai) Practice Base, the first practice base of smart maritime court in China, was formally established in Shanghai Maritime Court. The purposes of the construction of the Practice Base of Smart Maritime Court (Shanghai) are: "to meet the needs of the construction of an international maritime judicial center, attach importance to collecting maritime case information and judgment documents in the whole country, gather and conduct an in-depth analysis of judicial data, contribute Chinese wisdom and provide Chinese solutions to the improvement of the international maritime rule of law, and continuously enhance the international influence and discourse power of China's maritime justice".[3]

10.1.6 The Adoption of the First Five-Year Plan for the Development of Maritime Court in China

On April 12, 2017, Shanghai Maritime Court issued the Outline of the Five-Year Development Plan of Shanghai Maritime Court (2017–2021), which was the first five-year development plan issued by a maritime court in China. It clearly stated that the development of the Shanghai Maritime Court in the next five years will be characterized by "modernization", "innovation", "professionalism", "wisdom" and "transparency", and aimed at constructing a "smart court" and "data court", and building Shanghai Maritime Court into a national practice base for the informatization of maritime trial.

10.2 Index System and Assessment Methods

10.2.1 Assessment Targets

The 10 maritime courts covered by the 2017 assessment of maritime judicial transparency indices in China were the same as those covered by the previous four assessments, namely Shanghai Maritime Court, Tianjin Maritime Court, Qingdao Maritime Court, Dalian Maritime Court, Guangzhou Maritime Court, Wuhan Maritime Court, Haikou Maritime Court, Xiamen Maritime Court, Ningbo Maritime Court and

[3] "The first smart court practice base in China formally established", http://news.xinhouanet.com/local/2017-06/29/c_1121229594/c_1121229594.html, last visited on December 1, 2017.

Beihai Maritime Court. In order to truthfully reflect the situation and level of judicial openness of maritime courts, the method of horizontal comparison had been added in this assessment, that is, using the same modules, indices, and weights to assess and compare the judicial openness of the high people's courts (of municipalities directly under the Central Government) or intermediate people's courts (of other cities) where ten maritime courts were located. The 10 local courts were selected for this year's assessment were: Shanghai High People's Court, Tianjin High People's Court, Qingdao Intermediate People's Court, Dalian Intermediate People's Court, Guangzhou Intermediate People's Court, Wuhan Intermediate People's Court, Haikou Intermediate People's Court, Xiamen Intermediate People's Court, Ningbo Intermediate People's Court and Beihai Intermediate People's Court.

10.2.2 Emphases of Assessment

The emphases of maritime judicial transparency assessment in China in 2017 had been disclosed in the Report on Maritime Judicial Transparency Indices in China (2016: "In the assessment of maritime judicial transparency indices in China 2017, we will pay more attention to the quality and depth of judicial openness. The key points of the assessment will include but are not limited to the timeliness of information disclosure, analysis and application of big data, publication of white papers on maritime trials, publication of typical cases and excellent documents, effective links to national judicial information disclosure platforms, and updating of information on China Maritime Litigation Service Platform.[4]

10.2.3 The Index System

The assessment in 2017 was consistent with those in 2016 and 2015 in terms of the setup of index modules and their weights, that is, the openness of trial affairs (20%), the openness of the case-filing and court trial (30%), the openness of documents (30%), and the openness of enforcement (20%). Each module has a full score of 100 points. In terms of grade II indices and their weights, no new indices had been added and no changes made to the weights of various indices, only the index of document disclosure was fine-tuned: the indices of "integrity of judgment document content" (3.2) and "judgment document content information processing" (3.3) were merged into the index of "document content", and the indices of "online disclosure of data of judgment documents" (3.5) and "disclosure of information about judgment documents not disclosed online" (3.6) were merged into the index "data openness". The

[4] Li Lin and Tian He (eds.), *Report on the Development of the Rule of Law in China No. 15 (2017)*, Beijing: Social Science Academic Press, 2017, p. 270.

optimized and adjusted Assessment Index System of Maritime Judicial Transparency in China (2017) consists of four grade I indices (modules) and 21 grade II indices (see Table 10.1).

Table 10.1 Assessment index system of maritime judicial transparency in China (2017)

Grade I indices and their weights	Grade II indices and their weights
Openness of trial affairs (20%)	Platform construction (35%)
	Personnel information (15%)
	Financial information (15%)
	Annual reports and statistics (25%)
	Normative documents (10%)
Openness of case-filing and court trial (30%)	Litigation guides (20%)
	Announcements of court sessions (20%)
	Observation of court trials by members of the public (20%)
	Live broadcasting of court trial (20%)
	Information release system (10%)
	Trial transcripts (10%)
Openness of documents (30%)	Link to China judgment online (10%)
	Document content (30%)
	Typical cases (30%)
	Data openness (30%)
Openness of enforcement (20%)	Link to China enforcement online (10%)
	Enforcement guide (20%)
	Cases of termination of current enforcement proceedings (20%)
	Enforcement exposure (20%)
	Enforcement disciplinary actions (20%)
	Enforcement tip-offs (10%)

10.2.4 Methods and Principles of Assessment

The Project Team mainly adopted the method of observation and verification for the assessment in 2017. It carried out whole-process tracking of the situation of information updating on the websites of maritime courts and cooperated with the WeChat official account "Maritime Law Research Center" in selecting valuable information on the websites of maritime courts and in media reports. In addition, the Project Team assessed the web portals of 10 maritime courts in China and their information updating on the national judicial openness platforms. Whenever a member of the Project Team could not find a certain piece of information or open a certain webpage, other members of the Project Team would use major search engines on the Internet to search for the information or adopt such methods as changing computers, Internet connection, and time of visit to try to open the webpage and carry out multiple verifications. In order to ensure the accuracy, neutrality and objectivity of the results, the Project Team adhered to the following principles in the assessment: first, announcing the focuses and time period of assessment in advance, so as to give assessment targets sufficient time to prepare for the assessment and improve their work; second, objectifying assessment indices, that is, only "yes" or "no", the amount of effective information, the time of online disclosure, etc. were assessed; third, keeping the assessment indices relatively stable, basically making only some fine-tunings every year, and announcing in advance of any major change to the indices; and fourth, assigning different members of the Project Team to be responsible for assessment and verification.

10.3 Overall Assessment Results

In 2017, among the 10 maritime courts in China, the rankings of 7 maritime courts changed, and the scores of 8 maritime courts increased, with the average score crossing the passing line and increasing by 15.69% over the previous year. Two maritime courts scored above 90 points, two maritime courts scored between 80 and 90 points, two maritime courts scored between 60 and 70 points, one maritime court scored between 50 and 60 points, one maritime court scored between 40 and 50 points and two maritime courts scored 30 between 40 points (see Table 10.2).

In view of the fact that the modules, indices and weights in the 2017 assessment were basically the same as those in the 2016 assessment, the assessment results in 2017 were highly comparable with those in 2016. However, the followings need to be pointed out. First, portal websites were the focus of the assessment of maritime judicial transparency. Some maritime courts attached importance to information disclosure in traditional media, but did not disclose relevant information on their portal websites, and this had affected their final scores in the assessment. Second, the ranking of assessment scores reflects the relative levels of transparency. A court's decline in ranking might be caused by the faster progress made by other maritime

Table 10.2 Results of assessment of judicial transparency indices of maritime courts in China

Rankings	Maritime courts	Openness of trial affairs (20%)	Open of case-filing and court trial (30%)	Openness of documents (30%)	Openness of enforcement (20%)	Total score (out of 100 points)
1	Shanghai	93.5	95.0	95.0	80.0	91.7
2	Ningbo	95.0	86.0	95.0	90.0	91.3
3	Xiamen	88.5	80.0	95.0	65.0	83.2
4	North Sea	94.5	80.0	83.0	65.0	80.8
5	Guangzhou	79.5	40.0	88.0	55.0	65.3
6	Haikou	83.5	60.0	65.0	45.0	63.2
7	Tianjin	51.5	76.0	55.0	25.0	54.6
8	Wuhan	69.5	35.0	55.0	25.0	45.9
9	Qingdao	42.5	30.0	54.0	15.0	36.7
10	Dalian	54.5	20.0	35.0	15.0	30.4
Average scores		75.25	60.2	72.0	48.0	64.31

courts, or the insufficient attention paid by the court to judicial openness. Third, informatization and transparency are both related and different from each other. Some maritime courts might have a high degree of informatization, but their achievements were not reflected on their websites. As a result, their assessment scores were not satisfactory. This year's assessment was the fifth assessment of 10 maritime courts in China by the Project Team. See Table 10.3 for the ranking of courts in each of the five assessments.

Table 10.3 Ranking of maritime courts in the score of assessment of judicial transparency indices (2013–2017)

Ranking	2013	2014	2015	2016	2017
1	Ningbo	Ningbo	Ningbo	Shanghai	Shanghai
2	Guangzhou	Beihai	Beihai	Beihai	Ningbo
3	Beihai	Guangzhou	Guangzhou	Xiamen	Xiamen
4	Shanghai	Shanghai	Haikou	Ningbo	Beihai
5	Haikou	Tianjin	Qingdao	Guangzhou	Guangzhou
6	Xiamen	Xiamen	Shanghai	Qingdao	Haikou
7	Wuhan	Qingdao	Tianjin	Haikou	Tianjin
8	Dalian	Dalian	Xiamen	Tianjin	Wuhan
9	Qingdao	Haikou	Dalian	Dalian	Qingdao
10	Tianjin	Wuhan	Wuhan	Wuhan	Dalian

In 2017, the level of transparency of maritime justice in China had been steadily rising, successful experiences were popularized, bright spots were maintained, and the overall situation continued to improve. Firstly, more importance had been attached to transparency and the competition had become more intense. After the publication of the Report on Maritime Judicial Transparency Indices in China (2016), the maritime courts of Shanghai, Beihai and Xiamen quickly reported the assessment results on their web portals. A number of maritime courts took the initiative to contact the Project Team and expressed the hope to improve their work and continuously enhance the transparency of maritime justice. Some maritime courts had included the assessment results in their work reports, white papers on maritime trials, key points of work, and ten major events of the year. The Report on Maritime Judicial Transparency Indices in China continued to be valued by the Supreme People's Court. The leaders of the Supreme People's Court pointed out at the 25th National Seminar on Maritime Trial that China should pay attention to improving maritime judicial transparency, especially to the construction of "smart courts", and accelerate the modernization of maritime trial capacity.[5]

In 2017, some maritime courts carefully studied the maritime judicial transparency index system in China, improved their work according to the requirements of the index system, drew on the bright spots of other maritime courts, continuously increased the breadth and depth of judicial openness, and achieved satisfactory results. The assessment shows that the scores of maritime courts of Shanghai, Ningbo, Xiamen and Beihai all exceeded 80 points, higher than the highest score in the 2016 assessment. No maritime court had been able to keep its position in the top three in all five assessments. Two maritime courts (Ningbo and Beihai) had entered into the top three for four times, one maritime court (Guangzhou) three times, and two maritime courts (Shanghai and Xiamen) two times. From point of view of the trend of development, the competition among courts had become more and more intense, and an unsatisfactory score in any assessment module might affect the final ranking.

Secondly, maritime courts as a whole got higher scores than ordinary courts in the assessment of judicial transparency. As mentioned earlier, in order to truthfully reflect the level of maritime judicial openness, this year the Project Team also carried out an assessment of judicial openness of the high people's courts (of municipalities directly under the Central Government) or intermediate people's courts (of other cities) where the 10 maritime courts were located using the same assessment modules, indices and weights. The assessment results show that the judicial transparency assessment scores of maritime courts were higher than those of ordinary courts. In the horizontal comparison of ten pairs of courts, seven maritime courts scored higher than the high people's courts (of municipalities directly under the Central Government) or intermediate people's courts in cities where they were located.

Third, maritime courts had a broader vision of judicial openness. In 2017, the English websites of Shanghai Maritime Court, Guangzhou Maritime Court and Ningbo Maritime Court operated more stably, with richer content and more timely

[5] Zhang Zhiku, Yan Yina, and Li Hui, "The 25th National Seminar on Maritime Trial Held in Dalian", *People's Court News*, June 16, 2017, p. 1.

updates. In April 2017, Ningbo Maritime Court released the White Paper on Maritime Trial in Zhejiang Province in 2016 in both Chinese and English, introduced the content of the white paper in an English video on its portal website, and published typical foreign-related cases in a timely manner. In June 2017, Shanghai Maritime Court officially released the 2016 White Paper on Maritime Trials in Shanghai in both Chinese and English. In August 2017, Guangzhou Maritime Court published its white paper on maritime trials in three languages for the first time. In addition, maritime courts had attached more importance to publishing information on foreign language platforms. In addition to Chinese Maritime and Commercial Law Reports mentioned in the 2016 Report on Maritime Judicial Transparency, China Maritime Cases International Promotion Platform (www.chinesemaritimecases.com),[6] jointly created by Tulane Maritime Law Center and Shanghai International Shipping Institute, was officially launched in the United States. According to its introduction, the platform will establish linkages with 10 maritime courts in China, select 100 typical cases every year, translate them into English, add summaries and comments, and publish them for free reference by the public. In the future, the platform will publish a collection of cases in the United States every year.[7]

However, despite the obvious progress that had been made, the following problems still existed in the judicial openness of maritime courts in 2017.

First, the situation of numerous "zombie columns" had not been fundamentally improved. Some columns on the websites of maritime courts copied the templates of local courts without taking into consideration the characteristics of specialized courts. As a result, many columns had been idle for many years and some information was misplaced. Maritime courts should, in light of the characteristics of maritime trial work, reasonably set up the columns on their websites and update relevant information in a timely manner. For some columns, such as "Enforcement Exposure", if there is no content that can be updated in the current year, an explanation should be given and the explanation should be dated.

Second, the phenomenon of scattered openness platforms continued to exist. For example, in addition to their portal websites, some maritime courts had also opened trial information networks, sunshine judicial networks, litigation service platforms, etc., but no explanation of or link to these networks and platforms was given on their portal websites, and the information updating on these networks and platforms was not satisfactory. For another example, some maritime courts attached importance to WeChat push and media release, but the relevant contents were not disclosed on their websites in a timely manner, which not only weakened the status of the portal websites as the primary platforms for judicial openness but also increased the cost of information retrieval of the public.

---

[6] The original text uses the term "precedent". Considering that China is not a country with case law, this article uses "case" instead.

[7] "China Maritime Precedent International Promotion Platform" is launched to promote China's maritime precedents to the world", http://www.sh.chinews.com/spxw/2017-12-12/32791.shtml, last visited on December 26, 2017.

Third, the pattern of polarization was becoming increasingly obvious. The results of five assessments showed that the pattern of "the strong being always strong while the weak getting weaker" became more obvious. Some maritime courts strived for the first place and aimed to win the championship while some others had attached insufficient importance to the assessment and showed no enthusiasm for judicial openness and, as a result, their rankings had declined year after year or remained at a low level for a long time. Some maritime courts held the attitude of muddling along with the judicial openness work and were satisfied as long as they were not at the bottom of the ranking in the assessment.

10.4 Assessment Results of Various Modules

10.4.1 Openness of Trial Affairs

The indices and their weights in the assessment module of openness of trial affairs were: platform construction (35%), personnel information (15%), financial information (15%), annual reports and statistical data (25%), and normative documents (10%). Among the four major assessment modules, the openness of trial affairs was the one with the highest average score in the 2017 assessment. With the launching of the WeChat official account of Guangzhou Maritime Court on September 1, 2017, the WeChat official accounts of all 10 maritime courts in China had been put into operation. By the end of the assessment, the WeChat official account of one maritime court had not effectively pushed any message during the assessment period (from January 1, 2017 to October 31, 2017). The maritime courts of Shanghai, Xiamen, Ningbo, Guangzhou and Wuhan pushed a large amount of information on their WeChat official accounts, with relatively high click-through rates. From the mode point of view, the synchronization between WeChat official accounts and portal websites of the maritime courts of Shanghai and Ningbo was strong, which is worth drawing on by other maritime courts. The publication of the white paper on maritime trials was satisfactory. In 2017, nine maritime courts issued white papers on maritime trials. Ningbo Maritime Court and Shanghai Maritime Court issued bilingual white papers; Guangzhou Maritime Court issued a trilingual white paper; Qingdao Maritime Court issued the White Paper on Maritime Trial Work (2016); Xiamen Maritime Court issued the White Paper on Maritime Trial Work in 2016, Dalian Maritime Court issued the White Paper on Maritime Administrative Trial in 2016, Beihai Maritime Court issued the White Paper on Trial of Cases (2016), Wuhan Maritime Court issued the White Paper on Maritime Commercial Trial in 2016, and Haikou Maritime Court issued the White Paper on Maritime Administrative Trial (2012–2016). In addition to the Zhejiang Maritime Trial Report, Ningbo Maritime Court also issued a series of white papers on special or regional trials, including the Report on the Trial of Cases of Disputes over Marine Freight Forwarding by Ningbo Maritime Court (January 2012-December 2016), Notification on the Trial of Maritime and Commercial Disputes in Zhoushan Region, Report on the Trial of Cases by Wenzhou Tribunal of Ningbo Maritime Court, Report on the Trial of Cases by Taizhou Tribunal of Ningbo Maritime Court, and Report on the Trial of Cases of Dispute over Contracts on Financial Lease of Vessels by Ningbo Maritime Court.

In terms of data openness, the practice of Ningbo Maritime Court was recommendable. According to the information disclosed on its website, Ningbo Maritime Court had developed a relatively complete working mechanism, and the release time of some information was relatively fixed. For example, it releases on the 20th of each month the table of cases received in the previous month.

10.4.2 Openness of Case-Filing and Court Trial

Assessment indices and their weights in the module of openness of case-filing and court trial were: litigation guides (20%), announcement of court sessions (20%), observation of court trials by members of the public (20%), live broadcasting of court trials (20%), information release system (10%) and court trial transcripts (10%). In 2017, the openness of case-filing and court trial and the openness of documents were the assessment modules with the highest weights in the maritime judicial transparency index system, but unfortunately, the assessment scores of these two modules were not satisfactory, with the average scores barely crossing the passing line. In comparison, the situation of the openness of litigation guides was better. After the Supreme People's Court issued the Provisions on the Scope of Cases to Be Accepted by Maritime Courts on February 24, 2016, six maritime courts updated the litigation guides on their websites in a timely manner. Eight maritime courts classified their litigation guides to facilitate public inquiry. The live broadcasting of court trials was not satisfactory. According to the records of China Court Trial Online, during the assessment period, five maritime courts conducted live broadcasting of court trials, four maritime courts had no records on China Court Trial Online, and one maritime court had records on China Court Trial Online, but the records had not been updated during the assessment period. The situation of observation of court trials by members of the public was not satisfactory. The rules on the observation of court trials by members of the public could be found on the websites of six maritime courts. In 2017, the number of courts publishing court transcripts increased. The maritime courts of Shanghai, Ningbo and Beihai published trial transcripts on their websites.

10.4.3 Openness of Documents

Assessment indices and their weights in the openness of documents module included: link to China Judgments Online (10%), document content (30%), typical case (30%) and data openness (30%).

The openness of documents had always been the focus of the assessment of maritime judicial transparency in China. The openness of documents can guarantee the public's right to judicial participation and right to know, force judges to take every case seriously, promote the uniformity of law application and judgment standards, and guide people to solve disputes in a reasonable way.[8]

The assessment results of the integrity of document content were satisfactory: none of the 200 documents randomly selected for the assessment was found to be incomplete. However, some problems were found in the processing of document contents, such as not de-identifying the information about natural persons as required and not providing clear addresses of enterprises.

Compared with that in 2016, the situation of publication of typical cases had been significantly improved. In 2017, the overwhelming majority of maritime courts published more than ten cases and their analyses on their websites. In the maritime court information pushed by the WeChat official account "Maritime Law Research Center", the click-through rate and the number of comments on typical cases were relatively high, reflecting the increase in the public's interest in and demand for typical cases.

In terms of data openness, the situation of online data disclosure on China Judgments Online was better than that of reverse disclosure. Seven maritime courts disclosed the online data of judgment documents, and four maritime courts disclosed the data of judgment documents that were not disclosed online.

10.4.4 Openness of Enforcement

The indices and their weights in the "openness of enforcement" module were: link to China Enforcement Online (10%), enforcement guide (20%), cases of termination of current enforcement proceedings (20%), enforcement exposure (20%), enforcement disciplinary actions (20%) and enforcement tip-offs (10%). The enforcement disclosure module was the module that had the lowest scores in the assessment of maritime judicial transparency in China in 2017, with only 4 of the 10 maritime courts crossing the passing line.

The assessment scores of the index on the linkage to China Enforcement Online were relatively high. Among the 10 maritime courts, 8 had established effective links between their websites and China Enforcement Online.

With respect to enforcement tip-offs, eight maritime courts provided the tip-off email or telephone on their websites. The scores of other indices in this module were not satisfactory. For example, as with the results of the 2016 assessment, only two maritime courts disclosed information about enforcement procedures on

[8] Shi Hongju, "Making Fairness and Justice Visible by Publishing Judgments Online", *People's Court News*, January 6, 2018, p. 2.

their websites; only three maritime courts disclosed the information about enforcement disciplinary actions, and four maritime courts disclosed the data on cases of termination of current enforcement proceedings.

10.5 Suggestions for Improvement

The report to the 19th National Congress of the Communist Party of China clearly pointed out that efforts would be made to "adhere to the overall planning of land and marine development and build China into a major maritime power", "promote the formation of a new pattern of comprehensive opening up", "focus on the construction of 'the Belt and Road'", "turn China into a trader of quality" and "explore the construction of free trade ports". The advancement of the above work provides a historic opportunity for the construction of an international maritime judicial center in China. The core of building an international maritime judicial center in China is to build China into an international maritime litigation destination, and the key lies in improving the credibility and international influence of China's maritime justice.

Party General Secretary Xi Jinping pointed out: "The more open law enforcement and justice are, the more authoritative and credible they will be."[9] As the international window of Chinese justice, maritime trials have always been the focus of international attention. A large number of overseas visits to China Judgments Online, the launch of the English version of China Maritime and Commercial Law Reports and the launch of China Maritime Cases International Promotion Platform are all evidence of the real existence of this demand. Judicial openness can enhance the in-depth understanding of China's justice and rule of law construction by foreign countries, establish a good image of fairness, impartiality and authority, and enhance the credibility and international influence of China's maritime justice.

From the reports of visits to China by foreign guests and the visits to foreign countries by leaders of the Supreme People's Court, we can see that informatization, judicial openness, and case exchange have been frequently mentioned topics in the talks held during such visits. Driven by the Report on Indices of Judicial Transparency in China and Report on Indices of Maritime Judicial Transparency in China for many consecutive years, more and more maritime courts began to attach importance to judicial openness, and China's situation of maritime judicial transparency continued to improve.

In view of the problems identified in the assessment, the Project Team suggested that more attention be paid to the following aspects of the work.

First, making it clear that the president of a maritime court is the primary person responsible for the judicial openness of the court. The assessment results over the years show that the importance attached by the "top leader" of a court to judicial openness is closely related to the assessment results. If the "top leader" of a court

---

[9] "The Rule of Law in China in the Eyes of Xi Jinping", http://politics.people.com/cn/n/2014/1022/c1001-2589039. html, last visited on December 26, 2017.

attaches importance to judicial openness, the ranking of the court in the assessment is usually high. If the "top leader" does not attach enough importance to the work or the one who does so is replaced by someone who does not, the ranking of the court in the assessment will usually become stagnant or even decline. The maritime trial is of a strong foreign-related nature, which concerns the international image of China's judicial system. Therefore, more importance should be attached to maritime judicial openness.

Second, highlighting the status of portal websites of maritime courts as the primary platforms for judicial openness and improving the retrieval function of the websites. The assessment results show that currently few maritime courts are able to disclose all information on one platform. The Project Team has repeatedly suggested, but without much success, that the portal websites of maritime courts should be established as the basic platforms for judicial openness. In the era of information explosion, platform construction should develop in the direction of intensification. Meanwhile, the retrieval function of platforms should be improved to reduce the cost of access to information by the public. Maritime courts can release information on other platforms, but they should provide effective links to such information and corresponding explanations on their portal websites.

Third, publishing annual white papers on maritime trials and ten typical cases in both Chinese and English. With the continuous improvement of China's comprehensive national strength and the continuous expansion of the scope of its openness, the international trade, maritime and legal circles are paying more and more attention to China's maritime cases. China has a serious "deficit" in the openness to the outside world in the judicial field. A large number of maritime cases and rich experiences in the trial of these cases are the advantages of China's maritime justice. Publishing white papers and typical cases of maritime trials in both Chinese and English can export Chinese wisdom and provide Chinese solutions and Chinese rules to the international community.

China has started a new journey and will make new achievements in the new era. Maritime trial in China has entered the best development period in history. The advancement of the "the Belt and Road Initiative" and the strategy of building China into a major maritime power not only provide a historic opportunity for the construction of an international maritime judicial center in China but also raises higher demands on China's maritime justice. Judicial openness is always in the "progressive tense", and will never be in the "perfect tense". The Project Team will further improve the scientificity, neutrality and objectivity of the maritime judicial transparency index system in China, raise the level of the authenticity, accuracy and authority of the assessment, and work together with people from all walks of life to enhance the credibility and influence of China's maritime justice and promote the creation of an international maritime judicial center in China.

Chapter 11
Report on Indices of Maritime Judicial Transparency in China (2018)—From the Perspective of Information Disclosure on the Websites of Maritime Courts

Innovation Project Team on the Rule of Law Index

Abstract In 2018, the Innovation Project Team on Rule of Law Indices of Law Institute of Chinese Academy of Social Sciences conducted the sixth assessment of the judicial openness of 10 maritime courts in China. In order to assess the openness of various maritime courts in a more comprehensive way, the Project Team conducted for the first time a user experience survey by relying on professional platforms and consulting the data on new media big data platforms. The assessment shows that, in 2018, the transparency of China's maritime justice had steadily increased and the development trend was positive, as manifested in better website updating and continuous rise of the level of internationalization. However, some problems identified in previous assessments had not been fundamentally solved, the phenomena of "zombie columns" and doing a crash job in information updating remained to be prevalent, and the polarization pattern continued. With the deepening of reform and opening up, the importance of maritime justice has become increasingly prominent. Judicial openness is an effective way to enhance judicial credibility and influence. China should continuously improve the transparency of maritime justice and regularly publish typical cases, guiding cases and white papers on maritime trials.

Keywords Maritime courts · Judicial transparency · Judicial openness · Rule of law index

---

Leaders of the Project Team: Tian He, a research fellow at CASS Law Institute and the director of the Center for Studies of National Indices of the Rule of Law, Chinese Academy of Social Sciences, and Lv Yanbin, a research fellow at and the head of the Department of Survey and Study of National Situation of the Rule of Law of the Institute of Law, Chinese Academy of Social Sciences. Other members of the Project Team include: Wang Xiaomei, Wang Yiming, Liu Yanpeng, He Ouyang, Zhang Wenguang, Hu Changming, Li Yanjie, etc. Author of this report: Zhang Wenguang, an associate research fellow at the Institute of International Law, Chinese Academy of Social Sciences Deputy Director and Secretary General of "the Belt and Road Initiative" Judicial Research Base of Supreme People's Court. This report has received support and help from many experts, scholars, judges, and lawyers in the design of indices, investigation, research and preparation of the report, to who we would like express our deep appreciation.

Innovation Project Team on the Rule of Law Index (✉)
Institute of Law, Chinese Academy of Social Sciences, Beijing, China
e-mail: 13263169197@163.com

H. Tian et al. (eds.), *Report on the Rule of Law Index in China 2*,
Research Series on the Chinese Dream and China's Development Path,
https://doi.org/10.1007/978-981-19-9597-2_11

In 2018, in order to track the whole process, truthfully record and objectively assess the development of maritime judicial transparency in China, the Innovation Project Team on Rule of Law Indices of Law Institute of Chinese Academy of Social Sciences (hereinafter referred to as the "Project Team") conducted the sixth investigation and assessment of maritime judicial transparency in China from the perspective of information disclosure on websites and the updating of information on WeChat official accounts of maritime courts.

11.1 A Review of Important Policies and Events of Maritime Judicial Openness in China in 2018

The year 2018 marks the 40th anniversary of the reform and opening-up and the 5th anniversary of the construction of "the Belt and Road" and pilot free trade zones. According to the statistics released by China Foreign-related Commercial and Maritime Trial Network, foreign-related commercial maritime cases accepted by courts in the whole country involved nearly 70 countries and regions, and the international credibility of Chinese justice gradually improved in 2018.[1]

Reform and opening-up is China's basic national policy. With the further expansion of the opening up to the outside world, the service and guarantee function of maritime justice has become more prominent. It is an inevitable choice for China to strengthen its international influence of maritime trials, thoroughly implement the strategy of excellent trials, and solidly promote the construction of an international maritime judicial center.

The key to building an international maritime judicial center is to enhance judicial credibility and international influence. In 2018, the 10 maritime courts across the country continued to disclose trials and enforcement information through web portals, national judicial openness platforms, China Foreign-related Commercial and Maritime Trial Network and various other media and platforms, thereby continuously improving their maritime judicial transparency, judicial credibility and international influence.

As the highest adjudicative organ in China, the Supreme People's Court attached great importance to judicial openness. On March 9, 2018, the Supreme People's Court stated in its work report that Chinese courts "have adhered to the principle of taking disclosure as the rule and non-disclosure as the exception and expanded the scope of judicial openness to cover all fields and links of court work", "continued to deepen judicial openness and accelerated the construction of smart courts, expanded the scope of live broadcasting of trials, online disclosure of documents, information

[1] Documents of the Fifth National Conference on Foreign-related Commercial and Maritime Trial, pp. 5–6.

about the trial process and other judicial information, and comprehensively advanced judicial openness in breadth and depth."[2]

On March 27, 2018, the Guangzhou Base of International Maritime Justice of the Supreme People's Court was formally established in Guangzhou Maritime Court and inspected by the President of the Supreme People's Court of China and the presidents of the supreme courts of some Portuguese-speaking countries.[3] On June 12th of the same year, Shanghai Maritime Court held a press conference and issued the Implementation Opinions on Promoting the Construction of Shanghai Base of International Maritime Justice of the Supreme People's Court and the Implementation Opinions on Promoting the Construction of Smart Maritime Court (Shanghai) Practice Base.[4]

After the Supreme People's Court first released the top ten typical maritime cases in 2017, it released the top ten typical maritime trial cases again in August 2018, which attracted wide attention from the maritime and legal circles.[5]

On November 20, 2018, the Supreme People's Court issued the Opinions on Further Deepening Judicial Openness, which clearly put forward the basic principles of judicial openness, that is, active openness, law-based openness, timely openness, comprehensive openness, and substantive openness. In particular, the opinion pointed out that "maritime courts and courts with frequent foreign exchanges and many foreign-related cases should, based on their own conditions, advance the construction of foreign-language versions and sections of judicial openness platforms and carry out multi-language translation and foreign publicity and promotion."[6]

At the 26th National Seminar on Maritime Trial, the Supreme People's Court once again made it clear that all maritime courts should strengthen informatization construction, "actively use the work platform China Maritime Trial set up by the Supreme Court to exchange trial experience, carry out judicial cooperation and realize information sharing".[7]

---

[2] Work Report of the Supreme People's Court, http://www.court.gov.cn/zixun-xiangqing-87832.html, last visited on January 24, 2019.

[3] http://www.court.gov.cn/zixun-xiangqing-88402.html.

[4] "Shanghai Maritime Court Issued Opinions to Fully Promote the Construction of an International Maritime Judicial Center", http://www.court.gov.cn/zixun-xiangqing-101812.html, last visited on January 24, 2019.

[5] "The Supreme People's Court Issues Ten Typical Cases of Maritime Litigation", http://www.court.gov.cn/zixun-xiangqing-111541.html, last visited on January 24, 2019.

[6] Opinions of the Supreme People's Court on Further Deepening Judicial Openness, http://www.court.gov.cn/fabu-xiangqing-132411.html, last visited on January 24, 2019.

[7] "The 26th National Seminar on Maritime Trial held", http://www.court.gov.cn/zixun-xiangqing-131631.html, last visited on January 24, 2019.

11.2 Index System and Assessment Methods

11.2.1 Assessment Targets

The 10 maritime courts covered by the 2018 assessment of maritime judicial transparency indices in China were the same as those covered by the previous five assessments, namely Shanghai Maritime Court, Tianjin Maritime Court, Qingdao Maritime Court, Dalian Maritime Court, Guangzhou Maritime Court, Wuhan Maritime Court, Haikou Maritime Court, Xiamen Maritime Court, Ningbo Maritime Court and Beihai Maritime Court.

11.2.2 Emphases of Assessment

The emphases of maritime judicial transparency assessment in China in 2018 was disclosed in the Report on Maritime Judicial Transparency Indices in China (2017): "The emphases of the assessment of maritime judicial transparency indices in China in 2018 will include timeliness and synchronism of information disclosure, the retrial function of websites, data openness, publication of white papers on maritime trials, judicial recommendations, major events, typical cases and excellent documents, links to and updating of information on national judicial information disclosure platforms, and China Foreign-related Commercial and Maritime Trial Network, etc."[8]

11.2.3 The Index System

In 2018, the Project Team further optimized the index system of maritime judicial transparency in China in terms of the setup of assessment modules (grade I indices) and their weights. Firstly, the user experience survey was added to the system, and the data from big data platforms were used as references to improve public participation; secondly, considering that 2018 was the closing year of "basically overcoming enforcement difficulties", the weight of the openness of enforcement module was increased, and the weights of openness of case-filing and court trial and openness of documents were reduced. The adjusted setup of modules and their weights were as follows: the openness of trial affairs (20%), the openness of the case-filing and court trial (20%), the openness of documents (20%), the openness of enforcement (30%) and data openness (10%), with a full score of 100 for each module.

[8] "Report on Maritime Judicial Transparency Index in China (2017) officially released", *People's Daily Online*, http://legal.people.com.cn/n1/2018/0322/c42510-29883636.html, last visited on December 29, 2018.

With respect to grade II indices and their weights, some changes were also made in 2018. The optimized and adjusted assessment index system of maritime judicial transparency in China (2018) consisted of 5 grade I indices and 25 grade II indices (see Table 11.1).

11.2.4 Assessment Methods

The Project Team mainly adopted the methods of observation, verification and survey in the assessment in 2018. It carried out whole-process tracking of the situation of the updating of the websites of maritime courts to discover and record in a timely manner valuable information on maritime court websites and media reports. Whenever a member of the Project Team could not find a certain piece of information or open a certain webpage, other members of the Project Team would use various major search engines on the Internet to search for the information or adopt such methods as changing computers, Internet connection, and time of visit to try to open the webpage and carry out multiple verifications.

After completing the assessment of the first four grade I indices, the Project Team also conducted a user experience survey through the well-known WeChat official account Maritime Law Research Center. During the survey, a total of 23,137 accounts voted. In addition, the Project Team also acquired the annual report of Qingbo Big Data on WeChat official accounts of maritime courts, and extracted the annual reading data of WeChat official account of 10 maritime courts. In view of the fact that this assessment was the first one to demonstrate the influence of maritime courts with the help of platform data, the weight of this index should not be set too high. Therefore, the weight of the platform data index was set at only 10%, which was the smallest of the five grade I indices.

11.3 Assessment Results

In 2018, among the 10 maritime courts in China, the ranking of 6 maritime courts changed. As far as the score distribution is concerned, two maritime courts scored more than 90 points, two maritime courts scored between 80 and 90 points, one maritime court scored between 70 and 80 points, one maritime court scored between 60 and 70 points, two maritime courts scored between 50 and 60 points and two maritime courts scored between 40 and 50 points (see Table 11.2).

It should be pointed out that, firstly, portal websites have always been at the core of the assessment of maritime judicial transparency in China. If a court fails to disclose relevant information on its own portal website and does not provide an explanation for the failure, its final score in the assessment will be affected. Secondly, the ranking of assessment scores reflects the relative levels of transparency. A court's decline in ranking does not necessarily mean the decline of its level of judicial openness, but

Table 11.1 Assessment index system of maritime judicial transparency in China (2018)

Grade I indices and their weights	Grade II indices and their weights
1. Openness of trial affairs (20%)	1.1 Platform construction (25%) 1.2 Personnel information (15%) 1.3 Financial information (15%) 1.4 Annual reports and statistics (25%) 1.5 White papers on trial (10%) 1.6 Normative documents (10%)
2. Openness of case-filing and court trial (20%)	2.1 Litigation guides (20%)
	2.2 Announcements of court sessions (20%)
	2.3 Observation of court trials by members of the public (20%) 2.4 Live broadcasting of court trial (20%)
	2.5 Information release system (10%)
	2.6 Trial transcripts (10%)
3. Openness of documents (20%)	3.1 Link to China Judgments Online (10%)
	3.2 Timeliness (10%) 3.3 Document content (20%) 3.4 Typical cases (30%)
	3.5 Data openness (30%)
4. Openness of enforcement (30%)	4.1 Link to China Enforcement Online (10%) 4.2 Enforcement guides (20%) 4.3 Cases of termination of enforcement proceedings (20%) 4.4 Enforcement exposure (20%) 4.5 Enforcement disciplinary actions (20%) 4.6 Enforcement tip-offs (10%)
5. Platform data (10%)	5.1 Survey of website user experience (50%)
	5.2 WeChat official account data (50%)

Table 11.2 Results of assessment of judicial transparency indices of maritime courts in China (2018) (Unit: points)

Ranking	Maritime courts	Openness of trial affairs (20%)	Openness of case-filing and court trial (20%)	Openness of documents (20%)	Openness of enforcement (30%)	Platform data (10%)	Total score (out of 100 Points)
1	Shanghai	95.0	95.0	95.0	90.0	90.0	93.0
2	Ningbo	95.0	96.0	90.0	90.0	90.0	92.2
3	Guangzhou	93.0	95.0	90.0	85.0	55.0	86.6
4	Xiamen	90.0	84.0	90.0	85.0	80.0	86.3
5	North Sea	95.0	83.0	85.0	70.0	40.0	77.6
6	Tianjin	80.0	60.0	80.0	60.0	15.0	63.5
7	Wuhan	72.0	50.0	70.0	40.0	80.0	58.4
8	Haikou	70.0	60.0	65.0	45.0	45.0	57.0
9	Qingdao	61.0	35.0	65.0	40.0	25.0	46.7
10	Dalian	60.0	45.0	60.0	30.0	30.0	45.0

may be due to the faster progress made by other courts. Thirdly, the assessment standards are constantly rising. The same index, which was originally used only to assess whether the website of a court had been updated during the assessment period, is now also used to assess the number and time of disclosures. Fourthly, the assessment uses an index system in which each index and each module in the system has its corresponding weight. The final score of a court depends on its comprehensive performance in all indices and modules. Some courts attached importance to publicity work, and their websites were updated frequently, but their contents of openness were concentrated in a certain category, which fell short of the requirements of the assessment system and, as a result, their assessment scores were not satisfactory.

This year's assessment was the sixth assessment of the 10 maritime courts in China conducted by the Project Team. See Table 11.3 for the ranking of courts in each of the six assessments.

In 2018, the level of transparency of maritime justice in China had been steadily rising and the overall situation continued to improve.

Firstly, the awareness of openness had obviously been raised. After the publication of the Report on Indices of Maritime Judicial Transparency in China (2017), the assessment results were reported by online media such as Xinhuanet, People's Daily and Legal Network, and well-known We Media such as WeChat official accounts of Maritime Law Research Center, the maritime industry, the shipping industry and Xinde Marine, as well as on the front page of People's Court Daily, which further enhanced the social influence and industrial penetration of the report. After the report was released, many maritime courts held special meetings and took the initiative to contact the Project Team to discuss ways of improving their work and continuously enhancing the transparency of maritime justice.

Table 11.3 Ranking of maritime judicial transparency indices in China (2013–2017)

Ranking	2013	2014	2015	2016	2017	2018
1	Ningbo	Ningbo	Ningbo	Shanghai	Shanghai	Shanghai
2	Guangzhou	Beihai	Beihai	Beihai	Ningbo	Ningbo
3	Beihai	Guangzhou	Guangzhou	Xiamen	Xiamen	Guangzhou
4	Shanghai	Shanghai	Haikou	Ningbo	Beihai	Xiamen
5	Haikou	Tianjin	Qingdao	Guangzhou	Guangzhou	Beihai
6	Xiamen	Xiamen	Shanghai	Qingdao	Haikou	Tianjin
7	Wuhan	Qingdao	Tianjin	Haikou	Tianjin	Wuhan
8	Dalian	Dalian	Xiamen	Tianjin	Wuhan	Haikou
9	Qingdao	Haikou	Dalian	Dalian	Qingdao	Qingdao
10	Tianjin	Wuhan	Wuhan	Wuhan	Dalian	Dalian

In 2018, some maritime courts conducted an in-depth study of the index system of maritime judicial transparency in China. At the same time, drawing on the experiences summarized in previous assessment reports, they improved the setup of web columns, enriched the content of information disclosure, advanced judicial openness in breadth and depth, and achieved satisfactory results. During the assessment period, the maritime courts of Shanghai, Ningbo and Guangzhou revised their web portals, and Xiamen Maritime Court launched an English webpage on its website. After the assessment, some maritime courts took the initiative to provide the Project Team with a summarization of their judicial openness work in 2018. From the point of view of the development trend, with more importance attached by leaders of the courts to the judicial openness work, the improvement of the relevant institutions, and the availability of more funds and personnel, the competition in the ranking of maritime judicial transparency will become more intense, and the unsatisfactory score of one module or even one index may affect the final ranking of a court in the assessment.

Secondly, the bright spots found in the previous assessments had been maintained. Most of the unique practices and bright spots in judicial openness found in the previous assessments and summarized in the assessment reports of the Project Team, such as the disclosure of transcripts of court trials, the publication of typical cases, the issuance of special white papers, the regular disclosure of data, and synchronized information disclosure on WeChat and Weibo official accounts and websites, had been maintained, and some of the good practices were popularized. Take the white paper on trials, which had attracted extensive attention from the law circle, as an example. In 2018, eight maritime courts issued white papers on maritime trials. Ningbo Maritime Court issued three white papers, namely, Report on Maritime Trials in Zhejiang Province in 2017, Report on the Prevention of Water Traffic Accidents and Resolution of Maritime Disputes in Zhejiang Coastal Waters (2013–2017) and Current Situation of Trial of Cases of Marine Insurance Disputes in Ningbo Maritime Court (January 2014 to October 2018). It is particularly commendable that most maritime courts disclosed the full texts of their white papers online on the very day of their publication. Take the publication of typical cases as an example. Nine maritime courts published their typical cases on their websites. Among them, six published more than ten typical cases on their websites in 2018. Although one maritime court did not publish typical cases on its website, it pushed several typical cases through its WeChat official account.

Thirdly, the international color had become stronger. Considering China's status as a great power, the need for reform and opening up, and the international elements of maritime justice, the Supreme People's Court has always attached special importance to the international status of maritime justice. The purpose of building an international maritime justice center is to improve the international status and influence of China's maritime justice as a whole.[9] Portal websites are important windows for foreign parties to understand China's maritime judicial situation. In 2018, the English websites of Shanghai Maritime Court and Guangzhou Maritime Court, which were the two international maritime judicial bases of the Supreme People's Court, and Ningbo Maritime Court run more stably and their contents became richer. Ningbo Maritime Court and Shanghai Maritime Court continued to publish annual white papers on maritime trials in both Chinese and English, while Guangzhou Maritime Court continued to publish white papers on maritime trials in Chinese, English and Portuguese. Compared with 2017, Xiamen Maritime Court opened the English version of its official website and released the annual white paper on the trial work and annual typical maritime cases in both Chinese and English for the first time.

However, despite the above-mentioned progress, the following problems still existed in the judicial openness work of maritime courts in China in 2018.

First, the situation of numerous "zombie columns" had not been fundamentally improved. During the assessment, the Project Team observed every column on the website of each maritime court and clicked and read every piece of information disclosed during the assessment period. The assessment shows that some columns on the websites of some maritime courts had always been empty, with no information being disclosed in them since their creation, while some other columns had not been updated for a long period of time, with their latest update being made several years ago. The Project Team believes that the refinement of column setting is conducive to information inquiry by the public, and not updating the content in a column for a long period of time will lead to some unnecessary misunderstandings. For some columns, such as enforcement disciplinary action, if there is really no content to be updated in the current year, an explanation should be given and the explanation should be dated.

Second, the practices of not releasing information in a timely manner and doing a crash job in information updating were still common. The websites of some maritime courts were complete in content and released a considerable quantity of information. However, the situation of doing a crash job in information updating on these websites had not been significantly improved. Some websites had not been updated for a long period of time and then updated a large amount of content at a certain point in

[9] Documents of the Fifth National Conference on Foreign-related Commercial and Maritime Trial, p. 17.

time. Moreover, the timeliness of information disclosure needs to be strengthened. Take the release time of white papers on trials as an example. Generally speaking, a white paper released in 2018 should be about the situation or a certain topic in 2017. However, among the eight maritime courts that issued the white paper on trials in 2018, three issued it as late as in October 2018.

Third, the pattern of polarization among assessment targets judicial openness was becoming increasingly obvious. From the results of six assessments, we can see that the pattern of polarization has become increasingly obvious. In the 2018 assessment, the maritime courts of Shanghai, Ningbo, Guangzhou and Xiamen were in the first echelon in the ranking of judicial openness. At the same time, some maritime courts still had low awareness of and attached insufficient importance to judicial openness, and their scores in the assessments had been unsatisfactory in all the assessments.

11.4 Suggestions for Improvement

After more than 30 years of development, China is in a critical period of transformation from a maritime judicial power to a big maritime judicial power. A stable, open, transparent and predictable legal environment is one of the core elements of the business environment and an important guarantee for building an international maritime justice center. Judicial openness is always in the "progressive tense", and will never be in the "perfect tense".

Firstly, clarifying the positioning of websites and building a unified platform. In the assessment reports released in previous years, the Project Team has repeatedly suggested that portal websites should be clearly defined as basic platforms for maritime judicial openness. However, the suggestion had not produced a satisfactory result, and the phenomenon of information release on multiple platforms is still common. The Opinions of the Supreme People's Court on Further Deepening Judicial Openness require that "every endeavor should be made to build the websites of people's courts into timely, accurate, standardized and efficient judicial openness platforms, interaction and communication platforms, and public service platforms. The content construction and standardized management of the websites should be strengthened, the release and updating of information should be enhanced, and web columns and sections for which the updating of contents cannot be guaranteed should be consolidated or removed in a timely manner, so as to prevent judicial openness from being adversely affected by the delay in updating of contents, the release of inaccurate information, or non-response to opinions and suggestions" and that "maritime courts and courts with frequent foreign exchanges and many foreign-related cases should, based on their own conditions, advance the construction of foreign-language versions and sections of judicial openness platforms and carry out multi-language translation and foreign publicity and promotion".[10] The Opinions have pointed out the direction for the next step of judicial openness for maritime courts in China.

Secondly, implementing the system of responsibility for judicial openness. The assessment results over the years show that relying only on a certain internal department or a few staff members of a maritime court to carry out the judicial openness work will not produce a satisfactory result and that the level of importance attached by the "top leaders" of a maritime court to the work is one of the key factors in judicial openness. The president of a maritime court "should assume the leadership responsibility for judicial openness in the court, hear the report on the work of judicial openness at least once every year, conduct research on, make arrangement for, and carry out supervision over the implementation of the key tasks of deepening judicial openness."[11]

Thirdly, strengthening the publication of white papers on and typical cases of maritime trials. China is the country with the largest number of maritime adjudicative institutions and maritime cases in the world. Rich maritime cases and trial experience are the advantages of China's maritime justice, and they are also the public products that China can provide to the world. Publishing white papers on a regular basis enables the public to understand the key points of the work and trial situation of maritime courts, and to learn about the judicial attitude and adjudication rules of the courts. Publishing typical cases enables Chinese maritime courts to unify adjudication standards, actively participate in the making of international maritime judicial rules, and provide Chinese experiences and Chinese solutions for the development of an international civilization of rule of law. According to the requirements provided for in the Opinions of the Supreme People's Court on Further Deepening Judicial Openness, maritime courts should disclose typical cases on their own initiatives, "do a solid job in compiling, producing, publishing and publicizing white papers, and effectively enhance the authority, standardization and readability of white papers".[12]

In 2019, the Project Team will, in accordance with the requirements of the Opinions of the Supreme People's Court on Further Deepening Judicial Openness, the Guiding Opinions of the Supreme People's Court on Strengthening and Standardizing the Analysis and Reasoning in Adjudicative Instruments and other relevant documents, further improve the index system of maritime judicial transparency in China, carry out full-process tracking, observation and recording of the development of maritime justice in China, and work with people from all walks of life to enhance the credibility of China's maritime justice and expand its international influence.

---

[10] "Opinions of the Supreme People's Court on Further Deepening Judicial Openness", http://www.court.gov.cn/fabu-xiangqing-132411.html, last visited on January 24, 2019.

[11] Ibid.

[12] Ibid.

Chapter 12
Protection of the Rights of the Child in China and Third-Party Assessment Index System

Innovation Project Team on the Rule of Law Index

Abstract The rights of the child are an important part of human rights. Their protection depends on laws, and the strength and effect of their protection directly affect the future of the nation. At the level of international law, China is a member of the system of public international law protection of the rights of the child with the Convention on the Rights of the Child as the core and the system of private international law protection of the rights of the child coordinated by the Hague Conference on Private International Law; at the level of domestic law, the Constitution and major branch laws in China all contain special provisions on the protection of the rights of the child, and the system of special laws on the protection of the rights of the child, which takes the Law on the Protection of Minors and the Law on the Prevention of Juvenile Delinquency as its basis, is becoming more and more mature; in addition, some policy documents are also of great significance for the protection of the rights of the child. Constructing an index system to evaluate the legal protection of the rights of the child in China by empirical methods can objectively reflect the achievements made and problems faced by China in the legal protection of the rights of the child, and promote the related theory and practice to a higher level.

Keywords Rights of the child · Human rights · Rule of law safeguard · Positive jurisprudence

---

Leaders of the Project Team: Tian He, Director of the Center for Studies of National Rule of Law Index of Chinese Academy of Social Sciences, and a research fellow at the Institute of Law, and Lv Yanbin a research fellow and head of the Department of Survey and Studies of National Situation of the Rule of Law, Institute of Law, Chinese Academy of Social Sciences. Members of the project team: Wang Xiaomei, Wang Yiming, Li Yanjie. Hu Changming, Xu Bin, Liu Yanpeng, etc. Authors of the report: Wang Yiming, an assistant research fellow at the Institute of Law, Chinese Academy of Social Sciences, Tian He and Lv Yanbin.

Innovation Project Team on the Rule of Law Index (✉)
Institute of Law, Chinese Academy of Social Sciences, Beijing, China
e-mail: 13263169197@163.com

H. Tian et al. (eds.), *Report on the Rule of Law Index in China 2*,
Research Series on the Chinese Dream and China's Development Path,
https://doi.org/10.1007/978-981-19-9597-2_12

The 20th century is the century of children. In this 100-year history of human development, children and their rights received unprecedented attention and protection, and the legal protection mechanism for the rights of the child had been established in an all-round way and played an undeniable role in the promotion of the status of the child in society.

In the 20th century, the definition of the child had been gradually unified after continuous exploration by various international conventions, and the standard for distinguishing children from adults has changed from that based on both age and marital status to that based only on age.

The Convention of the 15th of April 1958 on the Recognition and Enforcement of Decisions Relating to Maintenance Obligations in Respect of Children provides that: "The purpose of this Convention is to ensure the mutual recognition and enforcement by States Parties of judgments handed down in international or domestic proceedings for the maintenance of unmarried legitimate, illegitimate or adopted children under the age of 21."[1] The 1965 Convention on Jurisdiction, Applicable Law and Recognition of Decrees relating to Adoptions contains a similar provision. The Convention on the Rights of the Child provides that: "For the purposes of the present Convention, a child means every human being below the age of eighteen years unless under the law applicable to the child, majority is attained earlier."[2] Because of the great international influence of the Convention on the Rights of the Child, the standard of defining children by age has been generally accepted by the international community since then. Although the definition of the child is simple, the hidden value behind it is of far-reaching significance to a nation. Why should we define children? Because adults are the present situation and established facts of a nation, whereas children are undoubtedly a special group with unlimited potential that determines the future destiny of a nation. From the perspective of population resources, the proper care of the growing children and the level of their quality training are the core factors that determine a nation's future direction of development and its international status. From the perspective of children themselves, due to the limitation of their capacity, they should receive special attention and all-round protection from adults. At the same time, this kind of attention and protection is also an important responsibility of the state and the government, and the rights of the child should be the top priority of a country's human rights protection strategies and actions. On the other hand, the protection of the rights of the child is the touchstone for testing the protection of human rights in a country. The state cares for children and protects their rights out of the considerations not only of its future interests but also of its obligation to protect human rights, as safeguarding basic human rights is the legitimacy basis of state power.

---

[1] The Central Committee of the Communist Youth League of China and Bureau of Legislative Affairs of the State Council of the People's Republic of China (eds.), *Compilation of Laws of the People's Republic of China on the Protection of Minors*, Beijing: Law Press China, 1992, p. 940.

[2] Institute of Law of Chinese Academy of Social Sciences (ed.), *International Human Rights Instruments and International Human Rights Bodies*, Beijing: Social Sciences Academic Press, 1993, p. 410.

Defining persons under the age of 18 as children, thus distinguishing them from adults, is only a logical starting point to providing special protection to the rights of the child. Only a part of the rights of adults can be classified as fundamental human rights, but almost all rights of the child are fundamental human rights. Currently, there is still no conclusive definition of human rights. There are only differences in the degree of acceptance between different concepts of human rights, and none of them is universally accepted. China's official definition of human rights is that: "Generally speaking, human rights are basic rights that everyone enjoys or should enjoy by virtue of their essence and dignity under certain social and historical conditions."[3] The difficulty in defining the concept of human rights is also generally acknowledged in academic circles. However, there is a high degree of consensus on the definition of the rights of the child as human rights. Article 25 Paragraph 2 of the Universal Declaration of Human Rights promulgated by the United Nations in 1948 and the Vienna Declaration adopted at the Second World Conference on Human Rights in 1993 both contain similar provisions on this issue. Giving special protection to the rights of the child under the framework of human rights has become a consensus of the international community. A large number of human rights documents specifically mention children and provide for special protection for them. In recent years, the mainstreaming of human rights has become a world trend, and human rights have become the mainstream discourse of society, both in developed and developing countries. In the field of the rights of the child, the mainstreaming of human rights is manifested in the fact that the rights of the child have been paid more and more attention to by the international community and governments of various countries, the research on and theoretical development of the rights of the child have been accelerated and great breakthroughs have been made in this field since the 20th century, and special legal documents on the protection of the rights of the child have been adopted in international law and domestic laws of various countries. The Convention on the Rights of the Child adopted by the United Nations General Assembly in 1989 is the first international convention that specifically guarantees the rights of the child, covering all basic types of human rights, including civil, cultural, economic, political and social rights. The far-reaching significance of this convention lies in the fact that it highlights the special status of the rights of the child, which are the most important human rights but often ignored by adults, clarifies the concept of the rights of the child, reminds the adult world to pay special attention to rights of the child, and becomes a solemn commitment made by adults to children. The Convention establishes four core principles of protection of the rights of the child: the principle of non-discrimination, the principle of best interests of children, the principle of respecting children's basic rights, and the principle of respecting children's views. These four basic principles later have become the guiding principles of international law and domestic legislation on the rights of the child in the state

[3] Jiang Wei: "Perfecting the System of Judicial Guarantee for Human Rights", in *Tutorial Reader on the Decision of the Central Committee of the Communist Party of China on Several Major Issues Concerning Comprehensive Deepening of the Reform*, Beijing: People's Publishing House, 2013, p. 222.

parties to the convention. Every right set forth in the Convention is indispensable to upholding and safeguarding the personal dignity and healthy development of children. Since the adoption of the Convention on the Rights of the Child, the survival and development of children in the world have been greatly improved.

12.1 Legal Framework of the Protection of the Rights of the Child in China

12.1.1 International Law Framework of the Protection of the Rights of the Child in China

12.1.1.1 Conventions on the Protection of the Rights of the Child in the Field of Public International Law

As far as the international conventions on the protection of the rights of the child to which China is a party are concerned, the Convention on the Rights of the Child is undoubtedly the foundation and core. The Convention was ratified by the Standing Committee of the Seventh National People's Congress at its 23rd meeting in December 1991, and entered into force with respect to China on April 2, 1992. The Convention provides for four kinds of most basic rights of the child: the right to subsistence, the right to protection, the right to development, and the right to participation. In May 2000, the UN General Assembly, in view of the key and hot issues of violation of the rights of the child in the world and on the basis of the Convention on the Rights of the Child, adopted two optional protocols to the Convention on the Rights of the Child, namely the Optional Protocol on the Involvement of Children in Armed Conflict and the Optional Protocol on the Sale of Children, Child Prostitution and Child Pornography, both of which have been ratified by China. Since its ratification of the Convention, the Chinese government has implemented all the provisions and obligations in the Convention, regularly submitting reports on the implementation of the Convention to the United Nations, and opening up its reports to the international community and the domestic public. Since its ratification of the Convention, China has put the principle of "the best interests of the child" first, consistently adhered to the principle in policies, laws and other dimensions, and implemented the strategy of giving priority to children's development, thereby greatly promoting the realization of various rights of the child in China. Driven by the Convention, the protection of the rights of the child in China has been improving continuously. China's latest report on the implementation of the Convention was the Third and Fourth Combined Periodical Reports submitted to the Committee on the Rights of the Child in 2010. The Committee considered the report and made corresponding recommendations in 2013. In addition to the Convention on the Rights of the Child, China has also ratified a series of important international instruments relating to the rights of the child in the field of public international law, including the 1985 United Nations Standard Minimum Rules for the Administration of Juvenile Justice (The Beijing Rules), the 1988 United Nations Guidelines for the Prevention of Juvenile Delinquency and the 1990 United Nations Rules for the Protection of Juveniles Deprived of Their Liberty.

12.1.1.2 Conventions on the Protection of the Rights of the Child in the Field of Private International Law

The private international law system of the protection of the rights of the child mainly relies on coordination by the Hague Conference on Private International Law, which is a global intergovernmental non-governmental organization committed to promoting family legislation and protecting children, and devoted to the solution of problems in the international protection of families and children. In the existing system of private international law conventions on the protection of the rights of the child, the Chinese government has ratified the Hague Convention on Intercountry Adoption in 1993, and the governments of Hong Kong Special Administrative Region and Macao Special Administrative Region of China have ratified the Hague Convention on Intercountry Adoption and the Hague Convention on Abduction of Children.[4]

12.1.1.3 Mechanisms for the Implementation of International Law on the Protection of the Rights of the Child

The domestic implementation of international law relies on the transformation of international law into domestic law, and China has a clear policy basis for the transformation of international conventions on the protection of the rights of the child.[5] The Hague conventions on the protection of the rights of the child establish a private international law and administrative cooperation mechanism with the central authorities of the States Parties as the core, and realize the protection of children in States Parties by stipulating the obligations and working procedures of the central authorities of the States Parties. The main subjects in China with the obligation to protect

[4] See Wang Jinlan, *Research on Conventions on the Protection of Rights of the Child in the Field of Private International Law and Their Implementation Mechanism—Taking the Hague Conventions as an Example*, Beijing: Law Press China, 2014, pp. 201–205.

[5] When China ratified the Convention on the Rights of the Child at the 23rd meeting of the Standing Committee of the Seventh National People's Congress, it made the following declaration: The People's Republic of China shall fulfill its obligations provided by Article 6 of the Convention under the prerequisite that the Convention accords with the provisions of Article 25 concerning family planning of the Constitution of the People's Republic of China and is in conformity with the provisions of Article 2 of the Law Protection of Minors of the People's Republic of China.

the rights of the child under international law include the Central People's Government, the Ministry of Civil Affairs and other central state organs, their subordinate or designated agencies, the governments of special administrative regions and related agencies, etc.

12.1.2 The Domestic Legal Framework and Legal System of Protection of the Rights of the Child in China

12.1.2.1 The Existing Legal System of Protection of the Rights of the Child

The Constitution is the fundamental law of a country. The fact that the state provides for the protection of the rights of the child specifically in the form of the fundamental law is a manifestation of the special legal status of children and the importance of their rights in the country. The Chinese Constitution contains many articles concerning the protection of the rights of the child. For example, articles 46, 48 and 49 of the Constitution contain basic provisions on the rights of the child to education, protection, support and be free from abuse, as well as girls' rights. The importance attached to and special protection given by the Constitution have laid the foundation and set the tone for the establishment of a sound and comprehensive legal system for the protection of the rights of the child. There are many provisions concerning children in basic laws such as the Criminal Law, the General Provisions of Civil Law, Civil Procedure Law, Marriage Law, Adoption Law, Anti-Domestic Violence Law, and Compulsory Education Law, all of which have been carefully reviewed to ensure that children get special protection different from that of adults. At present, there are two special laws on the protection of the rights of the child in China. One is the Law on the Protection of Minors adopted in 1991 and revised in 2006, which is known as the "mini-constitution" of the rights of the child. The second is the 1999 Law on the Prevention of Juvenile Delinquency, which aims at ensuring the physical and mental health of juveniles, cultivating good conduct of juveniles, and effectively preventing juvenile delinquency. In addition to laws, China has adopted a series of related administrative regulations, departmental rules, local regulations, judicial interpretations and other legal documents, thereby weaving a legal network and establishing a relatively complete legal system for the protection of the rights of the child.

Apart from legislation, some policy documents are also of great significance to the protection of the rights of the child in China. They include the Program for the Development of Children in China (2001–2010), the Program for the Development of Children in China (2011–2020), Human Rights Action Plan of China (2012–2015), Action Plan against Human Abduction and Trafficking (2013–2020), the Opinions of the State Council on Strengthening the Work of Protection of Children in Difficulties, and China Program for the Reform and Development of Education. Relevant government departments and social organizations have also formulated a series of targeted plans, such as the Outline of the Work for the Disabled in China During the Ninth Five-Year Plan Period, formulated by the relevant departments organized by the Coordination Committee for the Work for the Disabled under the State Council, the Diarrhea Control Plan of the People's Republic of China issued by the Ministry of Health, and the Outline of the National Plan for the Prevention and Control of Acute Respiratory Infection in Children, issued by the National Health and Family Planning Commission. The Outline of the Eleventh Five-Year Plan for National Economic and Social Development, formulated in 2006, stated that China will: "…implement the Program for the Development of Children in China, guarantee in accordance with law rights of the child to subsistence, development, protection and participation, improve the environment for children's growth, and promote children's healthy physical and mental development." Provincial-level governments have taken this program as a guide to adopting development plans for the protection of the rights of the child in their respective regions. The above policy documents are a series of targeted measures taken by the Chinese government to safeguard the rights of the child in light of the actual needs of a specific period and provide guarantee and impetus for the smooth implementation of relevant laws and administrative regulations on the protection of the rights of the child.

12.1.2.2 The Existing Implementation Mechanism for the Protection of the Rights of the Child

The National Working Committee for Women and Children under the State Council is a comprehensive coordinating body for the protection of the rights of the child at the national level. The Committee is composed of 35 member units and chaired by a vice-premier or state councilor. It specializes in women's and children's undertakings and coordinates and promotes the formulation and implementation of various laws, regulations, policies and measures concerning women and children by relevant government departments. In addition, there are national-level working institutions responsible for the children's work in specific fields, such as the Leading Group for the Prevention of Juvenile Delinquency. At the local level, "At present, 29 provinces, autonomous regions and municipalities directly under the Central Government and 71% of prefectures, cities and counties have set up committees for the protection of minors or committees for the protection and education of the youth, and working committees for women and children, leading groups for preventing juvenile delinquency, working institutions for ideological and moral construction of minors and working committees for caring for the next generation have been set up at all levels from top to bottom throughout the country."[6] The education, civil affairs, health,

[6] Report of the Law Enforcement Inspection Group of the Standing Committee of the National People's Congress on the Inspection on the Implementation of the Law of the People's Republic of China on the Protection of Minors, *People's Daily Online*, at http://www.chinacomcn/policy/txt/2008-09/16/content_16464513htm, last visited: December 2, 2017.

culture, human resources and social security departments of governments, as well as judicial organs at all levels have set up specialized agencies or mechanisms for dealing with affairs relating to children, adolescents or minors. At the national level and in 31 provinces, agencies for monitoring and evaluating the implementation effect of the Program for the Development of Children in China have been set up to monitor and collect statistical data on and evaluate various indices of the development of children in the country every year.

Protecting the rights of the child is not only the responsibility of the government but also the common responsibility of the whole society. Therefore, the mechanism for the protection of the rights of the child in China is also a linkage mechanism covering all levels of society. Women's federations, communist youth leagues and other social organizations have played an important role in this respect, and grassroots organizations such as villagers' committees and residents' committees have always been on the front line of the work of protecting the rights of the child. Moreover, the role of organizations for protecting the rights of the child has become increasingly prominent. In the future, China will establish a new model of participation by the whole society in the protection of the rights of the child characterized by "one body, two wings, two supports, one center and one guarantee", with "the government playing the leading role, non-governmental organizations as the main force, communities as the bases, families and schools as the supports, children as the center and society as the guarantee".[7]

12.2 The Current Situation of Protecting the Rights of the Child in China

12.2.1 Achievements Made by China in Protecting the Rights of the Child

China has achieved remarkable results in safeguarding the right to subsistence and the right to health of children in the country. According to the Interim Statistical Monitoring Report on the Program for the Development of Children in China (2011–2020) released by the National Bureau of Statistics in October 2016 (hereinafter referred to as the Monitoring Report), in 2015, the infant mortality rate in China was 8.1 ‰, and the mortality rate of children under 5 years old was 10.7 ‰, which were 5 ‰ and 57 ‰, respectively, lower than 2010; and the injury mortality rate of children under the age of 18 in China was 15.82/100,000, which was 6.59/100,000 points lower than in 2010. The quality of life of Chinese children has been improving year by year, and the protection of their right to life has become stronger and stronger. In 2015,

[7] "The 20th Anniversary of the Formal Entry into Force of the United Nations Convention on the Rights of the Child with Respect to China", *People's Daily Online*, at https://societypeople.comcn/n/2012/1120/c1008-19637530html, last visited: December 2, 2017.

China reduced the low birth weight rate of infants to 2.64%, and low weight rate of children under 5 years old to 1.49%, thus achieving ahead of schedule the established goal of "keeping the low birth weight rate below 4% and the low weight rate of children below 5%"; the exclusive breastfeeding rate of infants aged 0–6 months had exceeded the established target of 50% and the prevalence rate of anemia in children under 5 years old was 4.79%, which was obviously lower than the established goal of "controlling the prevalence rate of anemia in children under 5 years old below 12%". Moreover, China has actively adopted a number of measures, such as maternal health care, birth defect monitoring, neonatal health care and disease screening, which have effectively prevented and reduced the occurrence of birth defects and childhood disabilities.

China has made remarkable progress in the protection of children's right to education. The Monitoring Report shows that the Chinese government attaches great importance to children's education, is committed to promoting education reform, and has made all-round progress in preschool education, compulsory education, special education and high school education. The gross enrollment rate for three-year preschool education continued to increase, reaching 75% in 2015, exceeding the established target by 5 percentage points. The number of public kindergartens in cities and rural areas were 74% and 57%, respectively, higher than in 2010. The numbers of preschool education institutions, full-time preschool education teachers and preschool education students in China are growing rapidly. The popularization rate of nine-year compulsory education has been continuously improved. In 2015, nine-year compulsory education covered 100 percent of the national population, the completion rate of compulsory education reached 93%, the gross enrollment rate of high schools reached 87%, and the investment in senior high school education continued to increase. According to the Third and Fourth Combined Report of the People's Republic of China on the Implementation of the Convention on the Rights of the Child submitted to the Committee on the Rights of the Child, the Chinese government has taken special measures to ensure the equal right to education of girls, children with disabilities, children in poverty, sick children and children of ethnic minorities.

The welfare of children in China is improving day by day. Firstly, China has strengthened the administration of child welfare institutions, and issued such documents as Guiding Opinions on Formulating Minimum Fosterage Standards for Children in Welfare Institutions, Interim Measures for the Administration of Social Welfare Institutions, Basic Code of Social Welfare Institutions for Children, Opinions on Strengthening the Work of Providing Assistance to Orphans, and Notice on Formulating Minimum Fosterage Standards for Orphans. Secondly, China has improved the function of child welfare institutions, which have changed from simple fosterage to multiple functions of fosterage, medical care, special education, rehabilitation and skills training. Finally, China has innovated the fosterage mode and carried out trainings for social workers. China has made new progress in developing child welfare undertakings by increasing the number of child welfare institutions, reducing the number of orphans and improving the professional rehabilitation services for disabled children. In addition, the coverage of the national immunization program has been kept above 99%. The relief work for children in difficulties has been attached high importance by the Central Committee of the Communist Party of China and the State Council. Under the guidance of the Opinions of the State Council on Strengthening the Work of Assistance to Children in Difficulties, the pattern of the work for children in difficulties characterized by family responsibilities, government dominance and social participation is taking shape.

Chinese children are living in a safer social environment. The living environment of Chinese children has been continuously improved. With the development of the national economy and control of environmental pollution, the importance attached to children has been continuously increased, and the safety of children's living environment has been improved accordingly and, with the advancement of the rule of law in the field of education and the carrying out in a deep-going way the work of "running schools by law", the campus environment for children to receive an education is becoming safer and more orderly. New publications, music, film and television works for children are constantly emerging, and the popularity of the Internet and new media technologies has created excellent conditions for the improvement of children's cognitive ability. Meanwhile, the government has never slackened its supervision over children's information environment, and actions such as strictly examining and approving the contents of publications and purifying cyberspace have created a positive information environment for children.

China's judicial protection mechanism for children is improving day by day. In order to adapt to children's special physical and mental characteristics and development needs, public security organs, people's procuratorates, people's courts, detention centers and prisons have introduced special systems to realize special care and protection for children in the whole judicial process. For example, special judicial institutions for minors (juvenile criminal prosecution departments and juvenile tribunals) have been established, the mechanisms for providing legal aid and judicial assistance to children have been improved, and a social linkage mechanism for the judicial protection of minors has taken initial form. According to the Monitoring Report, in 2015, the number of minors who received assistance from legal institutions was more than 146,000, an increase of 66% from that in 2010, and the number and proportion of juvenile delinquency continued to decline.

12.2.2 Existing Problems in the Protection of the Rights of the Child in China

China's progress and achievements in protecting the rights of the child are obvious to all. However, it still has a long way to go in doing this work, which will never come to an end. There are still many problems and deficiencies in this development process, which need to be paid attention to and solved one by one in the future. Firstly, the awareness of protecting the rights of the child in the whole society needs to be raised. On the one hand, although it is a common tradition of the community with a shared future for mankind to give special attention and care to children regardless of race and culture, the concept and theory of protection of the rights of the child are constantly developing and updated from time to time. On the other hand, China has its own path and pace of development, as well as its own institutional design and long-term arrangement. In recent years, some hot events have reflected the tension between parents and children, the overreaction between adults caused by the conflicts between children, and the conflicts between parents, schools and the government, all of which are the results of the disorder of social consciousness in the process of transformation. China should always stand at the forefront of the world in the protection of the rights of the child under the precondition of adapting to its own national conditions. To this end, it needs to continuously renew and enhance the awareness of the protection of the rights of the child of the whole society.

Secondly, the problems in the equalization of protection of the rights of the child urgently need to be solved. First, the regional differences in economic development have led to the imbalance in the protection of the rights of the child among different regions. Regional differences and urban-rural differences are reflected in child mortality, popularization rate of compulsory education, medical resource distribution, social welfare, financial input, and many other issues. Second, there are differences in the level of satisfaction of the need for the protection of rights among children of different age groups. For example, at the preschool stage, public education resources are inadequate and there are still blind spots in the supervision of private educational institutions; at the stage of compulsory education, the issue of bullying on campus needs to be dealt with quickly by law; and at the stage of high school and vocational education, the quality of education needs to be improved. Third, the mechanism for and environment of individualized care for different groups of children are still not satisfactory. For example, the care system for various kinds of children in difficulties is not perfect. The needs of children in difficulties are complex and diverse, such as rehabilitation of disabled children, guardianship and education of left-behind children, education of and crime prevention among migrant children, medical assistance and guardianship of AIDS orphans, education and prevention of sexual assault against girls, and so on. All these require corresponding institutional arrangements, policy inclination, and a continuous increase of financial input.

Finally, the cultural environment for the protection of the rights of the child needs to be improved. The advent of the information age is a double-edged sword for children's growth. Its positive effects are obvious, and its negative effects need to be paid high attention to and actively prevented. Information explosion and cultural diversity can easily cause value confusion and psychological imbalance for growing children, while some "negative energy" and violent and obscene information are also spreading quietly in underground networks, directly endangering teenagers' mental health. How to effectively deal with the network information chaos, purify the cultural environment and enable children to grow up in a healthy cultural atmosphere is a question to be answered by the whole society.

12.3 The Index System for Assessing the Protection of the Rights of the Child

The Center for Studies of National Rule of Law Index of Chinese Academy of Social Sciences (hereinafter referred to as the "Center") has been actively carrying out empirical legal research for a long time by adhering to the fine tradition of being practice-oriented. In order to objectively evaluate the situation of protection of the rights of the child in China, the Center has developed the Index System for the Assessment of the Protection of the Rights of the Child in China (hereinafter referred to as "rights of the child index system"). The system, which took the Center one year to develop, is a part of the grand blueprint of the Center's human rights index system.

12.3.1 The Purpose of Establishing the Index System

The purpose of establishing the rights of the child index system is to truthfully reflect the reality of protection of the rights of the child in China. On the one hand, it shows the achievements made by China in the protection of the rights of the child and the overall improvement of children's lives and education in China; on the other hand, it tries to find out the problems existing in the practice of the protection of the rights of the child in China through objective data and comparative analysis, and put forward corresponding countermeasures, thus pointing out the direction for the future protection of the rights of the child in China. The ultimate social effect the Center hopes to achieve through the publication and application of the index system is to draw the attention of the whole society to the protection of the rights of the child, enhance public confidence in the legal system of protection of the rights of the child, enable relevant government departments to understand the effect of the implementation of laws and policies on the protection of the rights of the child in a timely manner, and provide basis and suggestions for them to adjust existing laws and policies or formulate new laws and policies, so as to push the protection of the rights of the child in China to a higher level.

12.3.2 Principles of Establishment of the Index System

12.3.2.1 Being Based on Law

The establishment of the rights of the child index system in accordance with law is the logical premise and the prerequisite for the legitimacy and scientificity of the index system. The principle of establishing the index system in accordance with law means that all indices in the system should be based on specific provisions or general principles of laws, administrative regulations and policy documents, rather than created at will. The bases for establishing the rights of the child index system include laws, administrative regulations, departmental rules, etc., such as the Constitution, the Law on the Protection of Minors, theRegulations on the Administration of the Circulation and Vaccination of Vaccines, and the National Standards on Child Health Care (for Trial Implementation). Some important policy documents relating to the protection of the rights of the child, such as the National Human Rights Action Plan (2012–2015), the Program for the Development of Children in China (2011–2020), and the Action Plan against Human Abduction and Trafficking (2013–2020), are also undoubtedly the bases of the rights of the child index system.

12.3.2.2 Being Objective and Fair

The rights of the child index system aims to accurately reflect the achievements and existing problems in the protection of the rights of the child in China through the collection and analysis of objective, truthful, verifiable and traceable data. On the one hand, it should be able to satisfy the public's right to know, so that they are not misled by false statements; on the other hand, it should be able to provide quantitative standards and0 objective bases for government departments to make strategic choices, assist them to effectively carry out the work of protection of minors, and improve their ability to cope with emergency public opinion situation and maintain social stability. Compared with the usual assessment methods, such as satisfaction survey, which are often subjective and biased, this objective assessment method has more scientific value and guiding significance.

12.3.2.3 Highlighting the Key Points

The concept of the rights of the child is rich in connotation and comprehensive in extension. It is impossible for the assessment to cover all aspects of this concept. Only the pillar framework rights and basic rights related to children's survival, development and daily life can be selected as the assessment objects, so as to give a macro description of the situation of protection of the rights of the child in China and a general judgment on its future trend of development. Any aspect of the existing index system may be developed into an independent index system. The actual operation and testing of this immature framework index system in practice can also reveal the direction of future development of the rights of the child index system.

12.3.2.4 Being Appropriately Forward-Looking

The original design of the rights of the child index system is not only based on the present situation but also focused on the future. Therefore, in the design of some indices, we took the more advanced or even ahead-of-the-time guiding provisions in the Convention on the Rights of the Child and relevant domestic laws and administrative regulations as benchmarks, so as to help assessment targets identify their problems and find the direction of future development.

12.3.3 A Brief Introduction to the Indices

Since the rights of the child index system is focused on the situation in China, the grade I indices in the system were designed by taking the target strategy established in the Program for the Development of Children in China (2011–2020) as the basic framework. They include the right to subsistence, the right to education, the welfare of children, the right to social environment and judicial protection, with each of them further divided into grade II, grade III, and grade IV indices. Altogether, there are more than 100 grade IV indices. The specific indices are all based on specific provisions of laws, administrative regulations and policy documents. In the assessment, which is expected to be officially launched in 2018, we will select some indices as parameters to examine the protection of the rights of the child in 31 provincial administrative regions, with the exception of Hong Kong, Macao and Taiwan.

12.3.3.1 Right to Subsistence

The right to subsistence is the primary human right and the most basic right of the child. Here, the index system adopts the narrow concept of the right to subsistence, that is, it only refers to the right to life and the right to an adequate level of health.

i. *The right to life*

The right to life is a prerequisite for children to enjoy all other rights. The Convention on the Rights of the Child stipulates that: "States parties recognize that every child has the inherent right to life. States Parties shall ensure to the maximum extent possible the survival and development of the child." The Program for the Development of Children in China (2011–2020) has set the objective of reducing infant mortality and child mortality for the first time in China.

ii. *The right to health*

The Convention on the Rights of the Child provides that "States Parties recognize the right of the child to the enjoyment of the highest attainable standard of health and to facilities for the treatment of illness and rehabilitation of health" and sets six concrete goals in this respect. In addition, it attaches special importance to the physical and mental health of the child by mentioning it in five different parts. The Program for the Development of Children in China (2011–2020) contains more detailed and specific goals, strategies and measures in the part of children's health than in any other part of the document.

12.3.3.2 The Right to Education

The right to education is the top priority of the right to development, and the level of education determines the course of life of a child. Both the Convention on the Rights of the Child and the Program for the Development of Chinese Children (2011–2020) contain clear provisions on the protection of children's right to education, because the future of children is the future of a nation and of the whole world. The growth of a child is divided into different stages. Children at each growth stage need the supply of educational resources suitable for their physical and mental development at that specific stage. Therefore, according to stages of children's education, the grade I index of the right to education is divided into three grade II indices: preschool education, compulsory education and high school education, with each of them further divided into sub-grades according to different requirements of education at different stages provided for by relevant laws, administrative regulations and policies.

i. *Preschool education*

The low development level of preschool education is an undeniable reality in China. There are many problems in kindergartens and preschool classes at the current stage of development of preschool education, including such inherent problems as shortage and uneven quality of teachers, the need to improve hardware facilities, potential safety hazards, imperfect management system, and the absence of relevant laws and administrative regulations. The Program for the Development of Children in China (2011–2020) puts forward the general requirements for preschool education, namely "promoting the early comprehensive development of children aged 0–3; basically popularizing preschool education, with the gross enrollment rate nationwide for three-year preschool education reaching 70% and that for one-year preschool education reaching 95%, increasing the number of public kindergartens in cities, and establishing and putting into effective operation public central kindergartens and village kindergartens in every township in rural areas." Some provincial-level governments have also formulated countermeasures against the problems existing in the preschool education in their respective administrative regions.

ii. *Compulsory education*

Compulsory education is the most important stage of all stages of education, and it is the basic education that determines the overall quality of citizens in the future. The Chinese government has always attached importance to the popularization and continuous improvement of the quality of compulsory education. However, currently China is faced with the problem of unbalanced regional development in compulsory education, and the situation of compulsory education for some children is not optimistic. For example, the schooling of left-behind children, migrant children and children with disability in rural areas is a problem that has been always plaguing local governments. In response to the requirements of the 12th Five-Year Plan, the Program for the Development of Children in China (2011–2020) puts forward the goal to be achieved in raising the retention rate of compulsory education,[8] and especially the task objective of ensuring that children in difficulties receive full compulsory education.

iii. *High school education*

The period of compulsory education is usually extended with the improvement of economic and social development. In recent years, Guangdong, Zhejiang and some other provinces have achieved good results in providing free high school education, and the call for popularizing 12-year compulsory education is becoming louder and louder. The popularization of high school education represents the development level of national education, and reflects the level of economic and social development in the country. It is also a manifestation of the expanding public demand for educational resources. The goal of raising the high school gross enrollment rate to 90%, set by the Program for the Development of Children in China (2011–2020), is reasonable for China today. Secondary vocational education, which belongs to high school education in a broad sense, is able to better suit the teaching to the aptitude of students, cultivate more professional and technical personnel for the country, and make up for the serious shortage of professional and technical personnel at present. For a long period of time, vocational education has existed as a by-product of high school education, with slow improvement in school quality and outdated personnel training mode, which makes it difficult for schools of vocational education to attract high-quality students and train a large number of professional and technical personnel with excellent quality. Based on a clear understanding of the present situation of vocational education, the Program for the Development of Children in China (2011–2020) puts forward the requirements for expanding the scale and improving the quality of vocational education.

12.3.3.3 Child Welfare

There are two concepts of welfare: one in the broad sense and one in the narrow sense. "Social welfare in the broad sense refers to a social security system of cash and services generally provided by the state to all citizens in accordance with law, aiming at guaranteeing a certain standard of living and improving the quality of life as much as possible; social welfare in the narrow sense specifically refers to social services provided to special groups of people such as the elderly, the disabled, women and children, and mental patients."[9] Correspondingly, there are also two concepts of child welfare: one in the broad sense and one in the narrow sense. In the rights of the child index system, children's welfare is used in its narrow sense in accordance with its customary usage in the context of China's national conditions, that is, the social services provided by the government to children.

---

[8] Retention rate of nine-year compulsory education = number of graduates ÷ number of students enrolled (including normal migrant students) × 100%.

[9] Xie Bing (ed.), *Introduction to Social Security*, Wuhan: Wuhan University Press, 2015, p. 327.

i. *Child health care*

With the continuous improvement of living standards, people are paying more and more attention to health and health care, especially child health care. However, problems and shortboards are constantly exposed in the field of child health care. Among them, the most prominent ones are the incidents of harmful vaccines used on children, which reflects the lack of a whole-process legal system and mechanism for guaranteeing child health care. The Program for the Development of Children in China (2011–2020) provides for some concrete measures for improving children's physical and mental health quality and points out the direction for further refinement of the legal system.

ii. *Relief for children in difficulties*

In 2016, the State Council issued the Opinions on Strengthening the Protection of Children in Difficulties, which attach special importance to "children who have difficulties in living, seeking medical treatment and schooling due to poverty of their families, children who have difficulties in rehabilitation, care, nursing and social integration due to their own disabilities, and children whose personal safety is threatened or violated due to abuse, abandonment, accidental injury and illegal infringement resulting from lack of family guardianship or improper guardianship" and provide them with all-round assistance and support in various aspects of life, such as medical care, education, guardianship, and social welfare services.

12.3.3.4 Right to Social Environment

Children's right to social environment is a broad concept involving all aspects of protection of and care for children by the whole society. According to the different time-space dimensions of a child's life, the above concept can be divided into physical social environment security and virtual social environment security, with the former mainly covering living environment security and campus environment security and the latter mainly involving the issue of whether information environments such as media and network are beneficial to children's growth.

i. *Safe living environment*

As children are physically and intellectually weak compared to adults, they need special attention and special social guarantee mechanisms with respect to food, clothing, housing and transportation. The outbreak from time to time of social conflicts caused by problems with the safety of children's food, drug, clothing and toys is a manifestation of the lack of relevant legal systems or inadequate law enforcement. The safety of basic necessities of life, such as food, clothing, housing and transportation, is the primary prerequisite for the care of children and guarantees of their healthy growth by the whole society. The achievement of this goal requires the double legal safeguards of legislation and law enforcement.

ii. *Safe campus environment*

Schools are the places where children spend for the longest time outside their homes when growing up, and, to some extent, children are more likely to be harmed on campus than at their homes. Phenomena such as bullying on campus and juvenile delinquency have gradually become thorny problems that give big headaches to parents, schools and government departments. Running schools by law is an effective measure for solving these problems, and local governments are exploring ways of refining and implementing the requirements for running schools by law. The beneficial experiences of the Government of Jiangsu Province and some other local governments are worth affirmation through assessment and promotion throughout the country.

iii. *Safe information environment*

The arrival of the Internet age has greatly changed people's lives, brought unprecedented high efficiency and fast pace to their work and daily life, and became an important means for children to know the world without leaving home. Meanwhile, the information explosion also brings some problems. The mixture of all kinds of information, both good and bad, and the lack of information classification and management technology have had a certain negative impact on public psychology. In particular, children, who lack abilities of discrimination and self-control, are more vulnerable to bad information, which can cause serious psychological problems and even deviations in behavior. How to protect children's mental health in the virtual world is an epic topic facing the rule of law. New media technologies, on the one hand, have aggravated the above adverse effects, but on the other hand, can also play a positive role in promoting children's all-round development if used properly. Giving full play to the advantages of information technology and curbing its adverse effects by legal means is the key point of the current work of protecting the rights of the child.

12.3.3.5 Judicial Protection

Judicial protection of children refers to the special protection of children who are involved in the judicial process. The subjects of judicial protection of children mainly include public security organs, people's procuratorates, people's courts, detention centers, and prisons. Article 50 of the Law on the Protection of Minors clearly provided for the obligations of public security organs, people's procuratorates, people's courts and judicial administrative departments to protect the rights of minors involved in judicial proceedings. Various judicial organs have successively issued their own special regulations, such as the Provisions on the Handling of Juvenile Delinquency Cases by Public Security Organs, Eight Measures for Procuratorial Organs to Strengthen Judicial Protection of Minors, Notice of the Supreme People's Procuratorate on Further Strengthening Procuratorial Work Related to Minors, and Interpretation of the Supreme People's Court of Some Issues Concerning the Specific

Table 12.1 Index system for the assessment of the protection of the rights of the child in China

Grade I indices	Grade II indices
Right to subsistence	Right to life
	Right to health
Right to education	Preschool education
	Compulsory education
	High school education
Child welfare	Child health care
	Assistance to children in difficulties
Right to social environment	Living environment
	Campus environment
	Information environment
Judicial protection	Judicial protection by public security organs
	Judicial protection by procuratorial organs
	Judicial protection by people's courts
	Judicial protection in detention centers and prisons
	Linkage mechanism for judicial protection of minors

Application of Law in the Trial of Criminal Cases Involving Minors. Special systems of judicial protection for minors mainly include the system of assigning specialized agencies or personnel to be in charge of cases involving minors, the system of legal aid and listening to lawyers' opinions, the system of the presence of appropriate adults at proceedings involving minors, the system of being cautious in prosecution, reducing the number of arrests and proving the necessity of arrest, the social investigation report system, the system of non-prosecution and conditional non-prosecution, the system of quick handling of cases, the system of sealing up criminal records, the social probation system, and the system of separate custody for minors and adults. On the basis of the above measures and systems, many pilot areas have established social protection linkage mechanisms for juvenile justice (Table 12.1).

MIX
Papier aus verantwortungsvollen Quellen
Paper from responsible sources
FSC® C105338
FSC
www.fsc.org

If you have any concerns about our products,
you can contact us on
ProductSafety@springernature.com

In case Publisher is established outside the EU,
the EU authorized representative is:
Springer Nature Customer Service Center GmbH
Europaplatz 3, 69115 Heidelberg, Germany

Printed by Libri Plureos GmbH
in Hamburg, Germany